LAW AND ECONOMICS
An Introductory Analysis

Third Edition

LAW AND ECONOMICS
An Introductory Analysis

Third Edition

WERNER Z. HIRSCH

Department of Economics
University of California, Los Angeles
Los Angeles, California

Academic Press
San Diego London Boston New York
Sydney Tokyo Toronto

Copyright © 1999, 1988, 1979 by ACADEMIC PRESS

All Rights Reserved.
No part of this publication may be reproduced or transmitted in any form or by any
means, electronic or mechanical, including photocopy, recording, or any information
storage and retrieval system, without permission in writing from the publisher.

Academic Press
a division of Harcourt Brace & Company
525 B Street, Suite 1900, San Diego, California 92101-4495, USA
http://www.apnet.com

Academic Press
24-28 Oval Road, London NW1 7DX, UK
http://www.hbuk.co.uk/ap/

Library of Congress Catalog Card Number: 98-89452

International Standard Book Number: 0-12-349482-6

PRINTED IN THE UNITED STATES OF AMERICA
99   00   01   02   03   04   EB   9   8   7   6   5   4   3   2   1

Transferred to Digital Printing 2004

To Esther, Dan, Joel, and Lani

CONTENTS

1

INTRODUCTION

2

PROPERTY LAW'S BASIC LEGAL PREMISES

3

ECONOMIC ANALYSIS OF LANDLORD–TENANT LAWS

4

ECONOMIC ANALYSIS OF ZONING LAWS

5

CONTRACT LAW

6

TORT LAW'S BASIC LEGAL PREMISES

7

ECONOMIC ANALYSIS OF TORT LAW

8

CRIMINAL LAW

9

ENVIRONMENTAL LAW

10

ANTIMONOPOLY LAW

11

DISCRIMINATION LAW

PREFACE TO THE THIRD EDITION

The field of law and economics, which originated as recently as the early 1960s, has proved vital and dynamic and has yielded many fruitful insights into the relationship between the two disciplines. It is of little surprise, therefore, that interest in the field has grown rapidly and spread among courts and legislatures. One would hope that as the economic underpinning for laws and legal institutions has been enriched, so has the quality of court decisions and legislation.

Although this book is arranged along legal topics, it makes use of microeconomic analysis to examine and deepen our understanding of laws and legal institutions uses and econometric tools to test hypotheses about their effects.

Following Calabresi and Melamed, laws and legal institutions are looked upon as a coherent system that focuses on the manner in which entitlements of economic actors are treated. When entitlements are freely traded, this action is guided and enforced by property and contract laws. When they are taken by force, though unintentionally, tort laws come into play. And when entitlements are intentionally taken by force, criminal laws are invoked. This view of transactions provides a powerful organizing principle.

The interface of economics and law is explored by making use of three approaches. One applies economic paradigms for rule formulation, designed to maximize an objective function. The second involves effect evaluation, that is, aims to deduce and empirically quantify the economic effects of particular laws or legal institutions. Finally, a perspective encompassing law, economics, and organization focuses on how legal forms of organization work, while making use of transaction cost economics.

The first edition appeared in 1979, and new editions have followed at intervals of about 10 years; thus it is possible to gain some understanding of how the field has progressed. The changes have been numerous enough that about a third of the material in the second edition had to be changed for this edition. The new edition of *Law and Economics* thus seeks to be sensitive to changes in the law, in society, and in technology and to reflect advances in legal theory, microeconomics, and the application of econometrics. More than ever, revolutionary advances have been occurring in information technology, communications, medicine, automation, and globalization. On the other hand, society is facing threats of increased inequality, balkanization, and discrimination, as well as imbalances among population, resources, and environment and between the right to personal security and the first amendment rights of defendants. Therefore, the future of society, including our own, will depend to no small extent on our capacity, education, personal skills, natural resources, informed choice, and, yes, caliber and acumen of our leaders, integrity of our legal institutions, and the wisdom of our laws to effectively advance justice and our peoples' productivity.

Since the appearance of the second edition in 1988, new scholarly contributions have been made, and new concerns have found expression by courts and legislatures. The new edition attempts to explore a number of them. For example, the law and economics of the Takings Clause of the Constitution is examined in the light of the Supreme Court's recently formulated nexus and proportionality tests, particularly as applied to land use and rent control issues. Examination of contract law seeks to take account of the high-tech communications revolution in, for example, determining what constitutes a legal contract. The discussion of tort law pays special attention to new developments regarding no-fault insurance systems and their economic effects.

In the criminal law chapter, new emphasis is given to deterring crime not only by increasing the cost of criminal behavior, but also by reducing the taste for criminal behavior by making legal activities more rewarding. Some available initiatives are subjected to cost–benefit analyses. The chapter on environmental law reviews new pollution control instruments and presents a number of empirical cost–benefit analyses.

Perhaps no area of law and economics is undergoing a more exciting transformation, and with it revival, than antimonopoly law. It had been in the doldrums for quite some time, until the emergence of high-tech industries, particularly communication and information, as well as the globalization of industry. An important question in relation to these circumstances, still unsolved, relates to the extent to which antitrust laws can protect consumers from predatory pricing without generating serious negative effects on innovation. Finally, the discrimination law chapter, newly added to the second edition, pays particular attention to the grave difficulties of reliably detecting and measuring discrimination and the policy implications for the law if these efforts are likely to be unsuccessful.

As was the case in earlier editions, no claim is made of a comprehensive coverage of all subjects in *Law and Economics*. Selection of topics has been guided by my judgment of where economists have made major contributions to a more profound and carefully reasoned understanding of laws and legal institutions and of where they have provided a solid and systematic intellectual underpinning to jurisprudence. Even though there is, for example, no chapter on constitutional law, some forays are made in that direction, e.g., an exploration of the Takings Clause of the Constitution in relation to zoning and landlord–tenant laws.

Some readers might be surprised at the disproportionate amount of space devoted to an analysis of property law. It is an effort at compromise between the approach of a generalized overview of all topics and a study of limited, selected topics in greater depth. Thus, the intent is to convey to the reader the broad contours as well as the depth of a major branch of the law and to demonstrate the use of powerful analytical and empirical economic techniques to derive significant policy implications. My hope is that some readers will be stimulated to apply this approach to other branches of the law.

In preparing the third edition of *Law and Economics*, I have benefited once again from discussions, comments, and advice of many students as well as a number of colleagues. Some of the students who took my course at the University of California at Los Angeles, by challenging ideas, constructs, and policy implications, have stimulated me to make some revisions. At the same time, colleagues' helpful comments and suggestions convinced me to rethink certain issues and strike out in new directions. I particularly benefited from discussions with Garry T. Schwartz on tort law, Jesse J. Dukemenian, Richard H. Sander, and Joel G. Hirsch on property law, Antonio Manzini on the economics of pollution control measures, and Anthony M. Rufolo and David Hoffman on the constitutionality of rent control. I thank all of them. However, once again the greatest gratitude must go to my wife, Esther Hirsch, for her thoughtful assistance and patience, without which this edition would not be possible.

Werner Z. Hirsch

PREFACE TO THE SECOND EDITION

Since the completion of the first edition of *Law and Economics* in 1978, major developments have taken place in jurisprudence, economics, and the field of law and economics. These developments alone would have justified updating and extending the material in the first edition. More important, however, in this decision have been certain changes in my own thinking about the interaction between law and economics and their joint use to provide the intellectual underpinning for many significant areas of jurisprudence.

The last ten years or so have seen a great expansion of research on productive uses of the study of law and economics in their interface and interaction. As more and more able scholars from both disciplines have been laboring in the growing field of law and economics, the quality and pace of the work have increased further.

These scholars are using three approaches. In some of their efforts, they apply economic paradigms for rule formulation. Here their objective is to construct carefully derived, rigorous rules toward maximizing an objective function, in most cases with allocative efficiency maximization as the main concern. In this exercise in normative economics, i.e., the quest for a Pareto optimum, it is crucial that scholars remind themselves continuously that the law's overriding concern is with distributional justice, and not merely efficient use of resources.

A second method of law and economics involves effect evaluation. This approach seeks to provide estimates of efficiency as well as distributional effects of a particular statutory or court-made law, on either an *ex ante* or *ex post* basis. Microeconomic analysis is applied to derive testable hypotheses that are then tested with the aid of econometric methods.

Quite recently a third approach has emerged, based in some respects on the institutional economics of John Commons. Neo-institutional rule formulation to date involves a descriptive theory of the law, focusing on transactions as the basic units of analysis rather than on firms, governments, or individuals. In carrying out their work, scholars using this approach seek to model the web of interrelated legal processes involved in transactions; no empirical analyses have so far been undertaken.

While this volume seeks to borrow the best of all three approaches, it is forced to give short shrift to neo-institutional rule formulation since so little scholarly work has been done under its banner. Rule formulation, which plays such a dominant role in the textbook of Judge Richard Posner[1], is utilized here in all those areas where the approach is powerful and appropriate, but on the whole somewhat less, particularly in the chapters on property and tort law. In my view, caution must be exercised before rules that maximize allocative efficiency are recommended for situations basically dominated by concern for distributive justice. The temptation to abandon caution is especially great, since economists have developed powerful paradigms from which allocative efficient rules can rather easily be derived.

The approach that seeks to quantify and evaluate the effects that specific laws have, or are likely to have, is not encumbered by this difficulty. Admittedly it is less ambitious, but at the same time it is applicable to a host of laws both at the time they are considered and after their implementation. Because of its broad applicability, this approach turns out to be prominent here.

It would be presumptuous to claim that this volume represents a comprehensive treatment of all aspects of the possible interface between law and economics. In fact, my effort has concentrated on selecting those areas of the law in which I felt economists can contribute to a more profound and principled understanding and where at the same time the legal profession appears receptive to such new insights. These criteria led to the selection of legal topics that are found in this book. The decision to exclude constitutional law, labor law, and tax law, among others, did not come easily, particularly since I have authored some articles on these areas.[2]

Another choice had to be made early on, and it turned out to be relatively easy. In the abstract, a textbook can be organized around economic concepts and principles, but such an approach is clearly inferior to structuring

---

[1] Richard A. Posner, *Economic Analysis of Law,* 3rd ed. (Boston, Mass: Little Brown, 1986).

[2] An example is Werner Z. Hirsch and Dan Floyd, "The Substantial Reason Requirement Under the Privileges and Immunities Clause: The Case of Residency Laws," *Southwestern University Law Review, 15* (3) (1985), pp. 431–471.

material around specific areas of the law. I consider the latter approach more likely to help economists get their teeth into real-life legal problems, and at the same time to stimulate in the legal profession an awareness and, I hope, an appreciation of how economics can contribute to the analysis of the law.

The reader is likely to wonder why there is so much more material dealing with property than with any other area of the law. My intent was to treat one area of the law, one about which the field of law and economics has much to say, in a most comprehensive manner, in the hope of using it as a showpiece. The purpose was to demonstrate to readers the scope and depth of the subject area, as well as to point out in detail the power and sophistication of operational methods of rule formulation and effect evaluation. Having seen how law and economics can effectively deal with a broad range of property law issues, it is my hope that readers will seek to emulate this effort in other areas of the law.

The second edition includes major changes and additions. An altogether new Chapter 11, on anti-discrimination law, has been added. A number of scholars, particularly Peter Asch of Rutgers University, had suggested, even urged, that I provide such a chapter since much has been happening in recent years in the anti-discrimination area. These developments made it possible to include a major chapter on this topic.

In addition to some changes in the introductory chapter, major additions were introduced in certain areas. In the development of property law and its economic analysis, much greater attention was paid to the topics of adverse possession and rent control. Since in recent years American society was forced to face some difficult issues in areas covered by tort law, especially medical malpractice and product liability, these topics were greatly expanded. In the development of criminal law, additional attention was paid to the insanity defense. The chapter on environmental law incorporates a more extensive discussion of regulation, together with a more careful comparative analysis of alternative methods to control the environment. Finally, much of the antimonopoly law chapter has undergone extensive revision. Specifically, tie-in arrangements, boycotts, damages, and resale price maintenance are topics that have been entirely redone.

In preparing the second edition of *Law and Economics*, I have incurred debts so numerous that it is impossible to identify and thank all those who deserve credit. Those whose contributions are especially hard to remember and mention individually are those numerous students who, during the last ten years or so, have taken my course at the University of California at Los Angeles. They frequently stimulated me to rethink and reformulate ideas, concepts, economic and legal theories, and policy implications.

Like the first, the new edition benefited greatly from discussions with and advice from friends and colleagues. They inspired me to reexamine issues, some small and others large, some new and others old, and some obviously obscure while others were on first blush incontrovertible. Special thanks go to Gary Schwartz. Discussions with him on tort law over the years have shaped the tort chapters in a major way. As already mentioned, Peter Asch, in his thoughtful manner, persuaded me to pay attention to discrimination as an area deserving major attention. Moreover, in addition to offering many helpful suggestions, he also critically read Chapter 11. Special thanks go to Joel Hirsch, who has collaborated with me in the area of property law. These efforts culminated in a number of law review articles on which the property law chapters draw extensively.

In the period during which the new edition was in preparation, I also benefited from help rendered by able research assistants—Unghwan Choi, Glenn Elder, Dan Floyd, Janet Green, David Mengle, and Steve Rivkin, the latter being especially helpful in the revision of Chapter 10.

Just as the manuscript of the first edition was ably typed by Lorraine Grams, so was this manuscript. Her outstanding efficiency and timely assistance were invaluable. Secretarial help by Kathy Martija is also greatfully acknowledged. However, by far my greatest gratitude must go to my wife, Esther Hirsch, who again provided insightful assistance, understanding, and patience, which made the preparation of this new edition a rewarding experience.

While the new edition has grown by a significant number of pages, it is my hope that it is not so much the lengthening of the volume but the new ideas and improved exposition that I hope will prove helpful to the reader.

Werner Z. Hirsch

PREFACE TO THE FIRST EDITION

"A lawyer who has not studied economics ... is very apt to become a public enemy." Thus wrote Mr. Justice Brandeis in 1916 in his *Illinois Law Review* article, "The Living Law." At this distance, it is not clear what kind of economics, or how much of it, Justice Brandeis considered necessary. He could not have read Lord John Maynard Keynes's essay on Alfred Marshall in which Keynes described his vision of a polymath economist, who "must understand symbols and speak in words. He must contemplate the particular in terms of the general, and touch abstract and concrete in the same flight of thought. He must study the present in the light of the past for the purposes of the future." But Brandeis might well have been thinking about a similar facility to deal with economic matters—concepts and tools— that need to be applied to legal problems.

Today the merit of applying economic analysis to legal matters has been widely recognized, though not necessarily by all lawyers or economists. More and more scholars are actively engaged in discovering areas where legal and economic concerns interface. Many are seeking to marry approaches of both disciplines to gain a deeper understanding of legal problems that have an economic dimension.

Who would suspect that law and economics have much in common and can assist each other? At first glance, prospects for fruitful cooperation appear unusually remote. The law's overwhelming concern is justice. It focuses on the distribution among different parties of rights, entitlements, obligations, income, and the like, and therefore on how a pie of a given size is divided. Economics, on the other hand—particularly that part of microeconomics that has developed the most powerful paradigms—is largely normative. Its preoccupation is with the efficient use of resources to produce the largest pie possible. To look at it in a somewhat different manner, underlying much of the law is the concept of the "reasonable" man. He is a person who not only is protective of his own rights, but also has a fair regard for the welfare of others. For example, the law holds that a person whose acts deviate from the standard of the "reasonable" man can be found negligent and held liable. Economics, on the other hand, is built around the concept of the "rational" man, who in the extreme is totally self-serving, seeking only to maximize his self-interest.

The antithesis of the two disciplines appears to go even further in relation to their rigidity of conclusions, at least so it appears on the surface. Law follows, by and large, a binary approach in its conclusions. Thus, a court tends to find a defendant either liable or not liable. Not so economics, which pursues an incremental approach. In negotiations between two parties to a transaction, the bargaining is about higher or lower prices and higher or lower quantities to be supplied or demanded, and the outcomes are also quantitatively different.

But before lawyers and economists conclude that there is a basic incompatibility between the two fields, they should look more closely. For there are likely to be some surprises. What on first glance appear to be grave fundamental differences in premises and approach turn out to be reconcilable and can often be brought into harmony. For example, it can be argued that the "rational" man in seeking his self-interest takes into consideration the effect of his decision on others to the extent that their reaction makes an impression. In this manner, we can explain how a person can be rational and at the same time altruistic. In the more technical language of the economist, we would say that the effect of one person's decision on others can enter as an argument into the first person's utility function.

In a similar manner, it can be shown that the binary approach used by the court in reaching conclusions can at times become almost as flexible as the overtly incremental approach of economists. First, many states have adopted a comparative-negligence system for many personal injury cases— compensation for losses is apportioned to the different parties to the extent that each was found negligent. Second, in a criminal case, a defendant charged with a particular crime may be found guilty of a crime of lesser severity, and the court has the leeway to apply incrementalism in sentencing. Thus, though the charge is murder, a court can find a defendant guilty of manslaughter; the penalty can be a prison sentence—which may be suspended—of various lengths, a fine of lesser or greater severity, or both.

Thus, what might appear to be fundamental differences in approach between the two disciplines turn out, on inspection, not to be major obstacles to collaboration. What, then, are the major facets of the alliance between law and economics? Where do lawyers and economists meet, and how do they join forces once they have agreed to meet?

Before offering this volume as a partial reply to these questions, I would like to pay my respects to the pioneers in the field of law and economics. Ronald Coase, Guido Calabresi, and Richard A. Posner, in particular, enabled the new field to take off in a fruitful and promising direction. As Posner has expressed it, "The new law and economics dates from the early 1960s, when Guido Calabresi's first article on torts and Ronald Coase's article on social cost were published."[1] Moreover, two journals have been particularly instrumental in advancing the new field of law and economics— the *Journal of Law and Economics*, which made its debut in 1960 under the able editorship of Ronald Coase, and the *Journal of Legal Studies*, which started publication in 1972 under its capable editor, Richard A. Posner. But it would be a mistake to underestimate the importance of various law reviews, which have published numerous outstanding contributions to the new field.

Those who have labored in vineyards of law and economics have sought to bring economics to bear on law in two distinctive ways. Posner is probably the foremost proponent of the first approach, the application of microeconomic theory to legal rule formulation. Here the focus has been on using microeconomic theory and paradigms to formulate new common-law rules and to interpret existing ones as consistent with efficiency considerations. The second approach has emphasized the application of microeconomic theory and econometric methods to the estimation of the effects of laws, both existing and proposed; this is the thrust of this volume. In the main, it will be concerned with effect evaluation in the light of a rather deterministic view of the universe.

The emphasis on economic effect evaluation was selected for a number of reasons. The intellectual justification for assuming that the common law is predominantly efficiency-based and that microeconomic theory can be successfully used to formulate laws rests on rather shaky grounds. As will be argued in Chapter 1, most of the essential assumptions underlying microeconomic theory are not met in real life. And why should judges, who in the first place do not know such theory, follow it and seek maximization of resource use, when their training and background seem to emphasize concern with justice and redistributional issues? But perhaps most persuasive is the fact that microeconomics and econometric techniques are particularly powerful and well suited for effect evaluation. From a theoretical point of view, such an effort looks upon the law as an important component

---

[1] Richard A. Posner, *Economic Analysis of Law*, 2rd ed. (Boston: Little, Brown, 1977): p 16.

of the environment within which transactions take place. The task, then, is to model the transactions in a changing legal environment and estimate the effects of these changes on the outcomes of transactions.

The world in which transactions take place is highly urbanized, industrialized, and mobile, and transactors interact continually. Thus, interdependencies abound and have to be reckoned with. In such a world, the entitlements and rights of some parties are frequently violated. And, although unwanted burdens are imposed on other parties, that is, as a result of violation of rights, compensation is often not forthcoming. Economists, as we shall see, then speak about the presence of externalities, and they have developed powerful theories for the analysis of these externalities.

These theories are helpful in examining legal relations where entitlements and rights are freely and voluntarily exchanged—the province of property law and contract law. Following Calabresi's lead, we can also apply them when entitlements and rights are forcibly violated. When this happens, we find ourselves in the domain of tort law and criminal law. Whenever the collective wisdom and values of society permit such encroachments on entitlements or rights to be remedied through the payment of appropriate compensation, tort law becomes applicable. If, however, society determines not to tolerate certain violations of entitlements and rights, such as killings and robberies, criminal law comes into play.

Within this framework (developed in some detail in Chapter 1), I first examine the basic legal premises of property law (Chapter 2). Concepts and ideas so developed are then given economic content and placed within an effect-estimating framework. Thus, in Chapter 3, certain landlord–tenant laws are presented and their effects on the welfare of landlords and tenants—especially indigent tenants—are analyzed. In Chapter 4, a similar effort is undertaken in relation to zoning laws.

The inquiry into property law is followed by a somewhat more limited effort with regard to contract law. One reason for the more limited scope is that contract law, rather than bringing forth side effects, is primarily supposed to facilitate transactions—a major concern of Chapter 5. In Chapter 6, the major basic legal premises of tort law are presented. They are subjected to an economic analysis in the following chapter, Specifically, Chapter 7 applies economic analysis to such pressing problems as malpractice, product liability, and accident law.

Chapter 8 looks at criminal law from the vantage point of protecting initial entitlements from criminal encroachment. Special attention is given to economic models that relate deterrence measures, including capital punishment, to the commission of crime. Thereafter, in Chapter 9, we come to the heart of the relations between law and economics in terms of the main theme of this volume—entitlements and externalities. Thus, environmental law seeks to define, allocate, and enforce environmental property rights and entitlements in a world replete with externalities. The response to this challenge of courts and legislatures is examined within an economic framework. Finally, in Chapter 10, I turn to the most venerable area of cooperation between lawyer and economist—antimonopoly law.

By no means do I wish to suggest that this is a comprehensive treatment of the interface of law and economics. Legal and economic concerns interact in innumerable ways, and the number of aspects of this interaction that can benefit from a joint approach of both disciplines is great. I have merely offered some examples in the hope of stimulating among legal scholars an awareness of the contribution that economists might make to the law, and among economists an interest in applying their discipline to the lawyers' problems. An important area of mutual concern has been omitted—the field of taxation, which has long been studied by both disciplines; a voluminous literature already exists. Moreover, I intend to address myself to this field in the future.

There are many friends and colleagues who have been most helpful during the preparation of this volume. I would like to express special thanks to Guido Calabresi, who not only inspired me during extended conversations but also critically read Chapters 1, 6, 7, and 9 and offered many helpful suggestions, and to Gary Schwartz, who critically read the entire manuscript. Thanks are also due to Marvin Frankel, who read and commented on Chapter 10, Donald Hagman (Chapter 2), Neil Jacoby (Chapter 10), Benjamin Klein (Chapter 10), Mitchell Polinsky (Chapters 2, 7, and 9), Arthur Rosett (Chapter 5), and Denis Smallwood (Chapter 7).

During the preparation of the manuscript, library research was carried out effectively by Byde Clawson, Berry Yoch, and Kenneth Sweezy. Moreover, extended discussions with Joel Hirsch proved most useful. The manuscript was ably typed by Lorraine Grams, whose efficiency and cheerfulness were especially appreciated. However, by far my greatest gratitude is due my wife, Esther Hirsch, for her everlasting patience, encouragement, and assistance, without which this volume could never have been written.

Finally, I would like to express my sincere appreciation to the Rockefeller Foundation, under whose auspices I was able to complete major portions of the final manuscript as a resident scholar at the Villa Serbelloni in Bellagio. Its study and conference center provided a uniquely stimulating and intellectually invigorating environment.

1

INTRODUCTION

LAW AND ECONOMICS

"A lawyer who has not studied economics ... is very apt to become a public enemy." Thus wrote Justice Brandeis in 1916 in his *Illinois Law Review* article, "The Living Law." This thought-provoking statement is most likely one of the earliest ones that point to the interconnectedness of the two disciplines. It stimulated and foresaw the emergence of law and economics as a fruitful field of inquiry. Though of quite recent vintage — the early 1960s — it has been claimed by one of its early pioneers to be "perhaps the most important development in legal thought in the last quarter century."[1] Moreover, Williamson has concluded that there is general agreement that law and economics is a success story.[2]

Although not all practitioners of law and economics agree altogether on its scope and methods of inquiry, most consider the application of economists' neoclassical framework as well as their theoretical and econometric tools to law and legal institutions as its hallmark. Ideally law and economics, as an intellectual enterprise, should inform and be informed

---

[1] Richard A. Posner, *Economic Analysis of Law*, 3d ed. (Boston: Little, Brown, 1986): XIX.
[2] Oliver E. Williamson, *Revisiting Legal Realism: The Law, Economics, and Organizational Perspective*, Working Paper No. 95-12 (Berkeley, CA: University of California School of Law, Center for the Study of Law and Society, 1996): 3.

1

by the law.[3] In the eyes of Johnston, "applying economics to the law shapes legal thought and language; in framing and detailing an order governed by law it necessarily frames the objectives of law."[4]

NATURE AND ORIGIN OF LAWS

In the narrow sense, laws can be looked upon as commands backed up by the coercive power of the state. A broader and perhaps more significant view is that laws are authoritative directives that impose costs and benefits on participants in a transaction and in the process alter incentives. They determine the environment within which transactions between two or more parties take place and as such can be made to contribute to overall efficiency and justice. In addition, laws as authoritative directives provide instruments by which questions of concern to different parties can be settled. Depending on the precision with which laws spell out the nature of the directive arrangements, laws provide a lower or higher degree of certainty about the law's implications for the performance of participants in a transaction. Transactions are thus facilitated or impeded, conflicts and court cases made more or less common; in turn, transactors' costs and returns are affected. Thus, laws can be looked upon as contracts — either voluntarily or involuntarily arrived at — adjudicated and enforced by government.

The making of laws is not costless. Their drafting and enforcement require real resources and involve the trading-off of costs and benefits to determine when to rely on written contracts and how detailed such contracts should be. We distinguish between *statutory* and *court-made* laws. The former include not only the statutes passed by the legislature but also the fundamental laws chiseled into the Constitution.

Increasingly, courts have made law by stepping in where, in their opinion, fundamental changes in social and technological conditions have not been reflected in legislation. Much of the debate among the more conservative and more liberal schools of jurisprudence centers around the issue of how far courts should go in assuming what is basically the responsibility of the legislature.

---

[3] Williamson distinguishes between law and economics on the one hand, and law, economics, and organization on the other. The latter's concern is the application of transaction cost economics to "figuring out how feasible legal forms of organization work" (*ibid.*: 3).

[4] Jason S. Johnston, *Law, Economics and Post-Realist Explanation*, Working Paper No. 137 — Post Realist (New Haven, CT: Yale Law School Program in Civil Liability, 1990): 5.

The debate is particularly fierce in relation to constitutional questions — the primary domain of supreme courts. In constitutional adjudication, the conservative approach is to search for "original intent" and apply it to the case at hand. One might study historical sources to search for what was on the minds of the framers and adopters of the Constitution. But such interpretations are not the same as knowledge of the direction the framers intended to impart by their phrasing. Nor is it clear that the framers, as some liberals would argue, merely expressed a principle with the intention of having future courts apply them in a manner consistent with social and political patterns and expectations of subsequent generations.[5]

But if there is no compass such as "original intent," what other reliable principle is available to courts? There is no easy answer to the question. Liberal judges tend to suggest that the prevailing mores of society can be defining guidelines allowing for change and growth of the law, while taking into consideration the impact of the law on society. In this spirit, Justice Grodin points to the image of a judge "as one who is charged with responsibility for painting scene in an ongoing mural — free to express his or her artistry, but within the constraints imposed by the context in which he or she paints."[6]

NATURE AND HISTORY OF ECONOMICS

As a scholarly discipline, economics is only slightly more than 200 years old, beginning with the publication of Adam Smith's *The Wealth of Nations*[7] in 1776. Smith emphasized the advantages of unfettered markets, i.e., the invisible hand, and extolled the virtues of capitalism. These virtues were seriously questioned by Karl Marx in his 1867 *Das Kapital*,[8] which was so influential that, roughly a century later, a third of the world's population lived under economic systems which basically did away with guidance by market prices. In the United Kingdom, however, Alfred Marshall showed in his *Principles of Economics*[9] the virtue of relying on market prices to affect beneficially consumers and manufacturers alike. This insight was further advanced by the Chicago School of Economics, which, as will later be seen, argued that unfettered markets for goods and services are essential for

---

[5] Joseph R. Grodin, "Do Judges Make Law," *In Pursuit of Justice: Reflections of a State Supreme Court Justice* (Berkeley, CA: University of California Press, 1989): 61–72.

[6] *Ibid.*: 65.

[7] Adam Smith, *The Wealth of Nations* (New York: Modern Library, 1937).

[8] Karl Max, *Das Kapital* (London: MacMillan, 1867)

[9] Alfred Marshal, *Principles of Economics,* 8th ed. (London: MacMillan, 1930).

efficiency and growth of the economy. Altogether, microeconomic theory in recent years has emphasized that prices can be used as incentives to action, with responses by households, firms, and, to some extent, governments depending on the types of incentives and their magnitudes. Interesting work has built models and analyzed the responsiveness of economic actors on prices.[10]

What is economics has perhaps been best defined by Samuelson and Nordhaus: "Economics is the study of how societies use scarce resources to produce valuable commodities and distribute them among different groups."[11]

What economists do has perhaps been best described by Lord Keynes, the most illustrious economist of the twentieth century:

The master-economist ... must understand symbols and speak in words. He must contemplate the particular in terms of the general, and touch abstract and concrete in the same flight of thought. He must study the present in the light of the past for the purposes of the future. No part of man's nature or his institutions must lie entirely outside his regard. He must be purposeful and disinterested in a simultaneous mood; as aloof and incorruptible as an artist, yet sometimes as near the earth as a politician.[12]

THE INTERFACE BETWEEN LAW AND ECONOMICS

Where did lawyer and economist first meet professionally? No doubt it was in the lawyer's rose patch. It happened when the lawyer first thought it propitious to have expert witnesses, some of whom were economists.

The most active area of cooperation for many economists has been the antitrust field. However, economists have gone beyond traditional areas to undertake research on criminal justice, pollution, poverty, racial discrimination, land use planning, accident prevention, landlord–tenant relations, and urban government, among others, where their interests often dovetail with those of lawyers.

The interaction between lawyers and economists gained scope in the 1980s and 1990s, when many business decisions appeared to be made in

---

[10] Phillip Lederer, *Perspectives on Operations Strategy Economics,* Working Paper OP-96-03 (Rochester: University of Rochester, 1996).

[11] Paul A. Samuelson and William D. Nordhaus, *Economics,* 13th ed. (New York: McGraw-Hill, 1989): 5.

[12] Maynard J. Keynes, *The General Theory of Employment, Interest and Money* (London: MacMillan, 1936). As quoted by Robert Heilbroner in *The Worldly Philosophers,* revised edition (New York: Simon and Schuster, 1972).

courthouses rather than in boardrooms. Some of those court decisions can have a bigger impact on sales and earnings than the marketplace itself.

The breakup of American Telephone and Telegraph, decreed by a federal court, is the biggest case of the early 1980s, but situations involving Texaco, E.F. Hutton, and Eastman Kodak are also of enormous proportions. Texaco, in the early 1980s the nation's third largest oil company, was forced to fight for its life after a jury found that Texaco interfered with Pennzoil's plans to merge with Getty Oil and awarded Pennzoil $11.1 billion in damages.

E.F. Hutton, a securities firm, suffered a devastating blow to its image and probably to its economic health after pleading guilty to mail and wire fraud. Eastman Kodak was forced from the instant camera market by a court decision. The asbestos and tobacco industries are deeply concerned about liability suits. Manville Corporation, once a mighty manufacturer of asbestos, was forced to seek protection under the bankruptcy laws because of an anticipated avalanche of suits connected with asbestos deaths. And tobacco companies are seriously worried about suits by state governments, health care providers, and long-term smokers afflicted by lung cancer. In order to avoid never-ending litigation and possibly punitive legislation, by early 1998 tobacco companies had settled massive lawsuits filed by four states and health care providers in them. The Texas settlement provides over a number of years for $15.3 billion; Florida, for $11.0 billion; Minnesota, for $6.6 billion, and Mississippi, for $3.4 billion. For example, in the Minnesota settlement of $6.6 billion, $6.17 billion goes to the state and the rest to Blue Cross and Blue Shield. (The state actions followed a failed national settlement proposed to amount to $368.5 billion.[13]

But there is another point of contact. It relates to the criticism voiced by some that legal scholars view the law too much from within — too much in terms of the law's own logical structure. When law steps outside itself, these critics claim, it lacks a well-developed theoretical or empirical apparatus with which to explore the world around it. Yet as legal scholars look outside law, they find that economics has developed paradigms that seem to provide a powerful analytic framework for the study of the law.

There exist three basic approaches to establishing a successful collaboration in intellectual endeavors that apply law and economics. One, which involves legal rule formulation, is akin to normative or welfare economics when its concern is maximization of an objective function, e.g., allocative efficiency. The second approach is one of effect evaluation and is akin to

---

[13] Henry Weinstein, "Big Tobacco Settles Minnesota Lawsuit for $6.6 Billion," *Los Angeles Times* (May 9, 1998): A1.

positive economics. It looks upon microeconomic analysis as a tool for deriving testable hypotheses that can be verified by empirical, often econometric analysis. With this approach, one seeks answers to the question of what is the likely effect of a particular law, be it court-made or statutory. Finally, a law, economics, and organizational perspective has been advanced. The focus is on transaction costs and the working of different legal forms of organization.

The interaction between lawyers and economists has benefited both sides. Law not only offers economists interesting problems, but also thinking in particularistic terms. At the same time, economics offers abstractions derived by microeconomic theory and mathematical economics, making possible generalization of goals, e.g., efficiency, and legal rules, e.g., the Learned Hand formula, which will be discussed in Chapter 6.[14] The use of economic and particularly mathematical models can increase the rigor of legal analysis. However, there is a risk when a host of limiting assumptions are relied upon in the model, at a time that the actual legal phenomena are frustratingly complex. The results can then be gravely misleading.

LEGAL RULE FORMULATION

Rule formulation seeks to maximize or minimize some specified goal, often alloactive efficiency. Normative or welfare economics is ideally suited for this task. This approach usually is applied after a failure to achieve a desired goal. Efforts are then undertaken to prescribe corrective solutions.

Efforts of rule formulation are in the rational intellectual tradition of William Blackstone[15] on the legal side and Adam Smith[16] on the economic side. They can also be traced to Jeremy Bentham's utilitarianism, "in its aspect as a positive theory of human behavior, ... another name for economic theory."[17]

A modern-day proponent is Posner. His view of the world of economics and to no small extent of law includes the assumption "that man is a rational maximizer of his ends in life,"[18] an assumption he correctly reminds us is "no stronger than that most people in most affairs of life are guided by what they conceive to be their self-interest and that they choose means

[14] Melvin A. Eisenberg, *An Overview of Law and Economics*, Working Paper No. 90-9 (Berkeley, CA: University of California School of Law, Center for the Study of Law and Society, 1991): 2–8.

[15] William Blackstone, *Commentaries on the Law of England*, 4 vols. (n.p., 1765–1769).

[16] Smith, *Wealth of Nations.*

[17] Jeremy Bentham, *Theory of Legislation*, R. Hildreth, Ed. (n.p., 1864): 325–326, 357.

[18] Posner, *Economic Analysis of Law*, 3d ed.: 1.

reasonably (not perfectly) designed to promote it."[19] On the basis of this assumption, three major fundamental economic concepts emerge.[20] The first is the inverse relation between price and quantity; the second is the economist's view of cost as opportunity cost, that is, the price that the resources consumed in making (and selling) the seller's product would command in their next best use — the alternative price; and the third is the tendency of resources to gravitate toward their highest value uses if exchange is permitted. If voluntarily exchanged, resources are shifted to those uses in which the value to the consumer, as measured by the consumer's willingness to pay, is highest. When resources are being used where their value is greatest, they are being employed efficiently; they produce the largest possible output. On the basis of microeconomic arguments — those that allegedly reflect the behavior of firms and households — Posner, for example, is convinced that "it may be possible to deduce the basic formal characteristics of law itself from economic theory";[21] consequently he argues that "the ultimate question for decision in many lawsuits is, what allocation of resources would maximize efficiency?"[22]

However, the application of microeconomic theory to legal rule formulation poses a number of serious problems. For example, microeconomic theory assumes that human beings are rational; whatever they do is in their best interest, given their tastes, market opportunities, and circumstances. This, in short, is the fundamental tenet of the *theory of revealed preferences*. By this theory, economists treat the actual behavior of consumers as faithfully reflecting preferences, and they consider preferences shown to be an extension of consumer behavior. Yet the theory is basically circular; it argues that since people are rationally self-interested, what they do shows what they value, and their willingness to pay for what they value is the ultimate proof of their rational self-interest. Some scholars have criticized the circularity of the argument; Leff, for example, points to the following difficulties:

> If human desire itself becomes normative (in the sense that it cannot be criticized), and if human desire is made definitionally identical with certain human acts, then those human acts are also beyond criticism in normative or efficiency terms; everyone is doing as best he can exactly what he set out to do which, by definition, is "good" for him. In those terms, it is not at all surprising that economic analyses have "considerable power in predicting how people in fact behave."[23]

---

[19] *Ibid.*: 5.
[20] *Ibid.*: 6.
[21] *Ibid.*: 393.
[22] *Ibid.*: 320.
[23] A. Leff, "Economic Analysis of Law: Some Realism about Nominalism," *Virginia Law Review* 60 (March 1974): 458.

The question has also been asked whether value is indeed determined by people's willingness to pay or whether it is not determined rather by people's ability to pay for a good or service. As Thurow sees it, "A market economy that starts with an unjust distribution of economic resources will yield an unjust distribution of goods and services, regardless of its efficiency."[24]

Additionally, there is an even more serious problem: The theory is best equipped to deal with resource-allocation efficiency, but justice and fairness, which relate to distributional issues, must also be considered.[25] Our task would be so much easier if efficiency could be rigorously defended as the only and ultimate objective. Instead we face two all-too-often opposing objectives — efficiency and equity. What is the most desirable distribution of income is a highly subjective decision. Nevertheless, legal rules must be concerned about both efficiency and income distribution.

Another problem is that efficiency must be related to a specific objective function. For example, if one were to assert that the purpose of criminal punishment is to deter criminal behavior, one therefore would like to see punishment commensurate with the committed crime. If, moreover, one were to find that the social costs of incarceration exceeded by far fines that might be imposed — because of the cost of running a prison, the loss of prisoners' productivity, and the prison's ill effects on prisoners — one would conclude that an efficient administration of justice should merely dispense fines. However, this conclusion results from the assumption of the existence of a single-valued objective function — deterrence. But what if society and therefore legislators and particularly law enforcement officers insist (as appears to be the case) not merely on deterrence but also on retribution through such punitive action as incarceration? Then the analyst will be forced to reach different efficiency conclusions about the criminal justice system, unless he turns preacher and calls to outlaw retribution. Furthermore, there are criminals who can neither be deterred by fines nor rehabilitated. Incarcerating them may be the only way to protect society. There is little evidence that economists or lawyers are particularly well qualified to select the most appropriate objective functions. As a matter of fact, many economists tend to have tunnel vision, since they find it more agreeable to engage in partial equilibrium, that is, piecemeal, rather than general equilibrium analysis — not because they are intellectually lazy,

---

[24] L. Thurow, "Economic Justice and the Economist: A Reply," *Public Interest* 33 (Fall 1973): 120.

[25] For a carefully articulated vision of justice, see John Rawls, *A Theory of Justice* (Cambridge: Harvard University Press, 1971).

but because the latter is so much more complex and often beyond their reach.

A final problem is that even for the determination of optimal allocative efficiency conditions, economists are forced to make a number of restrictive assumptions. At least three such assumptions are made in relation to Pareto efficiency: *zero transaction costs, zero redistribution costs,* and *convexity.* By transaction costs economists mean real resources employed in bargaining, getting information, and formalizing and enforcing agreements — costs that interfere with the working of competitive markets.[26] Thus, the assumption that all transactions are costless and that information about costs and prices is effortlessly available removes us far from real life.

The second assumption relates to the cost of redistributing incomes among consumers. Given that the initial endowment into which the population is born is considered inappropriate and redistribution is undertaken, virtually every redistribution scheme is costly in that it distorts incentives and behavior and imposes political as well as administrative costs. Thus, for example, efforts toward redistribution through an income tax that changes consumers' budgets, their spending habits, and their preferences for leisure are unlikely to be costless.[27]

The economic implications of the third assumption, convexity, circumscribe the structure of consumers' preferences and producers' technology. For example, with respect to households, convexity means, in the words of Arrow, that "if we consider two different bundles of consumption, a third bundle defined by averaging the first two commodity by commodity is not inferior in the household's preferences to both of the first two."[28] An example of nonconvexity would be the renter who has for years lived in the downtown area and then moves to the suburbs because of unchecked increases in downtown crime. Now a suburbanite, his interest in seeing crime combatted in the core city vanishes.[29] Nonconvexities are very common and lead to market failure, interfering with Pareto efficiency.

[26] See Werner Z. Hirsch, "Reducing Law's Uncertainty and Complexity," *UCLA Law Review* 21 (1974): 1239, and K. J. Arrow, "The Organization of Economic Activity: Issues Pertinent to the Choice of Market versus Non-market Allocation," in *The Analysis and Evaluation of Public Expenditure: The PPB System,* a Compendium of Papers of the Joint Economic Committee (Washington, D.C.: U.S. Government Printing Office, 1969): 47–63.

[27] T. C. Koopmans, *Three Essays on the State of Economic Science* (New York: McGraw-Hill, 1957).

[28] Kenneth Arrow, *The Organization of Economic Activity: Issues Pertinent to the Choice of Market versus Non-market Allocation* (Washington, D.C.: Joint Economic Committee of Congress, 1969): 49.

[29] M. Polinsky, "Economic Analysis as a Potentially Defective Product: A Buyer's Guide to Posner's Economic Analysis of Law," *Harvard Law Review* 87 (June 1974): 1655–1681.

EFFECT EVALUATION

Just as rule formulation draws heavily on normative or welfare economics, effect evaluation involves positive economic analysis. This approach seeks to estimate or predict the behavioral responses to a change in legal environment, one that is either contemplated or already in place. As with all positive economic analysis, legal effect evaluation seeks to make quantitative predictions and organizes data for empirical testing.

I would like to sound a note of caution: most positive economic models establish partial relationships. This reduces the universality and application of the analysis and leads to criticism from lawyers. From their point of view, effect evaluations of economists are often seen as simplistic and unable to capture the complexity of the legal phenomena at hand.

In spite of these criticisms, legal effect evaluation with the aid of positive economic analysis can make major contributions in providing answers to such questions as: What are the likely effects of a proposed law? What were the effects of an existing law? Have its objectives been obtained?

Thus, for the purpose of effect evaluation, it is necessary first to build a microeconomic model that represents as closely as possible the specific environment in which transactions take place and of which the law is an important part, a model that links the environment to various outcome dimensions. One of the great challenges is to model the specific law and its effects on important outcomes without doing too much violence to real-life conditions. Yet the model cannot be too complex, for complexity reduces the likelihood of its empirical implementation. The single most significant implementation step involves econometric techniques. When the modeling and the econometric work are successful, quantitative statements about the probable effects of the law, that is, statements within an inference setting, become possible. They will be presented throughout the rest of this volume in relation to property, contract, tort, criminal, environmental, antitrust, and discrimination law. Particularly, the quantitative undertakings serve either to help determine the nature of an appropriate legal rule, or to provide information to decide whether a particular act conforms with existing law.[30]

But, not infrequently, existing microeconomic theory and econometric methods and the availability of data limit the degree to which definitive quantitative statements about side effects can be made. In such instances we must be satisfied with deductive inquiries based on microeconomic models that can yield qualitative conclusions of major policy value.

---

[30] Isenberg, *Overview of Law and Economics.* 9–11.

Examples of the possible application of microeconomic theory and econometrics to the estimation of side effects are quite numerous.

LAW, ECONOMICS, AND ORGANIZATION PERSPECTIVE

A new institutional perspective that relates to law, economics, and organization theory focuses on how feasible legal forms of organization work.[31] It is based on the premise that legal institutions matter and lend themselves to analysis. The law, economics, and organization perspective relies on a firm-as-governance structure in which contracts are assumed to be incomplete and the action is concentrated on the mechanisms of ex post governance. It is positive and thoroughly interactive and makes use of transaction cost economics. Transaction cost economics considers transactions as the basic unit of analysis and focuses on aligning them with alternative modes of governance, e.g., markets and departments, with the objective of economizing transaction costs.[32] Its main application is to contract and antitrust law. With the help of transaction cost economics many economic phenomena can be reformulated as contracting problems. Then efforts can be undertaken to minimize transaction costs of contracts and organizations.[33] In the presence of inefficiencies, these efforts would seek to identify the contract that would remove the inefficiencies and the impediments to be overcome in its implementation.

WHERE LAW AND ECONOMICS MIGHT NOT MEET

Although lawyer and economist have much in common, there are also some significant differences in their approaches. Only two fundamental differences will be taken up — the law's reference to a *reasonable* man versus the economist's assumption of a rational man, and the incrementalism of the economist versus the binary aspect of the court, which finds a defendant either liable or not liable.

The lawyer's concept of a reasonable man is distinct from the economist's rational man. The reasonable man, according to the traditional tort literature, will ordinarily behave in a reasonable, prudent manner. Thus, he will act with fair regard for the welfare of others. Negligent conduct, for example, which departs from the standard of the reasonable man, is in a real

---

[31] Willimson, *Revisiting Legal Realism*: 42; Oliver E. Williamson and Scott E. Masten, Eds., *Transaction Cost Economics* (Brookfield, VT: Edward Elgar, 1995).

[32] Williamson, *Revisiting Legal Realism:* 13.

[33] *Ibid.*: 39–42.

sense subnormal and deviant; this deviance helps to justify the imposition of liability rules on tortfeasors, about which more will be said subsequently.

The rational man, according to traditional economic theory, seeks to maximize his own self-interest; he shows only limited concern for the well-being of others.[34] This self-centered drive produces outcomes in which private and social costs diverge. These outcomes can conflict with the overall societal interest. Attaining private net benefit (e.g., profit) objectives is often inconsistent with the attainment of societal net benefit objectives.

Court rulings — except when comparative-negligence tort standards are applied — are usually much more rigid and as a result extreme in their effects. A court finds a defendant liable or not; insofar as the defendant's reputation, for example, is concerned, the effects of the two outcomes are grossly different. Once the defendant has been found liable, however, the court has some leeway and can apply incrementalism in sentencing, that is, in the kind and severity of punishment.

ENTITLEMENTS AND EXTERNALITIES AND THE ROLE OF THE LAW

The law, as was stated earlier, provides guidelines for transactions between parties. It does so by explicitly stipulating and allocating rights and entitlements, and responsibilities, and by providing remedial rights. By so doing the law can help minimize conflicts; moreover, it offers rules by which conflicts, should they arise, can be resolved fairly. From the economist's point of view, certain classes of conflict are closely related to externalities in that a conflict is the direct result of an externality. But before we look at externalities, let us consider rights and entitlements that are violated in the presence of externalities.

The *Restatement of Property* defines a right as "a legally enforceable claim of one person against another, that the other shall do a given act or shall not do a give act."[35] Therefore, property rights may be thought of in terms of the legal relationships — rights and duties — between a property owner and another person. One has a property right when one is able to compel another legally to do or not to do a given act. Thus, when a person's activity cause damage to a landowner, the landowner is endowed with a property right that can be invoked to force the person causing the damage to cease the activity and to compensate the landowner for the damage incurred.

---

[34] *Ibid.*: 39–42.
[35] *Restatement of Property*, §1.

An entitlement is akin to a property right. It is the legitimate claim a person has and prevails in case of conflict. There exist two major views on entitlements. One is a natural and historical view that looks at entitlements as exogenously determined. Accordingly, entitlements are fundamental, exogenous claims that direct governments to pursue, for example, such goals as freedom of speech, protection against criminals, etc. In part this view is expressed by Ronald Dworkin, who states,

> Arguments of principle are arguments intended to establish an individual right; arguments of policy are arguments intended to establish a collective goal. Principles are propositions that describe rights; policies are propositions that describe goals ... I shall make ... a formal distinction that ... provides a guide for discovering which rights a particular political theory supposes men and women to have ... a political theory which holds a right to freedom of speech as absolute will recognize no reason for not securing the liberty it requires for every individual.[36]

Dworkin goes on to argue that individuals have rights and entitlements that exist prior to any explicit legislation, and the most fundamental of these is a person's entitlement to equality.

Robert Nozick states that the "historical principles of justice hold that past circumstances or actions of people can create differential entitlements. ... An injustice can be worked by moving from one distribution to another structurally identical one, for the second, in profile, the same, may violate people's entitlements."[37]

The second view looks upon entitlements as policy instruments that are endogenous. It is well expressed by Calabresi and Melamed, who maintain that

> the state not only has to decide whom to entitle, but it must also simultaneously make a series of equally difficult second order decisions. These decisions go to the manner in which entitlements are protected and to whether an individual is allowed to sell or trade the entitlement. In any given dispute, for example, the state must decide not only which side wins but also the kind of protection to grant. It is ... the latter decisions, ... which shape the subsequent relationship between the winner and the loser.[38]

[36] Ronald Dworkin, *Taking Rights Seriously* (Cambridge: Harvard University Press, 1977): 90–92. Similar views are taken by John Rawls, *A Theory of Justice* (Cambridge: Harvard University Press, 1971).

[37] Robert Nozick, *Anarchy, State, and Utopia* (New York: Basic Books, 1974): 155.

[38] G. Calabresi and A. D. Melamed, "Property Rules, Liability Rules, and Inalienability: One View of the Cathedral," *Harvard Law Review* 85 (April, 1972): 1092. Copyright © 1972 by the Harvard Law Review Association. Similar views are held by R. Coase, H. Demsetz, and R. Posner.

Examples of entitlements that are in fact endogenously derived policy instruments can be found in the Universal Declaration of Human Rights adopted by the United Nations General Assembly in 1948.

Article 23:

1. Everyone has the right to work, to free choice of employment, to just and favorable conditions of work and protection against unemployment.
2. Everyone, without any discrimination, has the right to equal pay for equal work.
3. Everyone who works has the right to just and favorable remuneration ..., and supplemented, "if necessary, by other means of Social Protection."

Article 25:

1. Everyone has the right to a standard of living for the health and well-being of himself and of his family....
2. Motherhood and childhood are entitled to special care and assistance.

Article 26:

1. Everyone has the right to education. ..."[39]

Now let us turn to externalities. An externality exists whenever the decision of such economic actors as a household or firm directly affects, through nonmarket transactions, the utility or production functions of other economic actors. An externality thus results as resources are exchanged in nonmarked situations commonly involving involuntary exchange.

A simple example of externality is shown in Figure 1—1, which depicts the demand and marginal cost curves for the product of a firm that emits smoke into the air in the course of production (the latter also is the firm's supply curve). The market equilibrium output and price levels occur at points Q' and P'. Yet this equilibrium is not efficient, for it does not consider the social cost imposed on residents who live near the factory and who must bear the discomfort caused by the smoke. If we assume that the discomfort to all the individuals equals T dollars per unit of production, then the full social marginal cost of production would be located T dollars above the firm's private marginal cost curve. The efficient equilibrium would be at output level Q and price P. In this case, the firm must pay for its true costs of production (we can assume that the firm directly compensates the individuals in the community).

---

[39] U.N.G.A. Res. 217A(III), U.N. Dec. A/810, at 71 (December 19, 1948).

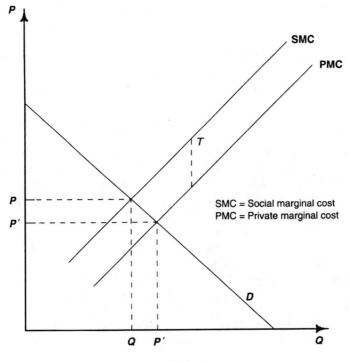

FIGURE 1—1

Technically, one individual's (household's, government's, or firm's) consumption can enter into another's utility (or production) function without proper market compensation because of imperfect appropriation of entitlements or rights.[40] *Imperfect appropriability of rights* means that because of a variety of reasons an individual, household, firm, or governmental unit is unable to appropriate (or capture) the full marginal value of the benefits each produces, or is unable to alleviate costs somebody else imposes.[41] Thus, even though from an economic perspective the holder of rights should be able to make decisions about resources and to claim the resulting rewards, there may be reasons why these rights cannot be asserted. Since these rights and entitlements help shape the individual's, household's,

[40] R. N. McKean, "Appropriability and Externalities in Urban Government" (paper prepared for the October 22, 1971, COUPE meeting in Cambridge, Mass.): 2.

[41] Ethical and institutional reasons may reduce appropriability, though to a lesser extent than do technological conditions.

firm's, and governmental unit's set of opportunities and trade-offs, and therefore their behavior, the effectiveness with which these rights and entitlements are enforced will also affect behavior.

When there is imperfect appropriability of rights, then Musgrave's "exclusion principle" cannot work. This principle postulates that an individual should be "excluded from the enjoyment of any particular commodity or service unless he is willing to pay the stipulated price to the owner."[42] When there is joint consumption, as in Coase's lighthouse case,[43] and exclusion is impossible or requires considerable resources, then rights will be imperfectly appropriated. In short, appropriability can be made easy or difficult because of technological and other characteristics of the phenomenon under consideration. It is the high cost of effectively excluding individuals from partaking in joint consumption without proper payment, that is, the high transaction cost, that interferes with the existence of a market and brings about externalities.

Since an externality is generated by one or more decision units directly affecting one or more units (often including the first unit) outside the marketplace, several important questions are raised. Which actors initiate the externality and which are affected by it? For example, in the case of congestion, many individuals participate in affecting others' utility functions, with virtually complete reciprocity. Thus they all contribute equally and are all equally affected. However, in the case of pollution, one or a few individuals (or firms) affect the utility (or production) functions of very many individuals without any reciprocity.

When economic activities are characterized by properties of positive externalities and nonexcludability, they give rise to public goods. They can be produced by government, controlled by it, or their production contracted out. Althougth there are relatively few pure public goods — for example, aircraft carriers — there are many public goods with varying degrees of purity.

In the preceding pages I have developed the concept of externalities and have suggested that in their presence public goods can arise and, more importantly, conflicts may occur. In either case, there is an important role for the law to play.

Whenever there are conflicting interests the law decides whose rights are entitled to prevail. As Calabresi and Melamed have pointed out, "the placement of entitlements has a fundamental effect on a society's distribu-

---

[42] Richard A. Musgrave, *The Theory of Public Finance* (New York: McGraw-Hill, 1959): 9.
[43] Ronald Coase, "The Lighthouses in Economics," *Journal of Law and Economics* 17 (1974): 357–376.

tion of wealth."[44] It is the country's constitution and its general values and mores that determine entitlements, such as to property, to free education, and to collective protection against crime and fire. Thus, private property can be looked upon as an entitlement that is permanently protected by a property rule. This rule involves a collective decision, based on the country's values, as to who is to be given an initial entitlement. The value of the property is determined not by the property rule, but by voluntary market transactions. These transactions are facilitated and enforced by property and contract laws.

Property rules stipulate and protect entitlements by ensuring that anyone wishing to remove an entitlement from its holder must buy it from him in a voluntary transaction in which the value of the entitlement and terms of the transaction are agreed upon by the relevant parties. Property law thus guides transactors of real property, that is, land and improvements, by providing rules than can help minimize conflicts among the transactors and can help resolve conflicts that arise, whether they are settled out of court or by the court. Contract law provides guidelines in relation to similar issues faced with respect mainly to other than real property. It provides for enforcement mechanisms, including rules on defenses and damages, in addition to procedures and institutions for enforcement. For example, compensation is paid if an agreed-upon voluntary transfer of entitlements is not carried out in full.

From the economist's point of view, a major role of contract law and property law is to reduce transaction costs. Either law does so by providing prospective transactors with a set of normal exchange conditions. Moreover, the law provides useful information about contingencies — externalities in association with partially or totally aborted exchanges — and about how the courts seek to cure losses resulting from these contingencies. As transaction costs are reduced, more transactions result and can be carried out with enhanced efficiency; social welfare is thus increased. Examples of property law applications are violations of a warranty-of-habitability law; examples of contract law applications are violations of an implied warranty-of-merchantability.

We can also look upon the courts as applying the guidelines of property and contract law in order to protect owners of entitlements against adverse externalities. They do so by playing the role of externality adjusters. Historically, the courts have been jealous of this role. Although adversary proceedings could be reduced in number and transactions made more efficient if the parties were to agree in advance on specified liquidated damages in

---

[44] Calabresi and Melamed, "Property Rules": 1098.

case of breach, courts have been reluctant to recognize liquidated damages. An overt stipulation could reduce uncertainties associated with a transaction. Each party could anticipate the gains and losses associated with a breach, rather than speculate what a jury would find to be an appropriate award.

Although the initial entitlement is protected by property rules, its destruction is protected by liability rules; the party responsible (e.g., the tortfeasor) pays an objectively determined value. Under a liability rule, an external, objective standard of value is applied in relation to the transfer of entitlements. Thus, if in the presence of externalities entitlements are forcibly taken (e.g., if the government alters the laissez-faire distribution of property rights or a steel plant imposes externalities on neighbors), liability rules go into effect and guide the payment of damages. Damage awards are established by unilateral public assessment rather than by private negotiation, and enforcement is the responsibility of government. The reason why a liability rule is invoked and government intervenes is that tortious acts would involve extremely high transaction costs if market valuation of entitlements were to be relied on. Examples are not only accidental damages, but government taking by eminent domain as well.

There are some special cases of entitlement transfers. For example, relative to crimes against persons or property, society refuses to convert property rules into liability rules and merely seek a compensation for the victim. Since society highly values respect for prevailing property rules, it opposes their violation by criminals. Therefore it imposes criminal sanctions in the hope of deterring future attempts to change property rules into liability rules.

Thus, society decides that certain entitlements are not freely transferable between willing buyers and sellers. The collective decision thus is that criminal conduct is not to be tolerated even though some individuals are willing to pay for the privilege of engaging in it. Society determines that the entitlement is inalienable and by so doing it limits or regulates the grant of the entitlement. Moreover, government may also establish mandatory minimum standards of conduct for permitted activities. For example, an inalienable entitlement might be for neighbors not to be disturbed by noisy bars and their drunken patrons after midnight. This in turn would mean that bars would have to meet a mandatory minimum standard of conduct, that is, they would have to close before midnight. The bar owner is prevented from undertaking a prohibited activity, even if he is willing to pay for its external costs. Mandatory minimum standards are based on collective directives in turn based on the community's values at the time. They can lead not only to orders to cease and desist but also to orders for affirmative action (e.g., a mandatory order included in a housing code).

In order to round out the discussion of four key law fields, we should point out that they also differ with regard to the conditions under which compensation is awarded to adjust for an externality. A contract or lease breaker is required to pay damages even if the breach results in an improved resource use. The same holds for trespassers, and the reasons are the same (i.e., more voluntary exchanges and greater efficiency of the exchange). Thus, parties are more likely to enter contracts if they are assured of legal protection in case of breach, and they are likely to own more real property if they are legally protected against unjustified impairment of the entitlement. Yet tortfeasors, who cause injury to a victim, are not liable to pay compensation if cost-justified precautions could not have prevented the accident, at least not under a negligence and contributory-negligence standard. This is because in accident cases compensation to victims of harm for which the injurer was not negligently responsible would raise transaction costs without producing benefits.

A further difference exists with regard to punitive damages, which, for example, in California, are allowable in personal injury cases. Punitive damages, unlike compensatory damages, are designed to deter and prevent one person from harming another. In some respects, they resemble sanctions imposed under criminal law. Thus, under tort law compensatory damages and sometimes punitive damages are levied, whereas under property law and contract law virtually always the former only are applied.

In summary, conflicts over property rights and entitlements are often resolved through the use of legal institutions. These conflicts can become severe when the property rights or entitlements are not well defined (e.g., when there are externalities present). The existence of externalities precludes the attainment of an optimal solution solely within the confines of the private marketplace. The use of legal as well as political institutions is often necessary in order to determine an acceptable allocation of resources, rights, and entitlements. Legal thought and economic analysis can be joined in the hope of attaining an insightful evaluation of laws and legal systems. This notion provides the intellectual underpinnings of many of the arguments that are presented in the following chapters.

2

PROPERTY LAW'S BASIC LEGAL PREMISES

INTRODUCTION

American property law has deep historical roots in English common law. From this beginning, property law has slowly changed to meet new conditions as they emerge in an increasingly urbanized and industrialized society. As we will see, the law has struggled to adjust itself to new circumstances.

In this chapter the basic legal premises of property law are examined.[1] First I discuss rights and entitlements to property, their permanent transfer, and their temporary transfer. Then I take up land use planning and development. Other chapters explore some of the economic aspects of certain property laws — landlord–tenant laws (Chapter 3) and zoning laws (Chapter 4). Three chapters are devoted to property laws to demonstrate in greater detail and depth the scope and methodology of law and economics.

DEFINING RIGHTS AND ENTITLEMENTS TO PROPERTY

Private property, under the American system of law, can be considered an entitlement protected by a property rule. Property law provides the rules with regard to the entitlement to land and improvements thereon. These

---

[1] American property law can be traced as far back as the Statute of Uses passed by Parliament in 1535. For a detailed treatment of property law, see A. James Casner and W. Barton Leach, *Cases and Texts on Property* (Boston: Little, Brown, 1969).

rules enhance the certainty of who owns a given property and under what circumstances. Moreover, they facilitate efficient transfer of title.

OWNERSHIP, POSSESSION, AND CONTROL

Of particular interest to lawyer and economist alike is the degree to which a given party has a right to a certain property under specified conditions. We can distinguish between ownership, possession, and control in an attempt to define the differing extent of a right to a particular property. An *ownership right* means that the enforcing party (e.g., the state) has determined that the holder of this entitlement has the benefit of the property for most uses. The owner will be able to transfer this right to others and accrue income from its use. However, there are certain restrictions on the owner's right to transfer. For example, an owner will not be allowed to limit the sale of his or her property to members of a certain racial group.

A *holder of possession* has more limited rights than an owner. He or she is temporarily entitled to the benefit of the asset or good while maintaining possession, but use is restricted, depending on whether the holder is a bailee or whether possession is constructive, adverse, involuntary, or unconscious. Although an owner is entitled to the property over a possessor, a possessor will be able to exclude one who merely *controls* a good, for example, a trespasser. An individual who is merely in control of a property has an extremely limited right.

THE ECONOMICS OF PROPERTY RIGHTS AND ENTITLEMENTS

The concept of property rights may be venerable, but that of entitlements is of more recent vintage. As discussed in Chapter 1, the latter concept is much broader than the first, referring to the legitimate claims possessed by a person.

Property Rights

The concept of property rights relates to the set of privileges and responsibilities accorded to a person in relation to the owning of property in general and real property in particular. These rights are determined by a long history of property laws, whether common laws or statutory laws. The right to property is the power to exclude others from or give them access to a benefit or use of the particular object. An elaborate system of property, liability, and inalienability rules exists to bolster an owner's claim to the property or good. Property rights to an unexplored area, such as the moon or the sea, are determined by international agreements entered into by

bodies that have the power to enforce them. A mere individual without
the coercive power of government could not hope to enforce a claim to,
for example, the Atlantic Ocean.

The presence of property rights furnishes incentives to use resources
efficiently. Given a legal system that enforces property rights, holders can
have confidence that they will obtain returns from the use of property.

Under what conditions is a system of property rights efficient? The conditions include universality, exclusivity, and transferability. *Universality* implies
that all resources should be owned by someone. *Exclusivity* is defined as
the right to exclude people who might want to take part of the property.
Transferability provides for voluntary exchanges that in general are value enhancing.

Universality is clearly preferred because the assignment of rights provides
the maximum amount of economic incentive to use resources efficiently.
The only exception is for goods so plentiful that everyone can consume
them without reducing enjoyment by anyone else.

The Coase Theorem The existence of externalities limits the extent to which
property rights are exclusive. Ronald Coase examined the relation between
externalities and Pareto-optimal resource allocation in the case of incompatible land uses. His work is often referred to as the Coase theorem, which,
based on limiting assumptions, produces the important result that in the
presence of externalities, the initial assignment of property rights will not
affect the ultimate use of the property. In fact, a Pareto-optimal resource
allocation of incompatible land uses can be obtained by bargaining parties
independent of the initial assignment of property rights. Here are some
of the assumptions underlying the Coase theorem (a few are explicit, while
others are implicit) — zero transactions costs, two agents to each externality
(and bargain), perfect knowledge of one another's (convex) production
and profit or utility functions, competitive markets, profit-maximizing producers and expected utility-maximizing consumers, and zero wealth effects.[2]

According to the Coase theorem, under the assumptions mentioned
above, the Pareto-optimal resource allocation in the case of incompatible
land uses will be obtained independent of the initial assignment of property rights.[3]

One important implication of the Coase theorem is that as long as the
various assumptions are met, particularly as long as transaction costs are

---

[2] Elizabeth Hoffman and Matthew L. Spitzer, "The Coase Theorem, Some Experimental
Tests," *Journal of Law and Economics* 25 (April 1982): 73.
[3] Ronald Coase, "The Problem of Social Cost," *Journal of Law and Economics* 3 (October
1960): 1–44.

zero, efficiency is unaffected regardless of which party is held liable. This is because both actors must consider the explicit cost of the activity itself as well as the implicit cost represented by the payment for not conducting the activity that the nonliable party could obtain. To demonstrate, suppose that A and B engage in incompatible land uses and A is given the right to pollute B's stream. This is worth $50 to A. However, B would pay $60 to A not to pollute. With no transaction costs, it is clear that both parties would agree not to pollute, even though the pollution is worth $50 to A. That is because the $60 payment he could receive from B represents a very real cost to A. Hence, he will bargain for a payment exceeding $50 from B. Similarly, if B was given the right to prevent the pollution, there would be no pollution, since A could offer B only $50 not to exercise his right and it is worth $60 to B to stop the pollution. Hence, the efficient result is reached in either case.

This result may be qualified depending on the initial distribution of wealth. Since A is richer in the first example and B in the second, such wealth distribution could alter demand for the pollution. Similarly, the initial assignment of the right could be determinative in an extreme case, for example, where two men negotiate for a bottle of water necessary for survival in a desert.

Coase also mentions that, in determining a government solution to a market-system imperfection, the possible inefficiencies in the government solution should also be considered, and a cost–benefit analysis of the two systems should be undertaken. A further point made by Coase is that placing liability on those who might be considered to have caused a negative externality, i.e., the active party (the polluter in our example), may lead to inefficient results.

Remember the crucial assumption of the Coase theorem: zero transaction costs. What can we say when these costs are not zero? When transactions are not costless, efficiency is advanced if the right is assigned to the party who would normally buy it, especially if transaction costs are so high that no exchange is likely. Then it is economically preferable to assign the initial property right to the party whose use is more valuable. Alternatively, liability could be imposed on the party whose use was less valuable, an assignment that would result in tort liability. Furthermore, even in cases where transaction costs are not zero, the Coase theorem should approximate reality whenever these costs are smaller than is the value of the transaction to the parties.[4] Often such a determination is hard to make and compromises are arrived at. Hence, a train that emits sparks that set fire to a farmer's crops

---

[4] Posner, *Economic Analysis of Law*, 4th ed. (Boston: Little, Brown, 1992): 51.

may be fitted with a spark arrester to reduce sparks, the farmer may remove some of his crops from the neighboring tracks, or he may plant crops that are more fire resistant.

The ability to shift a resource from a less productive to a more productive use via exchange provides economic rationale for the free transferability of goods. When these transaction costs are high it is often necessary to make property rights less exclusive.

Entitlements

Rather than argue in terms of property rights, it might be advantageous to rely on the notion of entitlements, as suggested by Calabresi and Melamed.[5] As was indicated in Chapter 1, there are two ways of looking at entitlements. On the one hand, they can be considered as policy instruments for government use in its pursuit of efficiency or income redistribution or both.[6] On the other hand, entitlements can be conceived of as bestowed on men and women in the form of natural or fundamental privileges that are to be protected by the state.[7]

Thus, we refer to entitlements as those privileges and responsibilities that accrue to an individual by virtue of his or her birth into a particular society at a given moment in time. These entitlements find their basis in the values and the mores and possibly in the constitution of the society. They include any and all human rights that might be assigned to persons, whereas property rights emphasize specific and more lasting rights associated with physical property.

Or, to put it differently, in the presence of major interdependencies among different persons' utilities, the values and mores of society determine entitlements in the light of externalities that come about. Just as these interdependencies can change over time, so can society's evaluation of the desirability and fairness of the externalities' impact. Consequently, human entitlements can and do change over time, whereas property rights tend to be much more stable. Thus, entitlements are good in a broader sense to indicate other rights that are not generally considered to be property rights. For example, the right to free education might be considered an entitlement rather than a property right, because education is not a physical object, nor are privileges of free public education venerable and immutable.

---

[5] Calabresi and Melamed, "Property Rules, Liability Rules, and Inalienability: One View of the Cathedral," *Harvard Law Review* 85 (April 1972): 1089–1128.

[6] Dworkin, *Taking Rights Seriously* (Cambridge: Harvard University Press, 1977): 90–92; John Rawls, *A Theory of Justice* (Cambridge: Harvard University Press, 1971); Nozick, *Anarchy, State, and Utopia* (New York: Basic Books, 1974): 155.

[7] Calbresi and Melamed, "Property Rules": 1092.

Occasionally there will be a conflict between the broader class of human entitlements and the narrower class of property rights. This might occur, for example, when a compromising picture of an individual is taken, with the photographer's right to dispose of his private property restricted by the other actor's entitlement to privacy. Hence, the property-right holder may be limited in his right by the extent of the entitlement granted. The right to privacy may so restrict the photographer's right to use the picture that at best only limited privileges to the exchange of the picture would be granted.

TYPES OF POSSESSION AND THEIR ECONOMIC RATIONALE

Let us next turn to the question of who has legal possession of a given property or good under various conditions. As we will see, some forms of possession (and ownership) are less obvious than others. In all six forms of possession that I will explore, I will seek to give economic content to the possession and ownership status.

Unconscious Possession Possession is unconscious when one of three situations holds — when a person is unaware that a particular item is in his control, when a person is aware that some item is in his control but has no idea what it is, and when a person knows that an item is under his control and thinks it is one thing but in fact it is something else. Thus in *Hannah* v. *Peel*,[8] Lance Corporal Duncan Hannah, serving during the early days of World War II in a battery of the Royal Artillery, was stationed in a house that had never been occupied by its owner, Major Peel. Major Peel had come into the ownership of the house late in 1938, and the house was requisitioned late in 1939 by the army. In August 1940, Hannah was adjusting the blackout curtains in a room when his hand touched something on the top of a window frame, loose in a crevice. Hannah thought it to be a piece of dirt or plaster and dropped it on the outside window ledge. The next morning he discovered it was a brooch covered with cobwebs and dirt. He informed his commanding officer, who advised him to hand it over to the police. When after 2 years the owner had not been found, the police handed the brooch to Hannah, who sold it for £66.

In a subsequent lawsuit brought by Major Peel, the court stated

> There is no doubt that in this case the brooch was lost in the ordinary meaning of the term, and I should imagine it had been lost for a very considerable time.... [Major

[8] King's Bench Division (1945) 1 K.B. 509.

Peel] was never physically in possession of these premises at any time. It is clear that the brooch was never his, in the ordinary acceptation of the term, in that he had the prior possession. He had no knowledge of it, until it was brought to his notice by the finder.[9]

The court ruled in favor of the finder Hannah.

Bailee   Quite often some property is left with a rather specialized agent so that he may perform certain services. During this period, the agent is the rightful possessor of an item but he is not the owner. He is a bailee. Examples include the railroad that is transporting freight, the watch repairman with whom a watch has been deposited, or the garage operator with whom a car has been left for repair. The bailee is absolutely liable for misdelivery and therefore can be looked upon as being the owner of the item as long as it is in his possession. Such rules give signals that can produce efficient resource use.

Yet the bailee is not liable when he could not reasonably have known that he was in possession of a valuable object. If you check a coat in a checkroom, for example, the bailee will not be liable for a missing unobserved ring. However, if the bailee is known to have seen the ring, he will be held liable. This standard gives the owner incentives to inform the bailee of the object and its true worth, so that the latter can take cost-justified precautions.

Lost Articles   The law treats lost articles differently depending on where the loss occurs. If the article is lost in a public place and the owner is not found, it goes to the finder; if in a private place, it goes to the owner of the premises. The individual who lost the object in a private place will most likely look in that place for the object. Where there is no obvious owner, as when the item is lost in a public place, the finder has some incentive to report the loss since he has a good chance to become the legal owner and the real owner has as good a chance to locate the finder as any other individual who might keep the find.

Involuntary Possession   Possession is involuntary when an individual is given a good that he does not want or accepts by mistake. The involuntary bailee is held liable if he exercises dominion by committing an overt act of interference with the real owner's possession. This offers the involuntary bailee the incentive to return the good immediately to the rightful owner before being held liable for conversion.

---

[9] *Ibid.*: 509.

Constructive Possession Constructive possession is essentially a legal assumption that an individual had possession, even if he did not have physical control over the property. Hence a bailor may constructively possess a chattel that is wrongfully converted while being transported by a bailee. This theory is more commonly used in the area of property law known as *constructive eviction,* and will be discussed later.

Adverse Possession Finally, there is adverse possession, which can ripen into ownership if an individual has unopposed occupancy of land for a period of time such as 5 or 10 years. More will be said about adverse possession later.

PERMANENT TRANSFER OF RIGHTS AND ENTITLEMENTS

At least four types of permanent transfers can be visualized — sale, taking by power of eminent domain, taking by police power, and adverse possession. They will be discussed next in some detail.

SALE

By far the most common method of transferring property in perpetuity is through sale. Therefore, it is little wonder that a large body of law has developed to provide guidelines for those who buy and sell property. Transferability of property by sale is normally efficient because it permits the reallocation of resources from lower- to higher-valued uses. However, some transfers may be restricted or at least complicated because of the existence of externalities, for example, a plant that pollutes an adjacent river.

EMINENT DOMAIN

Under the Fifth Amendment, "No person shall be ... deprived of property without due process of law; nor shall property be taken for public use without just compensation." The states have similar provisions in their constitutions. Moreover, the Fourteenth Amendment provides, "Nor shall any state deprive any person of life, liberty, or property, without due process of law; nor deny to any person within its jurisdiction the equal protection of the laws." These amendments must guide governments when they exercise their power of eminent domain, the power by which government can force involuntary transfers of property from private owners to itself, providing fair compensation. Exercising this power involves a taking by a public authority for a public purpose with just compensation and in accordance with due process of law.

An economic justification for the application of this power requires an investment or operation clearly related to a public good or the forestalling of a holdout monopoly. According to this point of view, government should be permitted to exercise its eminent domain power only to produce a good or service that has strong public good characteristics, that is, in the presence of externalities and high exclusion costs.[10] The latter occur, for example, when it is costly to eliminate free riders. If government is to produce a public good, and since it is mandated to serve everyone in its jurisdiction, it may have to locate a physical facility on a particular site. Likewise, in order to fulfill a social objective, such as providing military defense, it may have to use the power of eminent domain. These considerations come into play, for example, in the locating of military defense installations, fire stations, and flood control facilities.

Let us turn to the holdout monopoly.[11] Whenever a "public purpose" project requires the assembly of many lots, property owners may hike their prices when they know the location of the facility. Moreover, some owners do not want to sell and might hold out to the very end. This does not deny that virtually everyone will sell once the price is high enough. However, holdouts not only raise prices to levels that can exceed those that would otherwise prevail but they also retard the completion of important projects. Both elements can lead to inefficiencies when, for example, in the construction of airports, highways, and sewer lines, time is of the essence.

Exercising the power of eminent domain is only efficient when the expected collective valuation of benefits exceeds the expected total social costs of the taking. By and large, the taking should only be permitted when the market system fails to transfer real property for an important social purpose.

The scope and definition of "public use" in eminent domain procedures has undergone great changes in recent years. Specifically, the breadth of meaning attached to "public use" has been expanded, and so has the reach of the eminent domain power. In 1954, the Supreme Court, in *Berman* v. *Parker,* approved the taking of private occupied residential slums for transfer to private real estate developers in the name of urban renewal.[12] Justice Douglas, in delivering the opinion of the Court, held that:

---

[10] Werner Z. Hirsch, *Urban Economics* (New York: MacMillan, 1974): 218–221.

[11] An example of a holdout occurred when 1,362 households under condemnation procedures were willing to sell their property to the city of Detroit, but 10 homeowners were not. "Pushing the Boundaries of Eminent Domain," *Business Week* (May 4, 1981): 174.

[12] *Berman* v. *Parker,* 348 U.S. 26 (1954).

By §2 of the Act (District of Columbia Redevelopment Act of 1945) Congress made a "legislative determination" that "owing to technological and sociological changes, obsolete lay-out, and other factors, conditions existing in the District of Columbia with respect to substandard housing and blighted areas ... are injurious to the public health, safety, morals, and welfare; and it is hereby declared to be the policy of the United States to protect and promote the welfare of the inhabitants of the seat of the Government by eliminating all such injurious conditions by employing all means necessary and appropriate for the purpose."

Section 2 goes on to declare that acquisition of property is necessary to eliminate these housing conditions:

Congress further finds in §2 that these ends cannot be attained "by the ordinary operations of private enterprise alone without public participation"; ... and that the acquisition and the assembly of real property and the leasing or sale thereof for redevelopment pursuant to a project area redevelopment plan ... is hereby declared to be a public use...."

The power of Congress over the District of Columbia includes all the legislative powers which a state may exercise over its affairs. ...

The rights of these property owners are satisfied when they receive that just compensation which the Fifth Amendment exacts as the price of the taking.[13]

The power of eminent domain is often given to universities, hospitals, other nonprofit institutions, and even private corporations for redevelopment. However, usually the private entity must make a greater showing of right than a public entity.[14]

In the state of Michigan in 1981, creation of employment was considered to be satisfying the "public use" criterion. Thus, the city of Detroit successfully argued that meeting the demand of the General Motors Corporation to provide a rectangular area of 450 to 500 acres with access to long-haul railroad lines and a highway system as a condition for the company to build a new automobile assembly plant in Detroit justified it in exercising its power of eminent domain.

Finally, the California Supreme Court, in a condemnation suit filed by the city of Oakland against the Oakland Raiders football team, further broadened the "public use" definition to extend "to matters of public health, recreation and enjoyment," although the court ultimately ruled against Oakland.

Compensation under eminent domain should be at fair market value measured in terms of what the owner loses, not in terms of what the government gains. Thus, it would be appropriate to provide the people whose property was taken with compensation adequate to restore them to

---

[13] *Ibid.*: 26–75.
[14] *Linggi* v. *Garovatti*, 45 Cal. 2d 20, 286 P.2d 15 (1955).

their previous positions.[15] The difference between the first and second concept could in part be reconciled by adding relocation costs and reimbursement for sentimental value to the fair market value.

In some instances, the effect of exercising the power of eminent domain extends beyond the condemned property. For example, in *Los Angeles County, MTA* v. *Continental Development Corporation,* land was condemned to build an elevated rail line station.[16] Plaintiff, owning not only the condemned strip of land but also 86 adjacent acres of mainly office buildings sought compensation for the negative externalities on these buildings emanating from train noise. The California Supreme Court correctly held that while the new rail line would generate negative externalities on Continental, also benefits would accrue to it. For example, the station, being located within a 10-minute walk from Continental's property, would significantly increase rents and lower vacancy rates. The court, therefore, held that "Compensation for injury to the remainder is the amount of damage to the remainder, reduced by the amount of benefit to the remainder."[17]

The administration of acquisitions under the power of eminent domain differs among countries. For example, in the United Kingdom, heavy reliance is placed on technical experts, with disputes going to a quasi-administrative body — the Lands Tribunal. Courts can be appealed to only on a point of law — a most infrequent circumstance.

In the United States, the eminent-domain process is initiated by the local government, usually a municipality, sending to residents notices of its intent to acquire certain property for certain public purposes. Usually these notices contain an offer to buy the property for fair market value, a value arrived at by city officials. (It often reflects a value more than the amount shown on tax assessment records, but less than the property would bring on an open market.) If the property owner rejects such an offer, he can pursue administrative appeals, which are usually limited to the question of the value of the property. If informal administrative channels are not sufficient to produce an offer acceptable to the property owner, a complaint is usually filed by the governmental agency.

---

[15] F. Leary and E. D. Tucker, "The Injustice of Just Compensation to Fixed Income Recipients: Does Recent Relocation Legislation Fill the Void? *Temple Law Quarterly* 48 (Fall 1974): 1–45.

[16] *Los Angeles County, MTA* v. *Continental Development Corporation,* Cal. S051436, 1–23 (1997).

[17] *Ibid.:* 1. The *Continental* decision revisited the *Beveridge* v. *Lewis* [137 Cal. 619, 70 P. 1083 (1902)] decision, which had made the untenable distinction between general and special benefits to the remainder property. The *Continental* finding, no longer supporting this distinction, proceeded to insist that benefits to the remainder be considered.

POLICE POWER WITHOUT COMPENSATION

The police power is the right of the state to take action to protect the safety, health, and morals of the community. Under this power, the expropriation or extinction of private property rights become legally possible. Unlike under eminent domain, compensation of the property owner is not mandatory and often is not granted at all.

Under its police power, a public authority may take or destroy property in order to arrest the spread of fire, flood, or some other natural disaster; it may requisition property in time of war for national defense. In the latter case, compensation on similar principles to those of eminent domain will normally be forthcoming.[18]

The exercise of police power ranges from cases close to those of eminent domain to those very remote from it. At the latter end of the spectrum, police power merges into a host of administrative, legislative, and even judicial powers affecting property rights positively or negatively. Compensation rarely takes place. The courts have the right, though they seldom use it, to declare certain contracts contrary to public policy and hence unenforceable. Moreover, many statutes, including corporation laws, antitrust laws, and zoning laws, distinctly affect property rights, often without compensation.

When, under the police power, do we have a compensable taking, and when is compensation not warranted? The New York Court of Appeals in 1974 offered guidance:

> ... Such government interference as described is based on one of two concepts — either the government is acting in its enterprise capacity, where it takes unto itself private resources in use for the common good, or in its arbitral capacity, where it intervenes to straighten out situations in which the citizenry is in conflict over land use or where one person's use of his land is injurious to others. Where government acts in its enterprise capacity, as where it takes land to widen the road, there is a compensable taking. Where government acts in its arbitral capacity, as where it legislates zoning or provides the machinery to enjoin noxious use, there is simply noncompensable regulation.[19]

---

[18] Under the police power, the state may forbid use of property for the purposes of a gambling house or house of prostitution, or in a manner dangerous to public health. As a result, the value of particular properties may decline. No compensation is awarded, but neither is there a physical invasion of the property. Instead, the property remains physically intact in the hands of its owner. Although physical invasion almost always calls for compensation, its absence does not exclude compensation.

[19] *Lutheran Church in America* v. *City of New York*, 35 N.Y. 2d 121 (1974).

ADVERSE POSSESSION

Adverse possession functions as a method of transferring interests in land without the consent of the prior owner, even in spite of the dissent of such owner, who clearly is adversely affected.

The doctrine of adverse possession has been incorporated into the laws of all 50 states. The following justifications have been advanced:

1. Owners should face a penalty, i.e., loss of their land, for sitting on their rights and thereby preventing the land being used most efficiently. Thus, the process promotes efficient land use.
2. Evidence decays over time, interfering with the timely disposition of cases after some, and often a long, time has elapsed. The statutory period tends to be long; in the nineteenth century it was often longer than 20 years, while today in California it is 5 years.[20]
3. The elimination of old claims to property reduces transaction costs and thereby facilitates market exchange.
4. After occupying land for a significant period of time, the adverse possessor often has developed considerable reliance interests, all of which would disappear should the true owner succeed in retaining title to property.[21]

Economists have been particularly interested in the first justification that letting land lie idle prevents productive uses. The fourth justification of protecting the reliance interests of adverse possessors can encourage squatters unless inadvertent squatting, e.g., boundary errors, invalidates adverse possession. For this reason, a proposal has been made to impose penalties when possessors make boundary errors.[22] Helmholz, in a survey of actual adverse possession cases, found judges seldom to award title to those who intentionally occupied another owner's land, even though the statutory period had elapsed.[23]

A few select studies have shed light on some of the justifications in support of the doctrine of adverse possession. Miceli and Sirmans have developed a theory of adverse possession with the objective of boundary error cost minimization.[24] The third justification, i.e., minimization of

---

[20] J. M. Netter et al., "An Economic Analysis of Adverse Possession Statutes," *International Review of Law and Economics* 6 (1986): 217–228.

[21] Thomas J. Miceli and C. F. Sirmans, *An Economic Theory of Adverse Possession* (Storrs, CT: Center for Real Estate and Urban Studies, July 1993): 1–17.

[22] *Ibid.*

[23] R. Helmholz, "Adverse Possession and Subjective Intent," *Washington University Law Quarterly* 61 (1983): 331–358.

[24] Miceli and Sirmans, *Economic Theory:* 1–17.

uncertainty connected with land transfer, was empirically tested by Netter et al.[25] Merrill has analyzed the doctrine of adverse possession in the light of the distinction between property and liability rules.[26] A study by Ellickson has examined the determination of the optimal statutory period with the objective of minimizing the total costs of land transfer including the transaction, monitoring, and demoralization costs associated with the uncompensated loss of property by the true owner.[27]

In order to claim title to property through adverse possession, the claimant must show that he has some claim of rights and actually has possessed the land for an extended period of time.

Although the requirements for adverse possession differ among the various states, according to Dukeminier and Krier, "in all jurisdictions the courts have developed a series of requirements of their own. There must be (1) an actual entry giving exclusive possession that is (2) open and notorious, (3) adverse and under a claim of right and (4) continuous for the statutory period."[28] The possession that will give title by adverse possession is the actual use of property as the average owner would use it.

The leading case is *Ewing* v. *Burnett*, where both plaintiff and defendant claimed an unimproved lot in Cincinnati used principally for digging sand and gravel. Defendant Burnett had lived next to the vacant lot for 31 years, paid taxes on the lot for 24 years, maintained trespass actions, and operated a gravel pit. The plaintiff and his predecessor in title had never occupied or used the property. The statutory period for adverse possession being 21 years, the Supreme Court held for Burnett, who brought actions of trespass against others who had dug sand and gravel without his permission.[29]

However, in *Madison* v. *Cohn*, adverse possession was not established in the eyes of the court. The claimant had paid taxes on two unimproved city lots, visited the lots from four to six times a year, at which time he "looked around; figured on a few things to do with it," planted two rose bushes and four trees, and during one year cleaned the foxtails off the lots.[30]

Some states have further requirements, for example, that the adverse possessor pay the taxes assessed upon the land.[31] This is an almost impossible

[25] Netter et al., *Economic Analysis*: 217–228.

[26] T. Merrill, "Property Rules, Liability Rules and Adverse Possession," *Northwestern University Law Review* 79 (1986): 1122–1154.

[27] Robert Ellickson, "Adverse Possession and Perpetuities Law: Two Dents in the Libertarian Model of Property Rights," *Washington University Law Quarterly* 64 (1986): 723–737.

[28] J. Dukeminier and J. E. Krier, *Property* (Boston: Little, Brown, 1981): 94.

[29] *Ewing* v. *Burnett*, 36 U.S. 41 (1837) Supp.

[30] *Madison* v. *Cohn*, 122 Cal. App. 704, 10 P.2d 531 (1932).

[31] Cal. Code Civ. Proc. §325 (West 1976).

requirement since the tax assessment goes to the recorded owner of the property, but the court may "deem" that the taxes have been paid. For example, in *Duncan* v. *Peterson*,[32] the contesting parties had lived on their respective properties separated by a fence for 42 years before a survey detected that the true dividing line of the properties was 104 feet east of the fence. Since taxes were assessed based on section references, the plaintiff had not paid the taxes on the subject property as required by statute. However, the court held that "payment of taxes is not material as each coterminous owner is deemed to have paid the taxes according to his deed."[33]

TEMPORARY TRANSFER OF RIGHTS AND ENTITLEMENTS

LEASES: LANDLORD–TENANT RELATIONS

One of the most interesting and dynamic aspects of property law covers landlord–tenant relations. In this relationship, the landlord was historically favored over the tenant. Specifically, the doctrine of caveat emptor was applied to relieve the landlord of responsibility for warranting that a building rented for residential purposes was fit for that purpose at the inception of the tenancy. Likewise, the landlord had no responsibility to see that the building remained habitable during the term of tenancy. Repair of damage to existing facilities caused by ordinary wear and tear during tenancy was considered the tenant's responsibility.

In 1826, the doctrine of *constructive eviction* was first recognized in the United States.[34] Grounds for constructive eviction, which permitted the tenant to surrender possession and vacate premises, were the *covenant of habitability* and the *covenant of quiet enjoyment.* The covenant of habitability emphasized that premises were to be delivered in tenantable, fit, or suitable condition, where condition was assumed to be under the control of the landlord; and the covenant of quiet enjoyment emphasized that the tenant was to be protected — to the extent that a landlord can provide such protection — in the quiet enjoyment of the premises, particularly from direct intrusion by the landlord.

Constructive eviction, although an improvement for the tenant, did not ensure him habitable premises. Fit and suitable conditions were not defined

---

[32] *Duncan* v. *Peterson*, 3 Cal. App. 3d 607 (1970).

[33] *Ibid.*: 611.

[34] *Dyett* v. *Pendleton*, 8 Cow. 727 (N.Y. 1826), and M. P. Rapacz, "Origin and Evolution of Constructive Eviction in the United States," *De Paul Law Review* 1 (Autumn–Winter 1951): 69–90.

so as to ensure quality housing. Furthermore, the landlord had no duty to repair premises, since the covenant of quiet enjoyment could be breached by the landlord only by direct conduct and not by neglect to repair. Moreover, the only relief for the tenant was to vacate the premises within a reasonable time after the condition arose.

In the post-World War II period, some state statutes and court decisions modified and reinterpreted the doctrine of constructive eviction. The law began to make exceptions to the rule, first for short-term furnished apartments and then for defects reasonably discoverable by the landlord and not the tenant.[35]

Likewise, the early common-law rule that landlords were under no duty to repair and maintain residential premises leased to tenants had previously prevailed.[36] Moreover, since the rules of property law solidified before the development of mutually dependent covenants in contract law, a lessee's covenant to pay rent was considered independent of the lessor's covenant to provide housing. As a result, if the tenant's home became uninhabitable, even though it was through no fault of his own, he could neither demand

---

[35] In the post-World War II period the doctrine of caveat emptor was reinterpreted in relation to property. The reinterpretation took into consideration the great complexity and interdependence of present-day society compared with that of sixteenth-century England, where most landlord–tenant relations involved a piece of land and simple dwelling facilities. Not only was the prospective tenant usually well acquainted with the particular dwelling, but it was uncomplicated, relatively simple to repair, and expected to be maintained by the technical skills of the tenant himself. Thus on first inspection the tenant knew reasonably well what the overall state of the dwelling was. This is quite different from the housing of both poor and rich in the second half of the twentieth century. Complicated electric wiring, heating, and plumbing all are inaccessible for inspection on first visitation, and a renter tends to have no qualifications to do so [*Reste Realty Corp.* v. *Cooper,* 53 N.J. 444, 452, 251 A.2d 268, 272 (1969)].

As a result, for example, the Supreme Court of Wisconsin held that

"The need and social desirability of adequate housing for people in this era of rapid population increases is too important to be rebuffed by the obnoxiously legal cliche, *caveat emptor.* Permitting landlords to rent 'tumbledown' houses is at least a contributing cause of such problems as urban blight, juvenile delinquency, and high property taxes for conscientious landlords [*Pines* v. *Perssion,* 14 Wis. 2d 590, 595–596, 111 N.W.2d 409, 412–413 (1961)]."

A 1968 Michigan statute [Mich. Comp. Laws Ann. 554.139 (Supp. 1970)] and a 1969 decision by the Supreme Court of Hawaii [*Lemle* v. *Breeden,* 462 P.2d 470 (Hawaii 1969)] go in the same direction. This court ruling modifies the doctrine of caveat emptor by requiring the landlord to be responsible for "premises and all common areas [to be] fit for use" at commencement of tenancy.

[36] A lease at common law was considered to be the purchase of an interest in property, subject to the doctrine of caveat emptor. Since the lease agreement was considered a conveyance of property for a term, the tenant was deemed to have assumed the obligations and liabilities of ownership.

that repairs be made by the landlord nor escape liability for the rent due for the remainder of the term. Thus, the tenant had to pay rent regardless of whether he received any benefits from the residential premises.

A major modification of this traditional common-law landlord–tenant relationship began to occur in the early postwar period. Basically, two approaches have been pursued, mainly through laws ensuring that tenants have habitable housing and, to a lesser extent, continued tenancy.

Habitability Laws

By means of housing codes, many large American cities shifted to the landlord the responsibility for repairing leased premises and maintaining them in habitable condition. These codes impose the burden of repair and maintenance on the landlord and place the responsibility for the dwelling's cleanliness and for specified minor items of maintenance on the tenant.[37] Usually, the owner remains ultimately responsible for having housing code violations corrected. Parallel to these housing codes and in furthering their enforcement, courts and legislatures have created rights of actions of tenants. To this end, a number of legal remedies have been fashioned; they increase the property rights of tenants while reducing those retained by landlords. These remedies, designed to provide a minimum level of housing quality for tenants, include repair and rent deduction, rent withholding and abatement, and receivership. They are often supplemented by provisions that prohibit retaliatory eviction, facilitate return of the tenant's security deposit, and legalize rent strikes. Furthermore, courts have begun to rule that a warranty of habitability is implied in urban residential leases.[38]

These changes in landlord–tenant relations, by inferring and extending a warranty of habitability, revise the doctrine of caveat emptor. Since certainty about the law has declined, previously nonexistent legal risks have arisen, and the distribution of risks between landlord and tenant has been altered. For example, in the presence of caveat emptor, the landlord's obligations to repair and maintain premises are clear and he therefore faces few risks, regardless of how little repair and maintenance he provides. Under these conditions, tenants face many risks, all of which change when the doctrine of caveat emptor is modified.

---

[37] Still, the tenant is responsible for normal repairs and any waste or deterioration that he could have prevented.

[38] Key cases are *Pines* v. *Perssion,* 14 Wis. 2d 590, 111 N.W.2d 404 (1961), and *Javins* v. *First National Realty Corp.,* 138 U.S. App. D.C. 369, 423 F.2d 1071, cert. denied, 400 U.S. 925, 91 S. Ct. 186, 27 L. Ed. 2d 185 (1970).

Without a warranty of habitability, there is considerable potential for variation in the level of service delivered to the tenant. Thus, the tenant's lease agreement is, for him, a source of risk. There are two sources of this variability.

First, there is the risk that the tenant has not correctly assessed the attributes of the dwelling before leasing. Here the law would appear to economize on the cost of acquiring information, since the landlord is in the best position to evaluate his own property.

Second, there is the risk that some damage to the dwelling will occur and reduce the flow of services during the period of the lease. When a habitability law is passed, the risk is transferred from tenant to landlord. Let us next examine the major habitability laws.[39]

Repair-and-deduct laws offer a self-help remedy by permitting tenants, on their own initiative, to repair defects in their premises and deduct repair charges from their rent.[40] It is basically limited to relatively minor defects.[41] Wide application of this remedy in a large multiple-unit dwelling could be inefficient compared to repairs carried out by the landlord, who may benefit from scale economies.

A second form of remedy is *rent withholding*, through either *escrow* or *rent abatement*. In the first case, the tenant pays rent into a court-created escrow account. Rental income is withheld from the landlord until violations are corrected. Illinois, Michigan, and New York even authorize rent withholding by the state welfare department or some other agency.[42] An alternative is rent abatement, which is more consistent with the application of contract rather than property law principles.[43] Rent abatement permits a tenant to remain in possession of the premises without paying rent or by paying a reduced amount until the housing defects are remedied. The condition

[39] This section draws heavily on Werner Z. Hirsch et al., ''Regression Analysis of the Effects of Habitability Laws upon Rent: An Empirical Observation on the Ackerman–Komesar Debate,'' *California Law Review* 63 (September 1975): 1098–1143.

[40] The landlord must be notified after the fact, and only after he has failed to take action within an appropriate time period can the tenant contract for repair. In most states, the statute permits tenants to deduct no more than one month's rent to finance repairs.

[41] Repair-and-deduct laws can be applied relatively easily by tenants, since the law can be invoked without a prior judicial determination. Should a judicial proceeding later determine that the tenant was not justified in taking action, he would merely be liable for the outstanding balance of the rent (the deducted repair bill).

[42] As long as the violations continue, the welfare recipient is given a statutory defense to any action or summary proceeding for nonpayment of rent.

[43] A tenant utilizing a rent-abatement scheme takes the risk that by refusing to pay rent a court may later determine that his actions were unjustified. If the court so decides, the tenant may have to pay rent due, moving expenses, attorney fees, court costs, and even statutory penalties.

of the premises constitutes a defense either to an action of eviction or
to an action for rent. In most situations, the legal differences between
withholding and abatement are very small. Even under abatement, rent is
usually placed into escrow, either as a good-faith gesture by the tenant or
because courts so order pending a full investigation of the existence of
and correction of code violations. Therefore, we lump abatement and
withholding together as withholding laws.

A third remedy is receivership, that is, appointment by the court of
a receiver who takes control of buildings and corrects hazardous defects
after the landlord has failed to act within a reasonable period. By 1974,
this remedy had become available in 13 states. If large-scale repairs,
which cannot be financed through rental payments, are needed, some
statutes permit the receiver to seek additional loans. When this is done,
old first liens are converted into new second liens, imposing particularly
heavy costs on lenders and therefore ultimately on landlords. The
initiation of receivership is usually preceded by a hearing in which the
court determines whether the landlord has failed to provide essential
services. If the court so rules, the rent is deposited with the court-
appointed receiver until the violation is corrected. So long as the
tenant continues to pay rent into escrow, his landlord cannot evict him
for nonpayment.

Altogether, courts increasingly infer that warranties of fitness and habitability are implied in urban residential leases. This implied warranty of
habitability may be used as a defense in both action of eviction and action
for rent, if the tenant is able to show that a "substantial" violation of the
housing code existed during the period rent was withheld. In addition,
the tenant may take affirmative action against the landlord for breach of
contract, though remaining liable for the reasonable value of the use of
the premises.

Of the three remedies listed, receivership is potentially the most costly
to the landlord. It results in a complete stoppage of rental income to him,
since all tenants in the building, not only aggrieved ones, pay rents into
escrow. Moreover, the landlord loses control over his building altogether.
Instead, control is temporarily transferred to a receiver, who may be enthusi-
astic about fixing up the building, possibly even above minimum standards
established by housing codes. The repair decisions are thus made without
due consideration of their potential profitability. Finally, contrary to most
repair-and-deduct and withholding actions receivership is usually initiated
by government, which has vast resources behind it.

The three major remedies are often supplemented by laws that can
reinforce them. For example, there are *anti-retaliatory-eviction* laws, which
are designed to protect tenants from being penalized by landlords for

complaining about housing code violations.[44] Furthermore, a number of states have laws that facilitate the return of the tenant's security deposit at the end of the tenancy. Finally, a few states, for example, New Jersey and New York, have legalized rent strikes by tenants against a particular landlord.

Laws that prohibit retaliatory eviction, facilitate the return of the tenant's security deposit, and legalize rent strikes, together with the other three remedies, impose costs on landlords. Parts of these costs may result from reduced flexibility, imposition of high repair and maintenance levels, and the possibility of legal costs. Of these remedies, anti-retaliatory-eviction laws resembling temporary rent controls tend to be the most costly to landlords.

Rent Control Laws

A number of governmental bodies almost all on the local level, have enacted laws that regulate the price landlords may charge residential tenants for their property and services. Controls are of two types — first generation or hard controls, i.e., virtual rent freezes, and second generation or soft controls, which can allow for automatic rent increases (tied, for example, to the rate of inflation), cost passthroughs, vacancy decontrol, etc. The avowed purpose has been to protect tenants from excessive rent increases, particularly if such hikes could force them to vacate the premises. These controls were enacted in times of severe housing shortages, mainly during wartime and periods of hyperinflation. New York, for example, imposed rent controls during World War II and more than 110 municipalities did so during the inflation years of the 1970s. Likewise in California, when real estate prices skyrocketed in the late 1970s, a number of local jurisdictions (including the cities of Los Angeles, San Francisco, Oakland, Berkeley, and Santa Monica) adopted rent control ordinances. However, starting in the mid-1990s rent control lost some of its popularity. For example, California weakened controls and in 1994 Massachusetts eliminated all controls. In 1997, state and city legislation greatly reduced the scope of rent control in New York City.[45] In 32 states, municipalities are prohibited by state law to enact new rent restrictions.

---

[44] Although initially designed to make habitability laws work by protecting tenants who complain about housing code violations, retaliatory eviction statutes can also be looked upon as devices to ensure that tenants will have continued tenancy during a specified period.

[45] *The Rent Regulation Reform Act of 1997*, after a bruising fight between the legislature and the mayor of New York, extended controls until 2003. Yet apartments with monthly rents of $2,000 or more are deregulated for tenants with annual incomes of $175,000 or more. Moreover, vacancy allowances and succession rights were modified [Chapter 116 (S.5553 — Committee on Rules/A.8346 — Silver et al.)].

Many other countries have rent control, e.g., the United Kingdom,[46] Hong Kong,[47] Canada,[48] as well as a number of developing countries.[49]

Rent control laws differ in stringency and tightness, depending on their coverage and pass-through provisions, basis on which and manner in which permissible rent increases are calculated, the ease with which landlords can hope to get such increases, and whether the laws allow for vacancy decontrol, demolition of buildings, and use change. Stringent ordinances cover all premises, whereas the less stringent ones exempt single dwellings, luxury apartments, and apartment houses with fewer than four or three units. Also, the less stringent ordinances permit the cost for major repair and minor improvements to be passed on to tenants.

Great differences also exist in the manner that allowable rent increases are set and enforced. In the most extreme case, there can be rent freezes and even rollbacks to an earlier date.[50] Most laws provide for a formula by which annual "general adjustments" are made; some stipulate a fixed annual percentage increase, while others tie increases to changes in the Consumer Price Index (CPI) published by the U.S. Bureau of Labor Statistics.

Finally, some jurisdictions provide for vacancy decontrol, that is, when a tenant vacates, the landlord can charge a substantially higher rent. In the city of Los Angeles, for example, there are no restrictions on the new rent; in West Hollywood, a 10% rent increase is allowed, but only once every 2 years. Since rents are more in line with market rent under vacancy decontrol, total decontrol should be easier in its presence than in its absence.

Stringent rent control measures tend to be supplemented by provisions designed to prevent rent decontrol, for example, in the form of antidemolition and anticonversion provisions. Thus, for example, Santa Monica re-

[46] W. Z. Hirsch, "Landlord–Tenant Relations Law," *The Economic Approach to Law*, P. Burrows and C. G. Veljanovski, Eds. (London: Butterworths, 1982): 290.

[47] S. N. S. Cheung, "Roofs or Stars: The Stated Intents and Actual Effects of Rent Ordinance," *Economic Inquiry* 8 (March 1975): 1–21; Id., "Rent Control and Housing Reconstruction: The Postwar Experience of Prewar Premises in Hong Kong," *Journal of Law and Economics* 22 (April 1979): 27–54.

[48] Richard Arnott, "Time for Revisionism on Rent Control?," *Canadian Journal of Economic Perspectives* 9 (Winter 1995): 99–120.

[49] Stephen Malpezzi, "Can New York and Los Angeles Learn From Kumasi and Bangalore? Costs and Benefits of Rent Controls in Developing Countries," *Housing Policy Debate* 4 (Winter 1993): 589–626.

[50] The city of Santa Monica, for example, on April 10, 1979, froze rents for four months and, on September 10, 1979, it rolled back rents to April 10, 1978, while permitting a 7% automatic rent increase on the 1978 base.

stricts the ability of landlords to convert the form of their investment by taking rental properties out of the rental market by means of demolition or conversion. The city's conversion controls were constitutionally challenged in Phase III of *Baker* v. *Santa Monica.*[51] The court held that the only test that was acceptable was one requiring the landlord to prove he could not make a fair return on his property unless he was allowed to convert his apartment complex.

Rent control has typically been justified by local governmental entities as an exercise of their police power. In the 1920s, the United States Supreme Court held that the use of state police power to enact rental controls was consistent with the due process clauses of the Fifth and Fourteenth Amendments only if utilized in response to a housing "emergency."[52] In recent years, however, for some courts a crisis or extreme exigent circumstances are no longer required to justify rent controls. For example, the California Supreme Court, in *Birkenfeld* v. *City of Berkeley*, declared that it "is now settled California law that legislation regulating prices or otherwise restricting contractual or property rights is within the police power if its operative provisions are reasonably related to the accomplishments of a legitimate governmental purpose."[53]

Thus, one key constitutional issue is whether the rent control measure is reasonably related to a legitimate governmental purpose. Courts in the past interpreted broadly the existence of such a relationship. However, some courts, particularly in California, have now raised the question of whether indeed the control measure has accomplished the stated purpose, i.e., whether there is a "nexus" between outcome and statement of purpose. (The "nexus" test, developed by the Supreme Court beginning in the late 1980s, will be discussed in detail in Chapter 4.[54])

An example is a California Court of Appeal finding that the purpose of the rent control charter amendment of the City of Santa Monica had not been fulfilled, but, if anything, had proved counterproductive.[55] Specifi-

---

[51] *Baker* v. *City of Santa Monica*, No. WEC 058763 (April 14, 1982); *Nash* v. *City of Santa Monica*, 143 Cal. App. 3d 251, 191 Cal. Rptr. 717 (1983).

[52] See *Block* v. *Hirsh*, 256 U.S. 135, 156 (1921). See also *Woods* v. *Lloyd W. Miller Co.*, 33 U.S. 138, 141 (1948): Comment, *Rent Control and Landlords' Property Rights: The Reasonable Return Doctrine Revived*, *Rutgers Law Review* 33 (1980): 165–166. Even during a war crisis imposition of controls was usually justified only for a relatively short period. See *Block* v. *Hirsh*, 256 U.S. at 157.

[53] 17 Cal. 3d 129, 158, 550 P.2d 1001, 1022, 130 Cal. Rptr. 465, 486 (1976).

[54] *Nollan* v. *California Coastal Commission*, 483 U.S. 825 (1987); *Dolan* v. *City of Tigard*, 512 U.S. 374 (1994).

[55] *Santa Monica Beach Ltd.* v. *The Superior Court of Los Angeles* (96 Daily Journal D.A.R., 2155–2159).

cally, the Court reminded Santa Monica of the stated purpose of the charter amendment:

> A growing shortage of housing units resulting in a low vacancy rate and rapidly rising rents exploiting this shortage constitute a serious housing problem affecting the lives of a substantial portion of those Santa Monica residents who reside in residential housing. In addition, speculation in the purchase and sale of existing residential housing units results in further rent increases. These conditions endanger the public health and welfare of Santa Monica tenants, especially the poor, minorities, students, young families, and senior citizens. The purpose of this Article, therefore, is to alleviate the hardship caused by this serious housing shortage by establishing a rent control board empowered to regulate rentals in the City of Santa Monica so that rents will not be increased unreasonably and so that landlords will receive no more than a fair return.[56]

The court then presented the following results:

> Between 1980 and 1990, during which time the City's rent control law was continuously in effect, the City's stock of rental housing units declined by nearly 5 percent and ... low-income rental units [by] 12 percent ... notwithstanding that, during the same period, the rental housing supply and the number of low-income rental units *increased* in all comparable non-rent-controlled Southern California cities. The City also lost 285 very low-income rental units, the largest "exodus of economically disadvantaged renters" from *any* comparable Southern California city. At the same time, the City experienced a 37% *increase* in the proportion of households with very high incomes (while the proportion of very high-income households dropped by more than 8% in Los Angeles County as a whole).... In addition, rental housing in Santa Monica has become "increasingly unavailable" to young families, with the number of family households with children declining by 1,299, a 6% drop during a period when no comparable non-rent-controlled Southern California city lost young family households. ... female-headed households with children under 18 in Santa Monica fell by more than 27 [percent], despite an increase in such households in Los Angeles County as a whole.... Santa Monica's elderly population ... declined by 1.7 [percent] [while] ... the elderly population of Los Angeles County *rose* by more than 15 [percent] over the same decade. (Emphasis added.[57])

Consequently the Court concluded that "If, in fact, Santa Monica's rent control law has reduced rather than increased the number of rental units available to those intended to be benefited by that law, then the regulation has no relationship (nexus) at all to its stated [*1241] purpose."[58]

A second key issue is "whether rental regulations are fair or (unconstitutionally) confiscatory."[59] For example, the California Supreme Court in

---

[56] *Ibid.*: 2155.
[57] *Ibid.*: 2155–2156.
[58] *Ibid.*: 2159.
[59] *City of Berkeley* v. *City of Berkeley Rent Stabilization Board*, 27 Cal. App. 4th 984 (1994).

Birkenfeld v. *City of Berkeley* declared the Berkeley rent control ordinance invalid on its face since it did not give the board the discretion to avoid confiscatory results.[60] This conclusion was based on the fact that the maximum chargeable rent was set on a unit-by-unit basis.[61] The court concluded that "The mechanism is sufficient for the required purpose only if it is capable of providing adjustments in maximum rents without a substantially greater incidence and degree of delay than is practically necessary. Property may be effectively taken by long-continued and unreasonable delay in putting an end to confiscatory rates as by an express affirmance of them."[62]

Therefore, in order not to be confiscatory on its face, a rent control ordinance must permit the regulatory board to grant across-the-board increases based upon classifications enumerated by the board or statute. Or, alternatively, the rent control ordinance must institute a unit-by-unit procedure that will operate without what the court considers to be an unreasonable delay.[63]

The constitutional requirement for a "just and reasonable return" is a difficult concept. The California Supreme Court, for example, tried to enumerate the requirements of a "just and reasonable return" on property"[64] when such a provision is in effect. It concluded "whether a regulation of prices is reasonable or confiscatory depend ultimately on the result reached.[65] Obviously, this reasonable return standard is amorphous, and it has opened the door to much litigation. In *Baker* v. *City of Santa Monica*,[66] apartment owners successfully argued that the Santa Monica rental ordinance[67] denied landlords a fair return and was therefore unreasonable under the standard set fort in *Birkenfield*.[68] The ordinance provided that "it is the intent of this Article that upward adjustments in rent be made only when demonstrated necessary to the landlord making a fair return on investment.[69] The rent control board subsequently interpreted "invest-

---

[60] *Birkenfeld* v. *City of Berkeley*, 17 Cal. 3d at 169–172, 550 P.2d at 1029–1032, 130 Cal. Rptr. at 483–496 (1976).

[61] *Id.* at 169–172, 550 P.2d at 1030–1031, 130 Cal. Rptr. at 494–495 (1976).

[62] *Id.* at 169, 550 P.2d at 1030, 130 Cal. Rptr. at 494 (1976) [citing *Smith* v. *Illinois Bell Telephone Co.*, 270 U.S. 587, 591 (1926)].

[63] *Id.* at 173, 550 P.2d at 1033, 130 Cal. Rptr. at 497 (1976).

[64] *Id.* at 165, 550 P.2d at 1027, 130 Cal. Rptr. at 491 (1976).

[65] *Id.*

[66] *Baker* v. *City of Santa Monica*, No. WEC 058763 (Superior Court, Los Angeles County, July 27, 1983).

[67] Santa Monica, Cal. City Charter, art. XVIII §§1800–1812 (1982).

[68] *Birkenfeld* v. *City of Berkeley*, 17 Cal. 3d at 165, 550 P.2d at 1027, 130 Cal. Rptr. at 491 (1976).

[69] Santa Monica, Cal. City Charter, art. XVIII, §1805(e) (1982).

ment" to be equivalent to historic cash investment.[70] The *Baker* court ruled that this standard lacked the essentials of fair returns. Subsequent to this court determination, the rent control board in Santa Monica revised its standard.[71] It instituted a net operating income approach in which the net operating income equals gross income less operating expenses.[72] In the second phase of the *Baker* case, the landlords argued that this standard again did not take into account such items as appreciation.[73] The trial court judge, however, ruled that it was impossible to prove the actual long-term effects of this standard sufficiently to overcome the plaintiff's burden of proof in demonstrating the unconstitutionality of the ordinance and board regulations.[74]

Finally, some jurisdictions provide for vacancy decontrol, that is, when a tenant vacates, the landlord can charge a substantially higher rent.

Stringent rent control measures tend to be supplemented by provisions designed to prevent rent decontrol, for example, in the form of antidemolition and anticonversion provisions. Thus, for example, Santa Monica restricts the ability of landlords to convert the form of their investment by taking rental properties out of the rental market by means of demolition or conversion. The city's conversion controls were constitutionally challenged in Phase III of *Baker* v. *Santa Monica*.[75] The trial court, in June 1982, struck down Santa Monica's restrictions on apartment conversions, finding that, under the California Constitution, a person's right to alienate his property supersedes a city's right to regulate how that property may be used.[76] The court found that three of the four tests used by the rent control board to determine whether to permit property to be removed from the rental market were overly restrictive and therefore unconstitutional.[77] The court held that the only test that was acceptable was one requiring the

---

[70] *Baker* v. *City of Santa Monica,* No. WEC 058763, Memorandum of Intended Decision — Phase I, at 19–20 (March 6, 1981).

[71] Proposed Fair Return Regulation, §§4100–09.

[72] See *Baker* v. *City of Santa Monica,* No. WEC 058763, Announcement of Intended Decision — Phase II, at 5 (February 17, 1982).

[73] *Ibid.*: 16–17.

[74] *Ibid.*

[75] *Baker* v. *City of Santa Monica,* No. WEC 058763 (April 14, 1982).

[76] *Id.* (June 16, 1982). This intended order was revised on December 29, 1982, and the judgment in *Baker* was entered on July 27, 1983.

[77] The three criteria found unconstitutional by the court were: (1) the landlord must show that he has no low- or moderate-income tenants in the building; (2) he must show that the rent charged is not affordable for low- and moderate-income tenants; and (3) removal of property would not reduce the supply of rental housing. *Id.*

landlord to prove he could not make a fair return on his property unless he was allowed to convert his apartment complex.[78]

Just-Cause Eviction Laws

In order to enhance the effectiveness of rent control ordinances that include vacancy decontrol provisions, a number of jurisdictions have passed just-cause eviction statutes. Under these statutes, tenants can be evicted only for just cause, which is explicitly stipulated in the legislation. For example, a New Jersey statute delineates a number of legal grounds that constitute the sole basis for eviction:

1. Failure to pay rent
2. Disorderly conduct
3. Willful damage or injury to the premises
4. Breach of express covenants
5. Continued violation of landlord's rules and regulations
6. Landlord's wish to retire permanently
7. Landlord's wish to board up or demolish the premises because he has been cited for substandard housing violations and it is economically unfeasible for the owner to eliminate the violations[79]

A just-cause eviction law applying solely to senior citizens was passed by the California assembly in the 1973–1974 legislative session.[80] The bill, if enacted, was likely to have been counterproductive. Since it would have reduced landlords' freedom to terminate tenancies, and thereby impose a differential cost on them, many would have been reluctant to rent to senior citizens. Thus, it was fortunate that the bill died in the senate.

The theory behind just-cause eviction statutes is that if a landlord retains the ability to terminate tenancies at will, landlords will evict tenants to obtain the benefit associated with the rent decontrol of the unit caused by the vacancy. If the landlord were allowed freely to terminate tenancy at the end of the lease, the landlord could eventually rent all of his units at current rental prices.

Like habitability laws, just-cause eviction statutes reduce the property rights of landlords, particularly the landlords' flexibility in renting out their apartments. Hence, such laws impose costs on landlords. These costs come about because tenants who are assured of continued tenancy can feel free

---

[78] *Id.* Santa Monica's restriction on landlord demolition of rental property was challenged in *Nash v. City of Santa Monica*, 143 Cal. App. 3d 251, 191 Cal. Rptr. 717 (1983).

[79] N. J. Stat. (1974).

[80] A. B. 1202 (1973–1974 Regular Session) California Assembly.

to use all available legal remedies to obtain from landlords relatively high levels of repair and maintenance. Thus, just-cause eviction statutes reinforce the extension of the warranty of habitability and its enforcement and, as a result, further increase costs.

TIME-LIMITED RIGHTS

Patents and copyrights are rights that, although otherwise exclusive, are limited in duration. Therefore, although it is recognized that a property right in ideas provides incentives for their creation, there are time limits to the exclusivity of their ownership. Such time-limited rights, as sometimes bestowed on real property, can be efficient.

In this connection, the doctrine of inverse condemnation, which recognizes the power of eminent domain, is of interest. "Inverse condemnation is the popular description of a cause of action against a governmental defendant to recover the value of property that has been taken in fact by the governmental defendant, even though no formal exercise of the power of eminent domain has been attempted by the taking agency."[81]

The inverse condemnation doctrine requires a court to make a factual finding of a taking when the government insists none was intended. The term inverse condemnation is used since it involves a forced purchase of the plaintiff's property rather than a forced sale, as is the case under usual condemnation proceedings.

An example of inverse condemnation is the frequent low overflight by military planes alleged to interfere with the enjoyment of land. For example, in *United States* v. *Causby*,[82] military planes flew within 67 feet of the plaintiff's chicken farm, killing his chickens, reducing egg production, and damaging residential living. The court held that the government action could have constituted a taking, with the government becoming the owner of this easement of flight. Since it was a property interest, the easement had to be described accurately, and the court of claims awarded Causby $2000 for the taking of the easement. However, once the government flights ended, the easement could have reverted to Causby, since the United States no longer used that particular air base.

LAND USE PLANNING AND DEVELOPMENT

Government can take a number of direct actions that critically change the environment within which lasting changes in land use take place. I am

---

[81] *Thornburg* v. *Port of Portland*, 233 Ore. 178, 376 P.2d 100, footnote at 101 (1962).
[82] *United States* v. *Causby*, 328 U.S. 256 (1946).

referring to governmental zoning and regulation through various instruments by which transfer of land to new uses is restricted.

ZONING

The division of land into districts with different use regulations, usually in accordance with a comprehensive plan, is called *zoning*. It can take many forms, such as building and housing codes, permits, street ordinances, and architectural controls. As such regulation becomes more pervasive, the specific social policy it is designed to bring about becomes difficult to divine. Therefore, although an economic purpose of zoning might be to prevent external diseconomies, there may be other purposes, such as the exclusion of certain classes or groups, the maintenance of orderly development, fiscal advantage, the maintenance of property values, and the preservation of a neighborhood's character. Since zoning seeks to segregate uses and neighborhoods to reduce externalities, some of these results may be unavoidable. Still, the main objective is to prevent resource misallocation in the presence of major externalities associated with certain land uses.

We can distinguish between cumulative and exclusive zoning. A *cumulative zoning system* implies that externalities of activities are not limited to specified land uses and therefore permits activities in less-regulated areas up to a certain limit. The system is hierarchical in that any particular land use is prohibited in districts reserved for higher uses but permitted in its own district and in any district established for uses lower in the hierarchy. The typical ordinance places uses for single-family dwellings at the top, followed by various kinds of uses for multiple dwellings (e.g., two-family dwellings and walk-up apartments), followed in turn by various grades of commercial uses (e.g., neighborhood businesses, shopping centers, and central business districts), and ending finally with various grades of industrial use (e.g., light or heavy). From such an ordinance one infers that, in the opinion of its authors, any other use generates an external cost for owners of adjacent single-family dwellings. The inference continues through the hierarchy until, at the bottom, industrial uses generate an external cost for owners of all adjacent land not used for industry.

Exclusive zoning is based on the premise that in order to improve on the market's allocation of land, certain parcels must be set aside for particular uses. Not only must industry be excluded from residential zones but residences must also be excluded from industrial zones. Thus, exclusive zoning assigns a given district a single use, and all other uses are excluded.

Both methods of zoning — cumulative and exclusive — involve grouping particular uses of land. But it is not clear to what degree this results in a modification of the market, since such grouping often occurs naturally as a consequence of positive externalities that are present in unregulated markets (e.g., warehouses are grouped near terminals). Zoning is meant to emphasize and reinforce this market tendency toward specialization of uses and to thwart another market tendency toward intermingling of uses. More will be said on this subject in a later chapter.

Before going further, let us briefly review the history of land use control in the United States. Prior to the 1900s, land use was controlled primarily through nuisance laws and doctrines on covenants and easements. These still play a role today, but it was found that restrictive covenants, for example, could not effectively guide the rapid growth of big cities. When comprehensive planning replaced the piecemeal regulations of the nineteenth century, nuisance, covenant, and easement controls were found to be insufficient. Early in the 1900s, a few large cities established building-height restrictions to enhance public health and safety. Between 1909 and 1915, the city of Los Angeles enacted a series of ordinances that divided the entire city into zones and specified the types of industrial activities permitted in each.[83] New York City is generally credited with the first American comprehensive zoning program. Its 1916 ordinance classifies uses, assigns them to zones, and restricts structural height. One major reason for the New York ordinance was to keep glue factories and other dirty, noisy, or bustling plants away from residential and shopping areas. Soon other American cities began passing ordinances to regulate land use and building heights. However, 1926 was the watershed because of the Supreme Court's approval of zoning.[84] Although zoning already had been enacted by a number of states, zoning rapidly became adopted by more states, who promptly delegated the zoning power to local jurisdictions. Moreover, in the same year the federal government issued zoning guidelines.[85] Soon the zoning goals of segregating inconsistent uses, preventing congestion, and contributing to economical public-service delivery were extended into controversial areas: zoning out racial minorities, slowing the influx of urbanites to adjacent rural areas, and preserving open space. The new land use control techniques to slow down population growth included building moratoriums, population caps, open-space zoning ordinances, holding zones, and phased-growth ordinances. What started as an attempt to solve largely problems of incompatible land uses and crowding became an effort to solve much larger regional problems of population distribution and preservation of the environment.

---

[83] Jessie Dukeminier and James E. Krier, *Property* (Boston: Little, Brown, 1981): 1212.

[84] *Euclid* v. *Ambler Realty Co.*, 272 U.S. 365 (1926).

[85] U.S. Department of Commerce, 1926.

The 1926 Supreme Court position on the legality of local zoning ordinances in *Elucid* v. *Ambler Realty Co.* came about as follows. In 1924, a federal district court found a comprehensive zoning ordinance enacted by Euclid, a tiny suburb of Cleveland, Ohio, to be unconstitutional. The district court held that the Euclid ordinance would regulate the mode of living on 16 square miles of an undeveloped area by segregating people according to income or situation in life. The ordinance also had an esthetic purpose. However, the court ruled that the segregation "may not be done without compensation under the guise of exercising the police power."[86]

The district court was overruled in 1926. In a landmark decision, the U.S. Supreme Court held that a zoning measure would be constitutional if it were substantially related to "public health, safety, morals, or general welfare." Moreover, local zoning ordinances were clothed with a presumption of legal validity unless demonstrated to be "clearly arbitrary and unreasonable." Justice Sutherland, who wrote the majority opinion, indicated that the possibility should not be ruled out that in the future "the general public interest would so far outweigh the interest of the municipality that the municipality would not be allowed to stand in the way."[87] Since then, many aspects of life and many of the structural characteristics of cities have changed. Lower costs of transporting people first decentralized residence, then lower costs of surface transportation of goods decentralized employment. The megalopolis, a string of city suburbs extending even across state borders, now exists on the East Coast and is emerging elsewhere. Furthermore, increased specialization makes interregional migration a fairly common event.

On first blush, therefore, I would be inclined to conclude that the day foreseen by Justice Sutherland has arrived, and that today the general public interest need not correspond with that of the municipality. Yet the U.S. Supreme Court has retained the position taken initially in 1926. The Court has refused, as recently as 1974, to reexamine its scope of review of zoning cases. It did so in *Construction Industry Association of Sonoma County* v. *City of Petaluma*,[88] by declining in 1976 to review a ruling of the Court of Appeals. In this case, two landowners and the Construction Industry Association of Sonoma County filed suit against the City of Petaluma. They claimed that the Petaluma ordinance limiting housing development growth to a maximum of 500 dwelling units per year was unconstitutional. The district court ruled that certain aspects of the ordinance unconstitutionally

[86] *Ambler Realty Co.* v. *Village of Euclid,* 297 F. 307, 316 (N. D. Ohio 1924).

[87] *Elucid* v. *Ambler Realty Co.,* 272 U.S. 390 (1926).

[88] *Construction Industry Association of Sonoma County* v. *City of Petaluma,* 552 F.2d 897 (1975), cert. denied, 424 U.S. 934 (1976).

denied the right to travel insofar as they tended "to limit the natural population growth of the area."[89] It found that housing in Petaluma and the surrounding areas was produced substantially through goods and services in interstate commerce and that curtailment of residential growth in Petaluma would cause serious dislocation of commerce.

In reviewing this finding, the Appellate Court ruled that the Petaluma plan represented a reasonable and legitimate exercise of the police power and that the police power does not impermissibly burden interstate commerce where the regulation neither discriminates against interstate commerce nor operates to disrupt its required uniformity. It concluded, "Consequently, since the local regulation here is rationally related to the social and environmental welfare of the community and does not discriminate against interstate commerce or operate to disrupt its required uniformity, appellees' claim that the Plan unreasonably burdens commerce must fail."[90]

Some state supreme courts have taken positions quite different from that of the U.S. Supreme Court. Most notable is the ruling of the New Jersey Supreme Court in *Southern County of Burlington NAACP* v. *Township of Mount Laurel.* It held that zoning must promote the general welfare. A municipality cannot only look to its own selfish and parochial interest and in effect build a wall around itself, "but must consider the needs of the region as a whole and offer an appropriate variety and choice of housing."[91] A similar position was taken by the Pennsylvania Supreme Court in *National Land Investment Company* v. *Kohn,*[92] and the New York Court of Appeals in *Berenson* v. *Town of New Castle.*[93]

The lack of clear guidance from the court stems directly from legislative inaction. The only statutory guidance is found in Massachusetts and California. The Massachusetts Zoning Appeals Law states that "local requirements and regulations shall be considered consistent with local needs if they are reasonable in view of the regional need for low and moderate income housing."[94] A quota system is set out that mandates that local requirements are consistent with local needs when (*a*) the number of low- or moderate-income housing units exceeds 10% of the total housing units in the community, (*b*) the amount of land used for low-income housing equals or exceeds 1.5% of the total land area of the community, or (*c*) the application would

---

[89] 375 F. Supp. 57 (N.D. Cal. 1974).

[90] *Construction Industry Association of Sonoma County* v. *City of Petaluma, op. cit:*. 522.

[91] *Southern County of Burlington NAACP* v. *Township of Mount Laurel,* 67 N.J. 151, 363, A.2d 713 (1975)

[92] *National Land Investment Co.* v. *Kohn,* 419 Pa. 504, 532, 215 A.2d 597, 612 (1965).

[93] *Berenson* v. *Town of New Castle,* No. 430, December 2, 1975.

[94] *Mass. Gen. Law Ann.,* ch. 40B, §20 (1973).

result in the construction of low-income housing on "sites comprising more than .3 of 1% of such land area or 10 acres whichever is larger."[95] If the quotas have not been reached, the committee presumably balances the factor of need for low-income housing against such factors as the need to protect health and safety, the need to preserve open space, and the need to promote better site and building design.

California has adopted legislation requiring general plans for municipalities and counties to contain within their housing element adequate provision for the housing needs of all economic classes of the community. State Housing Element Guidelines are promulgated by the Department of Housing and Community Development.[96] The state housing goal is to provide a decent home in a satisfying environment. That goal is reached by policy objectives giving all classes of persons a selection of housing with access to employment, community facilities, and services. Each locality is required to prepare a housing element for the improvement of housing, for the provision of adequate sites for all economic segments, and for those whose housing opportunities are affected by the locality.

Some authorities maintain that master planning and zoning are more costly than alternative control systems.[97] Administrative costs are high, changes difficult, and inefficient use-dispersal is common. The system may also be inequitable. Furthermore, zoning cannot generally restrict preexisting uses; therefore, the greatest problems will often be unremedied. Land use controls may also redistribute income in unforeseen ways. Some of these issues will be explored later, when certain side effects of exclusionary zoning are examined.

CONCLUSION

In summary, property law has developed some basic legal concepts and rules, many of which can readily be given economic content. Much of the analysis can be advanced by reference to property rights and, to a lesser extent, to entitlements. Since landlord-tenant relations and zoning ordinances lend themselves especially well to an analysis of their economic effects, these two areas are explored in particular detail. An effect evaluation of these two areas is undertaken in the next chapters.

---

[95] *Ibid.*

[96] 25 Cal. Adm. C. 6400, 6402, 6418, 6424, 6478.

[97] See R. C. Ellickson, "Alternative to Zoning: Covenants, Nuisance Rules, and Fines as Land Use Controls," *Chicago Law Review* 40 (1973): 681–781.

3

ECONOMIC ANALYSIS OF LANDLORD–TENANT LAWS

INTRODUCTION

Economists have developed tools that can be applied to analyze some of the major economic effects of existing as well as proposed property laws. Such an analysis can be carried out on both a conceptual and an empirical level. In this chapter, the focus is on landlord–tenant laws. In the hope of providing an illuminating illustration of the power and limitations of economic theory and econometric methods, habitability laws are examined in detail; also discussed are just-cause eviction, rent control, and housing subsidy laws.

Some of the discussion is quite technical, particularly the analysis of the welfare effects of habitability laws, which requires knowledge of both microeconomic theory and econometric methods. Some readers may therefore want to skip this section (pages 53–64). They may be satisfied with the conclusion of this analysis that the most powerful habitability law — receivership — appears to have led to greater rental expenditures by indigent tenants than benefits from improved housing quality. Therefore, to the extent that the law was enacted to improve the welfare of indigent tenants, it has failed and may even have been counterproductive.

HABITABILITY LAWS

In the preceding chapter, I reviewed the evolution and present status of landlord–tenant relations in general and habitability laws[1] in particular. I pointed to the interest of legislatures and courts in expanding the warranty of habitability and redefining the doctrine of caveat emptor in relation to landlord and tenant law. The reinterpretation has taken explicit note of the inferior bargaining power of tenants, particularly indigent tenants, in relation to that of landlords.[2] The landlord is now the party held ultimately responsible for the condition of the building.[3] If he should fail in his obligation, courts and legislatures, as mentioned in the previous chapter, have provided at least four types of remedies: (a) repair and deduct, (b) rent withholding, (c) receivership, and (d) antiretaliatory-eviction laws. Not covered are those laws that regulate security deposits and legalize rent strikes. What has been the effect of these laws on the welfare of tenants, especially of indigent tenants?

An answer to this question is of particular interest in light of a statement made by Judge J. Skelly Wright. In his ruling in *Robinson* v. *Diamond Housing Corporation,* he declared: "We cannot expect judges to solve the housing dilemma, but at least they should avoid affirmative action which makes it worse."[4] Skelly Wright is the same judge who wrote one of the most important opinions affecting post-World War II landlord–tenant relations. In *Javins* v. *First National Realty Corporation,* he ruled that warranty of habitability is implied in urban residential leases.[5] Thus, because the increasing complexity of today's dwellings renders inspection by tenants most difficult and the inequality of bargaining power is in favor of landlords, the expectations of tenants, especially poor ones, for habitable housing deserve to be protected by law.

---

[1] For a fuller discussion of habitability laws, see Werner Z. Hirsch et al., "Regression Analysis of the Effects of Habitability Laws upon Rent: An Empirical Observation on the Ackerman–Komesar Debate," *California Law Review* 63 (September 1975): 1098–1143; Werner Z. Hirsch and S. Margolis, "Habitability Laws and Law-Cost Rental Housing," in *Residential Location and Urban Housing Markets,* Gregory K. Ingram, Ed. (Cambridge: Ballinger, 1977): 181–213; and Werner Z. Hirsch, "Habitability Laws and the Welfare of Indigent Tenants," *Review of Economics and Statistics* 63 (May 1981): 263–274.

[2] A. James Casner and W. Barton Leach, *Cases and Texts on Property* (Boston: Little, Brown, 1969).

[3] The tenant is liable only for specific acts that affect health, safety, or some other aspect of maintaining the building.

[4] *Robinson* v. *Diamond Housing Corporation,* 463 F.2d 856 (D.C. Cir. 1972).

[5] *Javins* v. *First National Realty Corporation,* 428 F.2d 1071 cert. denied, 400 U.S. 925 (1970).

In a letter to Professor Edward Rabin written in 1982,[6] Judge Wright provides interesting insight into his reasoning. Here is part of what he said in his letter:

> Why the revolution in landlord–tenant law is largely traceable to the 1960's rather than decades before I really cannot say with any degree of certainty. Unquestionably the Vietnam War and the civil rights movement of the 1960's did cause people to question existing institutions and authorities. And perhaps this inquisition reached the judiciary itself.
>
> I was indeed influenced by the fact that, during the nationwide racial turmoil of the sixties and the unrest caused by the injustice of racially selective service in Vietnam, most of the tenants in Washington, D.C. slums were poor and black and most of the landlords were rich and white. There is no doubt in my mind that these conditions played a subconscious role in influencing my landlord and tenant decisions.
>
> I came to Washington in April 1961 after being born and raised in New Orleans, Louisiana, for 51 years. I had never been exposed, either as a judge or as a lawyer, to the local practice of law which, of course, included landlord and tenant cases. I was Assistant U.S. Attorney, U.S. Attorney, and then U.S. District Court judge in New Orleans before I joined the U.S. Court of Appeals in Washington. It was my first exposure to landlord and tenant cases....
>
> I didn't like what I saw and I did what I could to ameliorate, if not eliminate, the injustice involved in the way many of the poor were required to live in the nation's capital.
>
> I offer no apology for not following more closely the legal precedents which had cooperated in creating the conditions that I found unjust.

I would like to examine landlord–tenant laws in general and habitability laws in particular with a view to ascertaining whether statutes and court actions have been consistent with Judge Skelly Wright's admonition and whether his ruling favorable to indigent tenants has been beneficial to them.

Economists have developed a number of rental housing models, including the following:

- Perfectly competitive static flow models, which assume the existence of an unobservable homogeneous commodity, i.e., housing services, and are the models most applicable to an analysis of habitability laws.
- Perfectly competitive static stock models, which treat rental housing as a homogeneous commodity, thereby neglecting such characteristics as location, quality, and size.[7] Rental housing has a variety of housing charac-

---

[6] E. Rabin, "The Revolution of Landlord–Tenant Law: Causes and Consequences," *Cornell Law Review* 69 (1984): 549.

[7] R. F. Muth, "Redistribution of Income Through Regulation in Housing," *Emory Law Journal* 32 (1983): 691–720; and E. V. Olsen, "What Do Economists Know About the Effect of Rent Control on Housing Maintenance?" *Journal of Real Estate Finance and Economics* 1 (November 1988): 295–307.

teristics, each of which has quantitative and price dimensions. This characteristics approach involved a demand and supply model and competitive market behavior, and lends itself especially to the analysis of housing quality. Many of these models assume a group of households and firms to be confined to the rental market and do not identify how quality changes come about, i.e., whether through maintenance, rehabilitation, or conversion.[8]

- Perfectly competitive flow models with select dynamic features[9] that allow for maintenance, construction, abandonment, and demolition of housing followed by construction of rentals.[10]
- Imperfectly competitive flow models, which recognize imperfections due to location, heterogeneity of housing units, neighborhood effects, and search costs.[11]
- Political–economic models, which theorize about the probability of a jurisdiction enacting landlord–tenant laws.[12] Such models take cognizance of the fact that landlord–tenant relations are significantly affected by the relative size, wealth, and political activity of the two groups to a bargain.[13]

In the perfectly competitive static housing flow model, as mentioned above, use is made of the abstract concept of housing service units and their prices. It is useful to look upon a dwelling — a housing stock concept — as generating, over time, a flow of housing services. The quantity of housing services that is delivered by a dwelling during a certain period is difficult to measure, mainly because the flow of such services is not a well-defined, homogeneous commodity. For this reason, a hedonic index of housing services has been developed.[14] It looks upon any particular aspect of the dwelling, be it paint, heat, size, or location, as a distinct economic commod-

---

[8] R. Arnott, "Time for Revisionism on Rent Control?" *Journal of Economic Perspectives* 9 (Winter 1995): 99–120.

[9] J. L. Sweeney, "A Commodity Hierarchy Model of the Rental Housing Market, *Journal of Urban Economics* 1 (July 1974): 288–323.

[10] R. Arnott, "Economic Theory and Housing," *Handbook of Regional and Urban Economics*, vol. 2, Edwin S. Mills, Ed. (Amsterdam: North-Holland, 1987): 959–988.

[11] P. Diamond, *A Search Theoretical Approach to the Microfoundations of Macroeconomics* (Cambridge, MA: MIT Press, 1984).

[12] G. Fallis, "Rent Control: The Citizen, The Market, and the State," *Journal of Real Estate Finance and Economics* 1 (November 1988): 309–320.

[13] Landlords tend to be richer but fewer in number than are tenants. A model by D. Epple, "Rent Control With Reputation: Theory and Evidence," *Regional Science and Urban Economics* 24 (1994), explicitly recognizes that a community has permanent and temporary residents, each with different interests.

[14] For details see Hirsch, "Habitability Laws and the Welfare of Indigent Tenants": 263.

ity. Variations in these commodities are variations in the amount of goods being consumed by the individual occupying the dwelling. Aggregating over these commodities and summarizing all those characteristics, we arrive at the concept of housing services. Then a better dwelling, be it larger, in better condition, or both, is said simply to deliver more housing service units. Thus, it is of higher quality.

The hedonic index of housing is designed to capture the special features of each dwelling and reduce them to a single value reflecting the consensus of the market about their relative importance. Construction of a hedonic housing price index involves empirical efforts at relating rent payments and specified dwelling characteristics.[15] If such quantification is carried out with the aid of regression analysis, then the regression coefficients can be interpreted as estimates of the market prices that consumers are willing to pay for the individual characteristics. Such prices are weights that can be used to combine any set of measured attributes into a one-dimensional measure of the total flow of housing services from a given dwelling. The index thus permits the comparison of quantities of housing services yielded by different dwellings.

Short-Run Models versus Long-Run Models

Because housing is a highly durable commodity, the length of the period during which adjustments are permitted to occur is important, especially on the supply side. The length of the adjustment period bears on the distribution of housing costs between landlord and tenant. Thus, in the legal landlord–tenant literature, two extreme assumptions have been made. B. A. Ackerman in the early parts of his paper employs a *short-run model*,[16] whereas N. K. Komesar has an extreme *long-run model*.[17]

A short-run model might be applied to certain housing pricing decisions, but it is less useful to an analysis of effects of habitability laws. Clearly, a short-run analysis that assumes no possible reaction by landlords will easily lead to the conclusion that landlords' reactions will not lead to higher rents.

For the analysis of habitability laws, a long-run model is needed to evaluate

---

[15] From a theoretical point of view, the hedonic index approach assumes perfectly competitive market conditions. Such an equilibrium is at best only approximated.

[16] B. A. Ackerman, "Regulating Slum Markets on Behalf of the Poor: Of Housing Codes, Housing Subsidies, and Income Distribution Policy," *Yale Law Journal* 80 (1971): 1093–1197; and "More on Slum Housing and Redistribution Policy: A Reply to Professor Komesar," *Yale Law Journal* 82 (1973): 1194–1207.

[17] N. K. Komesar, "Return to Slumville: A Critique of the Ackerman Analysis of Housing Code Enforcement and the Poor," *Yale Law Journal* 82 (1973): 1175–1193.

the effect of a change in legal environment on the housing market, particularly the low-cost rental housing market.

The allocation of housing services is complicated, since consumers must choose among heterogeneous commodities, especially with regard to location. Although location gives a landlord some monopoly power, there usually are many close substitutes. A landlord, it can be argued, tends to accept the highest bid for his dwelling unit and chooses a package of housing attributes so as to maximize his profits. Like a perfectly discriminating monopolist, the landlord will provide additional services as long as a tenant's marginal evaluation exceeds the services' marginal cost. See Figure 3—1.

EMPIRICAL ANALYSIS OF EFFECTS OF HABITABILITY LAWS

An empirical effort to estimate the effects of habitability laws on the welfare of indigent tenants as well as on their landlords can involve three sequential steps: First a set of hedonic housing price equations are estimated.[18] Second, by using the rental price and quantity coefficients of these rent equations, rental price and quantity indexes are calculated. Third, these indexes, which represent shadow rental housing prices and quantities, are combined with other data (including a dummy variable that reflects the presence or absence of a specific habitability law in a jurisdiction) to estimate rental housing demand and supply functions, respectively.

To demonstrate the methodological features of such an effort, an econometric study of 70 geographical areas with more than one-fourth of the 1974–1975 United States population is presented. Absence of a more recent study should not reduce the study's usefulness in demonstrating empirical efforts to test the welfare implications of habitability laws.

Rent Equations

A hedonic housing price approach is used to estimate rent equations of a set of geographical areas. In the equations, the dependent variable — monthly gross rent including utilities (R) — is regressed against a class of quantity variables (QUANT) and four classes of quality variables,

$$R = f(\text{QUANT, INDW, NEHDA, NEHDB, PUBSP}) \qquad (3.1)$$

---

[18] For the empirical analysis use can be made of SMSA Annual Housing Survey data collected by the Bureau of the Census under contract with the U.S. Department of Housing. The survey includes a large number of housing characteristics.

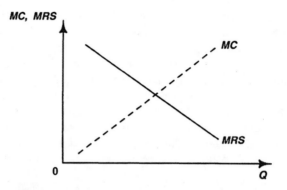

FIGURE 3—1 The equilibrium quantity of housing services Q where marginal cost MC and marginal rate of substitution MRS are equal.

Thirty-three housing quality variables are combined to derive four weighted quality classes — inside dwelling quality (INDW), physical neighborhood quality (NEHDA), public services neighborhood quality (NEHDB), and public space quality (PUBSP). (The specific variables of each class are presented in Table 3—1.) Rent is expected to have a positive relation with each of the five quantity variables and negative relations with each of the four quality variables, since the index number assigned to a dwelling increases with its shortcomings, that is, as its quality declines.

Rent equations were estimated for each of 70 geographical areas located in 25 states plus the District of Columbia with the dependent variable in log form. The statistical results can be summarized as follows: The coefficient of determination ranged from 0.15 to 0.73, indicating that the housing characteristics explained on average 15–73% of rents. Among the quality group, the inside dwelling quality (INDW) performed best in terms of both signs and statistical significance, followed by public space quality (PUBSP), physical neighborhood quality (NEHDA), and public services neighborhood quality (NEHDB).[19]

Rental Housing Price and Quantity Index

From the 70 rent equations, rental housing price and quantity indexes were estimated by specifying a standard bundle of housing services and

[19] Of the five quantity variables, number of rooms performed best, followed by age of building, number of bathrooms, presence of air conditioning, and renting of parking. The whole set of nine variables was found to be significantly different from zero at a 95% level (one-tailed test).

TABLE 3—1
Variable Descriptors

Variable name	Description
Quantity variables (QUAN)[a]	Age of building
	Number of rooms
	Number of bathrooms
	Air conditioning
	Rented parking
Inside dwelling quality (INDW)[a]	Working electrical wall outlets
	Complete kitchen facility
	Water breakdown
	Complete plumbing facility
	Additional heating equipment used
	Number of rooms without heat
	Number of heating breakdowns
	Rooms closed for warmth
	Type of air conditioning
	All wiring concealed
	Basement in house
Physical neighborhood quality (NEHDA)[a]	Noise bothersome
	Airplane noise bothersome
	Traffic bothersome
	Odors bothersome
	Trash, litter bothersome
	Abandoned structures
	Rundown houses
	Industry bothersome
	Streets need repair
	Street lighting bothersome
	Deter housing on street
Public services neighborhood quality (NEHDB)[a]	Street crime bothersome
	Inadequate public transportation
	Inadequate schools
	Inadequate shopping
	Inadequate police
	Inadequate fire protection
Public space quality (PUBSP)[a]	Passenger elevator
	Light fixtures in hall
	Light fixtures working
	Bad stairways
	Railing attached firmly
OREUT[a]	Mean annual rent and utility payments as percentage of median family income
FAMINCO[a]	Median renter family income in thousands of dollars
PRICELEV[a]	Price level proxy
PERPTAX[b]	Per capita property tax in SMSA in thousands of dollars, 1974 and 1975
LAND[c]	Per square foot land value of dwellings in SMSA, 1974
CONWAGE[c]	Hourly average union rates of building helpers and laborers, 1974

[a] From SMSA Annual Housing Survey, 1974–1975, U.S. Department of Housing and Urban Development and U.S. Bureau of the Census.

[b] From *Local Government Finances in Selected Metropolitan Areas and Large Counties,* U.S. Bureau of the Census, 1974–1975, 1975–1976.

[c] From Data for States and Selected Areas on Characteristics of FHA Operations under Section 203, *Handbook of Labor Statistics,* U.S. Bureau of Labor Statistics, 1977.

using hedonic values to calculate the cost of the standard bundle in each region.[20]

The Demand and Supply System

The functional form of the demand function can be expressed as

$$P_I = g(Q_I, L_I, Y_I, T_I, B_I) \qquad (3.2)$$

where L_I are the law variables of region I, Y_I are the income variables of region I, T_I is the taste variable of region I, and B_I is the price of the nonhousing commodities variable of region I.

In relation to the status of habitability laws, dummy variables were used to distinguish housing locations with active habitability laws from those without such laws — 1 if an active law was present and 0 if not. The dummy variables reflect not only the presence or absence of a habitability law but also, wherever possible, status of enforcement.

Three law variables in the form of dummy variables were used:[21]

REPAIR   identifies states with repair-and-deduct laws in 1974.
EWHOLD   identifies states with both withholding laws and anti-retalia-
            tory-eviction laws in 1974.
RECEIV   identifies states with receivership laws in 1974.

All three laws, if enforced, impose costs on landlords and should therefore be positively correlated with price.

The functional form of the supply function can be expressed as

$$P_I = h(Q_I, L_I, K_I) \qquad (3.3)$$

---

[20] The indexes are formulated as follows:

$$\overline{X}_k = \frac{\sum_{I=1}^{70} N_I \overline{X}_{Ik}}{\sum_{I=1}^{70} N_I}$$

where N_I is the sample size of geographical region I, $\sum_{I=1}^{70} N_I$ is the total sample size across the 70 geographical regions, that is, 28,753, $\overline{X}_{Ik}$ is the mean value of housing attribute k in geographical region I, and $\overline{X}_k$ is the mean value of housing attribute k weighted by the respective sample size in the 70 regions. For further detail and estimated indexes see Hirsch, "Habitability Laws and the Welfare of Indigent Tenants": 267–268.

[21] Rather than introducing retaliatory eviction as a separate variable, they were combined with withholding laws. The reason is that since withholding remedies are tenant initiated and impose substantial costs on landlords, whereas repair-and-deduct remedies do not, tenants who withhold payment often require protection from retaliatory eviction. Since receivership is not tenant initiated, no such protection is needed.

where K_I is the vector of cost production variables in region I; that is, PERPTAX, which is the per capita property tax in thousands of dollars; LAND, which is the per-square-foot land value of dwellings; and CONWAGE, which is the hourly wages of building helpers and laborers. Results are presented in Table 3—2.[22]

The demand function performed well. All variables, except REPAIR, which was not statistically significant, had the right signs. Three variables — quantity (QUANT), income (FAMINCO), and taste (OREUT) — as well as the constant were found to be statistically significant at the 99% confidence level (one-tailed test); the receivership law variable (RECEIV) and the price level variable (PRICELEV) were statistically significant at the 95% confidence level (one-tailed test). The other habitability law variables were not statistically significant.

Also, the supply function performed well. All variables had the right signs. Four variables — quantity (QUANT), receivership law (RECEIV), tax (PERPTAX), and land value (LAND) — and the constant were found to be statistically significant at the 99% confidence level (one-tailed test). Two other variables — eviction-withholding law (EWHOLD) and wages (CONWAGE) — were statistically significant at the 90% confidence level (one-tailed test). The other two habitability law variables — REPAIR and EWHOLD — were not statistically significant.

Thus of the three laws, only receivership laws had statistically significant effects on the housing demand and supply functions of low-income renters.

With the aid of the demand and supply functions thus estimated, specific habitability laws can be evaluated as to their welfare effects on demanders and suppliers of rental housing. For example, if tenants were unaffected by a habitability law, that is, if the net regression coefficient in the demand function relating price to the presence of a particular habitability law was statistically insignificant, no demand curve shift would have occurred. If, however, the net regression coefficient was statistically significant and positive, the presence of a habitability law would have increased the value tenants attached to their apartments. In a similar manner, a statistically significant positive habitability law coefficient in the supply function would indicate that the presence of a law, on average, increased the cost of an apartment.

Welfare evaluation requires comparing the relative magnitudes of vertical shifts of demand and supply functions, respectively, in relation to the presence of a particular habitability law. If the upward shift in the demand function associated with the presence of a given habitability law is signifi-

---

[22] Hirsch, "Habitability Laws and the Welfare of Indigent Tenants": 271.

TABLE 3—2

Regression Results for Demand and Supply Functions for 70 Geographical Regions (Inverse Semilog with Log Price as Dependent Variable)

	Demand		Supply	
	Coefficient	t-stat.	Coefficient	t-stat.
INTERCEPT	4.143	17.20*	3.118	6.57*
QUANT[a]	−0.0069	−4.87*	0.0079	3.25*
EWHOLD	0.022	0.98	0.072	1.43***
RECEIV	0.046	2.05**	0.156	3.27*
REPAIR	−0.0026	−0.14	0.019	0.43
PRICELEV	0.0093	1.96**	—[b]	
FAMINCO	0.063	3.19*	—[b]	
OREUT	0.0034	11.79*	—[b]	
PERPTAX	—[b]		0.561	2.40*
CONWAGE	—[b]		0.035	1.28***
LAND	—[b]		0.168	3.75*

*Significant at 0.01 one-tailed test level ($t_{1.62} = 2.33$).

** Significant at 0.05 one-tailed test level ($t_{1.62} = 1.64$).

*** Significant at 0.10 one-tailed test level ($t_{1.62} = 1.28$).

[a] Estimated from first stage.

[b] Variable not entered.

cantly larger than the shift in the supply function, the valuation by renters of improved housing exceeded the accompanying rent increase, and vice versa. Comparing the net regression coefficients that relate price and presence of habitability laws in the demand and supply function, respectively, we find that receivership laws raise the constant term of the supply equation by 0.074 log price units and of the demand equation by 0.022 log price units. The difference between the vertical shifts of the two equations is 0.052 log units (see Table 3—2 and Figure 3—2).

These supply and demand curve shifts can also be examined in terms of consumer's surplus, with point *C* being the equilibrium in the presence of a receivership law and point *E* being the equilibrium in its absence. The consumer's surplus is the area under the demand equation, bounded by the equilibrium price level from below and the vertical axis on the left. In the absence of a receivership law, the consumer's surplus is area *AEF* in Figure 3—2; in its presence, area *BCG*. The change of the consumer's surplus due to the law is the difference between areas *ABCD* and *DEFG* — a reduction of 3.7% of the consumer's suplus.

In conclusion, of the three major types of habitability laws available to tenants, only receivership had a statistically significant effect on both demanders and suppliers of low-cost rental housing in 34 large SMSAs with

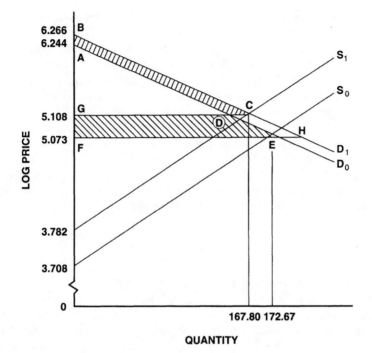

FIGURE 3—2 Comparison of consumer's surplus in the absence and presence of receivership laws.

more than one-fourth of the United States population. Its presence was found to be associated with a statistically significant increase in rental expenditures of indigent tenants and with expenditures outweighing benefits accruing to such tenants. To the extent that habitability laws are mainly designed to improve the welfare of indigent tenants, they have failed, at least in the sample studied. Receivership laws may even have been counterproductive.

An econometric analysis of black and aged indigent tenants, respectively, reveals that habitability laws affect them differently. For black indigents again the vertical shift of the supply curve related to a receivership law is more than three times that of the demand curve and the difference again is statistically significant.[23] Yet, for aged indigents, the vertical shifts of the two curves are

[23] Werner Z. Hirsch, "Effects of Habitability and Anti-Speedy Eviction Laws on Black and Aged Indigent Tenant Groups: An Economic Analysis," *International Review of Law and Economics* 3 (1983): 128.

about of equal size. In short, for black indigents, receivership laws were counterproductive, while for aged indigents they were of no consequence.

Why are habitability laws inconsequential or even counterproductive?
One reason is that these regulations are not accompanied by an increase
in the indigents' purchasing power, which should have permitted them to
pay for improved housing. Without income transfers, habitability laws can
be counterproductive. Schwallie recently concluded that habitability laws
have often failed indigent tenants. The main reason is that "the warranty
of habitability results in scarcer, more expensive housing for the poor.
Moreover, the quality of low-rent housing is a consequence of inadequate
demand due to the low incomes of renters."[24] The effects of making the
implied warranty of habitability compulsory on repairs, on maintenance
and safety, and on equity have been discussed by Singer.[25]

RENT CONTROL LAWS

Rent control laws reduce the freedom of landlords to set rent levels. An
exercise in positive economics reveals a host of effects on rental housing
supply, property values, maintenance and housing quality, new construction
and conversion, availability of rentals, potential mismatch of rental units
to households, and reduced housing mobility. Moreover, distributional
effects occur, not only between landlords and tenants, but also among
tenant groups with differing income, gender, race, and age characteristics.

It is helpful to recognize that rent control laws can apply to two major
classes of property ownership. Rent control of apartments, unless they are
furnished, involves single ownership, i.e., land as well as improvements
are owned by one and the same party. The second class involves divided
ownership, which occurs when the improvements are owned by one party
and the land on which they are placed is owned by another. Examples are
housing condominiums and cooperatives as well as mobile home parks on
leased land. In relation to an appraisal of effects of rent control, the two
ownership patterns differ.

RENT CONTROL OF SINGLE OWNERSHIP PROPERTY

First-generation, or hard, rent control laws, which involve a virtual rent
freeze, have usually been subjected to what Arnott refers to as "Textbook

---

[24] Daniel P. Schwallie, "Note: The Implied Warranty of Habitability as a Mechanism for
Redistributing Income: Good Goals, Bad Policy," *Case Western Reserve Law Review* 40 (1990): 525.

[25] Joseph Singer, *Property Law* (Boston: Little, Brown, 1993): 756–759.

Analysis.''[26] This analysis makes use of the first model discussed in an earlier section, i.e., a perfectly competitive static stock model. It focuses on rent and availability of rental housing. When, for example, inflation raises the cost of providing rental housing, controls prevent landlords from passing on cost increases to tenants. Using a housing stock model presented in Figure 3—3, where the two axes are rent (R) and number of dwellings (Q). Before the imposition of rent control on low-cost apartments, at equilibrium the number of dwelling units were Q_1 and their rent was R_1. As a result of, for example, increases in the price of input factors (whether repair and maintenance costs, utilities, or property taxes), the supply curve shifts to the left (S_2). Without a change in demand, a new equilibrium would be reached at Q_2 and R_2. Rent control would prohibit landlords from charging the rent that they would otherwise have sought; that is, their rent will be below R_2. In the most extreme case where no rent increase is permitted, landlords would supply $Q_1 - Q_3$ fewer dwellings than would be demanded in the short run. In the long run, rent control is likely to have a chilling effect on investors and therefore curtail the supply of housing. Thus, cumulative declines in low-cost dwellings could be anticipated, accompanied by housing shortages.

Some empirical estimates of the likely side effects are available. In an econometric study of 34 large metropolitan areas in the United States, the long-run price elasticity of housing supply related to land prices was found to be 0.20.[27] Thus, a 10% increase in the price of land per year would tend to increase rents by 6.5%. If no rent increases were permitted, supply would be reduced by 2.4% of low-cost housing units, and if only half of that increase were permitted, the shortage would be 1.2%.

The effects of rent control can also be examined from the demand side. For example, because income in a given low-cost rental housing market increases over time, the demand function tends to shift to the right. If we assume that in the short run the supply of low-cost housing rental units cannot change, a new equilibrium would be reached at a rent of R_2 and number of dwelling units Q_2. (See Figure 3—4.) Rent control does not permit this new price for housing units to be obtained. For example, if no increases in rent are permitted, then a shortage of $Q_3 - Q_1$ dwelling units will result. Landlords not permitted to raise rents may reduce repair and maintenance, that is, the quality of housing. Or they may withdraw dwellings from the market. This can be done by converting apartments into condominiums, convalescent homes, homes for the aged, or cooperatives. They

---

[26] Arnott, "Time for Revisionism on Rent Control": 99–120.
[27] Hirsch, "Habitability Laws and the Welfare of Indigent Tenants": 271.

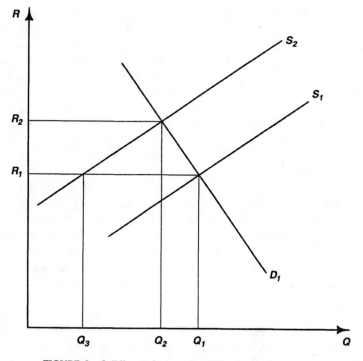

FIGURE 3—3 Effects of rent control laws (supply analysis).

may even be forced to abandon their properties because of the artificial imbalance between costs and rents.

Using the same econometric study of 34 large metropolitan areas, some empirical estimates can be offered. The income elasticity for low-cost housing was found to be +0.98 for 1974–1975. In an uncontrolled rental market, in the presence of an annual per capita income increase of 8%, for example, and on the assumption that the short-run supply of low-cost housing does not increase, annual rent increases of about 8.0% could be expected. If rent control were to be imposed and were to permit no increase whatsoever, an 8.0% shortage of low-cost rental units could be expected. If, on the other hand, rent increases were held to half the expected 8.0%, or 4.0% per annum, a shortage of about 4.0% would result. These shortages would be cumulative as long as income increases year by year.

This study makes use of a housing stock model in order to analyze the effect of rent control on the supply of housing. Rydell and his associates estimated that after rent control was in force for a number of years in the city of Los Angeles, rents were significantly lower than they otherwise would

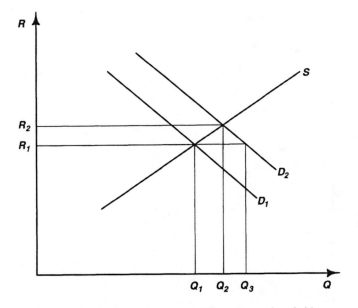

FIGURE 3—4 Effects of rent control laws (demand analysis).

have been.[28] But is the lower rent at least in part associated with tenants receiving lower quality housing? In order to examine this question, a housing services model must be used so that we can separate rent changes into changes in housing service units — quality changes — and housing service unit price changes.

I will present a housing services model developed by Mark Frankena.[29] He explored the effect of rent control as a ceiling on rent (or, equivalently, revenue) per dwelling as opposed to a ceiling on price per housing service unit. Frankena's model leads to a kinked supply curve when rent control, as is normal, takes the form of a revenue constraint, as shown in Figure 3—5. The horizontal axis measures housing services; equilibrium price and quantity occur at p_0 and q_0, respectively, in the absence of controls. If rent control limits revenue per dwelling to price–quantity combinations along the rectangular hyperbola AS_{sr2}, then the effective supply curve will become SAS_{sr2}. In this diagram, equilibrium occurs at a lower quality level

[28] C. Peter Rydell et al., *The Impact of Rent Control on the Los Angeles Housing Market* (Santa Monica, Calif.: RAND Corporation, August 1981).

[29] Mark Frankena, "Alternative Models of Rent Control," *Urban Studies* 12 (1975): 303–308.

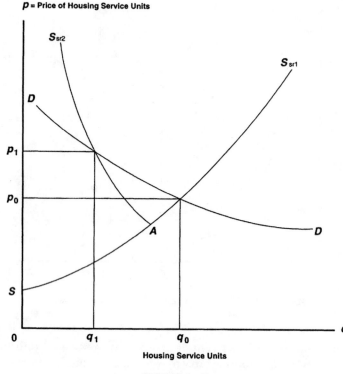

FIGURE 3—5

(q_1), but at a higher price per housing service unit (p_1). Increased demand, then, will lead to even more deterioration of quality.

Rydell and his associates built a model that permits the analysis of both the price and the quality effects of rent control.[30] They relied on the housing-services approach in which the variable of interest is a composite of the housing commodity's desirable attributes. If landlords charge the market rent for a dwelling with a certain number of housing services, a reduction in rents means that the landlords are now not being paid for all the services they supply. For example, if the rent declines by 5%, the landlord will be receiving payment for only 95% of what he offers. The landlord then will be tempted to reduce the quantity of services to only those for which he is paid. This is done for the least cost through deteriora-

[30] Rydell et al., *Impact of Rent Control.*

tion resulting from less maintenance, which, of course, is the result predicted by Frankena.

The empirical findings are that after rent control had been in effect for 4 years, the rents of controlled dwellings were estimated to be about 4% lower than they would have been if rent control had not been in force. Likewise, after 4 years, the price of rental housing services was estimated to be 3.2% lower than it would have been without rent control, and the quantity of rental housing services was 1.5% lower.

A temporal analysis indicated that rental housing services would only slowly bounce back after rent controls were abolished. Rent control was, moreover, found to confer its benefits early and to extract its costs late. The early effects of rent control were exclusively price reductions, whereas, as time passed, landlords reduced the level of rental housing services in line with the rent they were permitted to charge.

Finally, the study concluded that, in the long run, if rent control expired in 1982 after having been in force for about 4 years, the major effects would have been some rent relief for the tenants, with relatively small decreases in the number of rental housing services supplied. But should the law be continued until 1990, the study projected that it would reduce benefits to renters and also reduce supply. If the rent control ordinance were tightened, it would accelerate those reductions without providing proportionate increases in benefits to the renters.

Tenant gains and landlord losses that result from rent control have also been compared by Rydell et. al.[31] Gains are defined as net rent reductions after deterioration minus loss in consumer surplus due to reduced housing and rent control fees levied on tenants. Losses are the decrease in revenue due to rent reductions and decline in housing stock plus landlords' rent control fees, minus reduced maintenance expenditures. (The paper makes use of the Marshallian consumer surplus concept and assumes a constant elasticity aggregate demand function with a 0.7 price elasticity.) It concludes that the present value of landlord losses exceeds the present value of tenant gains, pointing to two reasons: (1) housing benefit losses to tenants due to quality declines outstrip landlords' savings from under-maintenanced units and (2) burden of rent control fees.

There exists further empirical evidence on the effect of rent control on housing quality. David Mengle[32] has studied eight large cities, estimating

---

[31] P. Rydell et al., "Analyzing Rent Control: The Case of Los Angeles," *Economic Inquiry* 29(4) (1991): 601–625.

[32] David L. Mengle, *Rent Control and Housing Quality: An Empirical Analysis of the Effect of Second Generation Rent Controls on the Quality of Rental Housing*, Ph.D. Dissertation, University of California, Los Angeles (1983).

that the presence of rent control was associated in 1974 with a 7.4% decrease in housing quality, while in 1977 it was associated with a 13.9% decrease. For indigent black tenants, the deterioration was even greater. Thus, rent control-associated housing quality deterioration for indigent black tenants was 18.6% in 1974 and 26.6% in 1977. Not only was the deterioration more serious for black tenants but also more serious for indigent aged tenants. Thus, in 1979 in the presence of rent control, the housing quality of all tenants had declined by 14.5%; of aged tenants 60 years and over, by 17.3%; and of indigent tenants 60 years and over, by 23.0%.

So far, the potential effect of rent control on each of a variety of rental housing dimensions has been examined in isolation. A more comprehensive framework, which seeks to take into consideration many of these dimensions, is the rent capitalization framework. In this framework, the expected future flow of revenues from rental properties determines their values, which, in turn, depend on supply and demand conditions and their modification by a changing legal environment. In a rent-capitalization model, we seek to represent those demand and supply factors that influence the expected future income stream and thus the value of rental income property. In order to implement a rent-capitalization model and test hypotheses about the effect of rent control on property values, I used pairs of sale and resale data of identical properties for nine middle-sized cities in Los Angeles County. Eight communities did not have rent control, while the ninth, Santa Monica, had enacted a stringent rent control ordinance in 1979. All sales data are for 1976–1978, while all the recorded resales occurred in 1981.[33]

Different specifications of rent-capitalization equations were used, all having relatively high degrees of explanatory power, with R^2 ranging between 0.56 and 0.60. All equations proved to be robust and confirmed the hypothesis that rent control decreases the appreciation rate of residential income property values. Specifically, rent control was associated with an annualized decline in property values of between 7.3% and 11.9%, *ceteris paribus*.

There are other side effects of which only two will be explored in relation to local ordinances. Since rent control ordinances induce landlords to skimp on repair and maintenance, tenants will find that their housing is deteriorating in quality. But the better-to-do and the affluent residents are willing to pay for good housing and are unlikely to put up with badly maintained dwellings. They will therefore tend to move to nearby communi-

---

[33] Werner Z. Hirsch, *Rental Housing Data Base* (State of California Department of Real Estate, 1987): 1–36.

ties that do not control rents. Thus, unless all cities impose rent controls, the city that has such an ordinance will lose middle- and upper-middle-income residents. It will be left with increasing percentages of low-income groups, who usually make disproportionate demands on fiscal resources. The result will be a deterioration of the city's fiscal health.

In addition to producing a shortage of rental units for low-income groups and providing a negative incentive for housing maintenance, rent control is likely to create difficult enforcement problems, which in all cases lead to a greatly enlarged bureaucracy. Moreover, as New York City as well as French and Italian cities have shown, rent controls once imposed are politically difficult to lift, and therefore generate many long-term ill effects — for example, on the tax base and on quantity and quality of housing stock.

For all these reasons, it is very likely that rent control ordinances designed to aid low-income groups are often counterproductive. In the long run, they are likely to hurt poor tenants rather than help them.

RENT CONTROL OF DIVIDED OWNERSHIP PROPERTY

Rent control under divided asset ownership has especially extensive effects. Here are some of the reasons — improvements, whether condominiums or mobile homes, are of no residential use without the land on which they are placed. Thus, land and improvements that jointly provide residential shelter are complementary goods. By and large, the tenant-owned condominium apartment or mobile home has a negative cross-price elasticity of demand for the stream of housing services associated with the stream emanating from the land on which the improvement is placed. Consequently, a decrease in rent for fee simple condominium or mobile home park land should increase the demand for condominium apartments or mobile homes, thus causing their prices to rise. In short, capping rents of land on which condominiums or mobile homes are placed will lead to an increase in their value, yielding for tenants a windfall profit which accrues in addition to benefits from reduced rents. When land rents are capped, owners of condominium apartments and mobile homes benefit from unearned appreciated values of their condominium apartments and mobile homes.

A capitalization model can be used to analyze, for example, the effect of changes in the rents for mobile home pads, i.e., the land parcels on which homes are placed, on the value of coaches. Since the supply of mobile homes is assumed to be inelastic at any point in time, in this model prices are basically demand determined in the short run.

$$P = f(U, V, W, C) \tag{3.4}$$

where P is the sales price of a mobile home or its assessed valuation; U is the flow of housing services derived from the home; V is the price per constant quality unit of pad services; W is the price per constant quality unit of alternative housing, mainly apartments; and C is the cost of transporting and installing the mobile home.[34] The price of a mobile home unit is assumed to be inversely related to C, the costs of transporting the coach and installing it in a park. A coach already located in a mobile home park should be relatively more expensive than a comparable one in a showroom, since for the former the costs of transportation and installation are negligible.

Coach prices should be positively related to the flow of housing services (U). The amount of housing services is an increasing function of a number of physical characteristics of mobile home units, including size, quality, and amenities contained in the coach. It is likely that consumers of mobile homes have a negative cross-price elasticity of demand for coach services with respect to services of pads (V). Consequently, any decrease in the rent for pads should increase the demand for coaches, causing the prices of coaches to rise.

Two econometric studies have applied the capitalization model to estimate the effect of rent control on the value of mobile homes. One covers the State of California in 1984–1986, where about 39% of all mobile homes were in rent control communities. Sales prices were on average about $8,800 or 30% higher in communities that had imposed rent control on mobile home park rents.[35] A second econometric study pertains to a particular mobile home park in Ocean City, California in 1987–1992. It found that during 1986–1992, sales prices of mobile homes under rent control were $3,531 higher than those in uncontrolled markets.[36]

When, under divided asset ownership, income from one asset is capped, the landlord's profit will be negatively affected in at least three ways. First, the annual rent savings benefiting tenants are losses incurred by landlords. Second, the lower rent adjustment resulting from rent control will be capitalized into lower prices potential buyers are willing to pay for the land on which the condominium or mobile home is placed. Third, there is the damaging effect of rent control on risks perceived by potential buyers of

[34] Werner Z. Hirsch, "An Inquiry Into Effects of Mobile Home Park Rent Control," *Journal of Urban Economics* 24 (1988): 212–226.

[35] Werner Z. Hirsch and Joel G. Hirsch, "Legal-Economic Analysis of Rent Control in a Mobile Home Context: Placement Values and Vacancy Decontrol," *UCLA Law Review* 35 (1988): 399–466.

[36] Werner Z. Hirsch, *Effects of Controlling Rent Under Divided Ownership*, Symposium on "Native Hawaiian Land Rights, Eminent Domain and Regulatory Takings" (Honolulu, 1995).

the land. Because of heightened risks, potential park buyers will use a higher interest rate, which they apply to capitalized expected rents into land values. The higher the risk, the lower the prices they are willing to pay for the land.

LAWS COMPLEMENTING RENT CONTROL

Rent control laws, particularly those of the first generation, tend to create conditions that often require followup legislation. They include vacancy decontrol, just-cause eviction laws, and anticonversion and antidemolition laws.

VACANCY DECONTROL LAWS

Rent controls, once imposed, are politically difficult to lift. Obstacles to terminating rent control are particularly formidable after controlled rents have fallen substantially below market levels. In order to mitigate this situation, some jurisdictions allow vacancy decontrol of the following major types — once a tenant vacates the premises, the landlord can charge higher rents, e.g., whatever rent the market will bear, and the premises remain decontrolled or rent control is reconstituted at the higher rent. Some jurisdictions prescribe by how much rents can increase once premises have been vacated.

Particularly the first type of decontrol would allow market forces to correct the disequilibrium created by rent control. The result would be particularly favorable under divided property ownership, e.g., when the tenant sells the mobile home or condominium.[37]

Vacancy decontrol of mobile home parks, in particular, raises the question of who gains and who loses. While the unearned windfall profits of sitting tenants will clearly be reduced, the effect on new tenants requires analysis, specifically whether potential mobile home buyers will be better off with or without decontrol. The existing resident is protected from unforeseen increases in pad rents, and new residents will pay a higher rental rate than older residents but, under some ordinances, would also be protected against future unforeseen increases in pad rents. Under vacancy decontrol the future sale value increment goes to zero since there is no longer a benefit associated with the existing unit.

Landlords would have an incentive to hold out for higher rents due to

---

[37] Hirsch and Hirsch, "Legal Economic Analysis."

the prospect of controlled rents in the future. In effect, the reduced supply of land for mobile home parks will still occur and this will lead to a higher rental rate than would exist in the absence of rent controls.

In this very simple model, the major issue is the distribution of value between the land owner and the owner of the mobile home. Even in this case there is a substantial distortion caused by the reduction in the land allocated for mobile home parks and the reduction in the number of sites available relative to an unconstrained market. However, in more complex analyses, the distortions due to rent control may be much greater. For example, the landlord may reduce the maintenance on common facilities since there is no longer any financial incentive to attract people to the park.

JUST-CAUSE EVICTION LAWS

Statutes designed to ensure continued tenancy for tenants are of recent vintage. They can be viewed as constraining landlords from exercising all the prerogatives usually associated with ownership. Eviction, except for one of the causes specifically enumerated in a statute, is considered illegal. As a result, tenants are supposedly assured some degree of permanence, should they wish it.

For policy as well as analytical purposes, two types of just-cause eviction statutes may be distinguished:

1. Universal just-cause eviction laws that apply to all tenants, for example, the 1974 New Jersey Law.[38]
2. Discriminatory just-cause eviction laws that single out a particular group for "favored" treatment, for example, the 1973–1974 proposed California statute, which would have given just-cause protection only to tenants 60 years and older who had been in continuous possession of their dwelling for at least 5 years.[39]

UNIVERSAL JUST-CAUSE EVICTION LAWS

A just-cause eviction law increases the security of tenancy. Within the hedonic price approach discussed earlier, security of tenancy is just another economic commodity traded between landlords and tenants. The demand

---

[38] N. J. Stat. Ann. §2A, 18–53 (West Supp. 1974).
[39] A. B. 1202 (1973–1974 Regular Session), California Assembly.

function for apartments with just-cause eviction guarantees is higher, that is, further to the right, than that without such guarantees, *ceteris paribus*. Thus, the law, by protecting tenants, provides benefits and enhances their utility.

Although just-cause eviction laws increase the welfare of tenants, they also impose costs on landlords. Specifically, such laws reduce landlords' rights and thereby their flexibility, and place greater risk upon them. For example, they reduce landlords' options to evict tenants in order to remodel their facilities for another class of tenants. Moreover, legal costs are likely to increase. As a consequence, the rental housing supply function shifts to the left in the presence of universal just-cause eviction laws, *ceteris paribus*.

In Figure 3—6, the effect of the imposition of a universal just-cause eviction law is illustrated. Rent, R, is on one axis and number of dwellings, Q, is on the other. Prior to the imposition of the law, landlords face demand function D_1 and supply function S. They lease Q_1 dwellings at R_1 rent. The benefits that result from just-cause eviction laws can be represented in an upward shift of the demand function from D_1 to D_2, which for simplicity's sake is assumed to be parallel. Costs imposed by the law on landlords may be viewed as the insurance they can purchase against the hazards that ensue from the law. This insurance is assumed to amount to $A-C$, and accordingly the new demand function, reflecting both benefits to tenants and costs to landlords, will be D_3. (Note that in this case costs exceed benefits.)

As can be seen in Figure 3—6, the just-cause eviction law has a chilling effect on landlords who consequently supply fewer dwellings, Q_1-Q_3, at a somewhat lower rent, R_1-R_3. The decline in the number of dwellings supplied in the face of universal just-cause eviction laws can be explained in the following manner: The law forces landlords to supply an additional economic commodity, security of tenancy. Since rent increases to compensate for the additional costs are not permitted, landlords will seek to reduce costs by cutting back on other housing services, particularly repair and maintenance. As a consequence, buildings will deteriorate and sooner or later reach a stage where they are abandoned. Should habitability laws not permit reduced maintenance, financial considerations will stimulate conversion of apartment houses to condominiums, cooperatives, or perhaps convalescent homes, all steps that reduce the supply of low-cost rentals.

The case discussed so far and presented in Figure 3—6 is only one of three possible cases. In a second case, the cost to the landlord is smaller than the increased value to the tenant. The result usually will be more dwellings, but at a higher rent. In a third case, law-induced benefit and cost increases are about equal. As a consequence, all parties are left in the same welfare situation as before, with no change in either the number of dwellings or their rent.

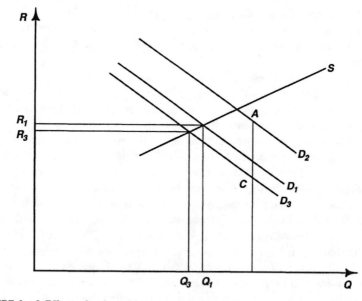

FIGURE 3—6 Effects of universal just-cause eviction laws. (Key: Q, number of dwellings; R rent; S, supply function; and D, demand function.)

A further side effect of universal just-cause eviction laws is their stimulus for rent controls. Clearly landlords working under just-cause eviction laws and incurring costs associated with such laws tend to raise rents. Rent increases will be contemplated for two reasons: to compensate for increased risk and cost, and to seek termination of tenancies of those who are protected by the law, since new tenants will pay higher rents. To counter such moves by landlords, government will be strongly tempted to institute rent controls, which will be examined subsequently.

DISCRIMINATORY JUST-CAUSE EVICTION LAWS

A just-cause eviction law, rather than protecting all tenants, can apply to a particular group of tenants. An example mentioned before is the bill that passed the California Assembly (but not the senate) in 1974, singling out senior citizens for just-cause eviction protection.[40]

Thus, in the presence of a law that applies only to a particular group, landlords face two classes of renters: those who are protected by just-cause

[40] *Ibid.*

legislation and those who are not. Separation of these two groups is not difficult when they are identifiably defined, and enforcement is facilitated by the prohibition of subletting. For example, aged tenants are likely to have rental housing demand characteristics that are distinctly different from those of young tenants. The difference stems from the aged tenants' desire for relatively easy access to various private and public facilities and their particular concern for a pollution-free environment and personal safety. These preferences are in part derived from the physical vulnerability of the aged, who by and large are risk-averse. As a consequence of these considerations, the rental housing demand elasticity for aged tenants can be expected to be lower than that for young tenants, *ceteris paribus.*

From a policy point of view, just-cause eviction laws singling out the aged tend to induce landlords not to rent to senior citizens. Also, in the long run, landlords are likely to refrain from building apartment houses with characteristics that appeal particularly to the aged. Moreover, landlords will be reluctant to remodel apartments in a manner that makes them especially attractive to the elderly. Under these circumstances, greater segregation in the housing market will tend to result. With landlords increasingly reluctant to rent to older people, the elderly will tend to end up in the least desirable places, and it is altogether likely that such laws will prove to be counterproductive.

ANTICONVERSION AND ANTIDEMOLITION LAWS

For the sake of protecting tenants from landlords who seek to circumvent rent control laws, some jurisdictions have enacted anticonversion and anti-demolition laws. The former prevent apartment house owners from converting properties into condominiums, cooperatives, or convalescence homes. The latter prohibit owners of residential rental property to go out of the housing business. While these laws protect tenants, they interfere with landlords' rights to seek the most efficient and profitable use of their property. Thereby they can create inefficiencies as well as inequities.

HOUSING SUBSIDY LAWS

Many low-income tenants cannot afford to pay rapidly rising rents, such as occurred at the end of World War II and again in 1977 in many parts of Southern California. If such low-income tenants cannot be helped by rent-control laws, what alternatives are available? Basically, income transfers are called for, and there exist various possibilities. Government income-transfer programs can be divided into those that provide subsidies to landlords and those that give payments directly to tenants. Moreover, tenants can be given welfare payments or earmarked payments, as are provided for in Sections 501 and 504 of the Housing and Urban Development Act of 1970.[41]

One of the differences between subsidies directed to landlords and those directed to tenants relates to the likelihood that the resulting benefits accrue to tenants in the form of improved housing. Clearly, subsidizing tenants' rents provides greater assurance of the benefits being reaped by them than by landlords.

However, even if tenants directly receive subsidies, not all of the monies will be used for housing, unless they are so earmarked. The housing allowance program with which the U.S. government has been experimenting seeks to make sure that the subsidy goes into improved housing. However, all earmarked subsidies, including rent subsidies, are less efficiently used by consumers than are general subsidies in the form of general welfare payments. Under the latter scheme, the poor are free to choose how they want to spend the subsidy and most likely will spend it more in line with their preferences than if forced to spend the entire subsidy on housing.

Under a housing-allowance program, tenants who meet an income test are paid a rent subsidy as long as they do not live in substandard housing. The rent subsidy amounts to the difference between the rent payments and 25% of the tenant's income. Such an earmarked subsidy is very different from a general welfare payment that can be used by recipients for whatever purpose they choose.

Decision makers who must decide for or against earmarked subsidies are heavily influenced by the magnitude of the housing income elasticity. To the extent that the income elasticity of rental housing is smaller than one, only parts of the subsidy will be applied by the tenant to housing.

There exists some evidence that the income elasticity of low-cost rental housing is less than one.[42] Because of these considerations, earmarked subsidies appear to be preferable to general subsidies. As tenants receive such a rent subsidy, their housing demand function shifts to the right. Depending on the demand and supply elasticities and the nature of the demand function shift (i.e., whether it is parallel or not), part, none, or all of the subsidy will be shifted to landlords in the form of rent changes.

Findings by I. S. Lowry in relation to the supply effects of some large-scale housing allowance experiments in Green Bay, Wisconsin, and South

[41] *Housing and Urban Development Act of 1970,* Pub. L. No. 91-609, §§501 and 504, 84 Stat. 1770, 1786 (codified as amended at 12 U.S.C.) 1701z-3 (1994).

[42] F. de Leeuw, "The Demand for Housing: A Review of Cross-Section Evidence," *Review of Economics and Statistics* 53 (February 1971): 1–10. The study of 34 large metropolitan areas referred to earlier revealed an income elasticity of +0.98 for 1974–1975.

Bend, Indiana, are summarized as follows: "We have tracked rents in each place ..., and find that they have risen less rapidly than in the midwest generally; moreover, virtually the entire increase during the first two years is attributable to rising fuel and utility prices."[43]

CONCLUSION

In summary, the rapid changes of landlord–tenant laws that have been witnessed can be subjected to an examination of their probable welfare effects. By building powerful microeconomic models of urban rental housing markets and applying econometric techniques to implement the models, much insight can be gained. Specifically, habitability laws that significantly extend the warranty of habitability are subjected to such economic analysis in order to estimate their welfare effects. Likewise, rent control and laws often enacted to complement rent control are examined. They include vacancy decontrol, just-cause eviction, anticonversion, and antidemolition laws.

---

[43] I. S. Lowry, *Early Findings from the Housing Assistance Supply Experiment*, P-6075 (Santa Monica, Calif.: RAND Corporation, January 1978): 4.

4

ECONOMIC ANALYSIS OF ZONING LAWS

INTRODUCTION

As was discussed in Chapter 2, a further important area of property law is concerned with zoning ordinances. Modern zoning began in 1916 in New York, but, by 1920, 35 cities had zoning ordinances.[1] In 1926, the federal government issued a standard state zoning enabling act, and today most cities have zoning codes.

Zoning is an area that lends itself more than some others to economic analysis, as we will see. In line with Chapter 2, zoning involves the division of land into districts or zones having different regulations. These regulations impose legal constraints under which the land market must operate and rights and entitlements can be exchanged. The constraints are made in accordance with a comprehensive plan, ostensibly designed to promote the health, safety, and general welfare of the population. It must be remembered that zoning in the United States derives its legal basis from the police power of state government. Unlike laws based on the right of eminent domain, zoning regulations do not require payment of compensation to a landowner whose property value is lowered as a result of zoning.

Just as landlord–tenant relations, discussed in the previous chapter, involve important economic issues in the area of applied welfare economics, so does zoning. Efficiency of resource allocation and equity in income

[1] J. Dalafons, *Land Use Controls in the United States* (Cambridge: MIT Press, 1969).

distribution are major considerations. The efficiency issue arises because, in the presence of externalities, land use controls in general and zoning in particular are designed to improve resource allocation. A major task is to assess the extent to which zoning does or does not accomplish this objective.

The equity issue arises because of direct and indirect influences of zoning. Direct influences relate to zoning's reallocation of rights and entitlements, with the result that some parties gain and others lose. At the same time, there are indirect effects because zoning influences patterns of local government finance, which in turn affect the distribution of income or at least the ability of local governments to redistribute income.

The major purpose of zoning, it is commonly argued, is to prevent offensive land uses (uses that impose negative externalities on neighbors). A second purpose often mentioned is fiscal in nature, reflecting a local government's desire to restrict land uses that result in larger expenditures than receipts. But the accomplishment of these objectives is made difficult because zoning ordinances commonly provide for but a partial assignment of property rights. A complete assignment of property rights would be possible only if government had all the following rights:

1. To exclude, through *controls*, certain economic factors from using specified land resources.
2. To enjoy income from the use of a resource by *leasing* it.
3. To transfer resources by *selling* them.

As Fischel points out, although zoning withholds part of the right to use property as private owners see fit and assigns this control to a local government, the assignment of property rights is far from complete.[2] Only one right can be fully exercised — the assignment of rights to local political authorities in the form of controls. Courts tend to go along with local zoning ordinances unless the plaintiff can prove that they are unreasonable in their public health, safety, and general welfare implications. One result of this partial assignment of property rights is that land subject to zoning is perceived as having a lower opportunity cost than it would have if all rights were assigned. Inefficiencies can therefore result.

Microeconomic theory can offer some further helpful insights — for example, into the relation between zoning and negative externalities. According to economic theory, the separation of land uses increases the efficiency of property markets to the extent that it causes the price of the

---

[2] W. A. Fischel, "A Property Rights Approach to Municipal Zoning," *Land Economics* 54 (February 1978): 65–81.

parcel of land to equal its true marginal product without causing the prices of equal parcels of land to differ. Thus, for a zoning ordinance to increase the efficiency of the local property market, it should remove any externalities that exist and yet do so without artificially constraining the supply of land in any given use. However, as we will see later, increasing efficiency of land use in this manner is not easy.

On the empirical level, economists can make contributions by determining whether unfettered land use generates major externalities, and, if so, how important they are. Furthermore, economists can help estimate some of the major economic effects of zoning ordinances.

I will deal with two major categories of zoning ordinances: zoning ordinances mainly designed to separate zones that can be put to different residential, commercial, and industrial uses, and zoning ordinances mainly concerned with prohibiting certain specified residential land uses in a community. I will refer to the former as residential–commerical–industrial (RCI) zoning ordinances and to the latter as exclusionary zoning ordinances. As was discussed in Chapter 2, either class of ordinances can involve cumulative or exclusive zoning systems.

RESIDENTIAL–COMMERCIAL–INDUSTRIAL ZONING ORDINANCES

Residential–commercial–industrial zoning ordinances do not simply divide land into residential, commercial, and industrial districts or zones. They also provide for separation of, for example, residential districts into various types of residential land uses. Examples are single dwellings, duplexes, and apartment houses of different sizes.

EFFECTS OF RCI ZONING ORDINANCES

Setting aside zones for specified land uses is designed to cure the market's imperfections. The existence of these imperfections is predicated on the assumption that certain land uses impose major negative externalities on surrounding land uses. A common notion is that, for example, factories, gasoline stations, and commercial laundries impose negative externalities on nearby residences. Zoning is supposed to reduce these externalities. But, if externalities are prevalent and burdensome, does RCI zoning significantly modify the allocation of land to various uses and therefore outcomes in the urban land market? Or do market forces perhaps negate the forces of regulation?

This question cannot readily be answered directly.[3] Instead, the effectiveness of zoning must be approached by seeking evidence on whether zoning has observable side effects. We can argue, for example, that if the amounts of land in the various zoning categories do not match the unregulated market allocations for uses in these categories, then prices of land in the overallocated categories will be depressed relative to prices in the unzoned market, and prices in the underallocated categories will be elevated relative to prices in the unzoned market. If zoning does not induce significant changes in the quantity of land allocated for various uses, we would expect to observe no such elevation or depression, respectively, of land prices attributable to zone category. Thus, one way to measure the effect of zoning is to look for price differentials. Such differentials would show that zoning does modify market outcomes by changing the amount of land allocated to various uses. If there is no price effect, then zoning probably does not affect the allocation of land by type of use, though it may affect specialization and location, and it may reduce or eliminate certain transaction costs.

Since RCI zoning is intended to allocate land differently from the market, the degree to which it succeeds will be reflected in price differentials and can be measured by them. But it is difficult to know a priori whether zoning regulation will modify market outcomes or conform to them. A number of economists have theorized about the effects of zoning regulations. For example, Ohls et al. have argued that it is not in general possible, using a priori theory, to predict the impact of zoning on aggregate land value in a community, regardless of whether the intent of the zoners is to control externalities or to achieve fiscal goals.[4] However, on plausible assumptions, they argue that zoning as practiced in the United States probably lowers aggregate land values in communities with zoning. Additional theoretical research has been carried out by White,[5] Stull,[6] Davis and Whinston,[7] and Davis.[8]

---

[3] Direct evidence would require the comparison of a map of land use in a zoned city with a similar (hypothetical) map of the same city unzoned. In the presence of such maps, it would be possible to identify precisely those changes resulting from zoning in the quantity and geographical specialization of land in various uses.

[4] J. C. Ohls et al., "The Effect of Zoning on Land Value," *Journal of Urban Economics* 1 (October 1974): 428–444.

[5] M. J. White, "The Effect of Zoning on the Size of Metropolitan Areas," *Journal of Urban Economics* 2 (October 1975): 279–290.

[6] W. J. Stull, "Land Use and Zoning in an Urban Economy," *American Economic Review* 64 (June 1974): 337–347.

[7] O. Davis and A. Whinston, "Economics of Complex Systems: The Case of Municipal Zoning," *Kyklos* 17 (1964): 419–446.

[8] O. Davis, "The Economic Elements of Municipal Zoning Decisions," *Land Economics* 39 (November 1963): 375–386.

On theoretical grounds, a variety of zoning effects can be deduced. For example, consider the supply of land for single-family use relative to the supply for other dwellings. The emphasis of most zoning ordinances on protecting single-family dwellings probably inspires planners to try to over-allocate land for single-family use. Yet competition among jurisdictions for land uses tends to influence planners to allocate land in a manner not different from the market. Likewise, owners of land currently zoned for commercial and industrial use prefer to limit the supply of such land. Owners of residential land may join them for fear of negative externalities. However, owners of land that is zoned for residential use but has industry or commerce as its best use may oppose such restrictions if those owners constitute a special interest that can hope to profit from an increase in the supply of such land. Whenever those who can best afford to pay prevail, zoning will tend to conform to the unregulated market outcome. Since political and economic concerns seldom coincide, it is difficult to theorize whether or not zoning modifies the market outcome. Therefore, an empirical determination is necessary.

There exist a number of such empirical studies; however, they reach conflicting conclusions. Among the studies concluding that zoning does not modify market outcomes are those by Reuter,[9] Crecine et al.,[10] and Maser et al.[11] More or less opposite results were obtained by Sagalyn and Sternlieb,[12] Siegan,[13] Stull,[14] and Avrin,[15] the last concluding that the effects of zoning are not consistent with efficient resource use. The reasons why different empirical studies appear to reach opposing conclusions are many. Perhaps the most important is that each study pertains to a particular geographical area and to a particular point in time. Another reason is the use of different methodologies.

---

[9] F. Reuter, "Externalities in Urban Property Markets: An Empirical Test of the Zoning Ordinance of Pittsburgh," *Journal of Law and Economics* 16 (October 1973): 313–350.

[10] J. Crecine et al., "Urban Property Markets: Some Empirical Results and Their Implications for Municipal Zoning," *Journal of Law and Economics* 10 (October 1967): 79–99.

[11] S. M. Maser et al., "The Effects of Zoning and Externalities on the Price of Land: An Empirical Analysis of Monroe County, New York," *Journal of Law and Economics* 20 (April 1977): 111–132.

[12] Lynne B. Sagalyn and George Sternlieb, *Zoning and Housing Costs* (New Brunswick, N.J.: Rutgers University Center for Urban Policy Research, 1973).

[13] Bernard Siegan, *Land Use without Zoning* (Lexington, Mass.: Lexington Books, 1972).

[14] W. J. Stull, "Community Environment, Zoning, and Market for Single-Family Homes," *Journal of Law and Economics* 18 (October 1975): 535–557.

[15] M. E. Avrin, "Some Economic Effects of Residential Zoning in San Francisco," in *Residential Location and Urban Housing Markets*, Gregory K. Ingram, Ed. (Cambridge, Mass.: Ballinger, 1977): 349–376.

The studies by Maser et al. and Avrin are particularly interesting — the first relates to Rochester, New York, and the second to San Francisco, California. They will be presented in some detail. They were selected because of their methodology rather than because of their conclusions about zoning.

The Rochester Zoning Study[16]

In most of the Rochester area, zoning systems are cumulative — single-family houses can be built in any district. However, in the city, industrial districts are exclusive. Data were available for 1950, 1960, and 1970 on sale, physical characteristics, and assessed valuation of property, as well as zoning, variance history, land use of neighboring properties, and average driving time to the central business district (CBD).

Ten samples were analyzed — nine from the city of Rochester and a tenth from the suburban towns. Within each sample, transactions included such residential uses as one-family and two-family uses. Moreover, there was one sample of commercial and industrial uses.

Tests were performed on regressions of the form

$$P = a_0 + a_B B + \Sigma a_{z_i} Z_i + \Sigma a_{v_i} V_i + \Sigma a_{A_i} A_i + \Sigma a_{X_i} X_i \qquad (4.1)$$

where

P = sale price per acre of land plus structure
B = equalized assessed value of structure divided by acreage
Z_i = dummy variables designating zoning category
V_i = dummy variables indicating that other land, visible from the observed parcel, was devoted to some use that might produce an externality for the given land
A_i = dummy variables indicating that land on either side of the observed parcel or directly across the street from it was devoted to some use that might produce an externality (A and V are mutually exclusive)
X_i = variables related to the value of land or the value of the structure, or in some way affecting P

Thus, the regression model of real estate prices contains basically three categories of independent variables: zoning variables Z, externality variables V and A, and a broad range of factors that jointly predict land prices in the absence of either zoning or externalities, that is, value-related variables X. If the predictive power of the regression model in Eq. (4.1) is significantly

---

[16] Maser et al., "Effects of Zoning and Externalities": 111–132.

decreased when the zoning variables are omitted, the study would support the conclusion that zoning has an impact on real estate prices independent of the other forces operating in the market. On the other hand, if omitting the zoning variables does not reduce the power of the model, one may conclude that zoning does not affect prices. In a similar manner, one can test a hypothesis about the impact on land prices of neighborhood uses of land that are thought to produce externalities.

To test these hypotheses, Maser et al. estimated for each of the ten samples a regression of the form of Eq. (4.1). However, instead of treating the effects of zone as simply additive, they consider the effects as varying with distance from the center of the city. Zone and access variables therefore appear in the equations as cross-products. As a result, it becomes possible to analyze the impact of zoning within each of the isoaccess bands surrounding the CBD.

Maser et al. undertook a number of powerful statistical tests. In all but one sample — the 1971 suburban towns — their tests consisted of dropping the zone variables from the regression and performing an F test to determine whether zoning had a statistically significant effect. The null hypothesis was not rejected in eight cases. In the ninth case — the 1960 two-family sample — the F statistic was significant, and the null hypothesis was rejected.

Accordingly, Maser et al. summarized their empirical analysis of the land value side effects of zoning as follows:

> Our principal conclusion is that comparisons we made reveal no price effects attributable to zoning. These comparisons are limited. We compared the several types of residential land and found no evidence of a shortage of multifamily land. We compared industrial and commercial land and found no evidence that either is scarce relative to the other. We did not compare residential land with commercial and industrial land, so we cannot rule out the possibility that zoning does modify the market allocation across that division. So in this case study at least, and within the limits of our tests, it appears that political forces, however much they originally aimed at modifying market outcomes, did not in fact do so.[17]

The San Francisco Zoning Study[18]

M. E. Avrin also sought to determine whether zoning affects land values with a view to reaching a conclusion as to whether zoning, once imposed, results in inefficiencies in the urban residential property market. Specifically, two different approaches were used to investigate whether zoning leads to nonoptimal pricing by misallocating land among different uses.

---

[17] *Ibid.*: 128.
[18] Avrin, "Some Economic Effects of Residential Zoning": 349–376.

The first approach relies on a time-series analysis based on repeat sales prices of given properties in each of four residential zoning categories in San Francisco. A major change in the residential zoning in San Francisco took place in 1960 and provided data to measure the zoning effects by using time-series data. Only three types of zoning existed in the city of San Francisco before 1960 — commercial, industrial, and residential with residential properties divided into two districts. The First Residential District allowed only single-family detached houses, whereas the Second Residential District was unrestricted as to residential use. The new zoning ordinance in 1960 divided the Second Residential District into new districts, with their essential differences taking the form of maximum-density restrictions.[19]

Using time-series methods, Avrin sought to estimate the effect of the 1960 ordinance on residential property values. She was specifically concerned with the following issues:

1. How did the 1960 restrictions affect the price of property in the new zoning districts? Did a differential effect occur among districts?
2. Are the prices of properties that are near less restrictive districts affected differently from those in the interior of a district?

An answer to the first set of questions involves determination of the total price effect of the zoning ordinance, whereas an answer to the second is concerned with the presence of broader effects.

The time-series analysis proceeded in two steps. First, four separate yearly housing price indices for 1950–1973 were constructed. Each index was based on observations of two sales prices of given properties whose zoning changed from Second Residential to one of the post-1960 categories. Use of repeat sales prices was designed to control for the effects of externalities and of neighborhood and housing characteristics on price. Second, each index was tested for a discontinuity at the time of the zoning change to provide evidence of any zoning-related changes in the value of property.

A second approach uses a cross-section analysis. In order to study the economic effects of zoning on sales prices of individual properties, a regression analysis was undertaken. In order to explain the variation in the sales price of individual properties, zoning was introduced as a dummy variable

---

[19] The Second Residential District was divided into five new districts: R1, one dwelling per lot, or one dwelling per 3000 square feet; R2, one two-family dwelling per lot, or one dwelling per 3000 square feet; R3, one dwelling per 400 square feet; R4, one dwelling per 200 square feet; and R5, one dwelling per 125 square feet. Space requirements for R3 were changed in 1963 from 400 to 800 square feet per dwelling.

in a regression. Other explanatory variables included structural characteristics of the house, lot, and neighborhood. According to Avrin, "The unique zoning situation in San Francisco makes it possible to determine what the price of residential land would be in an 'unzoned' equilibrium and, therefore, to measure the zoning caused distortion."[20] A reduced-form supply and demand equation for housing was estimated, with the value of a house assumed to be an additive function of its structural characteristics (i.e., lots and neighborhoods).

Both methods produced about the same general conclusions, which should give some confidence to the results. Thus there is strong evidence that residential zoning in San Francisco affected values in the urban residential property market and did so to different degrees depending on the zoning classifications. According to both the time-series and cross-section analyses, by providing stable neighborhoods and by limiting the growth of the city in general, zoning appears to have affected the demand for residential property. A direct result was an increase in the value of all properties. However, the effect of zoning on the relative supply of properties among different users caused differential levels of increase in property values in the various zoning districts. The magnitude of the effect increased with allowed density. Thus, the value of the R4 properties, on which high-rise buildings are permitted, was affected most. Based on the time-series analysis, there is some evidence that zoning increased property values in general to a much greater degree than it caused differential rates of increase among uses. Results of the cross-section estimation for each of the zoning districts separately show that zoning interacts with certain property characteristics to create value. A change in value caused by zoning appears to be directly dependent on the characteristics of the properties that are zoned in the various districts.

These results do not indicate optimality in the property market, leading to the conclusion that zoning in San Francisco creates inefficiencies in the urban residential property market by causing land to be allocated in a nonoptimal way among uses.[21]

Throughout this chapter, frequent reference has been made to the presumption that many land uses impose externalities on adjacent properties, particularly residential ones. Maser et al. found that the externality effects of different land uses are often insignificant.[22] This finding is consistent with that of Crecine et al. for Pittsburgh.[23] Likewise, Avrin could not find

---

[20] Avrin, "Some Economic Effects of Residential Zoning": 364.
[21] *Ibid.: 363.*
[22] Maser et al., "Effects of Zoning and Externalities": 128.
[23] Crecine et al., "Urban Property Markets": 79–99.

evidence that boundary externalities existed in the urban residential property market.[24]

The fact that both studies could not find significant zoning externalities could testify to the success of zoning, a not very convincing conclusion. More to the point is the need to reexamine the presumption of widespread boundary externalities in land markets. Should this presumption prove unwarranted, the call for RCI zoning could be unwarranted.

EXCLUSIONARY ZONING

In 1580, Queen Elizabeth I of England proclaimed,

> After the end of this session of Parliament, no person shall within this realm of England make, build, or erect, or cause to be made, builded, or erected, any manner of cottage for habitation or dwelling, nor convert or ordain any building or housing made or hereafter to be made, to be used as a cottage for habitation or dwelling, unless the same person do assign and lay to the same cottage or building four acres of ground at the least ... being his or her freehold [and] inheritance lying near to the said cottage, so long as the same cottage shall be inhabited.[25]

Clearly, this proclamation is the sixteenth-century precursor of modern exclusionary zoning. It must have been intended to reserve the countryside for the rich, while the poor concentrated in crowded central London. Although large-lot zoning is to this day an important exclusionary instrument, various other instruments exist and deserve examination.

As has been shown in Chapter 2, lawyers have been struggling with exclusionary land use problems in terms of the rights and obligations of the parties involved. Examples are *Euclid* v. *Ambler Realty Company*,[26] *Construction Industry Association of Sonoma County* v. *city of Petaluma*,[27] *Village of Belle Terre* v. *Boraas*,[28] *Southern County of Burlington NAACP* v. *Township of Mount Laurel*,[29] *National Land Investment Company* v. *Kohn*,[30] and *Berenson* v. *Town of New Castle*.[31]

---

[24] Avrin, "Some Economic Effects of Residential Zoning": 370.

[25] F. Bosselman et al., *The Taking Issue* (Washington, D.C.: U.S. Government Printing Office, 1973).

[26] *Euclid* v. *Ambler Realty Co.*, 272 U.S. 365 (1926).

[27] *Construction Industry Association of Sonoma County* v. *City of Petaluma*, 375 F. Supp. 574 (N.D. Cal. 1974).

[28] *Village of Belle Terre* v. *Boraas*, 94 S. Ct. 1536 (1974).

[29] *Southern County of Burlington NAACP* v. *Township of Mount Laurel*, 67 N.J. 151, 363 A.2d 713 (1975).

[30] *National Land Investment Co.* v. *Kohn*, 419 Pa. 504, 532, 215 A.2d 597, 612 (1965).

[31] *Berenson* v. *Town of New Castle*, No. 430, December 2, 1975.

The courts have also been concerned with the cost effects of exclusionary measures. They have held that, for example, restrictions on minimum lot size, which are closely related to the goals of public health and safety (as well as preserving the characteristics of a neighborhood), may be valid despite the exclusionary impact resulting from increased housing costs due to minimum lot size. However, where these adverse cost consequences become predominant, minimum lot size zoning may not stand, despite the fact that it bears some relationship to legitimate zoning purposes. This was basically the position of the Supreme Court of New Jersey in *Home Builders League of South Jersey, Inc.* v. *Township of Berlin.*[32] The court held that "Minimum floor area requirements bear a direct relationship to the cost of the house. The larger the house the more likely its cost will be greater. Living in a more spacious house will be more expensive due to higher taxes, mortgage payments, and expenses for heat, maintenance, and insurance." A similar argument had been made by the same court in *Southern County of Burlington NAACP* v. *Township of Mount Laurel.* In *Mount Laurel,* the court argued that the township's general requirements of minimum dwelling floor area of 1100 square feet for all one-story houses and 1300 square feet for all one and one-half stories or higher is without regard to required minimum lot size or frontage or the number of occupants. The court held, "it is evident these requirements increase the size and so the cost of housing. The conclusion is irresistible that Mount Laurel permits only such middle and upper income housing as it believes will have sufficient taxable value to come close to paying its own governmental way."[33]

THREE MAJOR EXCLUDING DEVICES

Three major classes of excluding devices will be examined as to their economic effects — large-lot zoning, population ceilings and construction quotas, and construction permits.

Large-Lot Zoning

In keeping with the long-run setting, it is assumed that laws are imposed on undeveloped land or land to be eventually redeveloped. Communities are not differentiated by their present land uses. Thus, every community can establish a minimum-lot-size requirement. To attract households that

[32] 81 N.J. 127, 405, A.2d 381 (1979).
[33] 67 N.Y. at 183–184, 336 A.2d at 7201 (1975).

build expensive structures, communities seek to make land (per acre) relatively inexpensive by requiring large lots. Thus, large-lot builders need not compete with higher-density builders who might value land very highly.

Although this strategy may work for a single community acting alone, it must fail when all communities take similar action to attract the rich, since there is a fixed number of rich households. Amenity-rich communities would have the highest prices for fixed-size lots. If these locational amenities are normal goods, the rich will seek them. The poor will get the least desirable locations, since large-lot zoning precludes high-density developments near places of employment. As long as incentives exist to segregate households by income, the emerging patterns will reinforce whatever motives caused the rich to locate in one jurisdiction and the poor in others. Since jurisdictions with expensive structures can support government services at a relatively low *ad valorem* tax rate, every household seeks to locate in the richer communities. But builders of expensive structures derive the greatest tax advantages and will bid highest for lots in communities with high per capita assessed valuation. Households will sort into communities according to housing values. Accordingly, every community seeks the largest legal minimum lot size with expensive structures.

Under large-lot zoning, the property tax approximates a lump-sum tax, with all households paying the same amount for any given level of services. As in a model built by Hamilton, in order to achieve a given number of choice levels for public goods, more communities are required than in the Tiebout case.[34] This first inefficiency is unimportant if the population is large relative to the efficient community size. Residents might also consider themselves better off under a smaller-lot-size constraint, since at the high-per-acre land prices, which capitalize tax savings, smaller lots would be chosen. However, this "cost" to the household is an illusion, since the purchase price of a lot reflects the price of the right to construct a residence in the community. If smaller lots were specified, the market clearing price for lots would fall by only the marginal evaluation of space itself, and the price per acre would increase. By adopting large-lot zoning, the community actually accomplishes a transfer of wealth from the previous nonresidential owners to prospective residents. With a large minimum lot size, the owner of undeveloped property must transfer a large amount of land in order to capture the prospective residents' evaluation of the right to locate in a community.

[34] B. W. Hamilton, "Zoning and Property Taxation in a System of Local Government," *Urban Studies* 12 (June 1975): 205–211.

There is a second inefficiency compared to the Tiebout case. Arbitrary lot-size constraints match the marginal evaluation of land with its opportunity cost (recreational uses, agricultural uses, etc.) for only a few residents. For most communities the largest allowable minimum lot size poses an inefficiency that could, however, be eliminated if they were to determine the optimal lot size for the residents that they would ultimately attract. Any jurisdiction acting alone in adopting a minimum lot size below the legal limit would attract smaller dwellings. Thus, where courts do not discriminate but allow all communities to set the same lot requirement, some loss must occur.

A third loss is that efficient community size with respect to public goods consumption is no longer ensured. Given fixed jurisdictional boundaries, population size is determined by the lot size. Incentives for adjusting lot-size requirements may result in a more efficient scale for local governments, but not necessarily for private consumption.

Population Ceilings and Construction Quotas

Population ceilings and periodic construction quotas have the political appeal of appearing not to exclude any particular income group but only to control population size or growth. Still, they affect the composition and size of the jurisdiction. An absolute population ceiling has effects similar to those of the minimum-lot-size requirement. Temporary constraints or moderate population restrictions may merely promote orderly growth. Where a community, acting alone, restricts the rate of growth, distortion toward more expensive structures results. In the long run, minor growth restrictions produce results similar to the no-exclusion case.

Small absolute population limits or new construction quotas allowing merely replacement of obsolete structures have effects similar to those of lot-size requirements — a sorting out of individuals into communities according to the values of their residences. The process is similar to the minimum-lot-size case.

Compared to the Tiebout model, a population ceiling imposes costs by requiring more communities than there are different packages of public output, since purchasers of a given level of service may prefer several different qualities of housing. Again, complementarity in consumption will limit the inefficiency. The population ceiling does not misallocate land between residential and nonresidential uses, since the builder is free to choose an efficient lot size once the right to build has been acquired. There does exist the possibility of inefficient scale, since no automatic forces exist that might produce a community size minimizing average costs. However, public officials could minimize average cost by adjusting the population ceiling.

The property tax without excluding devices will produce a distortion as decision makers reduce consumption to avoid the tax. Under large-lot zoning, the initial entry fees paid in the form of higher lot prices will be larger, the greater the value of structures in the community. Thus there is an excess burden generated by this scheme, since the price for additional units of housing services is equal to the cost of producing this service plus the increased entry fee that would be paid. The population ceiling scheme has similar effects, which governments could alleviate by auctioning off building rights and generating revenue for the community.

Construction Permits

Different construction permit fees (payments in cash or kind for the right to build) could be charged for different land uses in the same community. Mieszkowski has pointed out that if local governments can charge permit fees that are equal to the capitalized value of the difference between costs imposed by a land use and revenues generated by it, no incentive exists to zone out any particular land use.[35] Thus, all *ad valorem* taxes can be transformed into a lump-sum tax. A "fair" fee for a given structure is the capitalized value of the difference between actual tax payments and cost imposed on the community servicing an additional household. The latter could be approximated by the average tax payment in the community. Using the community's tax rate, the assessment of the new unit, and the average assessment in the jurisdiction, computation of the permit fee would be mechanical.

Construction permit fees pose problems where there is inflation, where costs of existing government services increase, or where local government expands services. When total revenue must be increased, those with low-value properties would pay less than a proportionate share of the increase. New services create a problem if financed by property taxes but not if financed by user fees. Special breaks could accrue to housing with limited service requirements (e.g., housing for bachelors or the elderly).

Why, then, do we not replace the property tax with a lump-sum tax? First, in jurisdictions with fiscal advantages, current residents probably have paid prices that reflect the capitalized value of these advantages; changing to lump-sum taxes can result in decreased capital values and wealth transfers. Construction permit fees have the advantage of countering incentives and justification for exclusion; they promote efficient choices for local govern-

---

[35] P. Mieszkowski, "Notes on the Economic Effects of Land Use Regulation," in *Issues in Urban Public Finance* (Saarbrücken, West Germany: Institut International De Finances Publiques, 1973).

ment expenditures. Furthermore, if higher levels of government want to provide low-income groups with particular goods — for example, education — they can readily subsidize these fees. In this way, distributional and allocative objectives can be planned specifically rather than determined by accident.

In summary, the efficiency losses of large-lot zoning are (a) an increase in the number of communities required to provide a given number of public goods choices, (b) inappropriate lot sizes for some communities, and (c) inefficient scale of local government operation. Two of these distortions are absent under population ceilings and all are absent under construction permits.

INCLUSIONARY ZONING

CONCEPT AND HISTORY

Inclusionary zoning, also often referred to as inclusionary housing, is of recent vintage. It originated as a remedy to exclusionary land use policies and is looked upon as a major urban land use innovation of the 1970s.[36] Its purpose is to force developers, who seek a building permit, to include low- and moderate-income households in new apartment and condominium projects. As a quid-pro-quo, developers are offered a variety of bonuses.

This affirmative land use control mechanism is implemented through a zoning ordinance and, in some instances, the housing element of a city's general plan.

The first mandatory inclusionary housing program was enacted in Fairfax County, Virginia, in June 1971.[37] State legislative action in California and judicial action in New Jersey around 1978 gave additional impetus to such programs. In January 1979, Orange County, California, adopted its inclusionary housing program with the following provision — 25% of the units within any applicable project had to be affordable to low- and moderate-income households. Specifically:

1. Ten percent of the units had to be affordable to "low-moderate income households," that is, those with incomes at or below 80% of the county's median income

---

[36] Paul Davidoff, "Zoning as a Class Act," *Inclusionary Zoning Moves Downtown*, D. Merriam et al., Eds. (Washington, D.C.: American Planning Association, 1985): 3, 5.

[37] G. E. Elder, *The Economics of Inclusionary Zoning* (University of California at Los Angeles, 1987).

2. Ten percent of the units had to be affordable to "median I" income households, that is, those with incomes between 80% and 100% of the county's median income
3. Five percent of the units had to be affordable to "median II" income households, that is, those with incomes between 101% and 120% of the county's median income

Developers who provided affordable units on site were offered a number of bonus incentives:

1. Density bonuses of 10% above the maximum density range allowed by the land use designation or 25% above that allowed by the zoning, whichever was greater
2. Modification of the zoning standards, usually those dealing with parking requirements and building setbacks
3. Special processing assistance and reduced processing times
4. Financial assistance through county revenue bonds and community development block grants, as well as aid in obtaining other forms of state or federal assistance

Two categories of price control were used to maintain the inclusionary housing units' affordability. For units built with the assistance of public funds, a 30-year deed restriction was used, which gave a preemptive first right to the county to buy the unit for the price that limited appreciation to the percentage increase in the county median income, adjusted for any substantial improvement or deterioration. Further, antispeculation controls in the form of income screening and certification of the buyer-applicant, in conjunction with a policy that for-sale homes needed to be both owner-occupied and the owner's only residential property, were imposed.

Inclusionary zoning, beyond any doubt, serves more a socioeconomic than a mere economic purpose. This fact was recognized in 1983 by the New Jersey Supreme Court. It stated,

> It is nonsense to single out inclusionary zoning ... and label it "socioeconomic" if that is meant to imply that other aspects of zoning are not ... [P]ractically any significant kind of zoning now used, has a substantial socio-economic impact and, in some cases, a socio-economic motivation. It would be ironic ... [to rule out inclusionary zoning] when its need has arisen from the socio-economic zoning of the past that excluded it.[38]

---

[38] *Southern Burlington County, NAACP* v. *Township of Mt. Laurel*, 92 N.J. 158, 272–273, 456 A.2d 390, 449 (1983) [hereinafter cited as *Mt. Laurel II*].

Mandelker has addressed[39] the constitutional question of whether inclusionary zoning ordinances interfere with substantive due process and equal protection. Particularly these concerns surround the ordinances' socioeconomic objectives when they include mandatory set-asides and density incentives. He concludes that "Inclusionary zoning raises constitutional problems ... however, [it] should survive under well-established principles applicable to due process, taking, and equal-protection objections."[40] His position is apparently influenced by the *Mt. Laurel II* holding, according to which inner cities have a duty to make sure that their zoning and housing policies are used in ways that assure housing opportunities for lower income families.[41] However, Bosselman interprets the very same court rulings differently, concerned that "the operations of government need to be tempered by a consciousness of individual rights."[42]

ECONOMIC ANALYSIS

The costs and benefits and their distribution in an inclusionary housing program can be analyzed with the help of a static partial-equilibrium demand and supply model for new housing, together with a partial-equilibrium demand and supply model for residential land.

Ellickson suggests that an inclusionary zoning program has three components — taxation of new residential housing for public purposes, spending public funds to provide in-kind subsidies to select income groups, and ironclad linkages of taxation and spending policies.[43] Relying on the nineteenth century land tax theories of Henry George, he is concerned that inclusionary zoning amounts to a tax on improvements, which can be offset by developers' bonuses. If there is a net tax, taxes on new construction would rise, and so would rents, thereby aggravating a housing problem the inclusionary program was designed to alleviate. Moreover, the tax would treat landowners inequitably. Ellickson finds the inclusionary spending program "plainly wrong-headed," since in his view in-kind housing compared to income subsidies is inefficient.

[39] Daniel Mandelker, "The Constitutionality of Inclusionary Zoning: An Overview," *Inclusionary Zoning Moves Downtown*, D. Merriam et al., Eds. (Washington, D.C.: American Planning Association, 1985): 31–40.

[40] *Ibid.*: 39.

[41] *Mt. Laurel II*: 272.

[42] Fred Bosselman, "Comments," *Inclusionary Zoning Moves Downtown*, D. Merriam et al., Eds. (Washington, D.C.: American Planning Association, 1985): 41.

[43] Robert Ellickson, "The Irony of 'Inclusionary' Zoning," *Southern California Law Review* 54 (1981): 1167–1216.

Elder addresses the question of who assumes the financial burden of subsidizing low- and middle-income households.[44] He suggests that an inclusionary program will initially impose one of three results on a developer: a net inducement (benefit), no effect, or a burden (cost), depending on whether net private cost is negative, zero, or positive.

Net private cost is the sum of two counteracting forces: private cost and inducement bonus. Private cost is composed of a number of elements, the principal one being the difference between the market value of the inclusionary unit and its selling price under the inclusionary restriction. To this amount is added the increased cost of the affordable unit due to production inefficiencies that may be experienced by the developer who does not normally produce lower-income housing. If forced combining of inclusionary and noninclusionary units decreases the market value of the noninclusionary units, a third element must be added — a prorated share of this decrease. Adding these elements results in the total private cost. The inducement bonus is determined by proportioning the total value of all the inducements used.

Private cost and inducements determine the amount and sign of net private cost. The restriction on the sales price, the inefficient production, and negative externalities affecting noninclusionary housing increase private cost, while inducements decrease it. When, for example, the value of inducements is larger than costs, the net private cost is negative and there is a net inducement, and vice versa. In an analysis of the demand for housing units by new home buyers and the supply of housing units by developers, net inducement can be treated as a subsidy for new housing construction, and a burden as an excise tax.

The burden can be represented by the vertical distance between the original and the "burdened" supply curve, with the burden borne by buyers and developers. However, there is the possibility of part of the burden being passed back to the landowners. The amount of the burden borne by buyers depends on the elasticity of the demand and supply curves, respectively, and the size of the net burden. The less elastic the demand curve and the more elastic the supply curve, the greater will be the proportion of the net burden borne by the buyers. The amount of the burden borne by developers depends on the same three factors, though here the more elastic the demand curve and the less elastic the supply curve, the greater the portion of the net burden borne by developers.

I will next turn to the distribution of the net inducement bonus, which can be shared by developers, new housing buyers, and landowners. Again,

---

[44] Elder, *Economics of Inclusionary Zoning.*

the distribution would depend upon the elasticities of the demand and supply for both new housing and residential land. Note that in the presence of such a bonus, the housing supply curve shifts to the right. The net adjusted supply curve for new housing moves less than the amount of the net inducement, since part of the net inducement is absorbed by the landowners.

EMPIRICAL FINDINGS

According to Elder's study of the mandatory inclusionary housing program in Orange County, California, inclusionary housing in the early 1980s was nominally subsidized by the housing developer by $3000 to $5000 per noninclusionary housing unit.[45] While the theoretical incidence analysis of this "tax" suggests that some or all of it may be passed to the new home buyers under noninclusionary zoning, empirical tests show no statistically significant increase in the price of new noninclusionary housing. Apparently, the inclusionary tax was not passed forward to the new home buyers. Although not proven by Elder's analysis, this finding is likely to have been related to a very elastic demand for housing caused by the availability of alternative housing outside the inclusionary jurisdiction. Only a portion of the community was subjected to an inclusionary program. (Housing in the incorporated part of Orange County, lacking such a program, appears to have been a ready substitute for housing in unincorporated Orange County, which had such a program.) This fact is likely to have prevented developers from passing the inclusionary tax forward onto the new noninclusionary home buyer in the Orange County program.

For somewhat similar purposes, commercial development exactions have been used in recent years. Examples are San Francisco's Office Housing Production Program and Boston's New Development Exaction and Housing Trust Fund Programs.[46] Under these programs, since the builder of new office buildings, especially in crowded downtown areas, creates also new housing demand, he must expand housing supply. Unlike inclusionary housing, however, these programs do not require a commitment to low- or medium-income housing, but rather to housing in general.

ZONING AS A TAKING?

Economists tend to look at zoning as a regulatory measure designed to advance resource allocation efficiency in areas where a significant public

---

[45] Ibid.

[46] Norman Marcus, "A New Era of Zoning Exactions?," Inclusionary Zoning Moves Downtown, D. Merriam et al., Eds. (Washington, D.C.: American Planning Association, 1985): 187–205.

purpose is to be pursued. As was pointed out earlier, the law justifies zoning when it is substantially related to "public health, safety, morals or general welfare."[47] Justice Douglas broadened the purposes when he held, "It is ample to layout zones where family values, youth values, and the blessings of quite seclusion and clean air make the area a sanctuary for people. . . ."[48]

Regulatory measures such as zoning are among a variety of devices used by government to intervene in the economic life of people. These devices differ widely regarding the extent to which they are intrusive and entail government participation in the economy. At one end of the spectrum are activities involving government production and tax financing (e.g., fire protection services). At the other end are regulation in general and zoning in particular. Regulation and zoning are much less intrusive than government production and tax financing.

Clearly, all government intervention has effects on the property rights of private citizens. Zoning is no exception; its effects on property values are sometimes positive and at other times negative.

Should a zoning action that has a negative effect on certain property values be allowed or held an unconstitutional taking that calls for awarding an appropriate compensation?[49] And under what circumstances does a taking occur, particularly in relation to regulations on the use and enjoyment of land, such as zoning? The U.S. Supreme Court's first major consideration of the question came in 1887 in *Mugler* v. *Kansas*.[50] The Court reviewed a Kansas statute against the brewing of beer that forced the defendant to close his brewery. It said that exercises of the police power that validly preserved the public health, safety, or welfare were never takings. Thus, *Mugler* stands for the proposition that police power regulations cannot be takings.

However, a different position was taken by the Court in 1922 in *Pennsylvania Coal Co.* v. *Mahon*.[51] Pennsylvania's Kohler Act prohibited coal mining that caused the surface to subside under a dwelling. This prohibition prevented the coal company from making any use of the underground layer of coal it owned in the vicinity of Mahon's house. The Court, declaring void a regulation that apparently totally denied an owner the use of its

---

[47] *Village of Euclid* v. *Ambler Realty Co.*, 272 U.S. 365 (1926).

[48] *Village of Belle Terre* v. *Boraas*, 416 U.S. 1 (1974).

[49] Whether a finding by the court of an unconstitutional taking requires merely invalidation or compensation was settled in the Supreme Court's 1987 decision in *First English Evangelical Lutheran Church* v. *County of Los Angeles* [482 U.S. 304, 107 S. Ct. 2378 (1987)]. It held that if a regulation causes a taking, the Fifth Amendment to the U.S. Constitution, which is directly binding upon the federal government and is binding upon the states through the Fourteenth Amendment, requires compensation.

[50] *Mugler* v. *Kansas*, 123 U.S. 623 (1887).

[51] *Pennsylvania Coal Co.* v. *Mahon*, 260 U.S. 393 (1922).

land, announced the doctrine that a land-use regulation that goes "too far" in diminishing rights of use and enjoyment is a Fifth Amendment taking. *Mahon* can be looked upon as the beginning of today's American regulatory takings jurisprudence, according to which zoning may be an unconstitutional taking.

In 1975, the California Supreme Court held (an appeal to the U.S. Supreme Court was denied) that inverse condemnation is not available to landowners alleging merely that zoning reduced the value of their property.[52] The court held that remedy in cases of unwarranted diminution in values is invalidation of the law or its applications. Moreover, even if the law is invalidated, interim damages for losses suffered during the period between enactment and invalidation may not be recovered because the government cannot be made liable for governing, even improperly.

In a second case, the California Supreme Court addressed the question of whether inverse condemnation would be appropriate in cases where government regulation forbade substantially all uses of particular land.[53] The 1979 ruling by the California Supreme Court (confirmed by the U.S. Supreme Court in 1980)[54] set forth the reasons for denying inverse condemnation in instances of harsh regulation. Agins, a dentist, bought a five-acre parcel of undeveloped land possessing a magnificent view of San Francisco Bay and the surrounding area. Shortly after the purchase, in 1974, Tiburon authorities placed Agins' land in a special zoning category for "open space." Under the restrictions placed on land in this zone, Agins could not build more than one house per acre on his property. Agins sought $2 million as compensation from Tiburon for the restrictions. Even though these were harsh regulations, the court held that to charge the government with the duty to compensate would inhibit community planning and chill exercise of police power by giving rise to threats of unanticipated financial liability. It would also usurp the legislative power to make decisions about public expenditures.

In *Keystone Bituminous Coal Association* v. *DeBenedictis*, the Court held that "two factors ... are integral parts of our takings analysis."[55] Citing *Agins* and *Penn Central*, these two factors leading to a conclusion that a regulation is a taking are as follows: (1) The land-use regulation does not substantially advance a legitimate state interest, or (2) the regulation denies economi-

[52] *H.F.H., Ltd.* v. *Superior Court,* 15 Cal. 3d 508, 542, P.2d 237, 125 Cal. Rptr. 365, cert. denied, 425 U.S. 904 (1975).

[53] *Agins* v. *City of Tiburon,* 24 Cal. 3d 266, 598 P.2d 25, 157 Cal. Rptr. 372 (1979), affirmed on other grounds, 100 S. Ct. 2138 (1980).

[54] 100 S. Ct. 2138 (1980).

[55] *Keystone Bituminous Coal Association* v. *DeBenedictus,* 480 U.S. 470, 107 S. Ct. 1232 (1987).

cally viable uses of an owner's property.[56] It found that the state act in question was designed to prevent a significant threat to the public welfare. The Court concluded that no unconstitutional taking had occurred.

Even though *Nollan* v. *California Coastal Commission*[57] does not directly involve a land-use regulation, it is of interest. As a condition to granting a demolition and rebuilding permit to a homeowner whose land fronted on a public beach, the California Coastal Commission required, without payment, the dedication of a public easement across the applicant's lot. The Court developed a "nexus" test. For the action to pass constitutional muster, a showing is required of an essential nexus between the stated ends and the means employed. This not being the case, it held it not to be a compensable taking.

A further case of interest is *Lucas* v. *South Carolina Coastal Council*[58] where plaintiff Lucas had purchased two beachfront lots in South Carolina with the intention of building single-family homes, a use for which the lots were then zoned. Before he began construction, however, the South Carolina legislature passed the Beachfront Management Act, which prohibited development of the land. Lucas filed suit claiming that because the regulation rendered his land essentially valueless, it was a taking under the Fifth Amendment of the Constitution. The state countered that the regulation was a legitimate exercise of its police power because it protected a valuable public resource. The Court overturned the South Carolina Supreme Court's ruling, which had denied compensation.

In a more recent decision, the U.S. Supreme Court appears to have added a further requirement to the nexus test. In *Dolan* v. *City of Tigard*[59] the Court added a "rough proportionality requirement." It held that the city's exactions for flood control purposes and a pedestrian bicycle path in return for a permit to expand a store were unconstitutional. Although both were legitimate public purposes, and there was a significant nexus between these ends and the exactions required by the city, the degree of the required exactions was disproportionate to the impact that the planned land development would have on problems addressed by the exactions. In short, it failed the "rough proportionality" test.

An economic basis for determining whether a taking requires compensation can be that compensation restrains excessive regulation on the one hand, but potentially leads to inefficient land use on the other. Miceli

[56] *Id.*: at 1242.
[57] *Nolan* v. *California Coastal Commission*, 483 U.S. 825, 107 U.S. 3141 (1987).
[58] *Lucas* v. *South Carolina Coastal Council*, 304 S.C. 376; 404 S.E. 2d 895; No. 91–453, slip op. (U.S. Supreme Court, June 29, 1992).
[59] *Dolan* v. *City of Tigard*, 512 U.S. 374 (1994).

and Segerson have argued that because of this trade off, a conditional compensation rule of two types can lead to efficient landowner and regulator decisions. "In the ... *ex ante* rule, compensation is paid for a regulation if it is determined that the landowner engaged in the offensive land use efficiently in an *ex ante* sense; and in the ... *ex post* rule ... if ... the regulator imposed the regulation inefficiently in an *ex post* sense."[60] Under such a set of rules, efficient landowner behavior is rewarded in the first case and inefficient regulator behavior is penalized in the second. Because the rules' conditional nature is instrumental in resolving the conflicting incentives of landowner and regulator, they involve different liability standards, which will be discussed in the tort chapters.[61]

Miceli and Segerson realize that both rules can be efficient and that selecting one over the other should depend on fairness and transaction costs.[62] When fairness is the guiding principle, they suggest that the *ex ante* rule be applied to cases that target individuals who must bear costs on behalf of society, and that the *ex post* rule be applied for general land-use regulations applied to particular land parcels.

EXPANDING AIMS OF ZONING

A number of statutory initiatives as well as judicial reactions have occurred that have expanded the scope of land-use control. They all have in common concern that certain land uses generate negative externalities that interfere with the quiet enjoyment of residents and, because of it, negatively affect property values. One initiative involves aesthetic regulations. Thus, for example, in *Stoyanoff* v. *Berkeley,* the Missouri Supreme Court faced the question of whether restrictions placed on building a residence of unusual design, yet complying with all existing building and zoning regulations, are permissible.[63] Note that the ruling did not rest on the legitimacy of aesthetics as a zoning aim, but on expected effects on property values. In short, the determinative issue was whether and, if so, to what extent aesthetical features generate property value losses.

A second expansion relates to the preservation of historic landmarks. In

[60] Thomas J. Miceli and Kathleen Segerson, "Regulatory Takings: When Should Compensation be Paid?," *Journal of Legal Studies* 23(2) (June 1994): 772.

[61] The *ex ante* rule parallels a strict liability with contributory negligence standard and the *ex post* rule involves a simple negligence standard.

[62] Miceli and Segerson, "Regulatory Takings": 773.

[63] *Stoyanoff* v. *Berkeley,* 458 S.W. 2d 305, Mo (1970).

Penn Central Transportation Co. v. *City of New York,*[64] the Court ruled on the constitutionality of New York City's Landmarks Preservation Law as it applied to land occupied by the Grand Central Terminal. It held in favor of preserving the Terminal as a historic landmark.

Finally, courts have tackled questions about zoning out land uses on the basis of household composition and a building's use purposes. For example, in *Village of Belle Terre* v. *Boraas,*[65] the Court reviewed *Belle Terre's* restrictions which allowed only one-family dwellings. The ordinance defined "family" narrowly as one or more persons related by blood, adoption, or marriage living together as one housekeeping unit. The Court upheld the zoning ordinance, arguing the merit of government designing "zones where family values, youth values and the blessings of quiet seclusion ... make the area a sanctuary for people...."[66] Some state courts, based on their state's constitution, have taken a somewhat less deferential position. Examples are *McMinn* v. *Town of Oyster Bay,*[67] *State* v. *Baker,*[68] and *City of Ladue* v. *Horn.*[69]

Courts also have been called upon to rule on the legitimacy of ordinances outlawing "group homes" in certain residential neighborhoods. Such homes include a variety of small, decentralized treatment facilities housing the mentally ill, foster children, juvenile offenders, ex-drug addicts, alcoholics, etc. They all have in common the fact that many residential areas consider such land uses to generate major negative externalities, which not only affect directly their quality of life, but also indirectly their property values. Thus, in *City of Cleburne* v. *Cleburne Living Center, Inc.,*[70] a municipality denied a special use permit to operate a group home for the mentally retarded pursuant to an existing zoning ordinance. The Court ruled the standard of the ordinance to be invalid as applied to this case, allowing the specific group a home.

CONCLUSION

In summary, municipal zoning ordinances are products of the twentieth century; most appeared only after 1926. Three major zoning categories have been singled out for economic analysis. In relation to the zoning

[64] *Penn Central Transportation Co.* v. *City of New York*, 438 U.S. 104 (1978).

[65] *Village of Belle Terre* v. *Boraas*, 416 U.S. 1 (1974).

[66] *Ibid.*: 3.

[67] *McMinn* v. *Town of Oyster Bay*, 66 N.Y. 2d 544, 488 N.E. 2d 1240, 498 N.Y.S.d 128 (1985).

[68] *State* v. *Baker*, 81 N.J. 99, 405 A.2d 368 (1979).

[69] *City* of *Ladue* v. *Horn*, 720 S.W. 2d 745 (Mo. App. 1986).

[70] *City of Cleburne* v. *Cleburne Living Center, Inc.*, 473 U.S. 432 (1985).

ordinances that assign land to residential, commercial, and industrial uses, theoretical and econometric inquiries raise questions about the efficacy of such ordinances. Exclusionary zoning, which through a number of devices restricts access to specific neighborhoods, is another zoning instrument. It poses serious constitutional as well as distributive questions. Equity issues arise when low-income families who cannot afford large lots and houses are kept out of a neighborhood. A third type is rather new. Inclusionary zoning, also often referred to as inclusionary housing, can be modeled as involving a tax that can be offset by concessions made to developers. If there is a net tax, construction costs would rise, and with them rents, possibly aggravating a housing problem the program is designed to alleviate. Empirical studies help determine who subsidizes whom — developer, land owner, condominium purchaser, or tenant. Finally, some new expanded aims of zoning are identified, e.g., aesthetics, historic land marks, and special use purposes.

5

CONTRACT LAW

INTRODUCTION

Contract law has developed over the centuries as a means of facilitating economic exchanges. By providing guidelines for transactions other than those involving real property, it helps increase the wealth of the nation.

To facilitate the assessment of contract law, its basic legal premises are first presented. After the nature of a contract is defined and related to the notion of "consideration," a number of formation defenses are explored. Thereafter, performance defenses, the notion of anticipatory repudiation, and damages rules are explored.

After setting forth the legal principles of contract law, I examine some of its economic aspects. The economic framework used allows the positions of the buyer and the seller in general, within credit transactions in particular, to be evaluated. The focus is on transaction costs in the formation and performance stages, and on evaluation of different contract clauses. The unconscionability of certain contract clauses and contract terms are also examined within this framework.

THE BASIC LEGAL PREMISES OF CONTRACT LAW

WHAT IS A CONTRACT?

A contract is a promissory agreement for a future exchange, freely and voluntarily arrived at. The law of contracts is designed to facilitate the process of exchange and to minimize breakdowns, and thus it contributes to transaction efficiencies. Within a system of contract remedies, incentives are provided to make good on promises. If the parties to the bargain agree, the law terms the agreement a contract, and for certain types of agreements society provides legal enforcement remedies should one of the parties decide to breach the contract. Contracts as a societal institution facilitate efficient exchange by providing a social mechanism for enforcing those agreements where aggregate value between the parties can be presumed to have increased. But not all promissory exchanges in society are enforceable as contracts. As we shall see, the law of contracts is structured foremost to enforce efficient exchanges and to deny enforcement to other types of deals.

As was argued in Chapter 1, rules provided by contract law protect initial entitlements, so that if others by their activities interfere with the enjoyment of the entitlement, they can be stopped or forced to compensate for damages. Anyone seeking to remove the entitlement to nonreal property must buy it from the entitlement holder in a voluntary transaction guided by contract law. These guidelines can reduce conflicts among transactors and can help resolve conflicts, whether they are settled out of court or in court.

Thus, contract law can help reduce transaction costs by providing transactors with information on normal exchange conditions and on rules that apply should conflicts arise and should parties not wish to fulfill their contractual obligations when the time for performance comes. Contract law usually is brought into play only when one of the parties to the contract no longer considers performance to be in its self-interest.

One of the primary tenets of contract law is the presumption of voluntary action by both parties. Evidence of duress or compulsion or other nonvoluntary behavior is thus a defense to a contract enforcement action.

Perhaps the most basic of all contract laws, also the most venerable, is the Statute of Frauds. Its full name is "An Act for the Prevention of Frauds and Perjuries," enacted in 1677.[1] In the United States it found its expression in the Uniform Commercial Code (U.C.C.), section 2-201(1), according to which

> a contract for the sale of goods for the price of $500.00 or more is not enforceable by way of action or defense unless there is some writing sufficient to indicate that a contract for sale has been made between the parties and signed by the party against whom enforcement is sought or by his authorized agent or broker.[2]

---

[1] Charles II, Ch. 3, Section 4 (Eng.), 1677.
[2] Uniform Commercial Code, Section 2-201(1).

The statute was designed to ensure against fraud through perjured testimony, as well as to safeguard the gullible and the unwary.[3] Yet, according to the Preliminary Editorial Board's comments on the Statute of Frauds, "§2-201 has generated considerable litigation without evidence that perjury on the making or terms of a contract for sale has been deterred."[4] Clearly, although the key reason for the Statute of Frauds was to promote the use of "writings" at contract formation, the writings also provided a record of specific terms agreed upon, thus reducing fraudulent claims based on alleged oral agreements.

However, in an age of rapidly changing technology, first the telegraph followed by the telefacsimile and various electronic communications technologies navigating on the "electronic superhighway," the insistence on written contracts poses serious problems. These new electronic devices — which can, and for efficiency's sake should, displace the conventional mode of contracting contemplated by the framers of the Statute of Frauds — require careful consideration.

Should, therefore, the Statute of Frauds and U.C.C. §2-201 be repealed or redefined? A universal repeal would appear uncalled for since there will continue to be many commercial transactions, where written evidence is available and the statute can provide major protection against fraud.

Redefinition might turn out to be difficult, if not impossible, because rapid technological progress in teleinformation will require continuous revision of provisions. This fact will make redefining "writing" or "signature" in relation to contracts virtually impossible. Moreover, should exceptions to the statute's application be attempted, they are likely to become so numerous and broad as to seriously threaten its deterrent effect. Marc E. Szafran has proposed the retention of the Statute of Frauds supplemented by a rule for cases with "writings" are impossible.[5] The focus is on the reduction of transactions costs and increasing procedural efficiency thereby.

A core concept for contracts to be enforceable is *consideration*, a legal term for the judicial inquiry of whether a bargain has been struck. The test of consideration is whether value has been exchanged between parties. The doctrine does not test the fairness of the exchange or the equality of the values exchanged. It seeks merely to ascertain whether an exchange of value has occurred. The maxim is that the law tests only to see if consideration, that is, exchange for value, exists. The parties to the exchange value

---

[3] Arthur L. Corbin, *Corbin on Contracts* (1950): §275.

[4] Preliminary Editorial Board Study Committee Executive Summary (1991): 11.

[5] Mark E. Szafran, *Contracts Formed in Cyberspace: A Day of Reckoning for the Statute of Frauds* (New York: Columbia Institute for Tele-Information, 1995): 1–48.

their respective contributions to the transaction autonomously, and the law determines only whether an exchange has occurred.

There can be no doubt that courts take seriously the existence of a consideration. An example is *Stelmack* v. *Glen Alden Coal Co.*, where the Pennsylvania Supreme Court held.[6] "We are satisfied that there is nothing in the present record to bring this case within any recognized exception to the well settled principle of contract law, that a promise unsupported by consideration is nudum pactum, and unenforceable."

On first blush, it might be disconcerting to find that courts inquire only about the existence of a consideration for a contract and not about its adequacy. However, this is a sound approach. First of all, courts are not in a good position to second-guess those who are actively engaged in specific economic transactions. Second, instead of imposing on experts the court's inadequate view of what a proper consideration should be, the court seeks to establish an environment in which fair and appropriate consideration is offered. Specifically, contract law provides a number of defenses that make it possible for a trading environment to emerge, within which fair and appropriate consideration is likely to be offered. Thus, as we will see, contract law provides for such formation defenses as duress and incapacity, and such performance defenses as commercial impracticability and mistake. These defenses should help create an environment in which transactions take place among more or less equal partners. To these defenses, antitrust laws and activities by such agencies as the Federal Trade Commission are added to increase the likelihood of a relatively fair balance of bargaining power between trading partners.

The corpus of contract law provides a carefully worked out body of information concerning certain contingencies that may defeat an exchange. This knowledge assists the parties in planning their exchanges. Uncertainty is decreased and efficiency increased; this can reduce the complexity and thus the cost of transactions. Thus the economic rationale for contract law is the creation of incentives for value-maximizing conduct in the future, encouraging a process by which resources are smoothly moved through a series of exchanges into successively more valuable uses. In this spirit, defenses have been stipulated. They are taken up next within the setting of the two major contract phases, formation and performance.

CONTRACT FORMATION AND FORMATION DEFENSES

The first phase of any contract involves the creation of a contractual obligation. During the formation stage various propositions may be advanced,

---

[6] *Stelmack* v. *Glen Alden Coal Co.*, 339 Pa. 410, 14 A.2d 127 (1940).

culminating at one point in a meeting of minds when an agreement is reached between the contracting parties. For the contract-formation stage to be completed successfully, an operative offer must be made by one party and an operative acceptance must be made by a second while the operative offer is still in force. However, after a contract is formed, it may not be binding under certain circumstances.

Within the law of contracts there exist certain *formation defenses* that allow a party to escape judicial enforcement of the contract. One such defense is termed *illusory promise.* Consider the promise: "I'll give you this car *when I feel like it.*" This promise is illusory — it is subject to a condition that makes its value uncertain or possibly nonexistent. An exchange of such promises is not efficient, since the deal is too vague, and a contract involving such vagueness defies enforcement.

Another formation defense relates to promissory exchanges made within *intimate relationships.* They are not legally binding contracts unless there is clear evidence that a legally enforceable contract was contemplated. The economic rationale of the doctrine is that imposing legal sanctions in this area would not facilitate efficient exchange. This was explicitly recognized in *Balfour* v. *Balfour.* Here the court decided that an agreement, reached in a friendly way, that the wife should be supported by £30 a month while detained in England on doctor's advice was not enforceable because the parties did not intend to have the bargain enforced, and courts do not enforce such an agreement.[7]

A further formaton defense is the doctrine of *duress.* The essense of the defense is that the contract was not voluntarily made by one of the parties. Instead, one of the parties agreed to the contract in response to an improper threat by the other party that left it with no reasonable alternative.[8] If a robber holds a gun to his victim's head and demands, "Your money or your life," the external format of a contract is complete when the victim hands over the money: A promise has been exchanged for a performance — the money was paid for the criminal's forbearance in not pulling the trigger.

A firm principle of Anglo-American law is that the courts will not permit themselves to be used as instruments of inequity and injustice. Courts will not enforce transactions in which the relative positions of the parties were such that one has unconscionably taken advantage of the necessities and distress of the other. Thus, as early as 1761, Lord Chancellor Northington wrote, "And there is great reason and justice in the rule, for necessitous

[7] *Balfour* v. *Balfour,* 2 K.B. 571 (1919).
[8] *Restatement (Second) of Contracts* §175 (1979).

men are not, truly speaking, free men, but, to answer a present exigency, will submit to any terms that the crafty may impose upon them."[9]

In *Atkinson v. Denby,* Cockburn, J. C. said that "where the one person can dictate, and the other has no alternative but to submit, it is coercion."[10] In this context, when a mortgagee under the pressure of financial distress conveys his equity of redemption to the mortgagor, the courts will scrutinize the transaction very carefully.[11]

Likewise, when a person heavily in debt, in order to obtain an additional loan with which to meet debts falling due, agreed to buy land at more than twice its value, the court as early as 1826 held that the lender had unjustly taken advantage of the borrower's necessity. It rescinded the contract. "The rule ... is ... [that when] a person is encumbered with debts, and that fact is known to a person with whom he contracts, who avails himself of it to exact an unconscionable bargain, equity will relieve upon account of the advantage and hardship."[12]

Also, a growing number of states recognize the doctrine of duress. Courts generally have held three elements necessary to a prima facie case of economic duress: (1) wrongful acts or threats by the defendant, (2) financial distress caused by the wrongful acts or threats, and (3) the absence of any reasonable alternative to the terms presented by the wrongdoer. For example, in *International Paper Co.* v. *Whilden,* the court struck down a third party's agreement to indemnify International Paper. The contract was held to have been executed under duress because International Paper wrongfully refused to pay accounts due to third parties unless it signed indemnity agreements.[13] Enforcing contracts entered into under duress would undermine confidence in our voluntary exchange system and reduce the general willingness to engage in market transactions.

Another formation defense is *incapacity.* Under this rubric, contracts that would normally be enforceable are denied legal sanction. The defense of incapacity arises when the party who breaches the contract seeks to prove that his assent to the exchange was made under undue influence or strain, or in the presence of mental illness, intoxication, or drug incapacity.

Thus, for example, undue influence was claimed in a 1966 California case. Plaintiff D. Odorizzi, a teacher, claimed that after he was arrested on criminal charges of homosexual activity representatives of the school board

---

[9] *Vernon* v. *Bethell,* 2 Eden 110, 113 (1761).

[10] *Atkinson* v. *Denby,* Hurlst. and N. 934, 936 (1862).

[11] *Villa* v. *Rodriguez,* 12 Wall. 323, 339 (1870).

[12] *Administrators of Hough* v. *Hunt,* 2 Ohio 495, 502.

[13] *International Paper Co.* v. *Whilden,* 469 So. 2d 560, 562 (Ala. 1985).

secured his consent to resign.[14] They used the high-pressure technique of assuring him that they were trying to assist him by securing his resignation. Otherwise, they said, the board would dismiss him and publicize the fact, all of which would jeopardize his chances of securing a teaching position elsewhere.

As the court stated in the Odorizzi case,

> Undue influence, in the sense we are concerned with here, is a shorthand legal phrase used to describe persuasion which tends to be coercive in nature, persuasion which overcomes the will without convincing the judgment.... The hallmark of such persuasion is high pressure, a pressure which works on mental, moral, or emotional weakness to such an extent that it approaches the boundaries of coercion. In this sense, undue influence has been called over-persuasion.... By statutory definition undue influence includes "taking an unfair advantage of another's weakness of mind; or ... taking a grossly oppressive and unfair advantage of another's necessities or distress [Civ. Code, 1575]."
>
> We paraphrase the summary of undue influence given the jury by Sir James P. Wilde in Hall v. Hall, L. R. 1, P & D 481, 482 (1868): To make a good contract a man must be a free agent. Pressure of whatever sort which overpowers the will without convincing the judgment is a species of restraint under which no valid contract can be made. Importunity or threats, if carried to the degree in which the free play of a man's will is overborne, constitute undue influence, although no force is used or threatened. A party may be led but not driven, and his acts must be the offspring of his own volition and not the record of someone else's.
>
> In essence undue influence involves the use of excessive pressure to persuade one vulnerable to such pressure, pressure applied by a dominant subject to a servient object. In combination, the elements of undue susceptibility in the servient person and excessive pressure by the dominating person make the latter's influence undue, for it results in the apparent will of the servient person being in fact the will of the dominant person.

Although it might be argued the *Odorizzi* was less a case of incapacity than of duress, this does not hold for *Ortelere* v. *Teachers' Retirement Board of the City of New York*.[15]

> This case involves the revocability of an election of benefits under a public employees' retirement system ... [because] ... of mental incompetency which may render voidable the exercise of contractual rights. The particular issue arises on the evidently unwise and foolhardy selection of benefits by a 60-year-old teacher, on leave for mental illness and suffering from cerebral arteriosclerosis, after service as a public schoolteacher and participation in a public retirement system for over 40 years. The teacher died a little less than two months after making her election of maximum benefits, payable to her

---

[14] *Odorizzi* v. *Bloomfeld School District*, 246 Cal. App. 2d 123 (1966).

[15] *Ortelere* v. *Teachers' Retirement Board of the City of New York*, Court of Appeals of New York, 25 N.Y.2d 196, 303 N.Y.S.2d 362, 250 N.E.2d 460 (1969).

during her life, thus causing the entire reserve to fall in. She left surviving husband of 38 years of marriage and two grown children.... The well-established rule is that contracts of a mentally incompetent person who has not been adjudicated insane are voidable.... [S]he acted solely as a result of serious mental illness ... Mrs. Ortelere's psychiatrist testified quite flatly that as an involutional melancholiac in depression she was incapable of making a voluntary "rational" decision.... [T]here should be a new trial under the proper standards frankly considered and applied.

The defense of incapacity has a persuasive economic rationale. The essence of the defense is that true preferences are not revealed in the exchange.

CONTRACT PERFORMANCE AND PERFORMANCE DEFENSES

Society has a interest in seeing contracts enforced once they are formed. If performance were not ensured, few contracts would be entered into and the number of value-creating exchanges would be reduced. Therefore, the law provides incentives to ensure performance.

Once a legally enforceable agreement between the parties exists, the law provides a social mechanism for its enforcement. A party to a contract who later breaches his deal will be held in breach and will be required to provide the nonbreaching party with compensation under specific damages rules. However, there are conditions under which the breaching party may be excused from performing or paying damages. Such conditions, which effectively excuse performance, are often referred to as *performance defenses*. For a performance defense to be invoked, the event claimed to be responsible for the performance inability must not have been preventable by the promisor at a reasonable cost.[16] A performance defense can only be raised where the contract does not explicitly assign the risk in question and the event responsible for claiming the performance defense could not have been avoided by cost-justified precautions. Posner and Rosenfield suggest that, when

> these threshold conditions have been satisfied, economic analysis suggests that the loss should be placed on the party who is the superior (that is, lower-cost) risk bearer. To determine which party is the superior risk bearer three factors are relevant — knowledge of the magnitude of the loss, knowledge of the probability that it will occur, and (other) costs of self- or market-insurance.[17]

[16] R. A. Posner and E. M. Rosenfield, "Impossibility and Related Doctrines in Contract Law: An Economic Analysis," *Journal of Legal Studies* 6 (January 1977): 83–118.
[17] *Ibid.*: 117.

A number of performance defenses have been identified in the law. One such defense is *impossibility*. Clearly, the risk of losses due to entirely unforeseen events that make delivery on a contract impossible can be assigned in various ways. If the seller assumes the risk, he will want to be compensated for it by including in the price a risk premium. And if the risk is assumed by the buyer, he will want to deduct the risk premium from the price he pays. There is an advantage in having a general risk assignment as under the impossibility defense, rather than writing special clauses into every contract. Such a rule will tend to reduce litigation and transaction costs.

One example is the death of a contracting entertainment performer. The performer's estate simply cannot provide performance of the terms of the contract between the decedent and another party. The law provides legal recognition of this fact, thus discouraging unnecessary suits when parties to the deal have not specifically made provision for the contingency. Here the doctrine promotes efficiency by decreasing the incentives for additional lawsuits and by providing incentives for parties to specify and think out future contingencies to the deal. Thus, efficient exchange is facilitated.

Or consider another unique resource, as in the case of *Taylor* v. *Caldwell*. Here a contract was signed for the use of the Surrey Gardens and the Music Hall. Just before the concert was to be given under the contract, the hall was destroyed by fire.[18] The court accepted the defense of impossibility, declaring that the hall had ceased to exist, without fault of either party. Therefore, it was impossible for either party to perform its promise.

When, under these circumstances, will the law excuse performance because of impossibility? Clearly, much depends on how financially ruinous and unforeseen the result of the erroneous underlying assumptions turn out to be. For example, a contract between two parties for the construction of a concrete bridge across the Arroyo Seco in South Pasadena, California, stipulated that all gravel and earth necessary for the project would come from the plaintiff's land, and a certain price would be paid for it by the defendants. When only about half of the gravel was taken from the plaintiff's land, he filed suit for breach of contract. However, the court found that "no greater quantity could have been taken by ordinary means except by the use, at great expense, of a steam dredger, and the earth and gravel so taken could not have been used without first having been dried at great expense and delay."[19]

---

[18] *Taylor* v. *Caldwell*, King's Bench, 1863.
[19] *Mineral Park Land Co.* v. *Howard*, 172 Cal. 289, 156 458 (1916).

Consequently, the court concluded,

> ... And, in determining whether the earth and gravel were "available," we must view the conditions in a practical and reasonable way. Although there was gravel on the land, it was so situated that the defendants could not take it by ordinary means, nor except at a prohibitive cost. To all fair intents then, it was impossible for defendants to take it.
>
> Judgment for defendants.[20]

Thus, if crucial assumptions underlie the deal as a foundation to the performance agreed upon, then failure of the assumption is a defense to actual performance. This rule clearly has an economic rationale, since enforcement of the performances agreed upon, once the underlying assumptions to the deal have been destroyed, would cause inefficient exchange.

The Uniform Commercial Code deals extensively with the doctrine of *commercial impracticability*. Section 2-615 indicates that a party seeking to be discharged from his contractual obligations must show all of the following and that the party seeking excuse has the burden of the proof:

1. A failure of an underlying condition of the contract must occur.
2. The failure must have been unforeseen at the time the contract was signed.
3. The risk of failure must not have been assumed either directly or indirectly by the parties seeking excuse.
4. Performance must be impracticable.
5. The seller must have made all reasonable attempts to assure himself that the source of supply will not fail.
6. Finally, the seller's own conduct must not have created the situation leading to the impracticability of performance.

An interesting examination of the claim by Westinghouse Electric Corporation in 1975 that it was not legally bound to honor fixed-price contracts to deliver about 70 million pounds of uranium by appealing to section 2-615 of the Uniform Commercial Code can be found in an article by Joskow.[21] The paper was written before the case had been disposed of by the courts. (In October 1978, a U.S. district court ruled that Westinghouse's claim of commercial impracticability was invalid, holding that it illegally had reneged on its uranium supply contracts.) Joskow correctly concluded

---

[20] *Ibid.*

[21] P. L. Joskow, "Commercial Impossibility, the Uranium Market and the Westinghouse Case," *Journal of Legal Studies* 6 (January 1977): 119–176.

that "Westinghouse appears to fail on all counts to justify a discharge of its contractual obligations under U.C.C. paragraph 2-615."[22]

In summary, formation as well as performance defenses invalidate a contract when it can be shown that actual agreement has not occurred. Under such a circumstance, the economic rationale of a contract is not met, and therefore efficient resource use is unlikely to result.

Anticipatory Repudiation

Anticipatory repudiation results when a party to a contract gives formal advance notice of his intention not to perform. It is a breach by anticipatory repudiation in contrast to a breach by failure to perform when due. Suppose two parties exchange promises to perform in the future. Specifically, one agrees to buy and another agrees to sell 100 widgets at $1 apiece one year from the date the contract is signed. Now that a contract exists, both parties have an enforceable obligation to perform or pay damages when the time of performance comes. During the intervening year before the seller's duty to deliver is due, he begins to have reservations about the deal and expresses them to the buyer, "I'm not sure I can perform."

The legal step of anticipatory repudiation is an expression of intention not to perform in the future, but to breach the contract. When the expression of intention not to perform in the future destroys the nonbreaching party's confidence in the reliability of the promise exchanged, a material breach of contract has occurred and the nonbreaching party has legal rights of action.

In connection with such anticipatory repudiation, the court stated in *Hawkinson* v. *Johnston,*

> The real sanctity of any contract rests only in the mutual willingness of the parties to perform. Where this willingness ceases to exist, any attempt to prolong or preserve the status between them will usually be unsatisfactory and mechanical. Generally speaking, it is far better in such a situation, for the individuals and for society, that the rights and obligations between them should be promptly and definitely settled, if the injured party so desires, unless there is some provision in the contract that, as a matter of mutual intention, can be said to prevent this from being done.[23]

According to the Uniform Commercial Code, the aggrieved party in the light of anticipatory repudiation may

---

[22] *Ibid.*: 175.
[23] *Hawkinson* v. *Johnston,* 122 F.2d 724, 729–730 (8th Cir. 1941).

1. Await performance for a commercially reasonable time
2. Resort to any remedy for breach
3. Suspend his own performance or proceed in accordance with the provisions of the seller's right to identify goods to the contract notwithstanding breach or to salvage unfinished goods.[24]

The economic rationale of the doctrine is clear. Efficiency in exchange is enhanced by certainty between the parties to the deal. Therefore, if one party is convinced that unforeseen circumstances make the deal unprofitable, being permitted to cancel the deal while leaving the other party no worse off than he otherwise would have been is efficient. As Vold has stated,

> The substantial practical reason for permitting the aggrieved promisee to sue at once for anticipatory repudiation is that allowing an action at once tends to conserve available resources and prevent waste.... Very often by such settlement through litigation, the controversy can be adjusted and the productive work of the business in hand continued without serious interruption.[25]

DAMAGES RULES

The law of contracts does not require parties to a contract actually to perform. Contracting parties are given the option of performance or breach. But if a contracting party breaches his deal, he is required to pay damages. As Oliver Wendell Holmes, Jr., has stated, "The only universal consequence of a legally binding promise is, that the law makes the promisor pay damages if the promised event does not come to pass."[26] Thus, a breach of contract is not a tort, and the party in breach is not held liable for consequences of nonperformance. Instead, the basic measure of damages for breach of contract is the *rule of financial equivalent performance*. Under this rule, a breaching party must pay the financial equivalent of his breach of the contract to the nonbreacher. The objective is to put the innocent party in the position he would have been in if the contract had not been breached. Suppose a party contracts to sell a buyer one sack of sand at $6. He then notifies the buyer that he will not deliver. The current market price of equivalent sacks of sand on the open market is $7. The financial equivalent performance of the deal from the buyer's perspective is the

---

[24] Uniform Commercial Code, section 2–610.

[25] L. Vold, "Repudiation of Contracts," *Nebraska Law Bulletin* 5 (February 1927): 269, 279–285.

[26] Oliver Wendell Holmes, Jr., *The Common Law*, Mark D. Howe, ed. (Boston: Little, Brown, 1963): 234–237.

difference between the market price and the contract price for the sand, or $1.

The underlying economic rationale for this rule is that if one party determines that breach is in its self-interest, actual breach is efficient, as long as the other party is not harmed. The rule of financial equivalent performance ensures such an outcome by giving the nonbreacher the value of his deal; it releases the breaching party from an actual performance that he believes would be more expensive for him than payment of damages. Thus, the party best able to evaluate the cost of actual performance versus the payment of financial equivalent damages is given the power to decide. The nonbreacher is given his full financial equivalent for performance of the deal and may purchase conforming performance on the market. Resources are saved, and the lowest-cost performance is revealed to the contracting parties.

Next, let us turn to a further damages rule, the *avoidable-consequences rule*, and demonstrate it. Suppose, as in *Rockingham County* v. *Luten Bridge Co.*, a construction company and a municipality contract to build a bridge.[27] As the company proceeds with bridge construction, the municipality reaches a decision to breach the contract. The bridge order is thereby canceled. Once notice of breach is given to the construction company, the law of contracts imposes the avoidable-consequences rule on the nonbreaching party. Specifically, the construction company is legally required to mitigate damages and minimize the loss from the breach. In this case, the construction company would be required to stop building the bridge. Its damages for materials expended and incidental costs in bringing the operation to a halt would be determined as of the time of breach. Any additional damages piled on after notification of the breach would be denied judicial enforcement.

As Judge Parker explained in the *Luten Bridge Company* case,

> There is a line of cases running back to 1845 which holds that, after an absolute repudiation or refusal to perform by one party to a contract, the other party cannot continue to perform and recover damages based on full performance. This rule is only a particular application of the general rule of damages that a plaintiff cannot hold a defendant liable for damages which need not have been incurred; or, as it is often stated, the plaintiff must, so far as he can without loss to himself, mitigate the damages caused by the defendant's wrongful act. The application of this rule to the matter in question is obvious. If a man engages to have work done, and afterwards repudiates his contract before the work has been begun or when it has been only partially done, it is inflicting damage on the defendant without benefit to the plaintiff to allow the

---

[27] *Rockingham County* v. *Luten Bridge Co.*, 35 F.2d 302 (1929).

latter to insist on proceeding with the contract. The work may be useless to the defendant, and yet he would be forced to pay the full contract price.[28]

The avoidable-consequences rule puts the burden on the nonbreacher to minimize damages and preserve resources for redirection toward other uses. This rule creates incentives for efficient use of resources once a deal has gone sour. To allow the innocent party to a breached contract to increase its award of damages via the courts by artificially increasing damages occurring from a contractual breach would be wasteful and inefficient in the use of resources.

Finally, there is the *rule of consequential damages,* which entitles the nonbreaching party only to those damages that are neither too speculative nor too remote. Instead it entitles him merely to those damages that flow naturally from the breach of contract. This is a very limiting rule, with the breaching party, according to *Hadley* v. *Baxendale,* liable merely for the foreseeable consequences of the breach.[29] In this famous case of the mid-nineteenth century, a mill was stopped by the breakage of a crankshaft. The shaft was taken to a well-known carrier for shipment to Greenwich for repair. The carrier was told that the breakage had stopped the mill and that the shaft should be shipped immediately. When the carrier delayed delivery by some neglect, the plaintiff claimed damages for the resulting loss in profits. Applying the rule of consequential damages, the court ruled,

It follows, therefore, that the loss of profits here cannot reasonably be considered such a consequence of the breach of contract as could have been fairly and reasonably contemplated by both the parties when they made this contract. For such loss would neither have flowed naturally from the breach of this contract in the great multitude of such cases occurring under ordinary circumstances, nor were the special circumstances, which, perhaps, would have made it a reasonable and natural consequence of such breach of contract, communicated to or known by the defendants. The Judge ought, therefore, to have told the jury, that, upon the facts then before them, they ought not to take the loss of profits into consideration at all in estimating the damages. There must therefore be a new trial in this case.[30]

Thus, the law of contracts generally denies recovery for consequential damages, unless the risk of consequential damages was specifically bargained for between the parties. If the buyer, for example, told the seller of the consequential damages that would result when nondelivery occurred and the seller and buyer made the deal with those damages in mind, such

[28] *Ibid.*
[29] *Hadley* v. *Baxendale,* 9 Exch. 341, 156 Eng. Rep. 145 (1854).
[30] *Ibid.*

that the seller bargained to take the risk for a price, the law of contracts would hold the seller liable for the ensuing consequential damages. If either party agreed to take the risk of consequential damages, any resulting consequential damages would be placed there. Normally, in the absence of an agreement to transfer risk from buyer to seller, the law presumes that the buyer takes the risks of consequential damages. He is the party best able to avoid any resulting damages. This rule thus has an economic rationale and the resulting signals should lead to an efficient use of resources.

The Damage Rule of Quantum Meruit

A plaintiff claiming damages under a breach of contract can often avail himself of an alternative to the rule of financial equivalent performance. According to Mueller and Rossett,

> ... a party to an agreement may have paid in advance, or expended money, materials and time in performing his part of the contract. In the event of a breach, such a party may just want his money back or compensation for what he has expended on a performance, the benefit of which the breaching party is enjoying. The law permits him to elect this form of relief if he wants it, and sue under the rule of quantum meruit. Under quantum meruit, the plaintiff is entitled to the fair market value of his performance until the time of breach, i.e., the judicial valuation of the performance given.[31]

Quantum meruit is well illustrated by the following instruction to the jury in *Mooney* v. *York Iron Co.*:

> It is the law that if an employer terminates a contract without any fault on the part of the employee or contractor, that then the employee or contractor may sue upon the contract to recover damages, or he may sue in *assumpsit* upon the common counts, as they are called — the *quantum meruit* — to recover what his services were worth. That does not mean what they were worth to the employer. It is the fair values; that is, the value of work and labor. Of course, the main question is first as to whether the contract was performed up to that time by the plaintiffs. If it was not, then the defendant had the right to stop the work, and discharge them, and they could not recover.[32]

Let us consider a hypothetical example. Suppose a painter made a contract to paint a house. During the negotiations he made a mistake and priced his services too low — he made a bad deal. His price is lower than

---

[31] A. Mueller and A. I. Rosett, *Contract Law and Its Applications* (Mineola: Foundation Press, 1971): 164.

[32] *Mooney* v. *York Iron Co.*, 82 Mich. 263, 46 N.W. 376 (1890).

the market price for similar work. Partway through the painting job the house owner breaches his deal. The nonbreaching party's options now include suit on the contract price (which is below the market valuation of similar performance) or suit under a *quantum meruit* theory for a fair market valuation of the performance given. He naturally takes the highest valued option — the *quantum meruit* theory. This option scheme of contract damages places a great incentive on the party making a good deal to perform his bargain fully and not breach.

Suppose, however, that the painter breaches his deal. In this situation, the nonbreaching party is entitled to financial equivalent performance, which would be the difference between the market price of the same performance and the contract price. He thus cannot escape the consequences of his deal by breach.

The *quantum meruit* option for breach of contract has an economic rationale. It gives the party who makes a sweet deal an incentive to perform in order to obtain the full value of the bargain. As long as he fully performs his side of the bargain, incentives are created to ensure actual performance of the contract. The other side cannot escape the consequences of a bad deal by breach, which would result in the payment of financial equivalent damages at the market price.

ECONOMIC CONSIDERATIONS OF CONTRACT LAW

EXCHANGES AND TRANSACTION COSTS

In order to explore certain economic implications of contract law, I propose a framework that focuses on the activities and costs associated with contract formation and contract performance. The intent is to clarify the transaction costs incurred by the seller–creditor and the buyer–borrower in these successive contract activities.

As a simplified case, assume that seller–creditor A has V goods, all of which he seeks to sell to buyer–borrower B. The transaction goes through three stages — in period t_0, before the contract is formed, A has V goods and B has no goods but usually has money or earning capacity; t_1 is the contract-formation stage, when both A and B incur certain transaction costs (FC); at its conclusion A no longer has a right to V, having incurred FC_A; B has a right to V and has incurred FC_B. In t_2 — the contract-performance stage — both A and B incur certain transaction costs in connection with performance C, for example, debt payment (collection). After performance is completed at the end of t_2, A will have been paid the agreed price for V goods and incurred an interest cost (I). However, he will have incurred transaction costs in both t_1 and t_2, that is, $FC_A + C_A$. At the same point in time, B will have V goods, but will also have incurred the interest costs plus transaction costs, that is, $FC_B + C_B$.

The length of t_2, that is, the duration of the contract performance period, which can extend from a day or two to a number of years, is important for various reasons. One reason relates to the risk of price-level changes (PC). By and large, the longer the period, the greater the price-level risk. The risk PC goes hand-in-hand with another risk in credit transactions, that is, the risk of default D. Both can be looked upon as involving transaction costs in a credit transaction. Thus, the transaction costs facing the seller A, for example, in the performance stage (C_A) can be written as follows:

$$C_A = C_{PC_A} + C_{D_A} \qquad (5.1)$$

Costs related to risk — for example, risk of default — can be evaluated by recognizing that the seller could contract with a third party for insurance against such a risk.[33] The insurance premium the seller would have to pay reflects the risk level transferred to the insurance company.

The relation between uncertainty (or risk) and costs was well stated by Arrow and Lind: "In private capital markets, investors ... choose investments to maximize ... the present value of returns properly adjusted for risk."[34]

Transaction Costs during Contract Formation

The transaction costs of both the seller–creditor A and the buyer–borrower B during contract formation, FC, have two main components:

1. Costs of negotiating the contract (a_1)
2. Costs of preparing and signing the contract form (a_2)

Thus,

$$FC = a_1 + a_2 \qquad (5.2)$$

Since the seller in consumer transactions has more knowledge, experience, and ability to spread cost over more transactions, FC_A usually is smaller than FC_B. Although in consumer transactions the seller usually benefits

[33] Frank H. Knight's distinction between risk and uncertainty is helpful. *Risk* refers to insurable liabilities and *uncertainty* to uninsurable liabilities and outcomes. See Frank H. Knight, *Risk, Uncertainty and Profit* (London: London School Reprints of Scarce Works, No. 16, 1933).

[34] K. J. Arrow and C. Lind, "Uncertainty and the Evaluation of Public Investment Decisions," *American Economic Review* 60 (June 1970): 364.

more from economies of scale than does the buyer, both tend to do so in nonconsumer transactions.

Transaction Costs during Contract Performance

In most instances the seller–creditor and the buyer–borrower perform as agreed upon in the contract. In such a routine case, both A and B incur bookkeeping costs and check-writing (collection) costs b_1. But in the absence of complete performance by both parties, additional costs can occur to A in each of three successive contract cases:

1. Default is threatened and A takes self-help measures and incurs costs b_2
2. Default occurs and A takes self-help measures and incurs costs b_3
3. Default occurs and A initiates judicial coercive collections under due process and incurs costs b_4[35]

Thus, the default-related transaction costs facing seller–creditor A during contract performance CD_A can be stated as

$$CD_A = b_{A1} + b_{A2} + b_{A3} + b_{A4} \qquad (5.3)$$

Likewise, the default-related transaction costs CD_B for the buyer–borrower B are

$$CD_B = b_{B1} + b_{B2} + b_{B3} + b_{B4} \qquad (5.4)$$

Clearly, each cost item can be very different for buyer and seller, with, for example, b_{B2} virtually nil in most instances. There are also price-level-related transaction costs (C_{PC}), which, as was mentioned earlier, change with the performance and/or length of the loan period.

Particularly in case of default, A and B are concerned about reducing their transaction costs. They would tend to take steps to write a contract that, should default become a possibility and occur, would minimize the ensuing transaction costs. Seller–creditors will seek contract terms that tend to persuade the buyer–borrower not to default. Such terms have been

---

[35] Coercive collection takes place under due process, with costs, according to Leff, substantial for four reasons: (*a*) due process requires a court that at the outset is altogether ignorant, and it is costly to educate it; (*b*) since each case is theoretically different, the process of education cannot be generalized but must be handcrafted; (*c*) this crafting, save in a court of small claims, is done by specialists (i.e., lawyers); and (*d*) in allocating docket space, the court disregards the size of the creditor's claim at stake. Thus those having very large claims at stake will queue behind plaintiffs with relatively small claims. See A. A. Leff, "Injury, Ignorance and Spite — The Dynamics of Coercive Collection," *Yale Law Journal* 80 (November 1970): 1–46.

of concern to the courts as possibly unconscionable, and I will say more about the matter subsequently.

Likewise, rational buyer–borrowers will seek terms that reduce their risk and transaction costs in case they themselves default or the seller defaults.

In connection with Case 1, self-help can take the form of the seller–creditor threatening to repossess the commodity or to initiate legal action. The ensuing costs b_2 can range from efforts at persuasion to lawyers' fees.

Once the buyer has defaulted, Case 2, the seller can rely on self-help. For example, in certain states, after due notice is given, the seller can repossess a car. If he does so, he will incur certain transaction costs associated with the repossession, such as hiring and manning a tow truck. Moreover, he may recover a value that is smaller than the outstanding debt plus transaction costs. Note that the value of the repossessed car depends on the down-payment and the rate of depreciation.

Commonly the costs of b_2, b_3, and b_4 are different for the seller–creditor than for the buyer–borrower. For example, in connection with b_2, the cost of repossession deprives the buyer of use and resale of the item bought on credit; the traveling salesman who has his car repossessed may be unable to make a living.

In Case 3, which involves judicial coercive collection, both A and B can incur court fees, attorney fees, time costs, and psychic costs. The seller–creditor faces an outside chance of losing the case, perhaps because of some technicality. In that case he will have incurred substantial costs not only in connection with the court case, but also in connection with his deprivation of debt repayment. The court may, however, call for such execution techniques as repossession, which has been discussed, or garnishment.

From a creditor's point of view, garnishment is a powerful technique for the noncooperative collection of debts. Like any lien, garnishment will interfere with the use of a liened property, be it a worker's wages or a businessman's bank account. Garnishment of wages imposes transaction costs on the employer, who is forced to organize and administer the withholding of wages at the risk of occasional error. As a result, employers tend to be outraged at their worker's apparent improvidence and seek steps to disassociate themselves from the complicated affair. Employers therefore tend to fire workers whose wages have been garnished. Thus garnishment of wages imposes relatively low costs on the creditor, some costs on the debtor's employer, and very high costs on the debtor himself.

Normally, costs associated with judicial coercive collection are higher for the buyer–borrower than for the seller–creditor, particularly in consumer transactions. The borrower may have his reputation damaged and may incur very high costs of repossession and/or garnishment.

It has been suggested that the contracting framework that emphasizes transaction costs be applied to contracts in cyberspace.[36] During contract formation, *FC*, in electronic transactions, costs in the presence of the Statute of Frauds include those due to unnecessary litigation, preventing enforcement of valid contract, inefficient business practices, lack of legal certainty, and courts' circumvention of Statute of Frauds regulations.

There, however, also exist three major benefits — deterrence of fraudulent practices, prevention of enforcement of questionable or nonexistent oral agreements, and enforcement of valid oral contracts despite absence of written proof.

Szafran has suggested that a benefit–cost analysis be undertaken in relation to contracts in cyberspace.[37] The objective is to determine whether under the circumstances U.C.C. §2-201 benefits exceed transaction costs that might have contaminated the agreement. If they do, the Statute of Frauds would be applicable. If they do not, selective repeal would be in order.

BARGAINING POWER IN EXCHANGE RELATIONS

The relative strengths of a buyer and a seller are seldom equal. This is particularly so in consumer transactions and even more so when low-income buyers are involved.

Retailers commonly have an advantage over consumers because a seller engages in many more repetitive transactions than does a buyer, particularly one who is poor. The retailer can spread his transaction costs in both the formation and the performance stages of the contract over many similar transactions, which greatly reduces his costs compared to those of the buyer, who has engaged in very few such transactions during his lifetime. The buyer's disadvantages are particularly great if he is poor, in which case his investment in signing a contract and knowing the law is large relative to his income. Thus, legal costs take a smaller percentage of the income and wealth of the rich than of the poor, and the poor tend to be less educated and have greater difficulty in interpreting laws than do the rich. Finally, the seller might be more accommodating to a wealthy person from whom he expects repeat purchases than to a poor person whose purchases are likely to be few. Thus, the seller's inclination to take full advantage of his legal rights might depend on the buyer's wealth.

---

[36] Szafran, *Contracts Formed in Cyberspace*: 39–48.
[37] *Ibid.*: 47–48.

Compared to the retail level, bargaining power tends to be more equal on the wholesale level and even more so on the manufacturing level. In relation to the comparative cost advantages and bargaining power of parties to a contract, Leff distinguishes three types of relationships between the buyer–debtor and the seller–creditor.[38] First, the buyer may be a consumer who also assumes the role of creditor, for instance, in a defective-products case. Second, the seller may be a professional creditor who sells to a consumer. Third, the buyer and the seller may be professionals, as might be the case on the manufacturing or wholesale levels. These three cases are of interest, since they have different effects on the transaction costs of the buyer and the seller.

Let us start with the case where the consumer acts as creditor. In the purchase by consumers of large-ticket-item durable goods it is not uncommon for the buyer to have fully or substantially performed on his contract although the seller has not.[39] For example, Leff discusses the case where a consumer

> has just bought a color television set from a retailer for $500 in cash. The consumer takes the set home, tries it, and finds that it is defective to the tune of $50; that is, that it would cost $50 to bring the television up to warranty. In these circumstances the consumer is a creditor; the retailer has possession of $50 of parts and services that belong to him. The consumer approaches the retailer and asks him to repair the set. The retailer refuses. This leaves the consumer with only coercive collection if he is to recover the $50.[40]

The consumer as creditor can recover through judicial coercion no more than the amount by which the seller is in default. As I have argued, the consumer–creditor is at a distinct disadvantage, because during his lifetime he engages in one or, at best, a very few such transactions, but the seller does so continuously. The seller has more knowledge and experience, and, because he engages in a larger number of similar transactions, he can spread parts of the legal costs. Moreover, repossession and garnishment affect professional debtors very little.

The same point is made in a somewhat different way by Mueller, when he states,

---

[38] *Ibid.*: 19–26.

[39] The consumer's position is likely to be the same whether he has paid cash or has "only" given a negotiable note. Because of the holder-in-due-course doctrine, he will probably have to pay cash to the eventual holder of the note, no matter what is wrong with the deal or the product.

[40] Leff, "Injury, Ignorance and Spite": 21.

Two factors combine to bring about the modern consumer's lack of effective legal power when he buys a product which is faulty but does not cause physical injury. Both of them stem from the fact that he is a little man in the scheme of things. First, there is an all-pervasive difficulty: our machinery of justice is simply not designed for easy use by the average citizen with a minor claim of any kind. It is especially frightening for the below-average citizen, for "the poor man looks upon the law as an enemy, not as a friend. For him the law is always taking something away."[41]

Most of his losing cards are colored "freedom of contract." Contract (says the jurisprudence) is a voluntary association, and the parties are therefore free within broad limits to adopt such terms as they see fit. The reasonably equal bargaining power that is manifestly required to support this basic principle is presumed.[42]

The second case is much more common. Here the seller, who is a large merchant, also serves as creditor and faces the probability that a consumer defaults. In the writing of a contract as well as the execution, the professional creditor has a distinct advantage over the buyer. He benefits from scale economics, mainly in the form of standardization and repetition. A lawsuit ordinarily requires an attorney; but at the summons and complaint stages the creditor needs only a little extra time or effort to file ten suits, rather than one. Likewise, specialization and standardization reduce costs in procuring a judgment by default or pursuing a regular lawsuit. By obtaining legal aid at relatively low unit costs, moreover, the creditor can readily shift some portion of the cost to others, including employers of delinquent workers who must in case of garnishment organize an installment plan.

In the third case, professionals are at both ends of the transactions. The buyer and the seller can have very similar knowledge and bargaining power, and if default is threatened there are strong incentives to work out a compromise while holding transaction costs to a minimum.

STRATEGIES TO REDUCE TRANSACTION COSTS

Within the microeconomic framework developed, we can identify a number of strategies that can be pursued during the contract-formation stage in order to reduce a party's transaction costs. Although transaction costs in this stage are relatively small, they can be reduced by using standard forms, often referred to as *boilerplate forms*. They make it unnecessary to draft a new contract form each time. As will be shown later, in consumer transactions reliance on standard forms usually gives the seller–lender an advantage over the buyer–borrower.

[41] Address by Attorney General Robert F. Kennedy on Law Day, University of Chicago, May 1, 1964. See Patricia M. Wald, *Law and Poverty* (Washington, D.C.: U.S. Government Printing Office, 1965): ch. 3.

[42] A. Mueller, "Contracts of Frustration," *Yale Law Journal* 78 (March 1969): 578–581.

More interesting are the strategies that can be used, particularly by the seller–creditor, to improve his position during the performance stage should default be threatened or occur. Within our microeconomic framework the seller–creditor can, if the buyer–borrower defaults, take steps that will increase the latter's costs, thus reducing the likelihood of default. Four major provisions have been incorporated into contracts in this connection:

1. Add-on clauses
2. Waiver-of-defense clauses
3. Due-on-sale clauses
4. Termination-at-will clauses[43]

Most of these clauses have been challenged under the rule of unconscionability, which is examined after these clauses are explored.

Add-On Clauses

Certain clauses provide that all previous goods purchased by the buyer from the seller will secure the debts incurred with the current purchase. Moreover, each payment made with respect to any of the items purchased is applied against all outstanding balances, allowing the seller in effect to retain his security interest in all the goods sold until all debts are discharged. Default on a single payment permits the seller to repossess all the goods subjected to the comprehensive security arrangement. Such clauses greatly reduce the risk of the seller of personal property, since the goods sold can lose value through use or abuse more rapidly than the purchase price minus the time payments. In turn, the buyer can end up having a negative equity in the goods. Thus, the seller who takes back a security interest only in the goods sold risks that, by repossessing the single item sold, he will be left with a loss on the transaction as a whole in the light of interest and transaction costs.

An alternative that could be used to reduce the seller's risk would be to insist on larger cash down-payments, which are often unacceptable to buyers with limited means. Thus, the add-on clause permits the buyer and the seller to benefit from a reduction in costs associated with the setting up of the security arrangements. The seller can collect on his unpaid debt without having to initiate costly procedures established for unsecured creditors. Moreover, the seller is assured that the value he has furnished the buyer will, should the occasion arise, first be used to satisfy his own claims and

---

[43] R. A. Epstein, "Unconscionability: A Critical Reappraisal," *Journal of Law and Economics* 18 (October 1975): 293–316.

not those of third parties. Yet the disadvantage to the buyer is that he will not be able to use any of the goods bought from the buyer, should he default on paying for any one item.

Waiver-of-Defense Clauses

In order to insulate itself from disputes between a buyer and a seller of goods, a finance company, having bought the right to collect the payments as they come due, favors original contracts of sale that include a waiver-of-defense clause. Such terms require the buyer to continue paying his installments to the finance company, even if the seller has not made good on his warranty obligation.[44]

Due-on-Sale Clauses

Some contracts allow a lender to call in the outstanding balance on the loan whenever the mortgagor either sells his interest in the property or further encumbers it with a second mortgage. Such a due-on-sale clause protects the lender against increased "moral risk" that might be associated with the new buyer and against undesirable price-level changes. The clause has been challenged as an unreasonable restraint on alienation.[45]

The due-on-sale clause allows the lender to use the natural turnover in real estate to become a relatively short-term lender, which is in his favor, should interest rates increase. Thus, the lender's risk associated with price-level changes is reduced; he should therefore be able to offer the borrower better credit terms. Moreover, the clause may reduce the risk of default faced by the lender, who at the time of sale would otherwise have to deal with an unknown party.

Termination-at-Will Clauses

In commercial transactions, a common provision to many franchise agreements allows the franchisor to terminate the franchise at will without having to give any justification for his action. The clause has been attacked because it allows the franchisor to act as a tyrant who can cut off his franchisee any time he chooses, in extreme cases even before the franchisee has recouped his start-up costs in the venture.[46] To the extent that in the formation stage a franchisee fully understands the implications of the

---

[44] *Ibid.*: 308–309.

[45] For example, according to California Civil Code §711 conditions restraining alienation when repugnant to the interest created are void.

[46] Epstein, "Unconscionability: A Critical Reappraisal": 314.

clause, and its potential inconvenience and losses are properly reflected in the terms of the contract, the clause can be efficient. It removes all uncertainty as to who has the exclusive right to terminate an agreement.

In summary, this framework considers credit costs to be composed of the pure interest rate that is related to a person's time preference, the risk of default, and the risk of price-level changes. The seller–creditor can reduce the risk of default he faces by including in the contract an add-on, a waiver-of-defense, and/or a termination-at-will clause. In order to reduce his risk of price-level changes, he can include a due-on-sale as well as a termination-at-will clause.

THE RULE OF UNCONSCIONABILITY

The Uniform Commercial Code and the courts have taken a strong interest in the possibility that an otherwise legal contract may involve unconscionable terms. Standards have been advanced to facilitate detection of unconscionability. Contracts containing oppressive clauses or ex-orbitant prices are considered unconscionable when more equal terms or lower prices would have been achieved had the bargaining process been adequate.[47] Unconscionability is thus related to imperfect markets that could produce oppressive terms or exorbitant prices compared to a perfect market. (Such terms or prices are not considered unconscionable if they result from fraud, duress, or misrepresentation.)

Using a perfect market, a market that has never existed, as a standard raises serious philosophical questions with regard to the economic determination of unconscionability. This issue will be taken up later. Here I will only say that two extreme policies are possible. One assumes that perfect market conditions are possible, and use of the law is therefore desirable to bring them about. A second policy realistically concludes that perfect markets cannot be attained and seeks to penalize seller–creditors who have written into a contract oppressive clauses or exorbitant prices. Remember that what may appear to be oppressive or exorbitant may not be so if careful consideration is given to transaction costs, particularly the risk of default and the risk of price-level changes. I will consider this issue in some detail.

The court's interest in unconscionable terms is perhaps best reflected in *Williams* v. *Walker-Thomas Furniture Co.*,[48] involving an appellant with limited education separated from her husband, maintaining herself and

---

[47] L. A. Kornhauser, "Unconscionability in Standard Forms," *California Law Review* 64 (September 1976): 1151–1183.

[48] *Williams* v. *Walker-Thomas Furniture Co.*, 121 U.S. App. D.C. 315, 350 F.2d 445 (1965).

her seven children by means of public assistance. During the period 1957–1962, she had a continuous string of dealings with appellee from which she purchased many household articles on the installment plan. These included sheets, curtains, rugs, chairs, a chest of drawers, beds, mattresses, a washing machine, and a stereo set. In 1963, appellee filed a complaint in replevin for possession of all the items purchased by appellant, alleging that her payments were in default and that the appellee retained title to the goods according to the sales contracts. By the writ of replevin, appellee obtained a bed, chest of drawers, washing machine, and the stereo set.

Appellant signed fourteen contracts in all. They were approximately six inches in length, and each contained a long paragraph in extremely fine print. One of the sentences in this paragraph provided that payments, after the first purchase, were to be prorated on all purchases then outstanding. Mathematically, this had the effect of keeping a balance due on all items until the balance was completely eliminated. It meant that title to the first purchase remained with the appellee until the fourteenth purchase, made some 5 years later, was fully paid.

The Appeals Court held,

The record reveals that prior to the last purchase appellant had reduced the balance in her account to $164. The last purchase, a stereo set, raised the balance due to $678. Significantly, at the time of this and the preceding purchases, appellee was aware of appellant's financial position. The reverse side of the stereo contract listed the name of appellant's social worker and her $218 monthly stipend from the government. Nevertheless, with full knowledge that appellant had to feed, clothe and support both herself and seven children on this amount, appellee sold her a $514 stereo set....

Accordingly, we hold that where the element of unconscionability is present at the time a contract is made, the contract should not be enforced.

Unconscionability has generally been recognized to include an absence of meaningful choice on the part of one of the parties together with contract terms which are unreasonably favorable to the other party. Whether a meaningful choice is present in a particular case can only be determined by consideration of all the circumstances surrounding the transaction. In many cases the meaningfulness of the choice is negated by a gross inequality of bargaining power. The manner in which the contract was entered is also relevant to this consideration. Did each party to the contract, considering his obvious education or lack of it, have a reasonable opportunity to understand the terms of the contract, or were the important terms hidden in a maze of fine print and minimized by deceptive sales practices? Ordinarily, one who signs an agreement without full knowledge of its terms might be held to assume the risk that he has entered a one-sided bargain. But when a party of little bargaining power, and hence little real choice, signs a commercially unreasonable contract with little or no knowledge of its terms, it is hardly likely that his consent, or even an objective manifestation of his consent, was ever given to all the terms. In such a case the usual rule that the terms of the agreement are not to be questioned should be abandoned and the court should consider whether the terms of the contract are so unfair that enforcement should be withheld.

In determining reasonableness or fairness, the primary concern must be with the terms of the contract considered in light of the circumstances existing when the contract was made.[49]

In short, although the court in *Williams* v. *Walker-Thomas* spoke in terms of unfairness, gross inequity of bargaining power, and no reasonable opportunity to understand the contract terms, it did not undertake an empirical evaluation of terms and prices. Basically, it refused to condone an add-on-clause, without examining whether such a clause produced substantially better terms for the borrower than she could have gotten had she made every purchase an independent contract.

An explicit attempt at establishing whether finance charges might be exorbitantly high was made in *Jones* v. *Star Credit Corporation:*

On August 31, 1965 the plaintiffs, who are welfare recipients, agreed to purchase a home freezer unit for $900 as the result of a visit from a salesman representing Your Shop At Home Service, Inc. With the addition of the time credit charges, credit life insurance, credit property insurance, and sales tax, the purchase price totaled $1,234.80. Thus far the plaintiffs have paid $619.88 toward their purchase. The defendant claims that with various added credit charges paid for an extension of time there is a balance of $819.81 still due from the plaintiffs. The uncontroverted proof at the trial established that the freezer unit, when purchased, had a maximum retail value of approximately $300....

The question which presents itself is whether or not, under the circumstances of this case, the sale of a freezer unit having a retail value of $300 for $900 ($1,439.69 including credit charges and $18 sales tax) is unconscionable as a matter of law. The court believes that it is....

No doubt, the mathematical disparity between $300, which presumably includes a reasonable profit margin, and $900, which is exorbitant on its face, carries the greatest weight. Credit charges alone exceed by more than $100 the retail value of the freezer. These alone, may be sufficient to sustain the decision. Yet, a caveat is warranted lest we reduce the import of section 2-302 solely to a mathematical ratio formula. It may at times, be that; yet it may also be much more. The very limited financial resources of the purchaser, known to the sellers at the time of the sale, is entitled to weight in the balance. Indeed, the value disparity itself leads inevitably to the felt conclusion that knowing advantage was taken of the plaintiffs. In addition, the meaningfulness of choice essentially to the making of a contract can be negated by a gross inequality of bargaining power. (*Williams* v. *Walker-Thomas Furniture Co.*, 350 F.2d 445.)

There is no question about the necessity and even the desirability of installment sales and the extension of credit. Indeed, there are many, including welfare recipients, who would be deprived of even the most basic conveniences without the use of these devices. Similarly, the retail merchant selling on installment or extending credit is expected to establish a pricing factor which will afford a degree of protection commensurate with the risk of selling to those who might be default

---

[49] *Ibid.*

prone. However, neither of these accepted premises can clothe the sale of this freezer with respectability.[50]

The court in the *Star Credit* case explicitly took cognizance of the social desirability of installment sales. As a matter of fact, it recognized that, except for credit, poor people could hardly hope to acquire certain durable goods.

Therefore, it is important to determine carefully whether the interest rate charged is or is not commensurate with the risk assumed by the merchant. Should merchants fear that they cannot be properly compensated for the risk they assume, credit sales will dry up, to the detriment of all those with low incomes.

However a few jurists, for example Judge Richard Posner, are bothered by the vague term "unconscionability." In his view, "Economic analysis reveals no grounds other than fraud, incapacity, and duress (the last narrowly defined) for allowing a party to repudiate the bargain that he made in entering into the contract."[51]

FORM CONTRACTS AND CONTRACTS OF ADHESION

There are strategies that can reduce transaction costs in the formation stage. One recognizes the presence of economies of scale that result when a seller uses standardized form contracts. Such forms, which standardize the terms on which exchanges are to take place, reduce the cost of drafting contracts and, more significantly, reduce the cost of negotiating agreements for each transaction. They also reduce the seller's transaction costs in the performance stage, because of the uniformity of exchange conditions.

These savings from standard form contracts may or may not be passed on to buyers. Moreover, buyers can face a number of possible efficiency losses. One would be from the take-it-or-leave aspect of the standard form, which will force consumers with varying tastes to buy a single undifferentiated product. A second efficiency loss can arise from asymmetric information, a phenomenon well analyzed by Akerlof in his "lemons" model.[52] In it sellers know the precise quality of their product while buyers only know the average quality of all items sold. Low-quality goods then tend to drive high-quality goods off the market, with the former goods unable to recover their costs. The result is an inefficient market equilibrium.

---

[50] *Jones* v. *Star Credit Corp.*, 59 Misc. 2d 189, 298 N.Y.S. 2d 264 (1969).

[51] Richard A. Posner, *Economic Analysis of Law*, 4th ed. (Boston: Little, Brown, 1992): 116.

[52] G. Akerlof, "The Market for Lemons; Qualitative Uncertainty and the Market Mechanism," *Quarterly Journal of Economics* 84 (1970): 488–500.

A third efficiency loss and possible consumer welfare loss associated with the standard form can result from the seller gaining monopoly power and, therefore, reduced competition. The anticompetitive and the unequal bargaining power issues dominate the concerns of Mueller, who fears that the consumer who buys a defective appliance or car often finds himself in the position of a creditor. He discovers that the seller has taken full advantage of the presumption that parties to a written agreement know, or ought to know, the terms of their agreement. In some cases, he will find that the printed contract with his dealer contained one or more conditions designed to give the dealer, and everyone above him in the distribution chain, maximum protection against consumer claims. He has, in short, entered into what has come to be called a *contract of adhesion*.

As Mueller has stated,

> Some of this printed boilerplate is apt to come in an envelope containing assorted other literature that is sealed in the carton or is taped to the chassis of the purchased equipment. In consequence it is seldom seen by the buyer until after delivery. Clearly, then, the buyer might persuasively claim that he cannot be bound by it because he never accepted it as part of his bargain.... The result of an attempt on his part to reject it would be no purchase.... And though theoretically the buyer could go elsewhere and buy from a merchant who did not so limit his obligations, he would almost certainly find that all competing goods were similarly limited.... A requirement that full disclosure be made concerning terms that can in face be accepted or rejected is a meaningful and important element of contract law. But standard disclaimers and limitation of remedy clauses such as make up the bulk of the printed boilerplate in contracts for the sale of consumer goods are not such choice-offering terms. The problem with such clauses is not lack of notice but lack of consumer power to bargain about them. The problem is that they are parts of contracts of adhesion.[53]

The implications of boilerplate contract forms in the presence of a buyer's limited bargaining power are extensively discussed in *Henningsen* v. *Bloomfield Motors, Inc.*[54]

> The conflicting interests of the buyer and seller must be evaluated realistically and justly, giving due weight to the social policy evinced by the Uniform Sales Act, the progressive decisions of the courts engaged in administering it ..., and the bargaining position occupied by the ordinary consumer....
>
> The warranty before us is a standardized form designed for mass use. It is imposed upon the automobile consumer. No bargaining is engaged in with respect to it.... The form warranty is not only standard with Chrysler but ... it is the uniform warranty of General Motors, Inc., Ford, ... the "Big Three" ... represent 93.5% of the passenger-car production for 1958....

[53] Mueller, "Contracts of Frustration": 578–579.
[54] *Henningsen* v. *Bloomfield Motors, Inc.*, 32 N.J. 358, 161 A.2d 69 (1960).

The gross inequality of bargaining position occupied by the consumer in the automobile industry is thus apparent. There is no competition among the car makers in the area of express warranty.[55]

THE ECONOMICS OF DAMAGES FOR BREACH OF CONTRACT

As was implied earlier, a major goal of common-law courts is expectation protection — that is, providing protection for agreed-upon expectations to be fulfilled.[56] The goal is to be attained through the rule of financial equivalent performance that is designed to restore the plaintiff to a position as good as if the promise had been honored. Another goal of contract law is the maintenance of incentives; parties should be motivated to honor their promises. However, courts do not explicitly recognize this goal.[57] Since, in line with Justice Holmes, the obligation imposed by a contract is not to comply, but either to comply or to pay damages, the goal of expectation protection is all too clear. The offended party is to be given a sum of money in damages to place him in as good a position as he would have enjoyed had the contract been honored.

Specifically, if a contract exists according to which one party sells 100 widgets at price p on a specific day and, on that date, the market price s is higher than p, a breach may result. The buyer will want to enforce the contract, whereas the seller will want to avoid its enforcement. Should the seller breach, the buyer is forced to purchase the widgets on the open market at price s. The difference between the two prices, d, would be the damages that would compensate the buyer for not obtaining the widget at price p. Thus, for each widget the damage measure d is equal to or larger than $s - p$. It can be larger than $s - p$ because of transaction costs.

Implementing the rule of financial equivalent performance requires an active market for the contracted commodity. In its absence, the plaintiff cannot find a replacement to make up for the breach, and the price for a reimbursement cannot be properly determined. Thus, for example, when a contract is entered into for the purchase and sale of a product manufactured to order, Barton talks about a nonmarket transaction.[58] Under such circumstances, there is no market by which a measure of damages can be defined or by which the injured parties can protect themselves. Costs and benefits to the different parties may not provide an unequivocal basis for

---

[55] *Ibid.*

[56] J. H. Barton, "The Economic Basis of Damages for Breach of Contract," *Journal of Legal Studies* 1 (June 1972): 277–304.

[57] *Ibid.*: 278.

[58] *Ibid.*: 280.

estimation of damages, mainly because the cost incurred by the injured party tends to be different from the benefit accrued to the breaching party. Under such conditions, completion of a transaction under all circumstances may not be efficient.

In nonmarket transactions, there is a strong incentive for parties to create rules to deal with this breach and, in the absence of such rules, courts are called upon to promulgate them. Clearly such rules will affect resource allocation by influencing the probability that parties will continue a performance that is not economically justifiable and by changing the manner in which parties allocate the cost of covering various risks. Under a number of simplifying assumptions — all markets are competitive except for the goods manufactured to order and sold under contract, parties have similar risk aversion, and parties have complete knowledge of each other's utilities — Barton produces a number of interesting propositions.

He shows that if parties have substantial and approximately similar knowledge of the risks involved in the transaction as a whole, any bargained-for allocation of risks incorporated in the contract should be enforced. Such clauses are also referred to as *liquidated-damages clauses*. Reasonableness of a liquidated damages provision must be determined freely by the parties as of the time of contract formation.[59] It should not be determined following the breach when the actual damage can be known. No evidence needs to be presented that indeed a loss occurred and what was its magnitude. The provision would have little usefulness, would be party against whom the breach occurred have to prove its losses. There exists a fuzzy line between penalty clauses and liquidated-damages clauses, where in the former losses and their magnitude must be proved, but not in the latter.[60]

In the past, courts have often rejected liquidated damages claims perhaps because courts look upon them as intruding upon their own prerogatives. Perhaps, however, Barton maintains that liquidated-damages clauses should only be rejected on the ground that the negotiation was unfair.[61] Altogether, when parties with equal bargaining power negotiate about risks that both understand equally, the court does best from an economic viewpoint to enforce their understanding much as it enforces a contract where damages are automatically ascertained in an organized market. By doing so, courts would help make efficient certain breaches.

[59] *Arduni* v. *Board of Education*, 93 Ill. App. 3d, 49 Ill. Dec. 460, 418 N.E. 2d 104 (4th Distr. 1981).

[60] *Lake River Corporation* v. *Carborundum Company*, 769 F. 2d 1284 (7th Cir. 1985).

[61] *Ibid.* 1280.

CONCLUSION

In summary, contract law provides guidelines by which voluntary exchanges of initial entitlements are expeditiously carried out and disputes in case of breach are settled. The process of contracting goes through a contract-formation stage followed by contract performance, and during each phase specified conditions serve as legal defenses. Financial equivalent performance and *quantum meruit* are the dominating damages rules. Economic analysis of contract law concentrates on the efficiency with which exchanges take place and on whether they are in fact voluntary. In connection with the former, strategies to reduce transaction costs, and in connection with the latter, unconscionable behavior of merchants and their use of form contracts and contracts of adhesion are of interest.

6

TORT LAW'S BASIC LEGAL PREMISES

INTRODUCTION

Tort law has a distinguished history, dealing with situations where an initial entitlement has been unintentionally destroyed. In this chapter, some major legal concepts and premises are explored, starting with the nature of a tort. The concepts of negligence, duty, and proximate cause are examined, and tort defenses are reviewed. Thereafter, major liability rules are presented and compared, before an examination of damages is undertaken.

WHAT IS A TORT?

Broadly speaking, a tort is a civil (seldom a criminal) wrong. Such a wrong occurs when one party, usually unintentionally, destroys another party's initial entitlement by imposing a negative externality on him. The courts can then provide a remedy in the form of damages. When externalities result in the forcible taking of initial entitlements — for example, when a slaughterhouse pollutes the air of the surrounding neighborhood — liability rules can be invoked. Concomitantly, government assumes responsibility for the imposition of objectively determined compensation and its prompt payment to the party harmed.

This issue can be related to transaction cost. Although property rules assume that voluntary transactions can be carried out at relatively low transaction costs, in many circumstances they cannot. When market evaluation of entitlements involves high transaction costs (i.e., market evaluation is either unavailable or very costly compared to collective valuation), and therefore is inefficient, a property rule can be replaced by a liability rule. Thus, for example, accidental damages are a special case of externalities with very high transaction costs, and such damages are covered by liability rules under tort law. As Calabresi and Melamed have stated, whenever "there is no reason to believe that a market, a decentralized system of valuing, will cause people to express their true valuations and hence yield results which all would *in fact* agree are desirable," an argument can be made for moving from a property rule to a liability rule.[1]

In relation to accidents, these authors argue,

> If we were to give victims a property entitlement not to be accidentally injured we would have to require all who engage in activities that may injure individuals to negotiate with them before an accident, and to buy the right to knock off an arm or a leg. Such pre-accident negotiations would be extremely expensive, often prohibitively so.... And, after an accident, the loser of the arm or leg can always very plausibly deny that he would have sold it at the price the buyer would have offered.[2]

The law treats a thief differently from an injurer in an auto accident or a polluter in a nuisance case. One reason is found in transaction costs. (A second reason is society's collective decision not to tolerate criminal conduct, even though some individuals are willing to pay to engage in it.) Since before an accident the injured person is unknown, transaction costs in negotiations with a potential victim for the transfer of entitlements are very high. Not so for the thief, who often knows what he is going to do and to whom. He could have negotiated for a good that is allowed to be sold. Likewise, relatively low transaction costs are incurred by a stationary-source polluter. It has control over externality-causing events. The polluter knows what it will do, how often, and whom it is likely to hurt. However, it faces a holdout problem; one or more potential victims may be unwilling to sell it their entitlement to clean air or water. Moreover, there may be a freerider problem — a very high exclusion cost. For example, once one polluter has bought all the entitlements, another may proceed to pollute without paying.

Tort law has a price-system rationale. Individual tortfeasors may meet their tort duties for a price, for an appropriate compensation. Thus, if

---

[1] G. Calabresi and D. A. Melamed, "Property Rules, Liability Rules, and Inalienability: One View of the Cathedral," *Harvard Law Review* 85 (April 1972): 1107; see also G. Calabresi, "Torts — The Law of the Mixed Society," in *American Law: The Third Century*, B. Schwartz, ed. (South Hackensack, N.J.: Rothman, 1976).

[2] Calabresi and Melamed, "Property Rules": 1108–1109.

enterprises unintentionally injure individuals they are not prohibited from operating; they need only pay compensation for the breach of their tort duty. (These principles, by the way, are substantially different from those of the criminal law system, which is little concerned with compensation of the injured individual against whom the crime is committed.) The civil action for a tort is commenced and maintained by the injured person, and its purpose is to compensate him for the damage he has suffered, at the expense of the wrongdoer. The tort system thus reallocates the costs of harm that are unintentionally imposed by a tortfeasor. It is the legal format created to protect the distribution of income from the interferences brought about by certain injurious interactions. If an individual breaches his tort duty to others — if he destroys an initial entitlement — he is required to pay for the imposition. The compensation is essentially an income transfer from one party to the other and creates a deterrent to wrongdoing. Specifically, incentives are created not to destory entitlements unless the expected gains from the destruction offset at a minimum the anticipated required compensation.

Let us look at the main elements in a tort suit, with an injured individual seeking compensation from his injurer (tortfeasor) for damages. To be awarded compensation in a tort suit, the plaintiff must prove that the following technical requirements are met:

1. That the defendant's actions were negligent, that is, that the defendant's actions fell below the standard of those of a "reasonable" man and thereby caused injury. An injury without proof of negligence and of defendant's deficient conduct is not compensable.
2. That the defendant owed the plaintiff a "duty," that is, an obligation to pay for any injuries the defendant caused with respect to this particular class of plaintiffs. Duties, as will be seen later, are defined by the statutes and cases of each particular jurisdiction and essentially define the class of persons to which the defendant owes an obligation not to injure without compensation.
3. That the particular defendant in fact caused the particular injury complained of. A further requirement, known as proximate cause, is the legal determination that a particular defendant was so intimately involved in causing the injury complained of that the legal system will hold him liable for the damage.

NEGLIGENCE

The tort of negligence is probably the most commonly known tort. It involves a failure to exercise the care of an ordinary prudent and careful person. Accident cases, mainly negligence cases, constitute the single largest item of business on the civil side of the nation's trial courts.[3]

Negligence as a legal concept has substantively changed over time. Until the nineteenth century, a person was liable for harm caused by his actions whether or not he was at fault. In the landmark case of *Brown* v. *Kendall*, Chief Justice Lemuel Shaw of the Massachusetts Supreme Court set aside the old application of a writ of trespass.[4] In turn, he formulated the beginnings of a doctrine of liability. This 1850 case dealt with a defendant seeking to separate two fighting dogs by beating them with a stick. Of course, the dogs moved about a good deal and, when the defendant raised his stick over his shoulder to strike them, he happened to hit the plaintiff in the eye. The report did not indicate whether the defendant or the plaintiff was in any way negligent. Shaw developed the principle that when harm occurs as the consequence of an unintended contact, it is actionable only on the basis of negligence. He thereby established that unintentional contact, achieved through the conduct of another, was not a trespass at all in the sense that it was a tort, even if damage ensued.

As C. O. Gregory concluded, "under this new principle the tort of trespass could occur *only* when there was an intentional invasion of one's interest ... no longer was there any theory of absolute liability without fault in our common law to govern the disposition of cases where one sustained harm unintentionally inflicted as a result of another's conduct."[5]

It appears that a major reason for Shaw's ruling was his interest in reducing the liability of the young industrial firms that were springing up by the hundreds in the mid-nineteenth century; in this way, he hoped to expedite the industrialization of Massachusetts in particular and of the United States in general. In a sense, Shaw's ruling amounted to subsidies for young industrial enterprises by removing the costs of compensating injured workers or employing expensive safety devices.

However, it did not take long for juries to become uncooperative and usually rule in favor of the plaintiff. In rural areas, in particular, juries tended to side with the local plaintiff, harboring strong feelings against remote corporate giants. To counteract "biased" juries, the courts began, particularly in New York State where most of the railway-crossing injury cases were initiated, to apply the doctrine of *contributory negligence*. Under this doctrine, as will be discussed later, any even minor negligence of the plaintiff that could be causally linked to the injury implied that the defen-

---

[3] Richard A. Posner, "A Theory of Negligence," *Journal of Legal Studies* 1 (January 1972): 29.

[4] *Brown* v. *Kendall*, 60 Mass. (6 Cush.) 292 (1850).

[5] C. O. Gregory, "Trespass to Negligence to Absolute Liability," *Virginia Law Review* 37 (April 1951): 367.

dant was not liable. The plaintiff therefore was bound to show that he did not, by his negligence, bring the misfortune upon himself. The argument of contributory negligence was used by the court to justify a nonsuit. It was an ingenious device that gave the court almost complete freedom to accept or reject jury participation at its pleasure.

Earlier claims that nineteenth-century law witnessed a major shift from strict liability to negligence and that the judicial motive was to subsidize emerging industries have been attacked on the basis of a careful review of court rulings in New Hampshire, California, South Carolina, Maryland, and Delaware.[6] A reading of these cases by Schwartz does not provide evidence that there was a moving away from the preexisting rules of strict liability. Moreover, he found that nineteenth-century tort law, except for employment injury cases, tended to affirm the tort liabilities of emerging industry.

At the end of the nineteenth century, the tort system was found wanting when tested against social needs. Particularly, tort law was found unacceptable to an industrialized society when applied to workers who were injured by a job-related cause.

Occupational injuries emerged as a serious problem after the Civil War. The rapid pace of industrialization brought a steadily increasing number of accidental injuries and deaths. The availability of both contributory negligence and assumption of risk defenses, to be discussed shortly, made it hard for workers to recover against their employers, particularly in the presence of the fellow-servant doctrine, which provided that respondent superior liability would not attach to the employer for negligence of plaintiff's coworker. Before the turn of the century, a number of states had sought to broaden the employer's liability by modifying or removing the above-mentioned defenses. Meanwhile, in Germany and in Great Britain, workers' compensation systems were taking shape, facilitated by the development of third-party insurance against legal liability that made it feasible to impose upon employers liability without fault. After some initial difficulties, today virtually all American workers are covered by workers' compensation. Accordingly, liability for the compensation without regard to negligence exists against an employer for any injury sustained by his employees arising out of and in the course of the employment and for the death of any employee if the injury proximately causes death. Workers' compensation should insure industrially injured workers prompt provision of adequate medical treatment and rehabilitative care. In the interim, money payment should be paid to them to tide them over until they have recovered.

---

[6] Gary T. Schwartz, *The Character of Early American Tort Law* (November 28, 1986, mimeographed).

In addition to human considerations, the extraordinarily high transaction costs of the existing system played an important role in the enactment of workers' compensation laws. They have also led to consideration of no-fault accident insurance.[7] Since motor vehicle injuries tend to involve very costly litigation, Robert E. Keeton and Jeffry O'Connell proposed a no-fault insurance system,[8] to be taken up in detail in the next chapter.

So far we have discussed the evolution of negligence in tort law in the face of prevailing social and economic conditions; it is time now to turn to more operational issues. A fundamental determination that must be made in the vast majority of tort claims revolves around the issue of the defendant's negligence. The question of actual negligence is almost always factual, requiring a jury determination. A key issue in determining liability relates to the defendant's conduct: Has it been such that under the same or similar circumstances a reasonable man would not have caused the resulting injury? Thus, would the conduct of a reasonable man have avoided the ensuing harm?

In *Osborne* v. *Montgomery*, Chief Justice Rosenberry carefully considered the dimensions of negligence:

> Every person is negligent when, without intending to do any wrong, he does an act or omits to take such precaution that under the circumstances he, as an ordinarily prudent person, ought reasonably to foresee that he will thereby expose the interest of another to an unreasonable risk of harm. In determining whether his conduct will subject the interests of another to an unreasonable risk of harm, a person is required to take into account such of the surrounding circumstances as would be taken into account by a reasonably prudent person and possess such knowledge as is possessed by an ordinarily reasonable person and to use such judgment and discretion as is exercised by persons of reasonable intelligence under the same or similar circumstances.[9]

Judge Learned Hand provided a more formal definition of the legal standard of negligence (i.e., the standard of care required by the law). In *United States* v. *Carroll Towing Company*, he offered the following algebraic formula: "If the probability be called *P*; the injury *L*; and the burden *B*; liability depends upon whether *B* is less than *L* multiplied by *P*; i.e., whether

---

[7] John G. Turnbull et al., *Economic and Social Security*, 3d ed. (New York: Ronald Press, 1968).

[8] For a very early statement see, Robert E. Keeton and Jeffry O'Connell, *Basic Protection for the Traffic Victim: A Blueprint for Reforming Automobile Insurance* (Boston: Little, Brown, 1965). A particularly thoughtful analysis of no-fault automobile compensation plans can be found in G. Calabresi, *The Costs of Accidents: A Legal and Economic Analysis* (New Haven, Conn.: Yale University Press, 1970).

[9] *Osborne* v. *Montgomery*, 203 Wis. 233, N.W. 372 (1931).

B is smaller than *PL*."[10] In short, in line with the Hand formula, the defendant is guilty of negligence if the loss caused by the accident multiplied by the probability of the accident occurring exceeds the burden of the precautions that the defendant might have taken to avert the mishap. Although the burden of precautions is the cost of avoiding the accident, the loss multiplied by the probability of the accident is the expected harm that the precautions would have averted. If a larger cost could have been avoided by incurring a smaller cost, Judge Hand would have preferred the smaller cost to be incurred.

The philosophy underlying the Learned Hand formula can be summarized as follows: A reasonable man, before taking any action, weighs the costs and benefits of that action not only from his own personal perspective but also from the broader perspective of all the individuals within the possible scope of any resulting harm. From the economist's point of view, the Learned Hand formula seeks a tort system that maximizes social welfare over the actions of all individuals involved in a given tortious act. When an individual's actions fall below the reasonable-man standards, he is assessed liability for any resulting harm. Knowledge of this compensatory requirement creates incentives for individuals to weigh their actions from a social welfare point of view.

Judge Hand's statement of his rule requires clarification to assure that his variables refer to marginal rather than total values. Also it needs to be interpreted as to which of three closely related negligence standards it relates. Brown suggests one as the *Literal Learned Hand Standard*,[11] which compares *total* costs and benefits of harm prevention with the expected costs of the accident. It can answer only the question of whether it is better to provide complete protection against potential harm or none at all. The second is the *Incremental Standard* of the Learned Hand formula. It assumes complete information and results in social cost minimization independently for both the injurer and the victim. It suffers from excessively stringent information demands that are relaxed in a third standard — the *Limited Information Incremental Standard*. It assumes the court to be able merely to investigate effects of small changes away from the preventive step actually chosen by the two parties on the probability of harm. Under the Limited

---

[10] *United States* v. *Carroll Towing Co.*, 159 F.2d 169 (2d Cir. 1947). Hand's formula's "utilitarian" origin can be seen clearly in H. Terry, "Negligence," *Harvard Law Review* 29 (November 1915): 40–54. In it, Terry defined fault as conduct involving unreasonably great risk, and isolated magnitude, principal object, collateral object, utility, and necessity of risk as determining whether a particular risk was so great as to be "unreasonable."

[11] J. P. Brown, "Toward an Economic Theory of Liability," *Journal of Legal Studies* 2 (June 1973): 331–335.

Information Incremental Standard, the court declares an avoidance level as negligent if it is below the optimal level in the light of the steps taken by the other party.

DUTY

One essential element of negligence is the demonstration of a duty. It relates to a person's responsibility not to destroy another person's initial entitlement. The defendant who owes no duty to the plaintiff cannot be negligent. Thus, the definition of the duties owed by defendants to plaintiffs in part determines the scope and range of the negligence tort. The scope and range of duties have been evolving and expanding over time. This expansion has been directed toward making individuals more concerned about the results of their actions on others.

As *Hynes* v. *New York Central Railroad Company*[12] reveals, the concept of duty of landowners and hosts toward trespassers and others changed as time passed. In *O'Keefe* v. *South End Rowing Club*,[13] the California Supreme Court in 1966 distinguished between varying duties toward a trespasser, licensee (or social guest), and invitee (or business visitor). Duties toward invitees are the greatest and toward trespassers they are the smallest. There is a special duty toward children. Although the distinctions are much finer in this case, the trend of the law is toward expanding the scope and range of the duty concept, giving rise to a greater scope of liability for a variety of acts. As the scope of duties expands, actors must internalize more and more costs and benefits and balance them in their choice calculus.

In the case of *Rowland* v. *Christian*,[14] the landowner and host's duty was further expanded. The plaintiff, while a social guest in the defendant's apartment, severed some tendons and nerves when the porcelain handle on a bathroom faucet cracked in his hand. Although the defendant had told the plaintiff about the handle some weeks earlier, she did not mention it before the plaintiff went to the bathroom. The California Supreme Court ruled that

> The proper test to be applied to the liability of the possessor of land ... is whether in the management of his property he has acted as a reasonable man in view of the

---

[12] *Hynes* v. *New York Central Railroad Co.*, 231 N.Y. 229 (1921).
[13] *O'Keefe* v. *South End Rowing Club*, 64 Cal. 2d 729 (1966).
[14] *Rowland* v. *Christian*, 69 Cal. 2d 108 (1968).

probability of injury to others, and although the plaintiff's status as a trespasser, licensee or invitee may in the light of effects giving rise to such status have some bearing on the question of liability, the status is not determinative.[15]

The court went on to hold that

where the occupier of land is aware of a concealed condition involving in the absence of precaution an unreasonable risk of harm to those coming in contact with it and is aware that a person on the premises is about to come in contact with it, the trier of fact can reasonably conclude that a failure to warn or repair the condition constitutes negligence.[16]

Courts not only have expanded existing duty concepts but also have imposed new duties where none existed previously. For example, in *Ellis* v. *Trowen Frozen Products, Inc.*,[17] a California court of appeals ruled in 1968 that a frozen food company is under a duty to watch out for small children using its services. It must use reasonable care to guard for their safety as regards the premises of the ice cream truck or face the prospect of civil liability for resulting injuries. The activity of providing ice cream bars to children must now bear the added expense of watching out for the children's safety by using lookouts or other devices to prevent accidents.[18] Creation of this duty of ice cream sellers has distributional effects. The burden of protecting small children buying ice cream from trucks has been shifted from the child and his family to the vendors. How much of this cost is shifted forward to the customer depends on the relative demand and supply elasticities of truck-catered ice cream.

Moreover, an additional major tort duty has been added, for negligently inflicted emotional distress and its consequent physical harm. In 1896, the Court of Appeals of New York held that individuals negligently exposed to fright or fear were not eligible for compensation.[19] However, in 1961, the same court reversed itself. In *Battalla* v. *State of New York*, the court considered the negligence of an employee of the state of New York who, placing an

---

[15] *Ibid.*: 319.

[16] *Ibid.*

[17] *Ellis* v. *Trowen Frozen Products, Inc.*, 264 Cal. App. 2d 499 (1968).

[18] In the mid-1980s, in Dallas, Texas, all neighborhood ice cream trucks were equipped with flashing red roof lights and rear doors that displayed octagonal red stop signs when open. Moreover, ice cream truck operators must participate in a school safety program and are subject to vigorous safety regulations.

[19] *Mitchell* v. *Rochester Ry. Co.*, 151 N.Y. 107 (1896).

infant in a chair lift at a mountain ski center, failed to secure and properly lock the belt intended to protect the occupant.[20] As a result, the infant became frightened and hysterical on the descent and "suffered severe emotional and neurological disturbances with residual physical manifestation." Although the *Mitchell* court had found that individuals negligently exposed to fright or fear were not eligible for compensation, the court here ruled that the inflictor of the fright must bear the cost.

Individuals exposed to fright or scare are in a poor position to avoid injury. The activity operator is usually in the best position to evaluate the most cost-effective steps to prevent emotional distress and resulting physical harm.

This extreme position, however, was substantially modified in *Tobin* v. *Grossman* by the same court. The court virtually returned to its position in *Mitchell* v. *Rochester Ry. Co.*, when a mother who witnessed a defendant negligently running down her son claimed to have suffered emotional distress and consequent physical injuries as result.[21] The court recognized that the problem was double-faceted. The first facet was the recoverability for injuries sustained solely as a result of an initial mental or physiological impact, but with ensuing mental illness and physical injury. The second was the scope of duty to one who is not directly the victim of an accident causing severe physical injury to a third person.

The court concluded,

> Every injury has ramifying consequences, like the ripplings of the waters, without end. The problem for the law is to limit the legal consequences of wrongs to a controllable degree. The risks of indirect harm from the loss or injury of loved ones is pervasive and inevitably realized at one time or another. Only a very small part of that risk is brought about by the culpable acts of others. This is the risk of living and bearing children. It is enough that the law establishes liability in favor of those directly or intentionally harmed.[22]

PROXIMATE CAUSE

Proximate cause "is that cause which, in natural and continuous sequence, unbroken by an efficient intervening cause, produced the injury (or damage

---

[20] *Battalla* v. *State of New York*, 10 N.Y. 2d 237 (1961).
[21] *Tobin* v. *Grossman*, Court of Appeals of New York, 24 N.Y. 2d 609, 249 (1969).
[22] *Ibid.*

complained of) and without which such result would not have occurred.[23] In an injurious event, the rules and doctrines of proximate cause seek to determine which actor is to be held legally responsible for the resulting harm. Often the combined negligence of many actors causes a given injury. The doctrine of proximate cause determines which of the actors must bear the cost of the resulting harm. As an example, suppose two negligent drivers collide and injure a pedestrian. Under the rules of proximate cause, both drivers would be held liable for the full extent of the injury, although in some states they would share the liability. They are both held liable because the resulting harm caused by their negligence was foreseeable; consequently, the expectation of it should have entered their choice calculus and affected their behavior. In terms of the Hand formula, when harm resulting from an actor's negligence is foreseeable, the burden that the defendant carries in order to avoid a judgment of liability due to his negligence is higher than if it were not foreseeable. (Since the resulting harm is foreseeable, the probability of occurrence to be placed in the Hand formula is higher than it would be otherwise.) Thus, whenever a resulting harm is foreseeable, the rules of proximate cause will impose liability on the actor, forcing him to be concerned about the foreseeable effects of his actions upon others.

However, suppose the resulting harm of an actor's negligence is unforeseeable, as in *Overseas Tankship Ltd.* v. *Morts Dock and Engineering Company Ltd.*[24] In this case, a ship-repairing firm repaired in its wharf the ship *Corrimal,* employing welding equipment to do so. At a different wharf, the ship *Wagon Mound,* while taking on bunkering oil, spilled a large quantity of it into the bay. Two days after the *Corrimal* had left, oil near the *Wagon Mound* was ignited, causing extensive damage to wharf equipment. The court's decision centered on the extent to which harm was foreseeable and made this issue the effective test. As this case illustrates, foreseeability of the resulting harm from an actor's negligence makes a substantial difference in determining the extent and scope of the negligent actor's liability. The court declared that "it is the foresights of the reasonable man which alone can determine responsibility."[25] The rationale for this legal doctrine is that an actor can only internalize a foreseeable result of his negligence into his choice calculus. Any other result, by definition unforeseeable, cannot be effectively brought into the actor's choice calculus and cannot affect his behavior. Consequently, the proximate-cause rule that liability only extends to foreseeable issues has a clear economic rationale.

---

[23] *Kettman* v. *Levine,* 115 Cal. App. 2d 844, 253 P.2d 102 (1953).

[24] *Overseas Tankship Ltd.* v. *Morts Dock and Engineering Co., Ltd.,* Privy Council, A. C. 338 (1961).

[25] *Ibid.* This case has not generally been accepted in the United States.

Another aspect of this general rule limiting liability to foreseeable harms concerns the rule that a negligent tortfeaser is not liable to the unforeseen plaintiff. This is essentially the rule of the famous 1928 New York Court of Appeals case of *Palsgraf* v. *Long Island Railroad Co.*,[26] in which the plaintiff was standing on a platform of defendant's railroad. A train stopped at the station. Two men ran forward to catch it. One of the men, who was carrying a package, jumped aboard the car but seemed unsteady, as if about to fall. A guard on the car, who had held the door open, reached forward to help him in, and another guard on the platform pushed him from behind. In this act, the package was dislodged and fell on the rails. It was a package of small size, about fifteen inches long, and was covered by a newspaper. In fact, it contained fireworks, but there was nothing in its appearance to give notice of its contents. The fireworks exploded when they fell. The shock of the explosion threw down some scales at the other end of the platform, many feet away. The scales struck the plaintiff, causing injuries for which she sued.

Writing for the majority Justice Cardoza stated,

> The conduct of the defendant's guard, if a wrong in its relation to the holder of the package, was not a wrong in its relation to the plaintiff standing far away. Relatively to her it was not negligence at all. Nothing in the situation gave notice that the falling package had in it the potency of peril to persons thus removed. If no hazard was apparent to the eye of ordinary vigilance, an act innocent and harmless, at least to outward seeming, with reference to her, did not take to itself the quality of a tort because it happened to be a wrong, though apparently not one involving the risk of bodily insecurity, with reference to someone else....
>
> One who jostles one's neighbor in a crowd does not invade the rights of others standing at the outer fringe when the unintended contact casts a bomb upon the ground. The wrongdoer as to them is the man who carries the bomb, not the one who explodes it without suspicion of the danger. Life will have to be made over, and human nature transformed, before prevision so extravagant can be accepted as the norm of conduct, the customary standard to which behavior must conform.[27]

Clearly, liability based on unforeseeable consequences is so unpredictable that a person cannot bring within his choice calculus such a system of legal responsibility. Thus, the probability of a freak accident is by definition very low, and the expected accident cost will usually be low. In a truly freak accident, such as that in *Palsgraf*, the expected accident cost may come close to zero.

[26] *Palsgraf* v. *Long Island Railroad Co.*, 248 N.Y. 339 (1928).
[27] *Ibid.*: 343.

William Landes and Richard Posner have attempted to offer an economic approach to the determination of causation in tort law.[28] They play down "foreseeability" as a useful determinant of proximate cause. Instead, their emphasis is on the probability of an accident occurring and the costs of legal administration.

Recently, the California Supreme Court has eased the standard on proximate cause. In *Mitchell* v. *Gonzales* it ruled that juries were no longer to be instructed to determine whether harm would not have occurred "but for" the defendant's actions.[29] This standard had been criticized because it tended to mislead juries into thinking that the defendant had to be in the proximity of the injured party or that his actions had to have occurred close in time to the harm. The new instructions ask the jury to determine whether the defendant's conduct was a "substantial factor" in bringing about harm. It would allow the jury to find defendant liable even in case his behavior was only a contributing factor in the injury.

DEFENSES

A number of defenses may be invoked to avoid a tort liability. These will be discussed under the headings Assumption of Risk, Immunities, and Contributory Negligence. But first a few words about custom as a defense are in order.

In medical malpractice cases, as will be discussed later in more detail, a special point is made of the defense of custom. The duty of care of a physician toward his patient is to comply with the *customary* standards of the medical profession in the *area* in which the physician is practicing. Thus, the physician implicitly promises to treat patients with the care customary among physicians in the area, and if he fails to do so, he is guilty of malpractice. However, customary compliance is more "some evidence" of nonnegligence than a complete defense.

ASSUMPTION OF RISK

People vary greatly as to their willingness to take risks. Some are risk-neutral, others are risk-averse, and still others are risk-preferring. A risk-preferring person may evaluate the dangers and decide that he can increase his welfare

---

[28] William M. Landes and Richard A. Posner, "Causation in Tort Law: An Economic Approach," *Journal of Legal Studies* 12 (January 1983): 109–134.

[29] *Mitchell* v. *Gonzales*, 819 Cal. P.2d 872, 525 (1991).

by taking the risk; he is thus held accountable for any resulting injury to himself.

For example, in *Murphy* v. *Steeplechase Amusement Co.*,[30] the plaintiff was injured in an amusement park. He stepped into a "Flopper," which is a moving belt running upward on an inclined plane. Jerking motions tend to throw visitors to a padded floor. The plaintiff, a vigorous young man, entered the "Flopper" with a young woman, later his wife, who said, when asked whether she thought that a fall might be expected, "I took a chance." The plaintiff took the chance with her, but was less lucky than his companion and suffered a fracture of the kneecap. Justice Cardozo, writing for the court, held that "one who takes part in such a sport accepts the dangers that inhere in it so far as they are obvious and necessary, just as a fencer accepts the risk of a thrust by his antagonist or a spectator at a ball game for the chance of contact with the ball."[31]

The rationale of this case is that a person who foresees the risks of his prospective activity and enters them into his choice calculus accepts the responsibility for the resulting outcome. He takes the risk only after being able to evaluate the relevant costs and benefits. The plaintiff's implicit or explicit evaluation of those risks apparently was such that he decided he could increase his welfare by his action and thus could be held to have assumed the risk and to have been accountable for any resulting injury to himself.

IMMUNITIES

In general, government officials and agencies have been granted sovereign immunity. It precludes them from being sued for tortious acts. However, a distinction prevails concerning the nature of the decision made by government. Sovereign immunity is granted for harm that governmental decisions cause if these decisions are discretionary policy decisions. However, to the extent that the decisions are ministerial in nature, no immunization is granted. In the following chapter, more will be said about sovereign immunity and its economic aspects.

CONTRIBUTORY NEGLIGENCE

If a defendant has been found to be negligent with respect to a particular plaintiff, he may still escape liability upon proof that the plaintiff was

---

[30] *Murphy* v. *Steeplechase Amusement Co.*, 250 N.Y. 479 (1929).
[31] *Ibid.*: 250.

contributorily negligent. To be contributorily negligent, the plaintiff must have failed to exercise due care and this breach must have contributed to the tortious result. A victim who is found contributorily negligent may then be barred from recovery, even though the defendant was negligent. Although contributory negligence involves an all-or-nothing (binary) approach to liability, comparative negligence also considers the contributory aspect. However, instead of being binary, comparative negligence reduces rather than bars recovery. Basically the reduction is by the percentage by which the victim's negligence contributed to the result of the tortious act.

LIABILITY RULES — INTRODUCTORY CLASSIFICATION

By what rule or standard should we determine whether a defendant, having destroyed an initial entitlement, is liable and therefore should pay for the tortious act? J. P. Brown has identified eight different liability rules.[32]

No liability (the victim is liable under all circumstances) and *strict liability* (the injurer is liable under all circumstances) are symmetrical.

Under the *negligence rule,* the victim is liable unless the injurer is found negligent. Under a *strict liability with contributory negligence rule,* the injurer is liable unless the victim is found negligent. Thus, these two rules, too, are symmetrical.

Under the *negligence rule with contributory negligence,* the injurer is liable if he is negligent and the victim is not, with the victim liable otherwise. Under *strict liability with dual contributory negligence,* the victim is liable if he is negligent and the injurer is not, with the injurer liable otherwise. Again these two rules are symmetrical.

A further rule is *relative negligence.* The injurer is liable under this rule if the increment to accident avoidance per dollar of avoidance by him is greater than that per dollar of avoidance by the victim — in short, if the money that could be spent by the injurer on avoidance is more cost-effective than that which could be spent by the victim.

Finally, there is the *comparative-negligence* rule. Under this rule, liability is apportioned according to the relative liability of the two parties. Under the comparative-negligence rule, negligence can be defined as a marginal or an average concept. In the former case, negligence is the incremental reduction in accident probability per dollar spent, and the liability of the injurer is his negligence divided by the negligence of both parties.

---

[32] J. P. Brown, "Toward an Economic Theory of Liability," *Journal of Legal Studies* 2 (June 1973): 323–349.

The different liability rules, except that of comparative negligence, are presented graphically in Figure 6—1. The graphs are taken from Brown, "Toward an Economic Theory of Liability."[33] Here, X represents the effort of the injurer to prevent harm, and Y represents the effort of the victim to avoid harm; X^* represents the legal standard of negligence for the injurer, and Y^* that for the victim. Finally, Ω is the optimal amount of protection from an overall point of view, where the marginal cost of protection is equal to the marginal expected benefit from the protection. The injurer is liable in the shaded area. Thus in part a (no liability), there is no shaded area since the injurer is never liable, but in part b (strict liability), the entire area is shaded with the injurer liable under all circumstances.

I will next discuss three major negligence rules in some detail — contributory negligence, comparative negligence, and strict liability.

THE RULE OF CONTRIBUTORY NEGLIGENCE

In terms of Figure 6—1, under the contributory-negligence rule the shaded area (indicating that the injurer is liable) covers the case where the victim has met his legal standard of negligence but the injurer has not done so.

As mentioned earlier, both orthodox and modified contributory negligence are affirmative defenses that are traditionally afforded by tort law. The defense of contributory negligence has a long history. It entered English law in the beginning of the nineteenth century;[34] *Brown* v. *Kendall* introduced contributory negligence as an integral part of American negligence doctrine in 1850.[35]

Let us examine the contributory-negligence rule and some of its complications. Assume a $100 risk that the defendant could prevent for $80, but that the plaintiff could prevent for $10. Although the defendant may be negligent, the plaintiff is more efficient in preventing the accident. The economic justification of the rule is to give the plaintiff an incentive to spend his $10, since he is the most efficient accident preventer.

Complications arise when we reverse the numbers. Now the plaintiff can prevent the risk for $80 and the defendant for only $10. Although the plaintiff is contributorily negligent, the defendant should be held liable since the defendant is in a better position to eliminate the risk. The modified contributory-negligence rule takes care of this matter, since the plaintiff's

---

[33] *Ibid.*: 330–331.

[34] *Butterfield* v. *Forrester*, 103 Eng. Rep. 926 (K. B. 1809).

[35] *Brown* v. *Kendall*, 60 Mass. (6 Cush.) 292, 296 (1850).

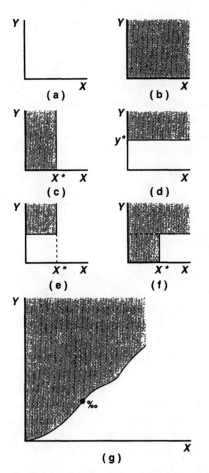

FIGURE 6—1 Liability rules: (a) no liability; (b) strict liability; (c) the negligence rule; (d) strict liability with contributory negligence; (e) the negligence rule with contributory negligence; (f) strict liability with dual contributory negligence; and (g) relative negligence. The shaded areas indicate where the injurer is liable when X represents the effort of the injurer to prevent harm; Y, the effort of the victim to avoid harm; X^*, the legal standard of negligence for the injurer; Y^*, the legal standard of negligence for the victim; and Ω, the optimum amount of protection. [From J. P. Brown, "Toward an Economic Theory of Liability," *Journal of Legal Studies,* (June 1973): 330–331. By permission.]

contributory negligence should bar his recovery only if his prevention costs are lower than the defendant's.

Thus, contributory negligence focuses on the fact that the plaintiff may be an efficient risk preventer. Although negligence law without any contributory-negligence defense is unlikely to be socially efficient, various scholars have argued that the contributory-negligence rule as a complete defense fails to produce efficient results.[36]

Although economists can build models that include risk neutrality and zero information costs under which contributory negligence is an efficient standard, in real-life situations, efficient results are unlikely to prevail. Some reasons follow.

For the Learned Hand formula to be applied effectively, all parties must be risk-neutral and know that this neutrality is a fact. If one party is indeed risk-neutral but the other is risk-averse or risk-preferring, no efficient accident prevention is likely.

Turning to the zero-information-cost assumption, it is in fact very costly for the potential victim to be able to predict that his injury will occur and that another party will assume tort liability. Moreover, it is costly for the potential victim to know and understand the contributory-negligence rule and its applications. And if such understanding is too costly, the rule will not reliably deter.

A further reason why contributory negligence is unlikely to generate efficient safety incentives relates to the probability that compensating damages will not cover the full cost of the accident. Reasons include the prevalence of contingency-fee arrangements in personal-injury litigations (if successful, the plaintiff receives only part of the award); the fact that the victim who files a tort claim subjects himself to the misery of litigation with its time costs and very real emotional costs; and the low probability that tort damages will fully compensate the victim.

In the literature, two additional claims have been made against the efficiency of contributory-negligence rules. G. Schwartz points to psychological complexities and specifically to the victim whose action was mindless rather than rational. As examples, he gives motorists who absentmindedly take their eyes off the road or who drive across well-marked railroad crossings without slowing down and pedestrians who jaywalk into the path of cars.[37] Although I do not deny such events, I wonder whether they cannot be placed within an economic benefit–cost framework. Thus, depending

---

[36] Gary T. Schwartz, "Contributory and Comparative Negligence: A Reappraisal," *Yale Law Journal* 87 (March 1978): 710.

[37] *Ibid.*: 713–719.

on the harm that jaywalkers must fear to befall them and the likelihood of such harm, it is more or less likely that they will absentmindedly jaywalk. Finally, it has been argued that "the plaintiff's unreasonable conduct may effectively be prevented by the defendant."[38] G. Schwartz offers a number of examples in which the defendant appears better able than the plaintiff to prevent conduct likely to result in accidents. Thus, the employee who is uncomfortable wearing protective goggles might wear them if comfortable ones were provided by the employer. Or the manufacturer can more easily design products that offer little opportunity for injuries due to carelessness.

Schwartz concludes, in relation to efficiency, that "in sum, there is inadequate reason to believe that any contributory negligence rule is a good idea in safety terms; the traditional rule, moreover, appears to be a distinctly bad idea."[39]

Though economists have been particularly interested in the safety rationale, and therefore the accident-prevention aspects, of negligence rules for the sake of resource-allocation efficiency, there are also fairness considerations. Fairness commands that if the defendant is found to have engaged in tortious acts, faulty, unreasonable, or wrongful behavior by the plaintiff should be reflected by either denying the plaintiff a defense or by reducing the plaintiff's damages. As long as an accident would not have occurred except for the plaintiff's faulty, unreasonable, or wrongful behavior, it is not fair to ignore the plaintiff's contribution to the outcome. Contributory negligence as a liability-denying rule raises serious questions as to its fairness, compared to a liability-dividing rule, such as comparative negligence. This will be taken up next.

THE RULE OF COMPARATIVE NEGLIGENCE

As mentioned earlier, comparative negligence can be looked upon as a special case of the broadly interpreted rule of contributory negligence. The all-or-nothing (binary) approach to liability adopted by the rule of contributory negligence has been widely criticized, with some justification. Harper and James state,

> There is no justification — in either policy or doctrine — for the rule of contributory negligence, except for the feeling that if one man is to be held liable, because of his fault, then the fault of him who seeks to enforce that liability should also be considered.

[38] *Ibid.*: 720.
[39] *Ibid.*: 721.

But this notion does not require the all-or-nothing rule, which would exonerate a very negligent defendant for even the slight fault of his victim. The logical corollary of the fault principle would be a rule of comparative or proportional negligence, not the present rule.[40]

In consequence, a significant number of jurisdictions have adopted general comparative-negligence schemes, among them 44 states,[41] Great Britain, all Canadian provinces, New Zealand, and some Australian states. These statutes or decisional laws provide that contributory negligence reduces, rather than bars, recovery. The reduction is by the percentage by which the victim's negligence contributed to the accident. Thus in California, for example, the rule is that in an action for negligence resulting in injury to a person or property, the contributory negligence of the person injured in person or property does not bar recovery, but the damages awarded shall be diminished in proportion to the amount of fault attributable to that person. Still, though "liability in proportion to fault"[42] is the slogan of comparative-negligence rules, several variations are possible. Thus, although in many United States jurisdictions, comparative-negligence standards generally call for a comparison of the extent to which the plaintiff and the defendant have departed from the standard of due care, in the United Kingdom the emphasis is on the parties' relative responsibility for the accident. Responsibility here is a concept that seems receptive to a number of considerations, including, for example, the relative extent to which the parties' conduct has caused the accident.

Some jurisdictions in the United States rely on a pure form of comparative negligence, whereas others use modified forms. Under the pure form, the recovery of the plaintiff is reduced by the proportion of his negligence to the sum of his and the defendant's negligence. Under the modified forms, the plaintiff's recovery is reduced in this very manner, but he receives no recovery whatsoever either if he was more negligent than the defendant or, depending on the variant of the modified form, if he and the defendant were equally negligent.

Matters are complicated by the fact that there are different ways in which the negligence of the plaintiff and defendant can be compared.[43] On the one hand, the comparison can be in terms of prevention cost. For example, if A could have prevented the accident for $20 and B for $60, A would

[40] Fowler Harper and Fleming James, Jr., *The Law of Torts* (Boston: Little, Brown, 1956), sec. 22.3: 1207.

[41] Christopher Curran, "The Spread of the Comparative Negligence Rule in the United States," *International Review of Law and Economics* 12 (1992): 317.

[42] *Li v. Yellow Cab Co.*, 13 Cal. 3d 804, 810, 532 P.2d 1226, 19 Cal. Rptr. 858, 862 (1975).

[43] Schwartz, "Contributory and Comparative Negligence": 705–706.

bear a liability three times as great as B. Each party's share of total liability could be determined as follows:

Party's share of liability
$$= \frac{(\text{total prevention costs}) - (\text{party's prevention costs})}{\text{total prevention costs}} \quad (6.1)$$

On the other hand, the comparison could be in terms of net losses incurred by the parties' failure to take preventive measures — the differences between A's and B's prevention costs and expected value of the risk that A and B allowed to materialize. For example, if the expected value of the risk is \$100 and again the respective prevention costs are \$20 and \$60, the differences are \$80 and \$40, respectively. Thus, A would bear a liability twice as large as B. The liability of A and B could be determined as follows:

Party's share of liability
$$= \frac{(\text{expected value of risk}) - (\text{party's prevention costs})}{2 \times (\text{expected value of risk}) - (\text{total prevention costs})} \quad (6.2)$$

The two methods of comparison can give very different results, especially when the difference between the prevention costs of A and B is either very large or very small. Thus, if the expected value of the risk is again \$100 and the prevention costs are \$1 and \$4, the first method would divide liability 80% to 20%, whereas the second method would divide liability 51% to 49%. However, should prevention costs be \$96 and \$98, the ratios would be 51% to 49% and 67% to 33%, respectively.

As to its accident-prevention and therefore efficiency aspects, comparative negligence in real-life situations differs little from orthodox or modified contributory negligence. The efficiency argument in connection with comparative negligence is similar to that made in the discussion of contributory negligence. Among the major reasons why comparative-negligence schemes are unlikely to be more efficient than contributory ones is high information cost. Thus, each party would have to invest heavily in order to learn about the prevention possibilities and costs of the other party. Only in the presence of information on the prevention possibilities of both parties can efficient decisions be made.[44] Efficiency is likely to be compromised because of payments of contingency fees and other expenses associated with the suit, the possibility of jury error, and the risk that defendant is insolvent.[45]

---

[44] For an analysis of the efficiency implications of comparative negligence, see David Haddock and Christopher Curran, "An Economic Theory of Comparative Negligence," *Journal of Legal Studies* (January 1985): 49–72.

[45] Richard A. Epstein, *Cases and Materials on Torts*, 6th ed. (Boston: Little, Brown, 1995): 383.

However, in terms of fairness, comparative negligence is much superior to contributory negligence. For this reason, Schwartz concludes that "the fairness criterion establishes a preference for a liability-dividing rule ... and, among liability-dividing rules for comparative negligence.... Comparative negligence is thus the proper rule."[46]

Comparative negligence can be looked upon as having the tort system provide insurance, for example, to accident victims. While a careless victim of a careless injurer gets no damages under contributory negligence, he may get some under comparative negligence.

THE RULE OF STRICT LIABILITY

In terms of Figure 6—1, under the strict liability rule the shaded area (indicating that the injurer is liable) is all-inclusive. Thus, the defendant is liable under all circumstances.[47]

Strict liability was first applied to cases involving trespassing animals and ultrahazardous activities — often referred to as *traditional strict liability*. I will take this up before turning to product liability.

TRADITIONAL STRICT LIABILITY

Traditional strict liability in tort holds that the defendant, even though he did not intentionally cause an injury, must pay damages if he did not live up to an objective, reasonable-care standard. For example, in regard to trespassing wild animals and domestic animals with known dangerous propensities, the owner is strictly liable for all injuries resulting from this dangerous propensity. Domestic animals that are not dangerous are usually entitled to one "free bite." The rationale, similar to the negligence theory, is that the utility of keeping a potentially dangerous animal is outweighed by the likelihood and possible extent of the harm.

Traditional strict liability for an ultrahazardous activity relates to an activity that involves a serious risk of harm to persons, land, or chattels of others that cannot be eliminated by exercising utmost care and is not a matter of common usage. Thus, blasting, explosive storage, crop dusting, water collection, tunnel construction, drilling of oil wells, and fumigation are considered to engender strict liability. The plaintiff must show that the

---

[46] Schwartz, "Contributory and Comparative Negligence": 727.

[47] G. Calabresi and J. T. Hirschoff, "Toward a Test for Strict Liability in Torts," *Yale Law Journal* 81 (May 1972): 1055–1085.

defendant committed the act or omitted to act and thereby breached his absolute duty, such breach being the cause of the damage sustained. The duty is limited to foreseeable harm to plaintiffs who are damaged from the normally dangerous propensity of the condition or act involved. Therefore, strict liability for blasting extends to the damage caused by flying debris, but not to completely unforeseen events.[48]

If the dangerous act is reasonable and permissible in cost–benefit terms, the actor is still held strictly accountable for the act's miscarriage. For example, in *Luthringer* v. *Moore*, fumigation was allowed, but the sprayer was held absolutely accountable, despite all possible precautions when his dangerous hydrocyanic spray poisoned people in the neighborhood, though he had left a notice warning of the danger.[49]

An economic rationale for strict liability is to deter uneconomical accidents. For example, in *Whitman Hotel Corporation* v. *Elliott and Watrous Engineering Co.*, the blaster who used dynamite was found to be able to limit the costs of such an activity better than the neighbor whose house was damaged by the vibrations.[50] Strict liability for ultrahazardous activities forces the actor to consider the social benefits and costs. Therefore, if the necessary activity can be performed by a similar but safer device at the same cost, there is incentive for the actor to adopt the safer method.

The only defense in ultrahazardous liability cases, other than causation, is that the plaintiff voluntarily participated in the ultrahazardous activity and that he negligently caused the harm.

PRODUCT LIABILITY

Accidental harm in general and from a defective product in particular comprise a special case of externalities. In the extreme, and usually at prohibitively high transaction costs, potential victims of harm caused by a defective product could be given an entitlement not to be injured accidentally. They would then negotiate with producers and/or distributors of products who would buy from them the right to impose on them accidental

---

[48] An example of the limitation of foreseeable damage is *Madsen* v. *East Jordan Irrigation Co.*, 101 Utah 552, 125 P.2d 794 (1942). The defendant was repairing a canal with the use of explosives, which disturbed the plaintiff's mother mink and caused the mink to kill 230 of their offspring. It is normal for mother minks to kill their offspring when they become excited, and a blaster is held strictly liable for damage caused by flying debris or vibrations. But the defendant was not held liable in this case. The court held that the act of the mother mink was so peculiar that it broke the chain of causation and the plaintiff had to prove negligence on the part of the blaster.

[49] *Luthringer* v. *Moore*, 31 Cal. 2d 489, 190 P.2d 1 (1948).

[50] *Whitman Hotel Corp.* v. *Elliott and Watrous Engineering Co.*, 137 Conn. 562, 79 A.2d 591 (1951).

damages. In this manner, externalities would be internalized, but at very high transaction costs. But there are alternatives, and I will review how product liability began as a negligence theory, was expanded under a contract-warranty approach, and now is considered a special case of strict liability.

Historical View of Product Liability

In the nineteenth century, product liability was predicated on a contract theory, and the seller was liable only to an individual with whom he was in privity of contract, that is, the immediate buyer. Therefore, a manufacturer would be liable to a wholesaler, a wholesaler to a retailer, and a retailer to a consumer. The seminal case was *Winterbottom* v. *Wright*, which involved damage caused by a carriage that overturned because of a defective wheel.[51] It was held that an injured coach passenger could not sue the manufacturer because he had no contract with the maker of the carriage. In the presence of competitive conditions, even under this privity limitation, the manufacturer had an incentive to reach an efficient safety level, since he feared to be sued along the contractual chain eventually. Therefore, he would seek to invest in the safety of his product to a point where marginal cost equaled marginal revenue. However, the courts later rejected the privity limitation. The first major basis of liability for negligence in the production of a product that could normally be expected to inflict substantial damage if it was defective occurred in *MacPherson* v. *Buick Motor Co.*[52] In that case, a car maker was held liable for negligence when a wheel was defectively manufactured, causing the car to collapse and injure the plaintiff. The case was unique because the product was not inherently dangerous; nevertheless, the defendant manufacturer was declared liable to a plaintiff who was not the immediate purchaser.

Under this negligence theory, the manufacturer is required to exercise the care of a reasonable man under the circumstances. This involves the familiar negligence test of balancing the likelihood and severity of the damage against the benefit of the product and the cost of safety devices. Today, negligence liability for defective products is primarily used to determine whether a manufacturer is negligent in designing a product. Such liability extends even to bystanders foreseeably within the scope of use of the defective product. The manufacturer is forced, therefore, to consider all possible repercussions of his negligence. However, repetitive and costly multiple suits along the chain of privity are eliminated. Still, when a dealer

---

[51] *Winterbottom* v. *Wright*, 10 M. & W. 109 11 L.I. Ex. 415, 152 Eng. Rep. 402 (1842).
[52] *MacPherson* v. *Buick Motor Co.*, 217 N.Y. 382, 111 N.E. 1050 (1916).

or middleman has no reason to know of the negligent defect, he is not held liable; to do so would not increase efficiency but merely effect a transfer from the dealer to the injured party.

Defenses include the injured parties' contributory negligence or assumption of risk. Both defenses create economic incentives for the injured party as well as the negligent manufacturer to avoid negligent behavior.

Because of the difficulty in proving negligence on the part of someone along the production chain and a desire to reduce litigation along the chain, courts next developed liability based on breach of warranty. *Breach of warranty* is a contract action based either on a warranty made expressly by the seller or on one implied in law that the product will do no harm in normal use. However, as a contract action, the injured party often had to show that he was in privity of contract with the alleged liable party.

Originally, the manufacturer's implied warranties covered only those to whom he sold his good. Therefore, the producer often could not be sued by the purchaser or consumer of the product because there was no contract between the two parties. Illustrative of this early court interpretation is *Chysky* v. *Drake Brothers Co., Inc.,* which involved a waitress working in a lunchroom who was badly injured when she bit into a nail hidden in the defendant's cake.[53] The court held the baker not liable because the plaintiff's employer had bought the cake from the defendant and the implied warranty ran only to those parties in privity of contract.

Finally, privity of contract in warranty cases was overriden, leading to the overruling of *Chysky* in *Randy Knitwear* v. *American Cyanamid Co.*[54] In this case a plaintiff consumer sued the wholesaler and manufacturer of a fabric that shrunk, contrary to an express representation within the garment itself. The court ruled that the ultimate consumer could sue the manufacturer despite the lack of privity.

Similarly, the scope of warranty liability was expanding. Originally a warranty of fitness was implied in law only to delicate objects such as food, as in *Chysky*. However, in *Henningsen* v. *Bloomfield Motors, Inc.,*[55] the implied warranty of fitness was extended to the manufacturer of automobiles despite the lack of a contractual arrangement between the manufacturer and the plaintiffs. The case signaled the end of the doctrine of privity of contract, and thereafter an implied warranty of safety was held to apply to a wide assortment of products.

---

[53] *Chysky* v. *Drake Brothers Co., Inc.,* 233 N.Y. 468, 139 N.E. 576 (1923).

[54] *Randy Knitwear* v. *American Cyanamid Co.,* 11 N.Y. 2d 5, 226 N.Y.S. 2d 363, 181 N.E.2d 399 (1962).

[55] *Henningsen* v. *Bloomfield Motors, Inc.,* 32 N.J. 358, 161 A.2d 69 (1960).

There are several possible reasons for the extension of warranty liability. One view is that the consumer is helpless to protect himself against dangerous products, and that the manufacturer is best able to defend against such hazards. Since only the manufacturer, barring a patent defect, is able to provide the optimal level of safety, he should be given the incentive to adopt cost-effective measures to reduce damage. If the two parties were free to bargain and had equal bargaining power, the duty to search for the hazard would often be placed on the manufacturer, since he frequently had a comparative advantage. If so, the law is merely trying to reinforce the likely market solution. Another view is that the manufacturer solicited the product's use and should not be able to disclaim liability by stating that he had no contract with the ultimate consumer. Theoretically, liability would force the manufacturer to stand behind his goods and advertisements. Finally, a direct action for warranty eliminates costly suits against intermediate suppliers that waste valuable court resources.

The defenses to warranty action were limited in many instances, and, since warranty was a contract action, the buyer had to give notice to the seller within a reasonable time after he knew or should have known of the breach.[56] However, the seller often included in the contract a disclaimer of liability that defeated the warranty.[57] Furthermore, courts have been reluctant to extend the rights of a two-party contract involving a good to all foreseeable users of that good. Therefore, a new basis of liability without these restrictions was needed.

Strict Liability for Products

The answer to these considerations has been the formulation of tort liability, which holds manufacturers and suppliers of defective products strictly liable in tort to consumers and users for injuries caused by the defect. Specifically, according to the *Restatement of Torts,*

> (1) One who sells any product in a defective condition unreasonably dangerous to the user or consumer or to his property is subject to liability for physical harm thereby caused to the ultimate user or consumer, ... (2) (*a*) although the seller has exercised all possible care in the preparation and sale of his product.[58]

Justice Traynor was the first to apply this theory to defective products. He did so in 1944 in his concurring opinion in *Escola* v. *Coca-Cola Bottling*

---

[56] Uniform Commercial Code, section 2-316.
[57] Uniform Commercial Code, section 2-607.
[58] *Restatement (Second) of Torts,* §420A.

Company.[59] In this case, a waitress was injured when a soda bottle broke in her hand as she moved it from the case to the refrigerator. While the bottler had used a nearly infallible test in relation to new bottles, used bottles were not tested at all. The court held that defects are likely to occur in used bottles and the bottler had a duty to make appropriate tests before refilling them with a charged liquid. Such a step was appropriate because there existed reasonable and practicable tests.

Justice Traynor developed his strict liability theory further in *Greenman* v. *Yuba Power Products, Inc.,* in which a power tool proved to be defective and caused injury. The plaintiff was foreclosed from suing on a warranty theory because he had failed to give timely notice of breach to the seller. A new rule of strict liability was formulated: "A manufacturer is strictly liable in tort when an article he places on the market, knowing that it is to be used without inspections for defects, proves to have a defect that causes injury to a human being."[60] Therefore, the defendant was held strictly accountable for the defect that made the product unsafe for its intended use. Within a short time, the doctrine of *Yuba* largely displaced the warranty theory.

In *Greenman* v. *Yuba Power Products, Inc.,* Justice Traynor also articulated reasons in support of strict liability. He emphasized cost internalization and insurance. Strict manufacturer liability was important in order to reduce the accident rate, because manufacturers were in a better position than "helpless consumers" to control safety. Morever, strict liability would serve to provide a form of insurance to injured victims, especially the poor, who might not possess other insurance coverage. Justice Traynor's view of strict liability is consistent with that of economists, who look at strict liability as forcing injurers to internalize the costs of accidents they caused. This rule can encourage a search for efficiency in incentives and risk-bearing, resulting in efficient outcomes.

In the 1960s courts began to recognize that product liability could stem from three types of injury causes — product design, manufacturing defects, and concealed dangers (or failure-to-warn). In product design cases, some courts have ruled that a design is defective if it fails to comply with "ordinary consumer expectations" of the product's likely safety.[61] The consumer expectation standard has lost favor because of the difficulty of defining and

---

[59] *Escola* v. *Coca-Cola Bottling Company,* 24 Cal. 2d 453 (1944).

[60] *Greenman* v. *Yuba Power Products, Inc.,* 59 Cal. 2d 57, 27 Cal. Rptr. 687, 377 P.2d 897 (1963).

[61] Schwartz, "Product Liability and Medical Malpractice in Comparative Context," *The Liability Maze,* Peter W. Huber and Robert E. Litan, Eds. (Washington, D.C.: The Brookings, Institution, 1991): 31.

measuring it. Thus, more recently the courts have held a design defective whenever the risks associated with that design exceed its benefits.

The claim of manufacturing defect relies on the criterion that a product is defective if it deviates from the norm of the manufacturers' other products. And in concealed dangers (or failure-to-warn) cases, courts could "scrutinize product warnings to determine whether their substance is sufficiently complete and also whether their style is sufficiently effective in conveying that substance to the product user.... Moreover, ... plaintiff in a failure-to-warn case must show that the inadequate warning is causal; that is, that a better warning would have resulted in his using the product more carefully or his declining to buy the product in the first place."[62] For example in the far-reaching asbestos case *Borel,* the court held that when a manufacturer sells a product to an employer, the manufacturer has an obligation to warn him of the extent to which worker exposure to that product might induce instances of occupational disease.[63]

Most strict liability cases center around actual defects in the manufacturing process. Manufacturers are liable if it can be shown that the defect is attributable to them and if the defect caused the injury. Often the proof is difficult. For example, in *Friedman* v. *General Motors Corporation,*[64] the issue was whether a defective gearshift that caused a car to start in the drive position could be attributed to the manufacturer of the 2-year-old car. Holding that reasonable minds could differ on the evidence, the court reversed a directed verdict for the defendant. It stated that it was possible for Friedman to prove that the car was defective, that the defect existed when the car left the factory, and that the defect was the proximate and direct cause of the injuries.

The major defense in strict liability cases is that the victim was engaged in unreasonable use of the product. The plaintiff has no duty to discover the danger and guard against it, but if he knows of the risk and continues to use the product unreasonably, then he has assumed the risk of the defect. He has also assumed the risk if he was adequately warned of the danger of continued misuse. The defense of mishandling has a solid rationale; the victim is not allowed to recover when he could have prevented the accident at lower cost than the producer. This is assumed to have happened when the victim knows of the danger yet continues to use the product in an unreasonable manner.

---

[62] *Ibid.*: 32–33.

[63] *Borel* v. *Fibreboard Paper Products Corp.*, 493 F.2d 1076 (5th Cir. 1973), cert. denied 419 U.S. 869 (1974).

[64] *Friedman* v. *General Motors Corp.*, 43 Ohio St. 2d 909, 331 N.E.2d 702 (1975).

In recent years courts have become reluctant to apply strict liability standards. One reason is that strict liability interferes with victims' incentives to avoid accidents. A second reason is that it transfers liability from consumer to manufacturer, i.e., from first- to third-party insurance, thereby providing consumers with greater coverage than they would have found worth buying in the form of accident insurance; a third reason is an unpredictable jury system that provides unpredictable awards, thus undermining manufacturers' incentives to avoid product defects. A final reason is the large and increasing number of payments made on the basis of an extremely expensive liability litigation system.[65]

PROBABILISTIC CAUSATION

Earlier in this chapter, I argued that in order to be awarded compensation in a negligence suit, the plaintiff must meet certain technical requirements, including one that the defendant proximately caused the alleged harm. There have always been those who have claimed that the traditional tort doctrine has overstated the ability of investigators to unequivocally determine causes. According to Glen Robinson, "In their more thoughtful moments legal scholars have laid bare the inherent ambiguity of causation and have shown that legal causation turns on more than mere factual investigation.... There is little judicial recognition of how indeterminacy and uncertainty pervade causal argument."[66]

Increasingly, many catastrophic injury, mass disaster, and toxic tort cases make it impossible to identify the specific source that caused the alleged harm. These difficulties stem from a long latency between exposure and the identifiable onset of harm (e.g., cancer and the lack of records on exposure). Moreover, there often exists a high degree of scientific uncertainty, which tends to weaken the association between, for example, a disease and particular chemical agent. There is also uncertainty about whether the person may have been exposed to more than a single contributing cause of the disease or malady in question.[67]

Under these conditions, legal scholars and courts have become interested

---

[65] Carl Shapiro, "Symposium on the Economics of Liability," *Journal of Economic Perspectives* 5 (Summer 1991): 6–7.

[66] Glen O. Robinson, "Probabilistic Causation and Compensation for Tortious Risk," *Journal of Legal Studies* 14 (December 1985): 780.

[67] E. Donald Elliott, "Why Courts? Comment on Robinson," *Journal of Legal Studies* 14 (December 1985): 800–801.

in arguing in terms of probabilistic causation.[68] In *Sindell* v. *Abbott Laboratories,* plaintiff claimed to have been injured as the result of a drug administered to her mother during pregnancy. While the mother knew the type of drug involved, she was unable to identify the specific manufacturer of the precise product. Thus, the plaintiff brought action against 11 drug companies (all having produced the identical drug, DES) on behalf of herself and other women similarly situated. The plaintiff claimed that companies had failed to test DES for efficacy and safety, and had disregarded test results of others that indicated that it was not safe. Moreover, the defendants had advertised assurances that taking DES was a safe and effective way to prevent miscarriage.

The California Supreme Court in 1980 applied the probabilistic causation approach. It accepted plaintiff's assertion that six or seven companies produced about 90% of the DES marketed. Therefore, the presence in the action of a substantial share of the appropriate market also provides a ready means to apportion damages among the defendants. Each defendant, thus, was held liable for the proportion of the judgment represented by its share of the market, unless the defendant was able to demonstrate that it could not have made the product that caused plaintiff's injuries (e.g., began to manufacture the product only after the plaintiff was born).

In 1989 the New York Court of Appeals in *Hymovitz* v. *Eli Lilly Co.,* 539 N.E. 2d 1069, 1078 (N.Y. 1989), accepted by and large the "Sindell" doctrine, while basing proportionality on the national market for DES used in pregnancy.

In summary, in a highly industrialized, high-technology society, it has sometimes become necessary to shift from the traditional causal standard of "more likely than not" to probabilistic risk assessment. There still remains the question of whether courts are equipped to handle the highly technical intricacies of probabilistic risk assessment or whether it would not be better to develop an administrative compensation system for probabilistic risk assessment and compensation of victims.[69] Both courts and administrative bodies could apply the Sindell rule to a variety of toxic, catastrophic injury, or mass disaster tort cases as long as liability is proportionate to the risks created by the defendant. This rule is applicable even in those instances, according to Robinson, where the cause litigated is likely to be

---

[68] Examples are Robinson, "Probabilistic Causation and Compensation": 779–798, and *Sindell* v. *Abbott Laboratories,* 26 Cal. 3d 588, 607 P.2d 924, 163 Cal. Rptr. 132, cert. denied, 449, U.S. 912 (1980).

[69] Elliott, "Why Courts?": 802–805.

complemented by additional, minor causes.[70] Admittedly, in such cases, the plaintiff would bear the costs associated with the unidentified causal agents.

DAMAGES

To compensate for the destruction of initial entitlements through the imposition of negative externalities, two classes of damages can be awarded by the court: *compensation* and *punitive damages*.

COMPENSATION

If accidental damages occur (i.e., negative externalities are imposed on a victim), the tortfeasor who is found guilty must compensate the victim. The role of the court is to provide the victim with appropriate compensation from the tortfeasor or his insurer.

The primary rule of compensation for nonintentional tort is that the defendant is required to compensate the plaintiff for the dollar value of the damages inflicted so as to maintain the earlier income distribution between the various parties. Calculating compensatory damages that provide just enough compensation to return the injured party to his prior condition revolves around the fundamental issue of evaluating the various component parts of a tortious injury. Some components are relatively easy to assess, such as medical costs and lost wages in injury cases. Other aspects of a tortious injury pose difficulties. For instance, in *Seffert* v. *Los Angeles Transit Lines,*[71] the plaintiff was dragged some distance by a bus. How does one place a value upon the pain and suffering incurred by such an accident?

Pain and suffering present problems of valuation as to both past and future. For example, *Seffert* involved not only the plaintiff's pain and embarrassment about limping and the permanent disfigurement of her thigh, but also her dread of needing an amputation. It is difficult to put price tags on such consequences, but if the law seeks to restore the plaintiff to her prior condition or its equivalent, these intangibles must be assessed.

---

[70] Glen O. Robinson, "Multiple Causation in Tort Law: Reflections on the DES Cases," *Virginia Law Review* 68 (1982): 713.

[71] *Seffert* v. *Los Angeles Transit Lines,* 56 Cal. 2d 498 (1961).

PUNITIVE DAMAGES

On occasion, the legal system awards punitive as well as compensatory damages. Punitive damages are generally awarded in cases involving concealable or intentional acts or in situations where the plaintiff's damages, though real, are not normally compensable under traditional legal standards. The economic rationale for punitive damages is thus multifaceted.

Some torts such as reckless driving are intentionally concealed by the actor. Here the probability of catching the appropriate defendant can be very small. If caught, the legal system imposes punitive damages as a bonus factor for both deterrent and compensatory reasons. By forcing the defendant to pay punitive damages, the law is in effect extracting compensation for the defendant's undetected torts. Substantial punitive damages can also effectively create a deterrent to future tortious conduct both in respect to this particular defendant and as a precedent with regard to possible future actors.

Another rationale for punitive damages is as an implicit compensation mechanism for damages and expenses not normally compensable under our legal system. Particularly in situations where mental anguish, personal discomfort, and damage to reputation are not normally provable or compensable under the usual compensatory damages standard, punitive damages can provide the plaintiff with some measure of relief. For instance, since under American law plaintiffs must pay their own attorney's costs, punitive damages are used to compensate for these expenses implicitly.

Perhaps the most fundamental rationale for punitive damages is their role of protecting the sanctity of the market system's structure of consensual exchange and production. Punitive damages are imposed to prevent the substitution of *post ad hoc* adjudications of legal rights for market transactions. Individuals in our society own property rights, and nonconsensual violations of those rights are punished by punitive damages to create a framework of consensual market exchange.

The imposition of punitive damages also reinforces the private property system. The fact that punitive sanctions are imposed for nonconsensual violation of property rights creates security in those entitlements and discourages encroachments. By maintaining the market system of consensual exchange, costs and benefits are internalized into each actor's choice calculus and through this mechanism a more efficient economic allocation of goods and services is achieved.

In recent years, however, increasingly strong objections to punitive damages have been voiced, particularly be business. The objections and proposals to change the punitive damages system are fueled by a concern that many damage awards are excessively large and can impair the competitiveness of

American business. The automobile industry often is cited as an example, since during 1981 and 1997 in at least five lawsuits, juries awarded punitive awards, in excess of $100 million.[72] In four of the five cases — two against General Motors and two against Ford — after appeal an out-of-court settlement was reached. The fifth case — against Chrysler — was only decided in October 1997.

High punitive damage awards tend to reflect the outrage of juries and courts about automobile firms' "conscious disregard" of known design defects that are likely to be life threatening. For example in relation to *Grimshaw* v. *Ford*, which involved a Pinto that burst into flames, a (reduced) award was upheld since "Ford's conduct constituted 'conscious disregard' of the probability of injury to members of the consuming public," and because "an award which is so small that it can be simply written off as part of the cost of doing business ... would have no deterrent effect."[73]

While this and a few other high profile cases gained much attention, reliable studies conclude that the punitive damages problem might be exaggerated. For example, Daniels and Martin concluded that charges of punitive awards' rapid increase in size and frequency in the United States, "are based on scanty empirical data and highly questionable interpretation of those data."[74] They find that "punitive damages were not routinely awarded," and "when they were awarded, the amount was generally modest."[75]

Still the perceived punitive damage crisis has caused more than 30 states during the 1980s to enact reforms designed to circumscribe both the circumstances in which punitive damages may be awarded and the size of

---

[72] According to the Center for Auto Supply, as reported in the *Los Angeles Times* (October 9, 1997, A3). The following facts pertain to the five cases: (1) *Jimenez* v. *Chrysler*, $262.5 million ($250 million punitive; $12.5 million compensatory), 1997, South Carolina Federal Court. Defective rear-gate latch in a 1985 Dodge Caravan resulted in death of a 6-year-old. (2) *Hardy* v. *General Motors*, $150 million ($100 million punitive; $50 million compensatory), 1996, Alabama State Court. Driver paralyzed, blamed on faulty door latch in 1987 Chevrolet Blazer. After appeal, settled for undetermined amount. (3) *Grimshaw* v. *Ford*, $128.5 million ($125 million; $3.5 million), 1981, California State Court. A 1974 Pinto exploded after being rear-ended, badly burning the driver. Eventually settled for $6.5 million. (4) *Durrill* v. *Ford*, $106.8 million ($100 million; $6.8 million), 1984, Texas State Court. 1974 Mustang burst into flames, killing driver. After appeal, settled for undetermined amount. (5) *Moseley* v. *GM*, $105.2 million ($101 million; $4.2 million), 1993, Georgia State Court. Child killed when pick-up gas tank exploded. After appeal, settled for undetermined amount.

[73] *Grimshaw*, v. *Ford Motor Co.*, 119 Cal. App. 3d 757, 774 (1981).

[74] S. Daniels and J. Martin, "Myth and Reality in Punitive Damages," *Minnesota Law Review* 75 (1990): 63.

[75] *Ibid.*: 43.

possible awards.[76] Reforms enacted in the different states vary "from outright abolition of punitive damages to tighter definitions of the kinds of conduct that may attract such awards, more stringent burdens of proof, monetary caps on the size of punitive awards or fixed ratios between punitive and compensatory damages, the partial escheat of awards to government agencies, and various procedural reforms such as bifurcated trials, or having judges rather than juries fix awards."[77]

Even if there is no punitive damage "crisis," it is important to assure that in meting out punishment there is need for careful procedural safeguards. Likewise, in relation to the deterrence rationale, safeguards against possible overdeterrence are needed. Some recent proposals to rein in punitive damage awards are likely to go too far. For example, some who would like to scale back the application of punitive damages would have them imposed only when there is "clear and convincing evidence of reckless disregard for the safety of others."[78] And still others would like to "exclude from consideration evidence of defendant's overall wealth."[79] It seems that such a step would be inconsistent with the deterrence rationale.

CONCLUSION

Tort law has been one of the most dynamic areas of the law. A number of forces have converged to result in this development. First and perhaps foremost has been the rapid increase in industrialization and urbanization, which has greatly increased the interdependence of each and every one of us. Thus, there has been a great increase in externalities, and many have become more severe. Another factor is the growth of social consciousness, dedicated to satisfying the economic goals of the "common person," which spread the desire to protect the common person from the destruction of his initial entitlements.

As a result, some major developments have taken place, particularly since 1960. For example, in California, defining changes in tort law occurred between 1961 and 1974, including extension toward stricter liability and reduced immunity of defendants. However, in 1975, the California Supreme Court indicated a change in direction away from strict liability.[80] It rejected a statutory rule of contributory negligence in favor of a rule of comparative

---

[76] The American Law Institute, *Study of Enterprise Liability for Personal Injury* (1990): 243, 246.

[77] *Ibid.*: 246–247.

[78] *Ibid.*: 283.

[79] *Ibid.*: 271.

[80] *Li* v. *Yellow Cab Co.*, 13 Cal. 3d 804 (1975).

negligence. Most and more states have legislatively established comparative negligence, and others have done so by court-made law. Moreover, the California Supreme Court, in *Sindell* v. *Abbott Laboratories,*[81] agreed in highly select cases to impose liability without the plaintiff showing that his injuries were caused by the act of the defendant. When DES, which was produced in identical form by a number of manufacturers many years ago, was found to have caused serious harm, it was clearly impossible for plaintiff to identify the specific manufacturer whose drug she has used. Under these circumstances, the court agreed to use a probabilistic liability to manufacturers, based on their market share.

There is a further area — medical malpractice — where major changes in tort law occurred by legislative action. As a result of the medical malpractice crisis of the early 1970s, which will be discussed in some detail in the next chapter, many legislatures enacted laws to limit the amount recoverable for pain and suffering, shortening the statute of limitations, informing juries about plaintiff's medical insurance, regulating legal fees, and requiring the plaintiff to inform the defendant of the suit in advance of filing.

Tort law has found increasingly many applications in a world of great interdependence and replete with externalities, many of which forcibly, though unintentionally, destroy initial entitlements. Some tort law concepts and standards lend themselves especially well to economic analysis, which will be undertaken in the following chapter, focusing on malpractice, industrial accidents, product liability, accident law, and sovereign immunity.

---

[81] *Sindell* v. *Abbott* Laboratories, 26 Cal. 3d 588, 607, P.2d 924, 411 (1980).

7

ECONOMIC ANALYSIS OF TORT LAW

INTRODUCTION

A number of concepts common to tort law were presented in the preceding chapter. An effort will now be made to infuse some further economic content into these concepts, in the hope of sharpening them and offering additional insight. Medical malpractice is examined first. Then effects of liability standards on industrial accidents are considered. The strict liability standard applied to product liability is then examined in terms of some of its economic effects. Thereafter, an economic analysis of accident law is undertaken. Sovereign immunity is then examined in an economic framework, and, the effects of the American and Continental rules of assigning liability for litigation cost are compared. Finally, economic effects of tort reform are examined.

The tort system, no doubt, has resulted in many benefits to society. However, it has also imposed major costs. Tillinghast has estimated that gross United States liability expenditures amounted in 1987 to $117 billion.[1] Transaction costs are estimated to constitute 30% of the costs of the workers' compensation system, but only about 1% of the Social Security system.[2] Tort costs in the United States have been escalating at a pace significantly faster than in any other modern economy.[3] Even after adjusting for inflation

---

[1] K. Tillinghast, *Tort Cost Trends: An International Perspective* (Simsbury, Conn., 1989): 16.
[2] *Ibid.*: 16.
[3] *Ibid.*: 12.

and population growth, tort costs have risen sharply in the past 30 years, and most especially in the past decade. For some industries, liability costs have been particularly heavy. For example, Martin has estimated that in 1987 the annual costs for product liability incurred by light plane manufacturers ranged from $70,000 to $100,000 per plane.[4] Thus, for light airplanes the product liability expense exceeded the cost of either raw materials or labor. In 1993, slightly less than 2 million tort law suits were filed in state courts and about 31,000 in federal courts.[5] In the 1980s, the number of civil lawsuits filed annually in state courts had been rising at about 3% a year. In the federal courts, the number of new civil filings had been declining since 1985 to head upward again in 1992.[6]

Plaintiffs win slightly more than half of all court cases. Their success is greatest, i.e., 66%, in automobile personal injury and business cases.[7] In medical malpractice and product liability cases, the success rate is significantly smaller, i.e., 33 and 44%, respectively. While product liability and medical malpractice cases had the highest median awards, automobile personal injury verdicts typically yielded the lowest median award. However, since 1985 medical malpractice and business awards increased most while product liability and automobile personal injury ones increased least, and some of the latter even decreased.[8] However, what more often stands out are the maximum awards. They occur particularly in business and product liability actions. For example, much national attention has focused on breast implant lawsuits against Dow Corning. After a federal court in Alabama announced a $4 billion class action settlement and allowed claimants to register, more than 400,000 claimants did so.[9]

Economists have been interested in tort rule formulation. These normative or welfare economics efforts have been made difficult by the multivalued objective function of tort law. In addition to the deterrence objective, there is the objective of compensation and its fairness as well as concern to minimize transaction costs.

As indicated already in Chapter 1, economists also have a great interest in effect evaluation, i.e., estimating the size and distribution of side effects.

---

[4] Robert Martin, "General Aviation Manufacturing: An Industry Under Siege," *The Liability Maze: The Impact of Liability Law on Safety and Innovation,* Peter W. Huber and Robert E. Litan, Eds. (Washington, D.C.: The Brookings Institution, 1991): 484.

[5] RAND Institute for Civil Justice, "Metaphors — and Facts — About Litigation Trends," *Fact and Trends* (RAND Institute for Civil Justice Spring 1995): 1.

[6] *Ibid.*: 2.

[7] Erik Moller, *Trends in Civil Jury Verdicts Since 1985* (Santa Monica, Calif.: RAND 1996): XV.

[8] *Ibid.*: XVI.

[9] RAND Institute for Civil Justice, "Metaphors and Facts About Litigation Trends": 2.

Among these side effects with far-reaching implications are safety and innovation. Safety concerns mainly relate to product design, and some studies have found that product liability has had a strong, positive safety effect on design.[10] They, however, also suggest that current liability law sends rather vague signals that do not indicate how safe the design of products should be. Priest has argued that liability laws, in addition to having a deterrent effect and therefore stimulating safety, may do the same also indirectly by amplifying the safety-enhancing implications of reputation and regulation.[11] Thus, the demand for a product might decline if serious assertions about its safety are widely disseminated.

In reviewing the relationship between liability laws and safety, Huber and Litan conclude that "on balance, however, the documented direct linkages between liability and safety thus far are weak."[12] Moreover, they suggest that such factors as regulation and bad publicity may generate more powerful incentives to manufacturers to improve the safety of their products.

Although the effect of tort laws on innovation is generally found to be substantial, there are variations across industries. A study in 1986 by the Conference Board, which asked 500 Chief Executive Officers of large U.S. corporations about the impact of the tort system on their companies, found widespread agreement.[13] Roughly one-third of all firms surveyed and about half of those claiming major effects made the decision not to introduce new products because of liability fears. Of firms having experienced a major impact from liability laws, 58% had discontinued some of their products for this reason.

Turning to the effects of tort laws on innovation, these are found to be particularly pronounced in relation to drugs and medical technologies. For example, in the 1970s, 13 pharmaceutical companies actively carried out research in contraception and fertility, but by 1988 only one U.S. company did so.[14] Similar developments can be identified in relation to

---

[10] G. Eads and P. Rueter, *Designing Safer Products: Corporate Responses to Product Liability Law and Regulation*, R-3022-ICJ (Santa Monica, Calif.: RAND Corporation, 1983).

[11] George Priest, "Products Liability Law and the Accident Rate," in *Liability Perspectives and Policy*, Robert E. Litan and Clifford Winston, Eds. (Washington, D.C.: The Brookings Institution, 1989): 184–222.

[12] Peter W. Huber and Robert E. Litan, "Overview," Huber and Litan Eds., *The Liability Maze: The Impact of Liability Law on Safety and Innovation* (Washington, D.C.: The Brookings Institution, 1991): 15.

[13] N. Weber, *Product Liability: The Corporate Response*, Research Report 893 (New York: The Conference Board, 1989).

[14] R. H. Weaver, *Impact of Product Liability on the Development of New Medical Technologies* (Chicago: American Medical Association, 1988).

vaccines. A further example is the small aircraft industry. The chilling effect of liability laws on innovations are exacerbated by uncertainty and the unpredictability of litigation.

It has been suggested that under certain circumstances tort law need not reduce safety or innovation, or only to a small extent. Thus, in the presence of a tort law that is highly and predictably specific, safety benefits are likely to occur without across-the-board industry deterrents that interfere with innovation.[15]

ECONOMIC ANALYSIS OF MEDICAL MALPRACTICE

LEGAL BACKGROUND

The first medical malpractice case reported in the United States was *Cross v. Guthrey* in 1794.[16] Malpractice was soon related to the standard of care applied by physicians, which was defined in the New York Supreme Court case of 1898, *Pike v. Honsinger:*

> The physician and surgeon, by taking charge of a case, impliedly represents that he possesses, and the law places upon him the duty of possession, that reasonable degree of learning and skill that is ordinarily possessed by physicians and surgeons in the locality in which he practices, and which is ordinarily regarded by those conversant with the employment as is necessary to qualify him to engage in the business of practicing medicine and surgery ... it becomes his duty to use reasonable care and diligence in the exercise of his skill and the application of his learning to accomplish the purpose for which he was employed. He is ... to use his best judgment in exercising his skill and applying his knowledge. The law holds him liable for an injury to his patient resulting from want of the requisite skill and knowledge or the omission to exercise reasonable care or the failure to use his best judgment.[17]

The locality rule of *Pike* not only established a standard for comparison, but also required that a medical expert testifying for the plaintiff in a malpractice action must have practiced in the defendant's community. Since, particularly in small communities, there are few physicians and, moreover, physicians are often reluctant to testify against colleagues, the locality rule greatly favors the defendant. Therefore, the Massachusetts

---

[15] D. E. Elliot, "Why Punitive Damages Don't Deter Corporate Misconduct Effectively," *Alabama Law Review* 40 (1989): 1058.

[16] *Cross* v. *Guthrey,* 2 Root 90 (1794).

[17] *Pike* v. *Honsinger,* 155 N.Y. 201 (1898).

Supreme Court in *Brune* v. *Belinkoff* in 1968 flatly announced that it was abandoning the locality rule.[18] Other states have followed suit.

Plaintiffs in the past have also been handicapped by the inadmissibility of medical treatises as evidence because what is written in the treatises was not given under oath. Pertinent here is the belief that the validity of testimony can be evaluated by jurors only if the witness is on the witness stand and can be subjected to cross-examination. Such states as Massachusetts, Kansas, Nevada, and Rhode Island have enacted statutes specifically to admit learned books and articles to establish the standard of care. The value of using medical treatises can be particularly great when used in conjunction with the examination of the defendant physician. In 1993, the United States Supreme Court decided that federal judges have the explicit responsibility of assuring that expert testimony be both reliable and relevant.[19] The reliability determination requires that the evidence be scientifically valid. This is a heightened standard over that of some states that have the vaguer "general acceptance" standard for determining scientific admissibility of evidence. The heightened standard is of particular interest to opponents of mass tort suits. Most states today have "adverse witness statutes," although they were long opposed. These statutes expressly permit a litigant to call the opposing party for cross-examination.

The doctrine of *res ipsa loquitur* ("the thing speaks for itself") is of particular interest in malpractice action. It can be viewed as simply a characterization of those conditions in which circumstantial evidence, by itself, is sufficiently strong to warrant the conclusion that the defendant was probably negligent and that the negligence was the proximate cause of the alleged damages. *Res ipsa* simply creates the presumption of negligence, which can, however, be overturned by evidence to the contrary by the defendant.[20] (For example, American courts almost always apply *res ipsa* to cases where sponges, and sometimes other foreign bodies, were not removed from the patient before the operation was concluded.) In many medical situations, particularly where the plaintiff has been given anesthesia, he is in no position to know whether the physician employed due care. Where there is little evidence of negligence, but the defendant knew about the likely harm and could have done more to avoid its occurrence than the plaintiff could, *res ipsa* is applied in ways that approach a strict liability standard.

---

[18] *Brune* v. *Belinkoff*, 354 Mass. 102 (1968).

[19] *Daubert* v. *Merrell Dow Pharmaceutical*, 509 U.S. 579 (1993).

[20] For an insightful discussion of *res ipsa loquitur* see Mark F. Grady, "Res Ipsa Loquitur and Compliance Error," *University of Pennsylvania Law Review* 142 (January 1994): 887–947.

It must be recognized that medicine is an imperfect science. Maloccurrences take place, with only some of them the result of negligence and incompetence. It is the court's responsibility to establish whether the maloccurrence could have been avoided. The court may do so with the aid of the Learned Hand formula.

An economic analysis of medical malpractice and the liability potentially associated with it must consider some unique aspects of medical markets. Patients are at a great disadvantage because doctors have significantly more information about available treatments and their likely outcomes. Thus, information is distinctly asymmetric. A second peculiarity of medical markets relates to the fact that most medical bills are covered by insurance, and thus are not directly paid for by the patient. According to Danzon,

> Over 80% of the population has some form of health insurance, typically with modest co-payment and premiums unrelated to past use [experience rating]. Consequently only roughly 10% of expenditure on hospital care and 26% of physicians' services are paid directly out-of-pocket. Because insurance drastically reduces the point-of-purchase price of medical care to patients, this distorts customary levels of use of services, relative to a first-best optimum, and may also distort customary "quality" defined as technologies typically used to treat a particular condition.[21]

These peculiarities of the medical markets must be considered while recognizing two primary factors that create security for patients seeking medical attention — the ethical commitment by the physician to pursue the good of the patient and the use of medical technology in line with the best scientific knowledge of the time. Ideally, tort law is designed to heighten physicians' sensitivity to these two concerns.[22]

Medical malpractice, which gained notoriety in the middle 1970s, is only one of a number of battlegrounds. Lawyers, architects, real estate agents, corporate officers and directors, and travel agents until recently have increasingly been subjected to malpractice suits and have seen their insurance premiums soar.

THE HAND FORMULA AND *HELLING* v. *CAREY*

Next, I will analyze a medical malpractice case, *Helling* v. *Carey*, which illustrates many facets and tensions within the field of medical malpractice

---

[21] Patricia M. Danzon, "Liability for Medical Malpractice," *Journal of Economic Perspectives* 5 (Summer 1991): 53.

[22] Stanley J. Reiser, "Malpractice, Patient Safety, and the Ethical and Scientific Foundations of Medicine," *The Liability Maze: The Impact of Liability Law on Safety and Innovation*, Peter W. Huber and Robert E. Litan, Eds. (Washington, D.C.: The Brookings Institution, 1991): 227–250.

in court, but in addition lends itself in part to an empirical implementation of the Hand formula.[23] The plaintiff Helling, who first consulted the defendant ophthalmologists in 1959 for myopia (nearsightedness), was fitted for contact lenses and became blind from glaucoma because no tonometry to detect glaucoma was performed. She experienced a minimal amount of irritation during the next 8 years, but, in September 1967, she consulted the defendants again, complaining of eye irritation. They diagnosed conjunctivitis (inflammation of the mucous membranes) and gave her a prescription. During several more visits in the course of the following months, the defendants decided Helling had corneal abrasions due to the contact lenses. In May 1968, the plaintiff returned, again complaining about irritation. On October 1, 1968, the defendants tested for glaucoma and found it.

Glaucoma can result in blindness; but it can be treated and ameliorated if detected early enough. There are few symptoms until the harm is irreversible. It can be detected by a simple tonometry test, the major cost of which is the ophthalmologist's time. The plaintiff contended that the defendants should have tested for glaucoma in 1967 when she was 32 years of age and that they ignored both their training and advances in the profession in not doing so.

The defendants presented evidence that, although there were some ophthalmologists who favored giving the glaucoma test to patients under 40 years of age, the accepted national practice did not require giving glaucoma tests to patients under 40 unless symptoms and complaints would indicate the presence of glaucoma. There was inconsistent evidence as to whether the defendants should have suspected glaucoma, and it was also unclear whether testing in 1967 would have made any difference.

The Washington Supreme Court held that the defendants were negligent *as a matter of law* for not administering the glaucoma test. The court stated,

> Under the facts of this case reasonable prudence required the timely giving of the pressure test to this plaintiff. The precaution of giving this test to detect the incidence of glaucoma to patients under 40 years of age is so imperative that irrespective of its disregard by the standards of the ophthalmology profession, it is the duty of the courts to say what is required to protect patients under 40 from damaging results of glaucoma.
> ... as a matter of law ... the reasonable standard that should have been followed ... was the timely giving of this simple, harmless pressure test.... In failing to do so, the defendants were negligent, which proximately resulted in the blindness sustained by the plaintiff.[24]

[23] *Helling* v. *Carey*, 83 Wash. 2d 514, 519 P.2d 981 (1974).
[24] *Ibid.*: 519.

To support its decision, the court cited two nonmedical cases, including the *T. J. Hooper* decision, in which Justice Learned Hand stated,

> ... In most cases reasonable prudence is in fact common prudence; but strictly it is never its measure; as whole calling may have unduly lagged in the adoption of new and available devices. It never may set its own tests, however persuasive be its usages. Courts must in the end say what is required; there are precautions so imperative that even their universal disregard will not excuse their omission.[25]

In justifying its holding, the court emphasized that the glaucoma test is "simple, harmless, and inexpensive."

Empirical evidence of the incidence of glaucoma was recognized by the court: For those under 40, the expected incidence is 1 per 25,000 persons; among all those over 40, it is around 1 to 2 per 100 persons. The test is not totally without risk, since any time an instrument is placed on the eye there is a risk of scratching the cornea.

Standards for the test were evaluated by R. P. Crick, an expert in the field, who concluded, "The prevalence of glaucoma is too low and the methods of detection such as to make population screening an uneconomic use of medical resources at present."[26]

Since *Helling* v. *Carey* has the distinction of citing generally agreed-upon quantitative estimates on the probability of harm occurring, it is useful to place these estimates into the Hand formula. Judge Learned Hand, it will be recalled, defined the legal standard of liability applicable to most unintended acts of negligence as follows: The defendant is guilty of negligence if the loss caused by the event, for example, an accident, L, multiplied by the probability of the event occurring, P, exceeds the costs of the precautions that the defendant might have taken to avert it, C.

In relation to glaucoma in general and *Helling* v. *Carey* in particular, the following numbers are illustrative: The medical profession indicates that P for persons below 40 is 1/25,000, and for persons above 40, 2/100. The cost of preventing the occurrence of glaucoma, C, is about 10 minutes of a doctor's time, let us say $30; the loss associated with the occurrence of glaucoma, namely blindness, L, is the most difficult parameter. Ideally, one would need to estimate the losses incurred by a person who goes blind, and do so year by year with each year reflecting the particular age. Since these losses constitute a flow over time, discounting would be necessary.

---

[25] *T. J. Hooper*, 60 F.2d 737 (1932).

[26] R. P. Crick, "Chronic Glaucoma: A Preventable Cause of Blindness," *Lancet* (February 9, 1974): 207.

We can use a bounding technique and estimate for the two age groups at what L value the Hand formula would find the defendant liable for the ill effects of glaucoma, should he have omitted an examination. For persons under 40 years of age, the defendant would be liable if the loss due to glaucoma was more than $30/(0.00004)$ or $750,000. For persons 40 years or older, the defendant would be liable if the loss due to glaucoma was more than $30/(0.02)$ or $1500.

Thus, the critical loss figure for young people is about 500 times as large as for older people. Younger people can look forward to a longer productive life than older persons, but the income difference is unlikely to be more than three to ten times on average.[27] Although, admittedly, there are other than income losses to be considered, such as mental anguish, or any harm from unintended scratching of the eye by the testing procedure, these harms are unlikely to offset entirely the 500-fold greater loss.

Another way of applying the Hand formula makes use of the average jury verdict for total or legal blindness in 1973–1977: $678,000.[28] Accordingly,

$$\$30 > \$678,000 \ (0.00004) = \$27$$

It would therefore be interesting to contemplate whether the Washington Supreme Court would have ruled in favor of plaintiff Helling had it explicitly placed its figures into the Hand formula. But perhaps it would have priced a tonometry test below $30.

In fact, the Washington legislature in 1975, a year after the Washington Supreme Court's ruling, enacted a statute that requires that, in judicial proceedings, standards of health care must be established by health care professionals only and not by the courts.[29]

THE MALPRACTICE SYSTEM'S EFFECTS

What are some of the major effects of medical malpractice laws on physicians, hospitals, patients, and insurors? While we can readily theorize about the likely effects, it has been difficult to estimate them empirically.

Studies of medical malpractice frequency are summarized by Schwartz,

[27] For example, if the average person starts to be gainfully employed at age 22 and retires at 65, and the average of persons 1 to 39 years old is 20, then those 1–39 years old could have been gainfully employed 17 + 26 or 43 years in the absence of glaucoma. With similar assumptions, the equivalent number of years is 15 for persons 40 years and older.

[28] "Injury Valuation Reports, Tables of Verdict Expectancy Values for Eye Injuries," in *Personal Injury Valuation Handbooks* (Cleveland: Jury Verdict Research).

[29] Washington Revised Code, §4.24.290 (1975).

who finds wide variation in results.[30] On the one hand, he points to a 1988 study of patients admitted to hospitals because of heart attacks, strokes, and pneumonia. Of the 48% who died during hospitalization, more than one-fourth of these deaths were probably caused either by errors in diagnosis or in management. On the other hand, he reports a study of 31,000 New York State patients who were hospitalized during 1984; 4% were found to have suffered unintended medical injury, and only a quarter of the injuries were due to negligence by doctor or hospital.

While there has been uncertainty about malpractice frequency and its possible rise, there has occurred since the late 1960s a steep increase in the severity of malpractice claims, that is, in the frequency of claims per physician and the average payment per paid claim (including both jury verdicts and out-of-court settlements). Leon Rosenberg, Dean of Yale School of Medicine, reported in 1986 that 60% of practicing obstetricians were sued for malpractice at least once and 25% could expect a suit in any one year.[31]

Physicians appear to have reacted in a number of ways. On the positive side, a Canadian study, for example, found that 15% of all surgeons spent more time discussing surgical risks with patients and almost 60% had modified their practices.[32] Furthermore, to reduce the chances that doctors leave surgical tools in patients when they close them up, about one-fourth of all hospitals have installed computers in their operating room to keep track of surgical instruments.[33] Also, according to Wiley, the level of glaucoma testing for patients under 40 by ophthalmologists in the state of Washington increased significantly between 1973 and 1977 as a result of the 1974 ruling in *Helling* V. *Carey*.[34] Schwartz also reported that in New York State the prospect of liability was a significant factor influencing physicians' "standards of care."[35] Although it is difficult to define "defensive medicine," there are many indications that physicians have increasingly engaged in such practices for fear of malpractice suits. Schwartz correctly concludes:

---

[30] Gary T. Schwartz, "Reality in the Economic Analysis of Tort Law, Does Tort Law Really Deter?" *UCLA Law Review* 42 (December 1994): 397–405.

[31] Leon E. Rosenberg and Guido Calabresi, *Law and Medicine in Confrontation: A Deans' Dialogue*, Working Paper No. 45 (New Haven: Connecticut Yale Law School Center for Studies in Law, Economics, and Public Policy, May 1986): 7–8.

[32] Gerald B. Robertson, "Informed Consent in Canada: An Empirical Study," *OSGOODE Hall Law Journal* 139 (1984): 144–146.

[33] Edward Felsenthal, "Forgotten Surgical Tools Spur Lawsuits," *Wall Street Journal* (Dec. 11, 1992): B-12.

[34] Gerry Wiley, "The Impact of Judicial Decisions on Professional Conduct: An Empirical Study," *Southern California Law Review* 55 (1981): 345–360, 363.

[35] Schwartz, "Reality in the Economic Analysis of Tort Law": 401.

"in the aggregate, then, these changes are beneficial to patients yet certainly costly."[36] Fear of malpractice suits also has induced physicians and hospitals to greatly improve the documentation for the treatment of patients. While mainly designed to assist in the defense of possible law suits against them, better documentation can reduce the frequency and severity of patient injury.

However, major negative effects have also resulted. For example, it was reported that in the mid-1970s, legislatures in virtually all states responded affirmatively by enacting far-reaching tort reforms. They had two purposes: to curb the rise in claims and to assure availability of malpractice insurance. The immediate results were encouraging. From 1975 to 1978, the claim frequency per physician slowed and, in some instances, even declined.

However, since 1978, claim frequency again increased.[37] A 55% increase in claim frequency occurred between 1980 and 1984, from 10.5 claims per 100 physicians in 1980 to 16.3 in 1984.[38] Between 1975 and 1984, claim severity increased at almost twice the rate of the Consumer Price Index. From 1979 to 1983, claim severity increased 95%, from $27,408 in 1979 to $53,482 in 1983. Moreover, between 1980 and 1984, the average malpractice jury award rose by 136%, from $404,726 in 1980 to $954,858 in 1984.[39]

These developments in turn lead to an explosion of medical malpractice premiums. For example, the average amount of money spent by physicians on medical liability insurance increased between 1982 and 1985 from $5800 to $10,500.[40] It would be a mistake, however, to look at the United States experience as unique. In Canada and the United Kingdom the rate of growth of malpractice claim frequency and severity has also been high over the past two decades, though not as high as that in the United States. Interestingly, this growth in Canada and the United Kingdom took place during a time in both countries that contingent arrangement fees for plaintiffs' attorneys were not permitted, there were limits on awards for pain and suffering, medical costs were lower, and so were rates of growth of medical costs — all factors often cited as explanations for the growth of U.S. malpractice claims.[41]

---

[36] *Ibid.*: 402.

[37] Patricia M. Danzon, *The Effects of Tort Reforms on the Frequency and Severity of Medical Malpractice Claims: A Summary of Research Results*, P-7211 (Santa Monica, Calif.: RAND Corporation, 1986): 1.

[38] Physicians' and Surgeons' Update, 1985 (St. Paul, MN: The St. Paul Fire and Marine Insurance Company, 1985).

[39] Danzon, *Effects of Tort Reforms*: 2.

[40] R. S. Shapiro et al., "A Survey of Sued and Non-Sued Physicians and Suing Patients," *Archives of Internal Medicine* 149 (1989): 2190–2196.

[41] Danzon, *Effects of Tort Reforms*: 58–59.

It has been suggested that tort liability in relation to malpractice should be looked upon as a system of medical quality control. In most industries, market signals can be relied upon as guides for consumers to make efficient decisions. However, in the professions, consumers are generally ill-informed about costs, risks, and benefits of alternative services, while the professional is trained to have superior knowledge and experience. As a result, consumers are unable to perceive and evaluate effectively the quality of services potentially available; in health care particularly, they cannot and do not monitor the quality of health care actually delivered. Moreover, in many acute and emergency situations the options of the patient are limited at best. Under these conditions, the argument goes, tort liability presents "a device to correct the inefficiencies that could result from market signals when consumers misperceive risk."[42]

Although tort law can have as its objectives deterrence, fairness, and loss spreading (compensation), a medical malpractice system from the standpoint of economic efficiency must concentrate on deterrence. (The goal of compensation can be achieved more equitably and at lower cost by first-party health and disability insurance, an arrangement that would have substantially lower overhead than the present system, make payments in a more timely fashion, and pay all victims regardless of cause of injury.)[43] As Danzon has argued,

> Our negligence-based system of liability for iatrogenic injury can be justified, if at all, only on grounds of deterrence — that is, assigning liability to those best placed to prevent injuries results in savings in injury costs that outweigh the added overhead costs of litigating over cause and fault.[44]

Because in the delivery of health services there is a high likelihood of market failure and there is evidence that a significant percentage of patients face harm due to negligence, relying on tort liability makes sense. A California study looked at the number of common medical mishaps due to negligence. The study found that about 1 in 126 patients admitted to California hospitals in 1974 suffered an injury resulting from medical malpractice.[45] Only 1 in 25 of these injured patients was compensated through the tort system. (It has been estimated that at most 1 in 10 of the injured patients filed a claim and less than half of those who filed a claim received any

---

[42] Patricia M. Danzon, *Medical Malpractice* (Cambridge: Harvard University Press, 1985): 9.

[43] *Ibid.*: 221.

[44] *Ibid.*: 221.

[45] California Medical Association, *Medical Insurance Feasibility Study* (San Francisco: Sutter Publications, 1977).

compensation.)[46] From these numbers, Danzon concludes that the cost of negligent injuries is several times larger than the cost of malpractice insurance premiums, making concern for quality control highly relevant.

It is important to recognize that the cost of operating our medical malpractice system is high, running into billions of dollars annually. These are the tangible costs composed of litigation costs and overhead (which absorb about two-thirds of every malpractice premium dollar), as well as the costs of defensive medical practices. To these must be added such intangible costs as the time and anxiety costs of physicians and plaintiffs, whether or not the case goes to trial.

Nonetheless, the cost of operating a malpractice system is small compared to the cost associated with injuries. These costs include medical treatment, rehabilitation, and lost wages. In addition, there are intangible costs of pain and suffering, and the diminution in the quality of life associated with physical impairment. Also, there are administrative and overhead costs of compensating victims. In recent years, overhead costs have been about twice as large as the compensation actually received by victims.[47]

While the costs of injury from medical malpractice are high, so are the costs of steps that can prevent injury. As with most activities, injury prevention encounters diminishing returns. In a world of finite resources, injury prevention takes away resources valued by society.

Here, too, we have a conventional trade-off problem. The general problem is that of providing for the maximization of the value of total societal resources. This social policy is attained (i.e., we have an optimum resource allocation) whenever the total value of the goods and services produced cannot be increased by rearranging the output mix. In relation to medical injury, resources are efficiently allocated when, at the margin, the last dollar spent on prevention saves exactly a dollar of injury cost. This principle should not only hold on an overall basis but, also in theory, for each prevention activity. Because of the complexity of the problem, the many actors involved, and the high transaction costs, injuries from medical treatment are subjected to a negligence rule of liability. Accordingly, a medical provider is liable for injury to a patient if the injury results from a failure to meet the "due care" standard discussed earlier. If the injury conforms to a normal risk of nonnegligent care, the medical provider is clearly not at fault and therefore not liable; instead, the victim bears the cost.

Earlier we referred to a negligence rule and sought to implement it with the aid of the Learned Hand formula. According to this formula, negligence

---

[46] Danzon, *Medical Malpractice*: 4.
[47] *Ibid.*: 10.

occurs if the loss caused by the accident times the probability of the accident occurring is larger than the cost of precautions the defendant might have taken to avert it. In the case of medical treatment, negligence is said to occur when physicians do not take precautions if their costs are less than those of the harm averted. This, by the way, is exactly the definition of efficient investment in malpractice prevention.[48] The negligence rule thus defined tends to create incentives for physicians to provide medical treatment of the exact nature that the patient would have chosen if fully informed, that is, in a perfectly competitive market.

We are now ready to indicate the four conditions that must be met before a tort liability system will provide both optimum deterrence incentives to physicians and optimum compensation to patients. They are:

1. The legal standard of due care must be optimally defined
2. Damage awards must be structured to provide optimal compensation to victims and optimal incentives to defendants
3. Patients must detect and file claims for all injuries due to negligence and unnecessary treatment
4. The courts must make accurate findings of liability and damages[49]

In real life, these conditions are, at best, only partially met. For example, rather than the courts seeking to define an optimum standard of due care, the customary standard of the profession, as discussed earlier in this chapter, is applied. Also, damage awards seldom provide full compensation for all monetary and nonmonetary losses. For one, it is virtually impossible to estimate properly what the appropriate award for pain and suffering should be. For another, even if the victim were awarded optimum compensation, he would tend to receive only about two-thirds thereof after paying his lawyer and court costs. Furthermore, there can be no doubt that many patients with valid claims fail to file them. As mentioned earlier, at most, 1 in 10 victims of medical malpractice file claims. On the other hand, we know that quite a few claims filed are not valid. Moreover, by far the largest number of claims that are filed are settled out of court, and little evidence exists that these out-of-court settlements reflect legal standards rather than compromises.

---

[48] Resource allocation efficiency requires that the legal definition of negligence takes cognizance of unnecessary treatments, those that are expected to benefit patients less than their expected costs.

[49] Rosenberg and Calabresi, *Law and Medicine*: 17.

REFORM OF THE MALPRACTICE SYSTEM

I will next review some reforms, evaluate them, and then examine some proposed reforms. However, before I do so, I would like to indicate that some scholars are extremely pessimistic about our ability to devise a tort system that will meet socially desirable objectives. One such scholar is Guido Calabresi, who has stated,

> the problem with malpractice law is ... that it fails utterly to achieve what are its only sensible justifications; a. to induce better medical care and b. to compensate efficiently those who suffer medical maloccurrences. Why does it fail to do the first of these? ... The reason is that the incentives created by malpractice law make no sense, and cannot be made to make sense.... In too many medical situations in which if something goes wrong the doctor may be held liable, there is an alternative course or treatment available whose extra costs either do not lie on the doctor or whose harm, if something does go wrong, lead to no malpractice suit.... Defensive Medicine is simply the tip of the iceberg. If a doctor is likely to be liable if she or he fails to take a seemingly unnecessary X-ray and a fracture goes undetected, why would a doctor ever fail to X-ray? The X-ray cost is, unlike the cost and stigma of a malpractice suit, borne by third party insurers. And even if over the years too many X-rays are taken and the patient gets leukemia, no law suits against any of the doctors who ordered the X-rays are likely to win.[50]

Calabresi's gloomy outlook for the efficacy of a medical malpractice system that relies on tort law is contradicted by Patricia Danzon. Her position is

> Reforms should be evaluated in the broader context of the fundamental purposes of the tort system, which are deterrence of medical negligence and efficient compensation of its victims. I believe that the tort system can be made cost-effective in performing these dual roles.[51]

Reform proposals relate to the standard of care, size and structure of awards, statute of limitations, cost of litigation, and change from a negligence to a no-fault system. An empirical study by Danzon and Lillard. By capping verdicts, eliminating specific dollar requests by plaintiffs (i.e., barring the *ad damnum* clause), or permitting payments of awards for future losses in periodic installments, the following changes were observed:
a) average verdicts or settlements were cut by 25% to 30%, b) the portion

---

[50] *Ibid.*: 18–23.
[51] Danzon, *Effects of Tort Reforms*: 10.

of cases dropped increased from 43% to 48%, and *c*) the share of cases going to verdict fell from 5.1% to 4.6%.[52]

Imposition of limits on contingent fees charged by the attorneys of plaintiffs also were effective. They cut average settlements by 9%, raised the portion of cases dropped from 43% to 48%, and reduced the share of cases going to verdict from 6.1% to 4.6%.[53]

Danzon carried out an updated empirical study for 1975 through 1984 that also should capture some of the long-run effects of reforms. Accordingly, cutting one year off the statute of limitations for adults reduced claim frequency by 8%. Statutes permitting or mandating the offset of collateral benefits reduced malpractice claim severity by 11% to 18% and claim frequency by 14%; capping on awards reduced severity by 23%; and arbitration statutes increased claim frequency while reducing average severity. However, providing for screening panels or limiting contingency fees had no statistically significant effect on either claim frequency or severity.[54] While Danzon concludes that caps on awards and collateral source offset have significantly reduced claim severity, Wencl and Brizzolara refute this conclusion.[55] In the 29 states capping in 1995 noneconomic damages, they neither find lower costs nor better access in rural areas. However, this study does not use the same quality of empirical techniques as does that by Danzon.

In spite of the various reforms that states have instituted, more can be done. One alternative involves a contractual approach that leaves questions of medical safety to free negotiation between patient and medical service providers. The most eloquent advocate of this approach is Richard Epstein. He has proposed that "we should both permit and encourage private agreements between physicians, hospitals and patients to set the terms on which medical services are rendered.[56] Epstein surmises that his proposal would lead to two types of contracts. First, some patients would opt for no rights to compensate by taking medical services on an "as is" basis. Clearly, under such an agreement, physicians and hospitals would be constrained only by market forces. Second, some patients might opt for a contract that protects them against willful harm or gross negligence.

[52] *Ibid.*: 2–4.

[53] *Ibid.*: 4.

[54] *Ibid.*: 6–9.

[55] A. Wencl and M. Brizzolara, "Survey of the States: Medical Negligence," *Trial* 32 (1996): 20–26.

[56] Richard A. Epstein, "Medical Malpractice: Its Cause and Cure," in *The Economics of Medical Malpractice*, Simon Rottenberg, Ed. (Washington, D.C.: American Enterprise Institute, 1978): 255.

This libertarian view argues that if a physician or hospital provides for unsafe medical services, people will seek out safer competitors, buy from them, and soon the unsafe health care provider will improve or be forced out of business. However, this approach to safety only works when both patient and health service provider have equal knowledge of the risks involved. Clearly, the patient all too often has distinctly inferior knowledge, which prevents him from choosing intelligently.

Danzon effectively summarizes the shortcomings of this approach.

> If patients systematically underestimate risks — and the financial incentives of physicians in the absence of liability discourage full disclosure — then private contracting will result in a lower quality of care and lower levels of compensation than patients would choose if fully informed; this is one reason for placing liability, by law, on physicians. Another reason is that patients cannot monitor the quality of performance, so tort liability is a way of requiring physicians to guarantee that their product conforms to the custom of the profession.[57]

A second alternative would be regulation, a method that, however, may turn out to be counterproductive, since doctors who are threatened by new procedures and new medication would tend to stay with the old and thereby hold back progress.

Rosenberg and Calabresi would establish a fund to pay those who suffer certain agreed-upon catastrophes on the basis of preestablished, inflation-protected schedules. This fund could be paid for from general revenues or by mandating a patient insurance fee.[58]

A third proposal involves a no-fault plan. Such a plan would rely on a negligence-based malpractice liability system of provider liability for medical injuries without regard to fault. Thus, patients could expect to be compensated for any injury arising out of medical care, even if negligence was not involved. The criterion for compensation would not be negligence but medical causation. In a sense, it would be a system of strict provider liability, akin to strict liability of employers for work-related injuries under workers' compensation. (This no-fault system is different from the one in the automobile context, which will be presented later. In no-fault automobile insurance, third-party liability through tort is replaced by mandatory first-party insurance.)

Proponents claim that, by eliminating the issue of negligence, litigation costs could be reduced and compensation made promptly. Also, this system

---

[57] Danzon, *Medical Malpractice*: 210.
[58] Rosenberg and Calabresi, *Law and Medicine*: 22.

would eliminate incentives to practice defensive medicine as long as no-fault insurance premiums are not experience rated. Savings on litigation costs could be applied to compensate victims of normal risks, who are denied compensation under the fault principle. Providing compensation on a no-fault basis might require a quid pro quo for some limitation on damage awards. Litigation would not be eliminated as long as there were compensable and noncompensable cases.

Danzon fears that the cost of a comprehensive no-fault system could be staggering. The number of potentially compensable events could be between 75 and 150 times the number of injuries currently compensated through tort.[59] Proponents hope to compensate for these increased costs by savings from reduced litigation per case; scheduled awards in place of unlimited, individualized tort awards; and offset of collateral benefits. Danzon, however, suggests that litigation savings per case may be negligible and benefits of scheduled awards can be realized without abandoning the negligence-based liability rule. Thus, she concludes that a no-fault compensation system "would simply add a costly compensation system that would largely duplicate the private and public insurance mechanisms already in place.[60]

A similarly negative conclusion about the merits of medical no-fault insurance is reached by Wencl and Strickland.[61] They review the performance of the two states that have limited no-fault medical practice insurance, i.e., Florida and Virginia. Their plans are narrowly tailored and apply only to newborns who suffer neurological damage caused by medical treatment during delivery.[62] It was found that "the no-fault systems have not performed as expected," having failed "to incorporate the positive attributes the current civil justice system provides."[63]

A fourth proposal involves experience rating, that is, relating doctors' insurance rates automatically to prior experience of malpractice claims taking into consideration medical specialty and geographic location. Danzon reports that the "distribution of claims against physicians within a given specialty is highly skewed, with a small number of physicians accounting for a larger number of claims than would be expected if the probability of a

---

[59] Danzon, *Medical Malpractice*: 216.

[60] *Ibid.*: 219.

[61] A. Wencl and D. Strickland "No-fault Medical Malpractice: No Gain for the Injured," *Trial* 33 (1997): 18–23.

[62] Florida. Stat. Ann. §766.301–316 (West 1996); Virginia Code Ann. §38.2 — 5000–5021 (Michie 1994; Supp. 1996).

[63] Wencl and Strickland, "No-fault Medical Malpractice": 20.

claim were constant and the judicial process entirely random."[64] However, she also concludes that "imposing more experience-rating or co-payment would entail real social costs in uninsured risks to physicians and possibly defensive responses, like a refusal to take high-risk patients."[65]

Shifting liability from physicians to hospitals is a fifth proposal. Doctors would be immune from liability for negligent injuries caused by them in a hospital, and the hospital would be required to assume the liability vicariously.[66] While there might be some economies of scale of having a hospital assume responsibility for malpractice of physicians on its premises, the deterrence effect wuld be diffused and, most likely, significantly reduced. Moreover, this proposal would place heavy financial burdens on hospitals, many of which are small and financially insecure. If hospitals were to institute experience rating of physicians and use probation and termination as penalties, heavy transaction costs would be incurred.

Finally, holding physicians liable only for willful negligence has been proposed. Penalizing physicians not when their negligence was inadvertent might cause them to choose inefficiently low levels of advertence.[67]

EFFECTS OF LIABILITY STANDARDS

Empirical evidence will be offered to show how a universal shift from a negligence rule with contributory negligence to a stricter negligence or strict liability standard (in the form of workers' compensation) has affected levels of accident risk in the United States. A second empirical study is offered to test whether the behavior of juries changes as liability standards change and, if so, whether the price of negligence changes also.

EFFECT ESTIMATION OF LIABILITY STANDARDS
ON INDUSTRIAL ACCIDENTS

It must be remembered that at the beginnig of the twentieth century negligence was the basis by which all states determined industrial accident costs. Under this system, the employer had an easy time invoking such defenses as the negligence of fellow servants, the assumption of risk by employees, and contributory negligence by injured workers. For example,

---

[64] Danzon, *Medical Malpractice*: 64
[65] *Ibid.*
[66] American Law Institute, *Study of Enterprise Liability for Personal Injury,* Vol. 2 (1990): 103.
[67] Mark F. Grady, "Why Are People Negligent? Technology, Nondurable Precautions, and the Medical Malpractice Explosion," *Northwestern University Law Review* 82 (1988): 333.

under the fellow-servant rule, an employer was not liable for the negligent acts of coworkers to each other unless a coworker was acting as the employer's representative.

Early in the twentieth century, states began to pass employer's liability laws, which greatly modified or altogether abolished the three employer's defenses just mentioned. As employer's liability laws were enacted, a further set of accident laws was considered in various states. Thus, in 1911, the first state introduced a system of strict liability — workers' compensation — and, by 1949, all states had switched to this standard.

An opinion written by Justice Cardozo in 1925 significantly broadened the meaning of accident for workers' compensation purposes. The opinion also helped to assure its general acceptance. in *Matter of Connelly* v. *Hunt Funiture Co.*,[68] claimant's son, Harry Connelly, was employed by an undertaker as an embalmer's helper. In the line of his duty, he handled a corpse, which was full of gangrenous matter. Some of this matter entered a little cut in his hand and later spread to his neck when he scratched a pimple with the infected finger. General blood poisoning set in and caused his death. His dependent mother obtained an award for death benefits.

Writing for the Court of Appeals of New York, Justice Cardozo stated,

> "Injury" and "personal injury" mean only accidental injuries arising out of and in the course of employment and such disease or infection as may naturally and unavoidably result therefrom" [Workmen's Compensation Law (Cons. Laws, ch. 67, §2, subd. 7)]. A trifling scratch was turned into a deadly wound by contact with a poisonous substance. We think the injection of the poisoin was itself an accidental injury within the meaning of the statute. More than this, the contact had itself occasion in the performance of the servant's duties. There was thus not merely an accident, but one due to the employment.

Fishback and Kantor found that even in fatal accidents 43% of the victims' families did not receive any payments under the negligence liability system.[69] The mean levels of compensation for all families of fatal accident victims ranged from about 38% of a year's income to 112%. Once, however, workers' compensation was in force, the average compensation went up to two to four times annual income, depending on the state. At the same time, increases in employer-mandated benefits often resulted in major wage declines to compensate employers' cost increase.

Specificially, they found that in over 20 states between 1907 and 1923, in the nonunionized lumber industry, annual earnings were reduced

---

[68] *Matter of Connelly* v. *Hunt Furniture Co.*, 240 N.Y. 83, 147 N.E. 366 (1925).

[69] P. V. Fishback and S. E. Kantor, "Did Workers Pay for the Passage of Workers' Compensation Law?," *NBER Working Paper No. 4947* (December 1994).

roughly by $1 for each dollar increase in expected accident benefits due to workers' compensation. In the nonunionized coal industry, the earnings' decline was $2 to $3 for every dollar increase from workers' compensation. For unionized workers the decline was smaller.

Under the workers' compensation system, which employs a strict liability standard, an employer must pay employees or their heirs a predetermined compensation, regardless of what caused the accident, as long as it was work related. Under the earlier standard, 6% to 30% of all industrial accidents were compensated, though court decisions could take up to 5 years and were highly uncertain. Under workers' compensation all accidents are compensated, though substantially below the employee's full accident cost. Litigation is sharply reduced. Only whether injury is work related and how serious it is can be contested. Moreover, employees covered by workers' compensation cannot sue an employer for negligence.

The political process has made workers' compensation laws increasingly generous. They have gone from providing injured workers with about half their lost earnings to an 83% recovery of last after-tax earnings.[70] But the obvious side effect has been to make the system increasingly costly, with compensation payments between 1980 and 1990 rising by 181%.[71] An analysis by Viscusi coincludes that benefit levels offer about an optimal level of insurance, from the worker's perspective. From a social point of view, however, the relatively generous benefits may be suboptimal once moral hazard problems are considered.

The question now arises whether employers modified work conditions when the switch to stricter tort standards increased their risk. Specifically, I would like to estimate the effect of this switch of tort standards on the level of accident risk. In a study by Chelius, the level of accident risk is approximated by the ratio of the machinery death rate for a state to the machinery death rate for the United States in a given year[72] (*Machinery death rate* is defined as the number of deaths caused by non-motor-vehicle machinery accidents per number of employees.)

In order to account for changes in factors such as per capita exposure to machinery, the business cycle, and the status of medical care, risk was measured as a ratio of the experience of a particular state for a particular year to the average experience in that year for the United States.

[70] W. K. Viscusi, "Product and Occupational Liability," *Journal of Economic Perspectives* 5 (Summer 1991): 81.

[71] *Ibid.*: 82.

[72] J. R. Chelius, "Liability for Industrial Accidents: A Comparison of Negligence and Strict Liability Systems," *Journal of Legal Studies* 5 (June 1976): 293–302.

Since safety regulations other than tort standards can also affect the risk level in work places, a dummy variable testifying to the presence or absence of such state regulatory efforts was introduced.

Chelius' model is as follows:

$$D_{ij}/D_{USj} = \alpha_0 + \alpha_1 \, (EL) + \alpha_2(WC) + \alpha_3(\text{Controls}) + \mu \qquad (7.1)$$

where

D_{ij}/D_{USj} = the ratio of the machinery death rate in state i in year j to the machinery death rate for the United States in year j

EL = a dummy variable representing the presence of an employer's liability law lagged 1 year

WC = a dummy variable representing the presence of a workers' compensation law lagged 1 year

Controls = a dummy vairable representing the presence of a regulatory system using safety standards lagged 1 year

μ = error term

The right-hand variables were lagged 1 year because laws went into effect during different times of the year and changes were not likely to be instantaneous. In using dummy variables for employer's liability and workers' compensation, the coefficients α_1 and α_2 are interpreted as the imapct of the laws on the death rate compared to the impact of the common law. Similarly, the coefficient α_3 measures the imapct of safety standard regulation compared to the absence of such regulation.

An ordinary least-squares analysis produced the results that are reproduced in Table 7—1. Specifically, it was found that although from 1900 to 1940 both employer's liability and workers' compensation laws were associated with significantly lower death rates, safety-control regulation was not. The larger value of the *WC* coefficient (1.4) in comparison with the *EL* coefficient (0.6) indicates that the strict liability system (workers' compensation) had a greater imapct on the relative death rate than did the employer's liability system.

There was the possibility that from 1900 to 1940 the 26 sample states had coincidentally developed a safer technology than was used by the average state. Should this be the case, the safety benefits of these changes would be inappropriately assigned to changes in liability systems. This possibility was investigated by alternatively restricting the sample to 1900–1930, 1900–1925, and 1900–1920 (Table 7—1, Eqs. II, III, and IV). Restricting the sample in this manner allows less time for technological change compared to the full period of 1900–1940. The results using each of the

TABLE 7 — 1

Impact of Liability Changes on Death Rates (D_y/D_{USj}) as Measured by
Coefficients on Employer's Liability (EL) and Workers' Compensation (WC)

	Coefficients and t values associated with the independent variables		
	EL	WC	Controls
I	−0.6*	−1.4*	+0.6
	(−4.0)	(−14.0)	(1.7)
	$R^2 = 0.29$, $F = 12.9*$, $n = 907$		
	Estimated using available data 1900–1940		
II	−0.8*	−1.4*	+0.6
	(−3.8)	(−10.8)	(1.3)
	$R^2 = 0.53$, $F = 8.3*$, $n = 621$		
	Estimated using available data 1900–1930		
III	−0.8*	−1.4*	+0.7
	(−3.5)	(−8.8)	(1.3)
	$R^2 = 0.51$, $F = 5.9*$, $n = 491$		
	Estimated using available data 1900–1925		
IV	−1.0*	−1.5*	+0.7
	(−3.0)	(−6.4)	(1.0)
	$R^2 = 0.50$, $F = 9.0*$, $n = 361$		
	Estimated using available data 1900–1920		

Source: J. R. Chelius, "Liability for Industrial Accidents: A Comparison of Negligence and Strict Liability Systems," *Journal of Legal Studies* 5 (June 1976): 305.

* Significant at the 1% level. All equations were estimated using dummy variables for each state except Connecticut as dictated by the covariance analysis. The coefficients for these dummy variables and the constant term are not presented.

restricted samples confirm the results of the full sample — employer's liability and workers' compensation were associated with lower death rates and safety-standard regulation had no imapct.

An analysis focusing more sharply on the changeover from a negligence to a strict liability system was undertaken. For this purpose, the average machinery death rate for the 5-year period before and the 5-year period after the change to workers' compensation was analyzed using a dummy variable to represent the difference in liability arrangements. The same was done for a 3-year period. In both cases, death rates were found to be significantly lower under a strict liability standard.

EFFECT ESTIMATION OF LIABILITY STANDARDS
ON JURY VERDICTS

In November 1975, California changed from one liability standard to another, specifically, from a negligence rule with contributory negligence to one of comparative negligence. As discussed in the previous chapter, this change came about as a result of the California Supreme Court's opinion in *Li* v. *Yellow Cab Company*.[73]

Using information from 582 civil cases involving rear-end automobile accidents in California from 1974 to 1976, Wittman used an econometric technique (logit analysis) to estimate jury behavior changes, if any, consistent with the change in liability standards.[74] Wittman found that, in a contributory negligence system, the more culpable the plaintiff the greater the probability of a defendant verdict. At the same time, he learned that, in a comparative negligence system, the plaintiff's culpability has no effect on the probability of a verdict in favor of the defendant. Specifically, the effect of plaintiff culpability under comparative negligence is only .015 as large as the effect of plaintiff culpability under contributory negligence. Yet, under comparative negligence, the greater the relative culpability of the defendant, the larger the award given to the plaintiff.

SOME ECONOMIC CONSIDERATIONS OF PRODUCT LIABILITY

The impression is widespread that we are witnessing an explosion in liability lawsuits. Most commonly cited in support is a 758% increase in product liability cases between the mid-1970s and mid-1980s.[75] However, this figure relates to filings in federal courts, where only a tiny percentage of liability cases are litigated. Liability filings in state courts reveal only a 10% increase between 1978 and 1984.[76] As a matter of fact, the number of personal injury, real estate, and contract suits in 21 states has declined from about 1,250,000 in 1981 to less than 1,200,000 in 1984.

While much publicity is given to large awards, creating the impression thay they are common, the facts are different. In a nation of 240 million

[73] *Li* v. *Yellow Cab Company*, 13 Cal. 3d 804 (1975).

[74] Donald Wittman, "The Price of Negligence Under the Differing Liability Rules," *Journal of Law and Economics* 29 (April 1986): 151–164.

[75] This figure is reported in *Business Week* (April 21, 1986): 24 as part of a study carried out by the U.S. Department of Justice's Tort Policy Working Group, chaired by Assistant Attorney General Richard K. Willard.

[76] National Center for State Courts (1986).

people, there have been, for instance, only 1,642 awards of $1 million or more in the last 14 years.[77] However, such awards have been on the increase. According to a RAND Corporation study San Francisco, California, and Cook County, Illinois, these changes are complex. For example, in San Francisco during the 1960s, only five cases had a value of $1 million (in 1979 dollars).[78] This was 0.3% of the cases that granted an award to plaintiffs. However, the awards amounted to 8% of all money awarded to plaintiffs. During the 1970s, 26 cases (2.3% of all cases in which plaintiffs received an award) produced awards exceeding $1 million, accounting for 30% of all money awarded in the first half of the decade and nearly half of all money awarded in the second half of the 1970s. During 1980 to 1985, these trends appeared to continue: Although million-dollar awards occurred in less than 4% of all cases won by plaintiffs during this period, they accounted for roughly two-thirds of all money awarded to plaintiffs.

Further research suggests two different trends in the size of verdicts awarded by juries.[79] For most lawsuits tried during the 1960s and 1970s, verdicts did not change much. After adjusting for inflation, the median jury award remained almost constant in both Cook County, Illinois, and San Francisco, California — less than $20,000 during both decades. In contrast to this stability for most suits, large jury awards more than doubled during the 1970s. The average jury award and the total amount of money awarded by juries also doubled in the 1970s, but these increased only because large awards increased in size. These differences arose in part because juries made bigger awards against "deep pocket" defendants — businesses, professionals, and government agencies — in product liability lawsuits. Government or business defendants were assessed, on average, 30% to 50% more than individual defendants when plaintiffs had similar injuries and brought the same type of lawsuit. If plaintiffs were seriously injured, businesses paid even more ($2\frac{1}{2}$ times as much as individual defendants did in similar cases). As a result, insurance companies and/or self-insured companies that are frequently involved in litigation have incurred great cost increases. They have to pay jury awards, and the total (and average) of these awards has increased.

The number and size of punitive damage awards also increased substantially.[80] In Cook County during the 1980s, for example, the number of

[77] A study by Jury Verdict Research Inc., quoted in *Business Week* (April 21, 1986): 25.

[78] Mark A. Peterson, *A Summary of Research Results: Trends and Patterns in Civil Jury Verdicts*, P-7222 (Santa Monica, Calif.: RAND Corporation, March 1986): 3.

[79] *Ibid.*: 2–3.

[80] *Ibid.*: 5.

punitive damage awards doubled, and the total amount of money awarded increased by 700%.

Although punitive damage awards were volatile, the typical award remained small throughout most of the period, and the total number of such awards in both jurisdictions was less than 200. Most punitive damage awards were made in cases involving intentional torts or business disputes. There were only eight awards in product liability suits in both jurisdictions during the entire 25-year period.

The increase in awards and in their size has led to a rapid rise in insurance costs. Much of the escalation in premium payments has been attributed to an increasingly broad application of strict liability standards. There may indeed be justification for this development, as suggested by *Morisett* v. *United States*, where the Supreme Court stated,

> The industrial revolution multiplies the number of workmen exposed to injury from increasingly powerful and complex mechanisms, driven by freshly discovered sources of energy, requiring higher precautions by employers. Traffic of velocities, volumes and varieties unheard of, came to subject to wayfarer to intolerable casualty risks if owners and drivers were not to observe new cares and uniformities of conduct. Congestion of cities and crowding of quarters called for health and welfare regulations undreamed of in simpler times. Wide distributions of goods became an instrument of wide distribution of harm when those who dispersed food, drink, drugs, and even securities, did not comply with reasonable standards of quality, integrity, disclosure and care.[81]

Another problem relates to courts holding manufacturers liable for the full life of their products and for "foreseeable" design defects that might not show up for years. Thus, for example, a tool manufactured 30 years ago and originally equipped with the required safety guard may presently injure a worker, with the manufacturer possibly held liable.

The position of legal scholars on foreseeability is not unanimous. Schwartz, for example, considers holding manufacturers liable under tort rules adopted after their allegedly improper conduct occurred as not necessarily unfair.[82] In his view, since a tort transaction, especially one related to a product with a long life expectancy, may occur long after the defendant has acted, the defendant should expect that governing laws may change before his conduct is examined and that this challenge may use new rules. For Schwartz, it is sufficient that these rules are "somewhat foreseeable," and therefore retroactivity does not unfairly interfere with reliance.

---

[81] 342 U.S. 246 (1952).

[82] Gary T. Schwartz, "New Products, Old Products, Evolving Law, Retroactive Law," *New York University Law Review* 58 (October 1983): 796–852.

Although a strict liability standard is designed to protect potential victims in general and consumers in particular, we must worry about the standard's side effects. In the presence of a strict product-liability rule, at least four major aggregate effects can result: distorted resource allocation, enhanced inflationary pressures, reduced competition, and slowed innovation.

How clear are the signals that product liability litigation give to the users and the producers of potentially unsafe products? A study involving interviews with corporate product safety officials in nine large manufacturing firms that were generally recognized as leaders in the safety field in the early 1980s offered the following conclusion.[83]

> Product liability ... conveys an indistinct signal. The long lags between the design decision and the final judgment on product liability claims (frequently five or more years), the inconsistent behavior of juries, and the rapid change in judicial doctrine in the area, all tend to muffle the signal.... The frequency of suits and the level of awards provide some idea of the costs of failing to design a safe product and hence the level of effort that should be devoted to assuring a safe design. Nevertheless, considerable uncertainty remains about the most appropriate method of assuring safety in product design.

With a view to providing clearer signals to users and producers of potentially defective products and reducing the cost of liability litigation to the economy while safeguarding the interests of injured parties, a number of reform measures have been suggested. One would cap awards for pain and suffering. Jury awards for pain and suffering in certain instances have become extremely large and therefore costly in terms of insurance rates paid by manufacturers. Yet limiting awards to economic damages would discriminate against the poor. A cap of $250,000 (in 1980 dollars) might be a reasonable compromise. In fact a number of states have adopted this cap.

A second step would be to modify "joint and several" liability, which can force the party with very little responsibility to pay the entire award if the parties with major responsibility are not financially able to pay. The rule is based on the reasoning that it is fairer to make the least responsible party pay the full amount than to deprive an injured person of compensation. In practice, this rule encourages plaintiffs to sue everybody in sight who can in any way be dragged into the case, especially those with "deep pockets," such as municipalities and large corporations. Amounts to payment should be related to the degree of responsibility.

---

[83] George Eads and Peter Reuter, *Designing Safer Products: Corporate Responses to Product Liability Law and Regulation* (Santa Monica, Calif: RAND Corporation, 1983): R-3022.

A third step would modify the strict liability rule. For example, only manufacturers "negligent in the design, production, distribution or sale" of a product would be liable, but there would be no liability for "any injury related to an unreasonable or unforeseeable use or alteration of the product." Proper warning would remove liability, as would any defect that could not reasonably have been discovered under existing technology.

As a fourth step, we have proposals to reduce greatly punitive damage awards and altogether bar them against airplane and drug makers for accidents that occur during the use of products approved by the Federal Aviation Administration or the Food and Drug Administration.

A fifth proposal involves either the abolition of contingency fees or reducing their percentage with the increase in the award.

Finally, proposals have been made to encourage injured parties to seek redress outside the courts. This could be done by providing financial incentives for both defendants and plaintiffs to settle out of court.

ECONOMIC ANALYSIS OF ACCIDENT LAW

The laws and institutional arrangements concerning automobile accidents are closely related to those dealing with malpractice and product liability, which similarly aim to protect against the destruction of initial entitlements. This analysis examines the goals of accident laws and evaluates various methods used toward their attainment.

The major goals of accident laws are, by general agreement, justice and accident-cost reduction. Justice through fair compensation of injured parties is an often-mentioned but elusive goal.[84] Posner finds compensation to be both costly and incomplete.[85] Economists can contribute to estimating compensation, but they are also interested in shaping accident law so as to reduce accident costs to efficient levels and in accomplishing this objective efficiently. In this connection, it is useful to define accident costs broadly, in terms of social costs of accidents. Furthermore, note that to protect against the destruction of initial entitlements can involve high administration costs.

Frequency and severity of accidents can be affected by the methods selected for risk distribution. Calabresi has identified three major risk-distribution methods — *risk-spreading, deep-pocket,* and *deterrence* methods.[86]

---

[84] G. Calabresi, *The Costs of Accidents: A Legal and Economic Analysis* (New Haven, Conn.: Yale University Press, 1970): 24.

[85] Richard A. Posner, *Economic Analysis of Law,* 4th ed. (Boston: Little, Brown, 1992): 202.

[86] Calabresi, *Costs of Accidents:* 21–23.

Risk spreading in its most extreme form seeks the broadest possible spreading of losses both over people and over time. Through social insurance schemes, the most universal spreading of risk is possible. The question remains, however, of how funds should be raised to cover all accidents. Social insurance could be paid out of general taxes. An alternative that involves high transaction costs is to tax people on the basis of their tendency to cause accidents, a scheme that would offer some incentive to avoid accidents; the first scheme would not do this. More commonly, risks are distributed through private or voluntary insurance. Most such insurance is a combination of intertemporal and interpersonal spreading, with some adjustment made in the rates for accident-proneness.

A further risk-spreading device is referred to by Calabresi as *enterprise liability*.[87] By placing losses on buyers of products or factors employed in their production, a fairly wide distribution of accident losses occurs. The analysis of these shifts is similar to that of tax shifting and heavily depends on the relative elasticity of the relevant demand and supply functions. Although it is difficult to determine precisely how much of the losses are shifted forward and backward, it is quite clear that those on whom the burden comes to rest are those who are engaged in the activity that produced the loss. A system of enterprise liability can therefore provide deterrence.

The deep-pocket method places losses on those who can afford to pay — the well-to-do. It is therefore an income-redistribution scheme. The method assumes that a dollar taken from a wealthy person causes less pain than one taken from a poor person.

Finally, the deterrence method places losses on activities that engender accidents. This method attempts to decide what the accident costs of activities are likely to be and then lets the market determine the degree to which and the manner in which activities are desired at such costs. The incentives might result in investments that produce a general reduction in the likelihood of accidents.

The deterrence method relies on the market to help make rational decisions. Accident costs are treated as one of the many costs faced by the automobile driver, who would trade off the costs and benefits associated with his driving activities and seek the most advantageous balance. The driver thus faces a conventional problem in welfare economics. Its solution assumes that he knows what is good for him, which, if correct, leads under ideal conditions to an optimal resource allocation. But the presence of monopoly, unemployment, and unequal income distribution, among other factors, will tend to prevent the attainment of Pareto optimum.[88]

---

[87] *Ibid*: 50–54.
[88] For a detailed discussion, see Calabresi, *Costs of Accidents*: 78–85.

Did the deterrence method work? The verdict is not yet in. A simplistic reading of national highway accident numbers can lead to quite reassuring conclusions. Thus, while in 1992 40,300 Americans were killed in highway accidents, comparable fatility numbers for 1972 were 56,278.[89] Schwarts reminds us that a host of other factors are likely to have contributed to the fatality decline.[90] They include federal regulation of vehicle design, state laws requiring safety belt use, increased public law sanctions of drunk driving, and changing public attitudes toward both drunk driving and safety belts. Regardless of the apparent decline in the number of serious automobile accidents, car-related suits have sky-rocketed.

REFORMS

In recent years, two major classes of reforms have been introduced in order to deal with rising insurance rates. One class has sought to modify the existing liability system. Its focus has been on control of noneconomic damages, especially through capping payments for pain and suffering, restricting the doctrine of joint and several liability, and limiting punitive damages. (Note that reducing punitive damages is unlikely to reduce insurance premiums, since few, if any, insurance companies are willing to insure drivers against punitive damages.)

Sweeping reforms have been enacted in Florida, for example, providing a cap of $450,000 on noneconomic damages and a limit on the level of punitive damages. In evaluating reforms, much can be learned from the Canadian provinces of British Columbia, Manitoba, Ontario, Quebec and Saskatchewan, as well as from New Zealand. The Canadian Supreme Court has set a $150,000 limit on pain and suffering awards across Canada, and lawyers' contingency fees are banned in most of the provinces.

The second major class of reforms is based on the application of a strict liability standard. Fault liability is removed from automobile accident law and in its place is substituted a system of first-party insurance. No-fault automobile insurance was first proposed by Keeton and O'Connell in an effort to rein in ever-rising transaction, i.e., attorney, cost.[91] They assumed, or more correctly hoped, that fear of self-inflicted bodily injury and of criminal prosecution can deter careless conduct. No-fault automobile compensation plans, regardless of their nuances, remove fault liability from automobile accident law and substitute in its place a system of first-party

---

[89] Schwartz, "Reality in the Economic Analysis of Tort Law": 393.
[90] Ibid.
[91] Robert E. Keeton and Jeffry O'Connell, Basic Protection for the Traffic Victim: A Blueprint for Reforming Automobile Insurance (Boston: Little, Brown, 1965).

insurance. Every motorist is required to carry basic protection insurance, which entitles him in case of accident to recover his medical expenses plus lost earnings, regardless of the injurer's negligence. In most plans, pain and suffering is not compensated and collateral benefits are deducted. Under most plans, victims may waive basic protection and sue in court, but only if they sustain more than a reasonable amount of damages — for example, $10,000 other than pain and suffering.[92] Basic protection is first-party (accident) rather than third-party (liability) insurance. The automobile driver pays premiums to and collects damages from his own insurer.[93] The injurer and his insurance company are liable only if the victim waives basic protection and sues in court.

As of January 1988, 14 states had no-fault auto insurance. In the other 36 states the traditional tort system governed compensation for auto injuries. Of the 14 states with no-fault systems, 11 had what is called a dollar threshold no-fault system. Under this system, a person injured in an automobile accident is not allowed to seek compensation for general damages from the other driver unless his or her medical costs exceed a specified dollar amount. The states of Michigan, New York, and Florida had verbal threshold no-fault systems in which the law contains an explicit list of injuries for which one is allowed to seek general damages. Injuries in the list tend to be serious, e.g., death, dismemberment, loss of a body part, or fracture.

Jeffrey O'Connell et al. reviewed various no-fault systems and their likely effects.[94] They concluded that costs associated with no-fault systems depend on the level of personal injury, protection benefits, the nature and size of barriers to pursuit of tort claims for pain and suffering, i.e., thresholds, and the litigiousness of the state's population. Compensation tends to closely match economic losses, principally medical costs and wage losses, and is more prompt than under other systems.

---

[92] A $10,000 economic loss as ceiling for unconditional reparation appears reasonable for the late 1960s in view of accident statistics. Thus, in the late 1960s, 99% of all persons injured in automobile accidents incurred losses below $10,000. The remaining 1% incurring $10,000 or more in economic losses accounted for 69% of the aggregate economic losses resulting from automobile accidents. The reason is that the gravest economic losses occur in a few, though very serious, accidents. See W. Blum and H. Kalven, "Ceilings, Costs and Compulsion in Auto Compensation Legislation," in Perspectives on Tort Law, R. L. Rabin, Ed. (Boston: Little, Brown, 1976): 269.

[93] Stephen Carroll et al., *The Costs of Excess Medical Claims for Automobile Personal Injuries* (Santa Monica, Calif.: RAND Corporation, 1995): 8–9.

[94] Jeffrey O'Connell et al., "The Costs of Consumer Choice for Auto Insurance in States Without No-Fault Insurance," *Maryland Law Review* 52 (1993): 1017.

No-fault plans also have major effects on the cost of excess medical claims for automobile personal injuries. Such excessive claims under the traditional tort system amount to 35–42% of all medical bills submitted in support of automobile injury claims.[95] These costs vary depending on whether the state has a verbal or dollar no-fault system. Specifically, dollar no-fault systems have been found to reduce incentives to submit claims for minor or non existent injuries. Yet, they provide strong incentives to build claims on real injuries. Verbal no-fault systems appear to weaken incentives to submit excess medical bills.[96]

In addition to reducing the costs of excessive medical claims, no-fault insurance can also greatly reduce transaction costs, mainly those related to litigation. Savings will vary dependent on the no-fault system's design, i.e., the level of personal injury protection (PIP); on tort claim thresholds for pain and suffering; and whether the state has a verbal or dollar no-fault system. It has been estimated that depending on the system's design, transaction costs can be reduced by between 22 and 83%.[97] For example, providing unlimited personal injury protection benefits for economic losses, together with a ban on all noneconomic losses, has been estimated to result in savings in personal injury compensation costs of about 29%. This saving would translate into about half that percentage savings in total auto premiums covering personal injury and car damage.[98]

To demonstrate potential savings from no-fault insurance, California's Proposition 200, though defeated at the polls in early 1996, will be analyzed. The proposal would have eliminated tort liability for auto accident personal injuries, while establishing first-party, no-fault insurance covering all of an accident victim's economic losses up to policy limits. The minimum limits option would have required motorists to carry $50,000 of personal injury protection coverage, while the standard limits option would have raised coverage to $1 million. Compensation of accident victims would have been limited to the personal injury protection, and no compensation could be sought from another driver. Savings would have come from two sources — no compensation for noneconomic losses and lower claim processing and legal costs due to resulting liability claims. These savings could have been substantial. For example, it was estimated that under the present system about 56% of the compensation paid by auto insurers to accident victims in California was for noneconomic loss, while the transaction costs associ-

[95] Carroll et al., *Costs of Excess Medical Claims*: 3.

[96] *Ibid.*: 24.

[97] Jeffrey O'Connell et. al., "The Comparative Costs of Allowing Consumer Choice for Auto Insurance in all 50 States," *Maryland Law Review* 55 (1996): 162.

[98] *Ibid.*: 163.

ated with claim processing and litigation accounted for about 17% of total insurers' costs.[99] The study estimated

> that the proposed plan with a $50,000 personal injury protection limit would reduce the cost of compensating auto accident victims for personal injuries by about 54 percent.... If the PIP limit were $1 million, the cost reduction would be about 21 percent.... If the premium an insurer charges for a policy varies in proportion to the compensation costs the insurer can expect to incur on behalf of the policyholder, the 54-percent savings on personal injury coverages under the $50,000 (personal injury protection) version of the plan would result in a 29 percent reduction in the average California drivers' auto insurance premiums. Under this assumption, the average California driver's insurance premium would be reduced 11 percent under the $1 million personal insurance protection version of the plan.[100]

Although most observers agree that no-fault automobile insurance should reduce transaction costs as well as overall costs, there is disagreement about how much, if any, of these savings will be passed on to motorists. There exists also disagreement among observers about a potentially negative effect on deterrence of unsafe driving conduct.

Sloan et al., when they compared fault states to no-fault states, found that no-fault plans that function so as to bar 25% of all tort claims have the effect of increasing automobile fatality rates by 18%.[101] On the other hand, four studies carried out between 1985 and 1992 found no increase in the accident or fatality rates in states that had adopted no-fault insurance.[102]

Another negative effect is an unwarranted differential incentive to various groups to reduce the likelihood of accidents. For example, an insurance company might favor relatively low premiums to drivers of large, heavy automobiles, since they tend to sustain less serious losses than drivers of small, vulnerable cars. These comparatively low premiums would reduce the incentive of drivers of heavy cars to avoid accidents while unduly increasing the incentive for drivers of small cars to do so. Avoidance measures taken in light of the incentives given to the two groups are likely to lead to distortion and inefficiency. Nevertheless, if transaction costs can be

[99] Stephen Carroll and Allan Abrahamse "The Effects of A Proposed No-Fault Plan on the Costs of Auto Insurance in California: An Updated Analysis," *Issue Paper* (Santa Monica, Calif.: RAND Institute of Civil Justice, January 1996): 2–3.

[100] *Ibid.*:3.

[101] Frank A. Sloane et al., "Tort Liability Versus Other Approaches for Deterring Careless Driving," *International Review of Law and Economics* 14 (1994): 53–69.

[102] Schwartz, "Reality in the Economic Analysis of Tort Law": 395.

reduced greatly and fear of self-inflicted injury and of criminal prosecution is a major deterrent to unsafe driving, no-fault compensation plans can provide efficient means of protecting against the destruction of initial entitlements.

Finally mention should be made of objections raised by Judge Richard Posner. He argues

> A surprising feature of these laws from an economic standpoint is that they are not at all concerned with creating better incentives for accident avoidance. They do not seek to make the tort system a better deterrent of unsafe conduct but instead seek to increase the coverage of the system and to reduce the cost of insurance. These goals are inconsistent with each other as well as with the goal of reducing the number of accidents.... Why exclude damages for pain and suffering and require deduction of collateral benefits? Apparently not because the authors do not consider pain and suffering to be real losses, or consider collateral benefits to be pure windfalls, for they do not exclude these items in serious accidents. But they needed some way of reducing the average damages award in order to prevent the plan from increasing the cost of insurance.... The strategy of the plan, however, is clear: to increase the number of accident victims who are compensated but to reduce the average compensation. The plan is inimical to proper safety incentives.[103]

Why not offer motorists choices between no-fault plans, which offer costs savings as well as speedier and more certain compensation to victims and traditional tort rights? "Choice of auto insurance" proposed by Abrahamse and Carroll would permit drivers to elect insurance under either the traditional system or a no-fault one. Drivers electing the former retain traditional tort rights and liabilities, while drivers choosing the latter neither recover nor are liable to others for noneconomic losses for minor injuries incurred in auto accidents.[104] The study estimated that in tort states costs of compensating accident victims on behalf of drivers who elect no-fault would drop at least 60% compared to those under the traditional tort system. For those who remain with the tort system under choice, costs would increase, but probably no more than 10%. To the extent that insurance premiums are proportional to insurers' costs, drivers who select a no-fault plan could buy personal injury coverage for about 40% of what they would pay under the tort system. Drivers preferring their full tort rights would incur costs essentially similar to those under the tort system.[105]

---

[103] Posner, *Economic Analysis of Law*: 205.
[104] Allan F. Abrahamse and Stephen J. Carroll, *The Effects of A Choice of Auto Insurance Plan on Insurance Costs* (Santa Monica, Calif.: RAND Corporation, 1995): 1–55.
[105] *Ibid*: 14.

SOVEREIGN IMMUNITY

LEGAL BACKGROUND

From the beginning of judicial history in the United States, there has been great confusion about sovereign immunity. It was a rule that began in England as the personal prerogative of the king. The basic position was that "the king can do no wrong," but even local governments were held not liable for tort. *Russell* v. *Men of Devon* involved an action in tort against an unincorporated county.[106] The court ruled that, since the groups were unincorporated, there was no fund out of which the judgment could be paid, and, moreover, it was more appropriate for an individual to sustain an injury than for the public to suffer an inconvenience. This ruling of an English court was first applied in the United States in *Mower* v. *Leicester.*[107] Although the county was incorporated, could sue, and had corporate funds out of which a judgment could be satisfied, the Massachusetts court used *Russell* as a leading case, and it became the basis for the treatment of governmental tort liability in the United States. *Russell* has been attacked on all three levels of government; on the federal level, the Federal Tort Claims Act of 1946 waived the government's general tort immunity.[108]

On the state level, too, there has been much action. In 1963 the California legislature enacted the first general law dealing with governmental liability.[109] This legislative action followed two important California Supreme Court decisions. In *Muskopf* v. *Corning Hospital District,* the court held that

---

[106] *Russel* v. *Men of Devon,* 100 Eng. Rep. 359 (1788).

[107] *Mower* v. *Leicester,* 9 Mass. 247, 249 (1812).

[108] Under the Federal Tort Claims Act, the federal government is made generally liable for money damages, for injury or loss of property, or for personal injury or death caused by the negligent or wrongful act or omission of any employee of the government while acting within the scope of his office or employment, under circumstances where the United States, if a private person, would be liable to the claimant.

There are three principal exceptions to this general rule of suability. First, the government is absolutely immune from suit for torts occurring while it is engaged in a set of specific tasks, including collecting taxes and fighting wars. Second, the government is granted immunity from a set of causes of action, including any claim arising out of assault, battery, false imprisonment, false arrest, malicious prosecution, abuse of process, libel, slander, misrepresentation, deceit, or interference with contract rights. Third, the United States may escape liability if it can show that the acts or omissions complained of were based on the exercise or performance of or the failure to exercise or perform a discretionary function or duty on the part of a federal agency or an employee of the government, whether or not the discretion involved be abused. Federal Tort Claims Act, 28 U.S.C. 1291, 1346, 1402, 1504, 2110, 2401–2404, 2411–2414, 2671–2680 (1970), as amended by Act of March 16, 1974, Pub. L. 93–253, 2, 88, Stat. 50, 28 U.S.C. 2680 (h) (Supp. IV 1974).

[109] California Tort Claims Act (1963).

the doctrine of sovereign immunity would no longer protect public entities from civil liability for their torts.[110] In *Lipman, v. Brisbane Elementary School District*, the court stated that the doctrine of discretionary immunity might not protect public entities from liability in all situations.[111] Other states that enacted sovereign tort immunity acts in the early 1960s include Illinois,[112] Minnesota,[113] and Oregon.[114]

Sovereign immunity has been based in the past on two classes of distinctions: governmental versus proprietary activities, and discretionary versus ministerial functions. Wherever legislatures have acted, the governmental-proprietary distinction has been discarded, most likely for good reason. There never was a logical reason why, for the same tortious act, for example, a private hospital could be sued but a government hospital could not.

Much of today's argument in favor of sovereign immunity is based on the distinction between discretionary and ministerial functions of government. Discretionary acts have been defined as "those wherein there is no hard and fast rule as to the course of conduct that one must or must not take."[115] Thus, discretionary activities relate to basic policy decisions as well as planning operations, as opposed to operational-level day-to-day decision making, which involves ministerial functions.

The distinction between discretionary and ministerial functions has been elucidated in *Ramos v. County of Madera*.[116] In September 1967, the Madera County schools were closed so that pupils could assist in the grape harvest. The county welfare department, although lacking the authority to so act, announced that Aid for Families with Dependent Children (AFDC) recipients aged 10 years and older must work in the fields or face aid termination. When 19 families refused to send their children to the harvest, their assistance payments were halted immediately. Consequently, the California Supreme Court reversed the finding. The court ruled that "a public entity may be liable in tort ... where it knows or should know that its failure to exercise its duty to reasonably supervise employees will result in coercing others to violate state laws, and where such violation proximately results in an injury of the kind the law was designed to prevent."[117]

[110] *Muskopf* v. *Corning Hospital District*, 359 P.2d 457 (1961).
[111] *Lipman* v. *Brisbane Elementary School District*, 350 P.2d 465 (1961).
[112] Illinois Tort Immunity Act (1965).
[113] Minnesota Tort Claims Act (1963).
[114] Oregon Tort Claims Act (1967).
[115] *Elder* v. *Anderson*, 205 Cal. App. 2d 326, 331.
[116] *Ramos* v. *County of Madera*, 4 Cal. 3d 685, 94 Cal. Rptr. 421, 484 P.2d 93.
[117] *Ibid.*: 695–696.

Moreover, the court held that governmental immunity did not protect defendants, since immunity is only for decisions of a policy-planning nature, not for the operational level of day-to-day decision making. Since welfare-eligibility standards are determined at state and federal levels, the court decided that the defendants' actions were not discretionary in the statutory sense, even though welfare employees often exercise judgment in determining whether individual recipients fulfill aid eligibility requirements. The court, realizing that almost all actions involve some element of discretion, rejected any rule of law based on such a semantic distinction and opted for a rule considering whether policy reasons justified immunity. Local welfare departments, for example, are not protected by governmental immunity when they merely enforce and administer mandatory eligibility standards established at state and federal levels. They do not perform the policymaking function necessary for governmental immunity, and their actions leave no room for discretion.

A similar position was reached by the Court in *Berkovitz by Berkovitz* v. *United States.*[118] The case involved a 2-month-old infant who had been given Orimune, an oral polio vaccine, and who promptly developed a severe case of polio. The Court agreed with a lower court that neither the licensing of Orimune nor the release of a specific lot of the vaccine to the public was a discretionary function. Thus, the government was not immunized.

The opposite position was held by the Court in *United States* v. *Gaubert*[119] by allowing the discretionary exception function to apply and so protect the Federal Home Loan Bank from the charge of being negligent in its supervision of the bank it managed. The Bank Board was accused of responsibility for losses in value of Gaubert's stock. The Court offered a set of insightful considerations for the determination of government immunity:

> [I]f a regulation mandates particular conduct, and the employee obeys the direction, the Government will be protected because the action will be deemed in furtherance of the policies which led to the promulgation of the regulation. If the employee violates the mandatory regulation, there will be no shelter from liability because there is no room for choice and the action will be contrary to policy. On the other hand, if a regulation allows the employee discretion, the very existence of the regulation creates a strong presumption that a discretionary act authorized by the regulation involves consideration of the same policies which led to the promulgation of the regulations.

A similar denial of immunity was reached in *Gordon* v. *Lykes Bros. S.S. Co., Inc.*[120] Here the court faced a claim that the government had not established

---

[118] *Berkovitz by Berkovitz* v. *United States*, 486 U.S. 531 (1988).
[119] *United States* v. *Gaubert*, 499 U.S. 315, 324 (1991).
[120] *Gordon* v. *Lykes Bros. S.S. Co., Inc.*, 835 F.2d 96 (5th Cir. 1988).

a safety program to warn servicemen about the dangers of working with asbestos to build ships during World War II. The court held that government's use of asbestos was consistent both with its policy of building ships rapidly and the existing standard design.

A FRAMEWORK OF ANALYSIS

Tort law reallocates the costs of unintentional harm, and we need a framework within which we can weigh the circumstances under which government should be held responsible for a tortious act or should be held immune. Moreover, we would like to inquire into the circumstances under which, if ever, public employees or officials, rather than public entities, should be suable. Clearly, there is a difference as to whether a public official or only a public agency can be sued, although even if an official is immune personally, heavy burdens can be placed on him when his agency is sued. Public agencies, unless they are immune, must fear the possibility of fines, large amounts of time being required in the discovery and trial stages of suits, adverse publicity, and the like. In the face of such a threat, public agencies are likely to be induced to consider seriously whether their action or inaction is likely to result in litigation. Though considering these issues will require resources, these costs under certain circumstances are likely to be small compared to the benefits that can result from more careful decision making.

Under the doctrine of *respondeat superior,* the government agency *and* the employee are responsible. As a practical matter, however, government, with its deeper pocket, will be sued. This arrangement takes advantage of government's unique ability to spread the cost of harm. However, the concept of strict liability inherent in *respondent superior* can result in inefficient solutions to conflicting resource use problems. In the narrow sense, the doctrine gives the public official relatively little incentive to take steps to prevent harm. In order to counteract this tendency, government would have to devote resources to monitor the activities of employees so as to eliminate careless individuals and carelessness. Moreover, it might have to impose sanctions for carelessness. In short, the doctrine of *respondeat superior,* weakens the incentive of public officials to make every effort toward the best possible solution and its implementation.

Yet refusing personal immunity to public officials under most circumstances would be a mistake. Most people, particularly the ablest ones, would tend to refuse public employment, should they be suable. For these reasons, the total absence of sovereign immunity would tend to reduce the caliber of persons who fill top government positions. The chilling effect would be even more significant in relation to the filling of positions on boards where renumeration is insignificant or plays a minor role.

Thus, the costs to government, in the absence of sovereign immunity, of being served by generally less qualified public servants and the costs of legal action must be balanced against the benefits that can be expected from conditions that give decision makers incentives and signals conducive to the best possible decisions.[121]

Spitzer has argued that since tort law "is a system of reallocating the costs of accidents, when one of the parties in an accident is the government, sovereign immunity in tort may preclude any reallocation. Hence, the government and private citizens face different structures of incentives to be careful (or to take risks)."[122] He advances "the preferred rule ... that the government should be suable to tort for monetary damages."[123]

Spitzer, by having picked the example of the locomotive sparks that can burn up a farmer's wheat field, first used by Coase, misses many of the public-goods aspects of government immunity. He fails, for example, to place sufficient emphasis on the social costs that are incurred in the absence of immunity in the case of essential public services for which there are only very costly alternatives. Yet, for many public goods there exist few substitutes. The social costs can be great, as I stated earlier, when key government jobs cannot be filled by the best people because of fear that their agency might be sued and their own reputations tarnished by adverse publicity. In addition, the administrative cost of providing a record for evidence that alternatives have been weighed and discretion exercised, and the expense of defending the agency in court, can become very high. Spitzer finally modifies his Simple Welfare Maximizing model into one of Welfare/Tort Balancing, in which the "bureaucrat wants to do the best that he can for the citizens, ... [but he] dislikes tort judgments against his bureau."[124] In this model, which is perhaps his most realistic one, Spitzer finds that "immunity is the preferable rule."[125]

---

[121] In a more general way, this issue has already been stated in 1969 by the California Appeals Court, when it stated that immunity be given "flexible definition which balances the harm that may be caused by inhibition of the governmental function against the desirability of providing redress for wrong that may have been done." See *Jones* v. *Oxnard School District*, 270 Cal. App. 2d 587 (1969).

[122] M. L. Spitzer, "An Economic Analysis of Sovereign Immunity in Tort," *Southern California Law Review* 50 (March 1977): 515.

[123] *Ibid.*: 548.

[124] *Ibid.*: 538.

[125] *Ibid.*

SOVEREIGN IMMUNITY AND PAROLE DECISIONS

When a felonious act is committed, the shock and outrage expressed is particularly strong if the crime was perpetrated by a parolee. One of the first questions often asked under such circumstances pertains to preventability. If there were no sovereign immunity, would parole boards and parole agencies not make more careful parole decisions and would they not implement them more efficiently? Then, would not fewer crimes be committed by parolees?

Most states provide explicit immunity to all those who deal with parolees. However, some court decisions appear to limit sovereign immunity. Thus, for example, according to California case law, although parole boards are basically immune, many activities of associated agencies may not be immune.[126]

As long as decisions by parole boards involve descretion and are therefore immunized and most other parole decisions are not, the efficiency of parole decisions is increased if all parole and prison functions are vertically integrated. Then boards would look upon themselves, the prison agency, and the parole agency as parts of a single integrated system through which criminals move after conviction by the courts. The board would stand in the middle of this vertically integrated system whose overall costs and benefits it would seek to balance. The more supervisory functions of the parole agency (though not of the board) are classified as ministerial and known to be so, the more efficient the parole decisions that will result. This statement, however, should be tempered by the possibility that as parole agencies enjoy fewer immunities, recruiting of able probation officials will become more difficult.

The board should take into consideration the various cost and benefit elements associated with paroling a convict on the one hand and with keeping him incarcerated on the other. Costs of paroling include losses to victims of crimes committed by parolees, to parole boards and parole agencies resulting from a dissatisfied public, to parole officials as their reputations are beclouded, and to parole agencies in defending themselves in court and possibly being forced to pay damages.

Benefits of paroling include those to parolees whose sentences are shortened, who are able to leave early the often-damaging prison environment,

---

[126] In *Elton* v. *County of Orange*, California Appeals Court held that "while the ... Probation Department performs functions ... which could be classified as involving basic policy decisions (such as recommending a child be, or not be, declared a dependent child), and hence warrants immunity, it does not follow [that] its subsequent ministerial acts in implementing such decisions rise to the same level [53 Cal. App. 3rd 1058, 54 Cal. Rptr. 30 (1970)]."

and who may thus be more successfully rehabilitated, and to prison authorities who will have fewer prisoners to look after and who can effectively use parole as a means to elicit good behavior from prisoners.

The last two issues deserve some elaboration. First, although the capacity of the prison system is more or less fixed and all too often inadequate, the number of prisoners that require incarceration varies over time. Strong evidence exists that parole decisions today are heavily influenced by prison vacancy rates. Thus, one cost of not paroling prisoners is overburdened prisons in the short run and adding prison space in the long run. Second, costs are incurred when the paroling of prisoners is altogether abandoned. Then a potent inducement to good behavior is lost. No doubt, the administration of prisons has been made easier by prisoners' knowledge that their term might be shortened for good behavior, and prison authorities are likely to be reluctant to give up this valuable enticement.

Two extreme, and less efficient, solutions would virtually disappear from the scene — parole boards being influenced by prison occupancy rates, which can lead to premature paroling of prisoners, and boards becoming increasingly reluctant to grant parole for fear of being sued. Since within the proposed framework boards would seek to consider the difference between benefits and costs of incarcerating versus paroling prisoners, they would not necessarily vote against parole.

RULES FOR ASSIGNING LIABILITY FOR LITIGATION COSTS

Once courts have determined that a negative externality has been imposed on a plaintiff and initial entitlements have been destroyed, they can assess compensatory and punitive damages. But should the assessment of damages also include the payment of the plaintiff's litigation costs? And if so, what are the effects of rules that assign liability for litigation costs to the unsuccessful party in tort (and contract) cases?

As one surveys the legal scene, one finds two major rules for allocating litigation costs — mostly attorney fees — in civil cases. The American rule, prominent in all states but the state of Alaska and applicable to most types of litigation at the federal level, directs each party to pay its own fees, regardless of which litigant prevails. Admittedly there are some exceptions. For example, U.S. equity courts reserve the right to assign litigation costs as a punitive measure where a party has willfully disobeyed a court order or has engaged in an oppressive activity. Moreover, litigation fees have been awarded to successful plaintiffs for bringing litigation that promotes the effective implementation of public policy.

The second rule — the Continental rule — is specified in 29 federal statutes and is in force in the state of Alaska and in the United Kingdom, Canada, and other Western countries. It awards to the prevailing litigant some or all of his litigation costs, according to some predetermined schedule.

What are some of the effects of these two rules? These rules have serious incentive effects, which in the literature are often discussed under the heading of fee shifting.[127] One result is the amount and intensity of litigation. The American rule, it has been argued, leads to an excessive initiation of suits, an inordinate amount of litigation relative to settlement, and prolongation of litigation.[128] Since it is also said to encourage nuisance suits and to discourage plaintiffs with strong but small suits without legal aid, the American rule may be inefficient and inequitable.

Yet the American rule has been supported by the courts because it "allegedly" places the parties "on a footing of equality" and because it avoids the problem of adopting a "fixed standard" against which reasonable fees would be measured.[129] Chief Justice Warren has defended the American rule on grounds that "since litigation is at best uncertain one should not be penalized for merely defending or prosecuting a law-suit."[130]

In Britain a losing litigant pays not only his own legal fees, but those of his opponent. This means that no sensible lawyer would pursue an absurd case in the hope that his opponent will settle out of court — as many do in the United States. The risks are too great.

The British system reduces the number of cases that are tried in court. Its approach to costs provides a lawyer who has a reasonable but not cast-iron case with a powerful incentive to settle before trial, which is where the tort system gets really expensive.

A number of proposals have been offered to change the rules so as to assure that they elicit more efficient and equitable responses from aggrieved parties.

The American Law Institute in 1990 proposed that a successful plaintiff be awarded "reasonable attorney fees and other litigation expenses" as part

---

[127] Useful surveys of work in this field can be found in R. D. Cooter and D. L. Rubinfeld, "Economic Analysis of Legal Disputes and their Resolution," *Journal of Economic Literature* 27 (1989): 1067–1097; and D. A. Anderson, Ed., *Dispute Resolution: Bridging the Settlement Gap* (Greenwich, Ct.: JAI Press, 1996).

[128] C. McCormick, "Council Fees and Other Expenses of Litigation as an Element of Damages," *Minnesota Law Review* 15 (May 1931): 619–643, and John Tunney, "Financing the Cost of Enforcing Legal Rights," *Pennsylvania Law Review* 122 (January 1974): 122, 632–635.

[129] *Oelricks v. Spain*, 82 U.S. (15 Wall.) 211, 231 (1972).

[130] *Fleischmann Distilling Corp. v. Maier Brewing Co.*, 383 U.S. 714 (1967).

of compensatory damages.[131] In calculating these fees, the court "should use a contingency-based percentage of the recovery formula as the standard approach," with "possible variations downward" for "especially large or quick recoveries" and variations "upward ..." in cases of appeal and "contested smaller claims" that meet with "strong defense resistance [that leaves the] plaintiff no alternative but to make a seemingly disproportionate investment in legal services."[132]

Jerry J. Phillips points to two major shortcomings of this proposal.[133] He expects that substantial secondary litigation could be expected over the contested upward- and downward-adjustment situations. Even more damaging is a severe conflict-of-interest problem for plaintiff's attorneys in settlement negotiations. With more than 95% of all tort claims settled rather than tried to verdict and judgment, the fact that in the settlement process attorneys are not prohibited from waiving or compromising their attorney fees must be of concern. Phillips points out that "The defense attorney will naturally, and understandably, apply pressure on the plaintiff's attorney to accept a reduced attorney's fee in return for a larger client settlement, or, conversely, the defense may offer the plaintiff's attorney an especially attractive fee settlement, in return for a reduced client settlement." Both of these situations are likely to occur frequently in the settlement process, and they place the plaintiff's attorney in an untenable conflict-of-interest situation.[134]

A further and rather forward-looking reform would add to the American contingency fee system the British system whereby the losing litigant pays all legal cost. Then the losing lawyer would not only have no compensation for his own time, but would have to pay his opponent's costs as well. The presence of American contingency fees put the market to work in dispensing civil justice. Britain's cost and award-setting system prevents the market from being a travesty — one in which lawyers win exorbitantly and lose painlessly.

These conclusions clearly neglect a number of important considerations. For example, the American rule may often be circumvented by juries who include in their awards to plaintiffs some equivalent of litigation costs. Moreover, court costs are often deductible for federal and state income tax purposes, and many defendants fall into distinctly different income categories than do plaintiffs.

---

[131] American Law Institute, *Study of Enterprise Liability*: 349.

[132] *Ibid.*: 331, 333, 350.

[133] Jerry J. Phillips, *Comments on the American Law Institute Study of Enterprise Liability for Personal Injury* (Knoxville, TN: University of Tennessee, 1991): 74–77.

[134] *Ibid.*: 75–76.

TORT REFORMS' ECONOMIC EFFECTS

In this and the preceding chapter a number of measures that can reform the tort system have been discussed. Quite a few have been implemented and their effects, especially on productivity and employment, are of interest. Econometric analysis of these effects is facilitated since different reforms were introduced in different states and they possibly affected industries in varying ways.

An empirical study by Campbell et al. is particularly helpful in appraising recent tort reforms' effects.[135] In order to study effects on 17 industries they identified six types of tort reform as likely to reduce liability and two types as increasing liability. The former class included

1. Caps on contingency fees
2. Relaxation of the collateral source rule, which held the defendant liable even if the plaintiff was compensated by an independent or "collateral" source
3. Caps on damages
4. Reforms that require future damages to be paid periodically, rather than in a lump sum
5. Elimination or limitation of joint and several liability, which held each of many defendants liable for the whole damage, regardless of the defendant's contribution to the damage
6. Limits on punitive damages

Tort reforms that increase liability included

1. Replacing a contributory negligence by comparative negligence standard
2. Shifting to prejudgment interest so that plaintiff receives interest on a loss either from the time of the loss or from the time the plaintiff files suit, rather than from the date of the judgment.

Campbell et al. found that in 13 out of 17 industries they studied decreases in liability were followed by productivity increases. Specifically adopting one additional tort reform measure that reduces liability resulted in productivity increases of 3% in retail trade, 7% in miscellaneous repair services, and 9% in amusement and recreation.[136] At the same time, in 14 of the 17 industries adding a reform measure led to a productivity decline.

---

[135] Thomas Campbell et al., "The Causes and Effects of Liability Reform: Some Empirical Evidence," *NBER Working Paper No. 4989* (1995).

[136] Campbell et al., "Causes and Effects of Liability Reform."

The impact of liability on employment was even more pronounced — in 14 of their 17 industries, as liability decreased employment rose. Thus on average, adding an additional reform measure that reduces tort liability led to job growth of 23% in amusement and recreation and 25% in motion pictures. Conversely, in 14 of the 17 industries, adding a liability-increasing measure resulted in job losses.

CONCLUSION

In summary, microeconomics and, to a lesser extent, econometric methods are employed in examining both rule making and effect evaluation in relation to torts. Medical malpractice suits, which had gotten out of hand in the United States, are examined with the aid of the Learned Hand formula, and with a view of developing acceptable reform. Liability standards are examined in terms of their effects on malpractice and industrial accidents. Another tort area — accident law — has developed strong interest in applying no-fault policies. While they can reduce insurance costs, their effects on the number of accidents is a problem. Finally, sovereign immunity, with its emphasis on discretionary acts, can benefit from economic analysis.

8

CRIMINAL LAW

INTRODUCTION

In the past, the discussion of criminal justice was often the domain of philosophers, civil libertarians, and politicians; law enforcement officers and lawyers, obviously, also played a major role. But economists have also developed an interest in the field, and they have begun to produce analytic work.[1] This work casts new light on important policy issues and may even call into question some of the basic assumptions of criminal law and some current criminal justice practices. At the same time, economic analysis is providing a useful underpinning for basic concepts found in criminal law.

The scope of the field is well described by Greenwood:

> The problems of crime and justice are important public policy issues because they touch so many lives and because they involve such fundamental values — personal safety, property rights, privacy, due process and punishment.[2]

Crime and efforts to combat it can seriously affect our private lives and our public institutions, particularly when victimization is as widespread as it has been in the United States. How do we know the levels of crimes and victimization? Three data sources exist: the Federal Bureau of Investigation's annual *Uniform Crime Reports*, the *National Incident-Based Crime Re-*

---

[1] Some of the more important work will be presented here.

[2] P. W. Greenwood, *Criminal Justice Research at RAND*, P-5886 (Santa Monica, Calif.: RAND Corporation, 1977): 1.

porting System, and the *National Crime Victimization Survey* of the Bureau of Justice Statistics. The last exists only since 1993 and is the most reliable.[3] According to it, in 1993 U.S. residents aged 12 or older experienced a total of 43.6 million crimes, including nearly 11 million violent crimes (25%) and over 32 million property crimes (75%). There were 52 violent victimizations per 1000 persons and 322 property crimes per 1000 households.[4]

For many years, annual levels of crimes have been published in the form of an overall crime index which, using *Uniform Crime Reports* data, presents the number of serious crimes committed in the United States per 100,000 inhabitants. The serious crimes include murder, forcible rape, robbery, aggravated assault, burglary, larceny, and motor vehicle thefts. They do not include white-collar crimes. For the period 1965 to 1997, we find astounding fluctuation. Thus the index rose from less than 2,400 in 1965 to a peak of almost 6,000 in 1980, and after declining for a number of years, reached again about 8,000 in 1991.[5] However, since then it has fallen year by year to below 5,000 in 1997. In some of America's largest cities the decline of crimes had been particularly large. In New York City, for example, crimes have steadily declined from a high of 700,000 in 1988 to a low of 350,000.

Many reasons for the decline in crimes during the last decade have been suggested, including novel policing methods, America's changing age distribution, prosperity, mandatory minimum sentences, and high imprisonment rates.[6] The last two reasons relate directly to the legal environment.

A country's criminal law reflects and also determines governmental roles or objectives in curbing crime. Key issues are whether penalties for those who are caught should be severe, in the hope of deterring others, and how the conflicting aims of punishment and rehabilitation should be resolved.

To facilitate the understanding of criminal law, this chapter begins with a discussion of the premises and tenets on which it is based: what makes an act a crime, defenses that may be employed by those accused of a crime and the imposition of penalties and sanctions. The discussion also touches

[3] Bureau of Justice Statistics, *Criminal Victimization, 1993* (Washington, D.C.: Bureau of Justice Statistics, May 1995).
[4] These data can be compared with those reported by the FBI for 1993, i.e., 14.1 million crimes, including 1.9 million violent crimes (13%) and 12.2 million property crimes (87%).
[5] *Crime in the United States, 1965–1997,* Uniform Crime Reports, U.S. Department of Justice: (1998).
[6] The number of persons in jails or other correctional facilities has skyrocketed. In 1994, the total correctional population amounted to 5.1 million, of which about 1/2 million were in jail, a million in prison, 700,000 on parole and almost 3 million on probation. Between 1993 and 1994 alone, the prison population increased by 10%. Bureau of Justice Statistics, *Correctional Populations in the United States* (Washington, D.C.: Bureau of Justice Statistics, April 1995).)

on the economic rationale of these premises. Next, a comprehensive theoretical framework is presented, within which crime and its motivation and deterrence can be given economic content, and the role and effect of criminal law can be evaluated. Empirical studies of crime deterrence are reviewed and evaluated and some public policy implications deduced. The scholarship is divided into deterrence that raises the cost of criminal behavior and is likely to reduce potential criminals' taste for it and deterrence that reduces the taste for criminal behavior by making legal activities more attractive and rewarding. Regarding the latter, the focus is on improving labor market and educational opportunities.

BASIC LEGAL PREMISES OF CRIMINAL LAW

THE LEGAL DEFINITION OF A CRIME

American criminal law is founded upon certain basic premises concerning what constitutes a crime. Thus, a crime consists of an act, a mental state, concurrence of the act and the mental state, and causation of harm. Crimes are socially responded to by prosecution and punishment. Underlying the criminal law in both its individual and social aspects is an economic rationale, which I shall examine next.

As argued in Chapter I, the destruction of initial entitlements by acts that meet the requirements for a crime is protected by criminal laws. Society, since it places a high premium on human life and on respect for the prevailing property rules, is unwilling to tolerate the negative externalities imposed by persons who commit a crime. Opposing the unleashing of such externalities, society refuses to convert property rules into liability rules and merely to seek compensation for the victim. Instead, for the sake of deterring future externalities of this sort, criminal sanctions are imposed.

Let us next look at the legal requirements necessary for an act to be considered a crime.

Volitional Act

The criminal law imposes liability only when there has been an act of commission or when there has been an act of omission at a time that there is a legal duty to act. An act is defined as a volitional bodily movement. Reflex actions, for example, are not criminal acts regardless of the harm they cause. This definitional requirement of a crime may be said to have an economic rationale. The criminal must have had a choice between action and inaction. Since the criminal law seeks to guide human behavior by the imposition of costs on certain types of activities, it would be inefficient to impose penalties on activities that either do not occur or are not subject to a person's choice calculus. Enforcement bodies have limited resources, which must be efficiently used.

J. G. Murphy has stated that

> an act or omission [is] involuntary (and thus excusing liability) ... if and only if the behavior or the failure in question is explainable by factors which causally prevent the exercise of normal capacities of control or eliminate such capacities entirely. By "causally prevent" here I mean simply the following: that the factors and the incapacity can be related by submission under a scientific law. Thus: Prince Miskin (who, in an epileptic seizure, flails his arms and breaks a valuable vase) acted involuntarily (or really did not act at all, if you prefer) in breaking the vase, because epilepsy is a factor we know to be related (in a lawlike way) to capacities of control. The switchman who fails to pull the lever omitted to do so involuntarily if, for example, he was having a seizure at the time he was supposed to be pulling the lever. The merely negligent man, however, has the normal capacities. He simply did not exercise them.[7]

Some crimes are defined in terms of a duty to act or an omission to act. For example, a father has a legal duty to save his child from drowning in a small stream if he is physically able. Such crimes are always defined in terms of circumstances when the omission sought to be punished must clearly have entered the actor's choice calculus. Any objective observer of an omission to act would perceive that the criminal actor involved must consciously have taken account of the costs and benefits of the omission to act. Thus, the nonaction was volitional and would be responsive to the imposition of criminal penalties.[8]

Criminal State of Mind

To be a crime, an act must not only be volitional but also have a criminal mental element. Most crimes require some sort of subjective fault. Others require only an objective fault and still others are defined in terms of strict liability crimes. For instance, the crime of receiving stolen property may be defined in terms of "knowing that such property is stolen." Thus, the prosecutor must prove that the criminal actor knew in his own mind that

[7] J. G. Murphy, "Involuntary Acts and Criminal Liability," *Ethics* 51 (1971): 332.

[8] For instance, in *Jones* v. *United States*, 308 F.2d 307, the defendant was found guilty of involuntary manslaughter through failure to provide for the ten-month-old illegitimate baby of Shirley Green, who had been placed with the defendant, a family friend. According to medical evidence, the baby had been shockingly neglected and died of malnutrition, although the defendant had ample means to provide food and medical care. The court concluded that the defendant's nonaction was clearly the result of a volitional choice not to act, and therefore liability was upheld.

the particular property was stolen. If the crime is defined as "having reason to know" the property was stolen, the proof required is an objective determination of whether a reasonable person would have known the property was stolen. If the crime is defined as "received stolen property," no mental element other than the volitional action of receiving property is necessary.

Within the criminal law, such gradations of fault for crimes are correlated closely with the severity of the crime and, as we will see, with the types of punishments imposed. In crimes requiring a subjective fault, the prosecutor has to prove that the criminal consciously weighed the costs and benefits of his act in his mental calculus.

Objective-fault crimes are defined as acts that would have entered the choice calculus of an "objective person." For example, a reasonable person would have known that the property received was stolen. The law is less certain that the act entered the actor's choice calculus. However, the act would have entered an average or objective person's choice calculus.

Strict liability crimes do not require a determination of fault. They are crimes that usually carry light penalties and often involve high transaction costs. With such crimes it is not efficient, given the types of lesser penalties that are imposed, to make a judicial inquiry into whether the act entered the criminal's conscious choice calculus. It is assumed to have so entered and the penalty is imposed if the act occurred.[9]

Concurrence of Act and State of Mind

A further requirement of a criminal act is that the act and the mental part concur; the state of mind must actuate the commission or omission. Likewise, if the crime requires certain attendant circumstances, these circumstances must exist at the time of the conduct; thus no criminal act occurs when the bad state follows the physical conduct, for here it is obvious that the subsequent mental state is in no sense legally related to the prior act of commission or omission of the defendant. Thus, it is not criminal battery for A accidentally to strike and injure his enemy B, though A, on realizing what has happened, may rejoice at B's discomfiture.

---

[9] For example, in *State* v. *Arizona Mines Supply Co.*, 107 Ariz. 199 (1971), the county attorney's office charged the Arizona Mines Supply Co. with two counts of "air pollution," a misdemeanor. The information charged that the defendant–respondent did discharge into atmosphere, from a single source of emission, air contaminants in violation of Section IV, Regulation 1, Maricopa County Air Pollution Control Regulations, February 9, 1970, and ARS §36–779 and §36–789.01, May 18, 1970. At trial, the state contended that it did not need to prove intent or knowledge since this offense was more in the nature of *malum prohibitum* or strict liability. The doing of the inhibited act constitutes the crime, and the only fact to be determined in these cases is whether the defendant did the act.

Clearly, the criminal law seeks to impose penalties only in situations where the actor's choice calculus will be affected — when the actor has made a conscious decision to commit the act. The requirement that the act and the mental part concur ensures that the act in question is the result of the actor's conscious choice calculus. This has an economic rationale since penalties on criminal acts will tend to result in an efficient redirection of human behavior.

Causation of Harm

Most crimes require not merely conduct but also a resulting harm — the defendant's conduct must be the proximate cause of the result that turns out to be harmful. Proximate cause, as was discussed in Chapter VI, denotes a legal determination that the specified actor is responsible for the cause that produced the harm complained of, without which the result would not have occurred. Then the imposition of a criminal penalty would serve some social purpose. The criminal requirement of causation thus has a rationale in that the imposition of a penalty on a particular actor serves no purpose if that actor did not cause the harm. Thus, A is not liable for murder if he shoots at B intending to kill but misses. The question of causation is whether there is sufficient causal connection between the defendant's conduct and the result of his conduct so that the imposition of a penalty will affect the actor's choice calculus and thereby tend to redirect his behavior.

The goal of the criminal justice system and its system of penalties is thus the creation of a pattern of costs that will create incentives against criminal acts. Therefore penalties are in order only when an actor's prior conduct has caused the crime in question.

DEFENSES TO CRIME

In line with the legal requirements necessary for an act to be considered a crime (discussed earlier in this chapter), a number of defenses suggest themselves. If successfully applied, they can prevent criminal prosecution. A number of the defenses are designed to show that the act was not volitional. This is an issue of particular importance to economists, who are concerned about a defendant's ability to make a rational choice. Several defenses will be taken up here and particular emphasis will be placed on the defense of insanity, which claims that the actor was unable to control his conduct because of circumstances beyond his control and that the act had no criminal mental element.

Insanity

Fletcher has argued that

> With respect to ordering questions within the concept of culpability, insanity is both the easiest and the most recalcitrant of issues. The criteria of insanity sound unmistakably in the idiom of blameworthiness. The issue is whether the accused is responsible, whether he knew that his act was wrong, whether a mental disease or defect prevented him from conforming his conduct to law.[10]

If it has been established that a person committed a particular criminal act, the demanding question is how to distinguish whether that person can be considered responsible for his action. Should this determination be made by experts or is it a question of common sense? If it is a question for experts, why do they persistently disagree? If it is a matter of common sense, why is the issue so difficult to resolve?

The defining case in the history of the plea of insanity is that of James Hadfield, who, in 1800, shot King George III as he entered the royal box at Drury Lane Theatre. Hadfield pleaded insanity and was acquitted. Some of the crucial issues are well debated in *The Queen* v. *M'Naughton*.[11] In his speech for the defense, Mr. Cockburn stated,

> The defense upon which I shall rely will turn, not upon the denial of the act with which the prisoner is charged, but upon the state of his mind at the time he commited the act. There is no doubt, gentlemen, that according to the law of England, insanity absolves a man from responsibility and from the legal consequences which would otherwise attach to the violation of the law ... the deprivation of that reason, which is man's only light and guide in the intricate and slippery paths of life — will absolve him from his responsibility to the laws of God as well as to those of men. The law, then, takes cognisance of that disease which obscures the intellect and poisons the very sources of thought in the human being — which deprives man of reason, and converts him into the similitude of the lower animal.... The law, therefore, holds that a human being in such a state is exempt from legal responsibility and legal punishment; ...
> ... That which you have to determine is, whether the prisoner at the bar is guilty of the crime of willful murder. Now, by "willful" must be understood, not the mere will that makes a man raise his hand against another; not a blind instinct that leads to the commission of an irrational act, because the brute creation, the beasts of the field, have, in that sense, a will; but by will, with reference to human action, must be understood the necessary moral sense that guides and directs the volition, acting on it through the medium of full reason.

[10] George Fletcher, *Rethinking Criminal Law* (Boston: Little, Brown, 1978): 539.
[11] *The Queen* v. *M'Naughton*, Eng. Rep. 718 (H.L. 1843).

The all-consuming issue, thus, is to determine scientifically the presence or absence of insanity. Perhaps the most pessimistic view was expressed by Lawrence Kolb, a past president of the American Psychiatric Association and the author of a textbook on modern clinical psychology. According to Kolb, "It is beyond the capacity of a psychiatrist to comprehend the defendant's capacity to define the rightness or wrongness of his action taken at the time the act was committed. At best, he has only the recollections of the individual — distorted as we often know they may be — on which to base his judgment."[12] His conclusion was that much of the psychiatric testimony about a defendant's state of mind at the time of the crime is invalid.

The criteria for finding a defendant insane have changed over the years. Under the M'Naughton rule, a defendant is not culpable if he "was labouring under such a defect of reason, from disease of the mind, as not to know the nature and the quality of the act he was doing; or, if he did know it, that he did not know he was doing what was wrong."[13]

In 1954, the Court of Appeals for the District of Columbia adopted the Durham test, which placed great weight on the assumption that insanity can be scientifically determined. This test reduced the question of insanity and nonresponsibility to a determination of whether the act was "the product of a mental disease or defect."[14]

In 1972, in the *United States* v. *Brawner,* the same court of appeals suggested a test that required jurors to assess whether the accused was suffering from a mental disease to the extent that he could not "justly be held responsible."[15] *Brawner* requires the finding of a "mental disease or defect." In line with the Model Penal Code, it requires a finding that the accused "lacks substantial capacity either to appreciate the criminality [wrongfulness] of his conduct or to conform his conduct to the requirements of law."[16] For a time, the Brawner rule was widely adopted by federal courts as well as many state courts.

Until the early 1980s, the plaintiff had to prove that the defendant was sane. However, as a result of the attempt on the life of President Ronald Reagan in the early 1980s, Congress enacted a statue that places the burden of proof on the defendant; if he chooses the defense of insanity, he must prove insanity. Within 3 years after the verdict in the assassination attempt

---

[12] Quoted in R. Jeffrey Smith, "The Criminal Insanity Defense Is Placed on Trial in New York," *Science* 188 (10 March 1978): 1049.

[13] *The Queen* v. *M'Naughton.*

[14] *Durham* v. *U.S.*, 214 F.2d 862 (D.C. Cir. 1954).

[15] *United States* v. *Brawner*, 471 F.2d 969 (D.C. Cir. 1972).

[16] Model Penal Code, Section 4.01.

on President Reagan, 15 states also had shifted the burden of proof onto the defendant.

In the Insanity Defense Reform Act of 1984, Congress provided a statutory formulation of the insanity defense for the first time:

> (a) *Affirmative defense.* It is an affirmative defense to a prosecution under any Federal statute that, at the time of the commission of the acts constituting the offense, the defendant, as a result of a severe mental disease or defect, was unable to appreciate the nature and quality or the wrongfulness of his acts. Mental disease or defect does not otherwise constitute a defense.[17]

Changes in the definition of insanity have continued. For example, in 1985, the California Supreme Court ruled that a person is insane when he is incapable of understanding the nature of the criminal act or is incapable of distinguishing right from wrong in connection with the act.[18]

Courts also have recognized "diminished responsibility." Thus, the California Supreme Court, in *People* v. *Conley,* held that a defendant's capacity for reflection might be so diminished temporarily (as by intoxication) or permanently (as by disease or defect short of insanity) that even if the act of killing were willful, deliberate, and premeditated, it was committed without malice aforethought, the killing therefore being not murder but manslaughter.[19] Thus, in the United States as well as in England,[20] diminished responsibility has been allowed as a defense to a charge of murder — a conviction of manslaughter being substituted.

Duress

In some instances, a criminal confronts a person with a tragic choice. A person's unlawful threat, which causes a defendant reasonably to believe that the only way to avoid imminent death or serious bodily injury is to engage in conduct that violates the literal terms of the criminal law and which causes the defendant to engage in that conduct, allows the defense of duress. An exception is the case where the violation of the criminal law consists of the equally great cost of intentionally killing an innocent third person. Thus, the duress rule — with this one exception — allows a person caught in the predicament of a threat of imminent death or serious bodily harm to choose the lesser evil in order to avoid the greater evil threatened by the other person. This rule, it can be argued, is socially beneficial in

---

[17] Insanity Defense Reform Act of 1984, 18 U.S.C. §17(a).

[18] *People* v. *Jesse Skinner,* Crim. 23783.

[19] *People* v. *Conley,* 64 Cal. 2d 310, 49 Cal. Rptr. 815, 411 P.2d 911 (1966).

[20] Homicide Act 5 & 6 ELIZ. 2, c. 11 §2 (1957).

that it reduces the costs incurred by the threat of intentional death or serious bodily injury, both of which involve extremely high costs. However forbidding such a defense for any lesser violation of the criminal law, one that avoids such high costs increases social benefits. Note, however, that the defense is inapplicable when the actor has only the alternative of intentionally killing an innocent third person. In a formal way, in such a situation the intentional killing of an innocent third person would merely amount to a wealth transfer, a transaction between the defendant and the third person, without any likely net social benefit.

Necessity

The tragic choice may have an impersonal origin. Thus, pressure of natural physical forces sometimes confronts a person in an emergency with a choice of two evils: Either he may violate the literal terms of the criminal law and thus produce a harmful result, or he may comply with these terms and thus produce great harm. For reasons of social policy, if the harm that will result from compliance with the law is greater than that which will result from violation of the law, he is justified in violating it.

United States v. *Kroncke* well summarizes this defense:

> The common thread running through most of these cases in which the defense of necessity was asserted is that there was a reasonable belief on the part of the defendant that it was necessary for him to act to protect his life or health, or the life or health of others, from a direct and immediate peril. None of the cases even suggests that the defense of necessity would be permitted where the actor's purpose is to effect a change in governmental policies which, according to the actor, may in turn result in a future saving of lives.[21]

The rule of necessity has an economic rationale in that it allows the actor to weigh the costs and benefits of a particular action even though it violates the criminal law. He should act in a manner that maximizes social welfare.

Defense of Another Person

This defense is well stated in *People* v. *Williams*, where the court held

> A person is justified in the use of force against another when and to the extent that he reasonably believes that such conduct is necessary to defend himself or another against such other imminent use of unlawful force. However, he is justified in the use of force which is intended or likely to cause death or great bodily harm only if he

---

[21] *United States* v. *Kroncke*, 451 F.2d 697.

reasonably believes that such force is necessary to prevent imminent death or great bodily harm to himself or another, or the commission of a forcible felony.[22]

By encouraging value-enhancing behavior over the aggregate of individuals, total social welfare is increased.

Self-Defense

One who is not the aggressor in an encounter is justified in using a reasonable amount of force against his adversary when he reasonably believes (*a*) that he is in immediate danger of unlawful bodily harm from his adversary and (*b*) that the use of such force is necessary to avoid this danger. Notice that the key emphasis is on the term *reasonable*.

In general, courts hold that it is not reasonable to use deadly force against a nondeadly attack. Thus, the courts' dealings with the term *reasonable* implicitly value the costs and benefits of each response to the threatening attack and give judicial sanction only to those responses that over the aggregate of the parties decrease the net social costs of the resulting harm.

Defense of Property

A person is justified in using reasonable force to protect his property from trespass or theft when he reasonably believes that the property is in immediate danger of such an unlawful interference and that the use of such force is necessary to avoid that danger.

This legal rule creates incentives and sanctions costs that tend to minimize the resulting harm from criminal conduct and encourage the defender of property to use the minimum force necessary to defend his property. It thus minimizes the aggregate of costs over all the parties. Thus, it is not efficient to use deadly force to protect mere property since the value of human life is greater than that of property. Furthermore, it is most efficient for the defender to use the minimum force necessary to achieve his desired result, and the rule encourages the defendant actor to use a minimum force consistent with the judicial determination of whether such force would be reasonable. The determination of reasonableness relates to the costs and benefits of an action.

ECONOMIC ANALYSIS OF CRIMINAL LAW

The model presented in this section provides a rational explanation for criminal activities. It also provides a framework for the examination of

[22] *People* v. *Williams*, 56 Ill. App. 2d 159 (1965).

some early econometric attempts at estimating crime-deterrent effects and for the exploration of police production functions and deterrence.

ECONOMIC MODEL OF A CRIME

There are many sociological and psychological explanations of crime, relating criminal behavior to relative deprivation, deviancy, and socially disorganized environments. For example, Mario Merola, the district attorney of the Bronx (New York City), is reported to have said, "Kids view it as the haves versus the have-nots. They can't cope educationally."[23] He believes that many of the criminals he prosecutes are "monstrous": "They will kill you for nothing.... They're cold and callous. They have no remorse." A view that "Criminals are born and not made" is attributed to Wilson and Herrnstein, although their work is concerned only with street crime.[24] They suggest that crime is in the genes and cannot be changed by conscious social action. Therefore, understanding of street crime should focus on differences among individual people. These, they argue, often reflect biological and genetic differences; moreover, different types of family upbringing also play a role. In short, "bad families produce bad children."[25] Wilson and Herrnstein cite hundreds of scientific research reports. However, the quality of much of this research and its interpretation is strongly and persuasively attacked by Kamin, who, among others, points to their "fallacy of confusing correlation and cause."[26]

The Wilson-Herrnstein stark view of criminals is very different from that of economic determinists. One of them is former U.S. Representative Jack Kemp, who is reported to have said, "Seventy-five to eighty-five percent of the social problems of the country are being caused by the shrinking of the economy ... crime and social problems, to a larger extent than I thought, result from economic problems."[27]

In line with this second view, economists have developed an economic theory of crime. Though admitting that the propensity to commit a crime is possibly rooted in an individual's background and personality, they have offered a complementary explanation of crime and criminals. These econo-

---

[23] Reported by Ken Auletta in "The Underclass," *The New Yorker* (16 November 1981): 162.

[24] Q. Wilson and R. J. Herrnstein, *Crime and Human Nature* (New York: Simon and Schuster, 1985).

[25] *Ibid.*: 215.

[26] L. J. Kamin, "Is Crime in the Genes? The Answer May Depend on Who Chooses What Evidence," *Scientific American* 254 (1986): 26.

[27] Reported by Ken Auletta in "The Underclass," *The New Yorker* (30 November 1981): 148.

mists argue that the decision to engage in crime is rational and does respond to incentives. Accordingly, they claim that there is an economic-choice calculus with regard to criminal activity. Based on work by Becker, a framework has been developed that seeks to explain how rational persons trade off expected returns from legal and illegal activities.[28] Becker's economic-choice framework views crime, with the exception of crimes of passion, as an economic activity with rational participants. They engage in criminal acts if their expected utility exceeds the level of utility they can derive from alternative (legal) activities. They may choose to be criminals, therefore, not because their basic motivation differs from that of other persons, but because their options and the evaluation of their benefits and costs differ. In other words, the close association of violent crime with lower-class urban life is a direct result of the opportunities that are *not available*.[29]

Thus, in the simplest terms, crime can be explained as a matter of rational choice, in which criminals weigh the expected gains against expected cost of potential punishment. The penal code in conjunction with past behavior by the criminal justice system provides a sort of price list for various crimes. We can look at the criminal justice system as designed to influence human behavior by imposing costs on criminal activities, thereby offering the individual an economic incentive to choose not to commit a criminal act, that is, a deterrent incentive.

Within Becker's framework, the number of crimes committed by an individual depends on his probability of conviction, the expected severity of his punishment, and variables reflecting his legal-income-earning potential, environment, and tastes. This can be represented as

$$O_j = O_j(p_j, f_j, u_j) \tag{8.1}$$

where O_j denotes the number of offenses committed by the jth individual in a given period, p_j is the probability of conviction per offense, f_j is his expected punishment per offense, and u_j is a composite variable represent-

---

[28] Gary Becker, "Crime and Punishment: An Economic Approach," *Journal of Political Economy* 78 (1968): 169–217.

[29] The economic model of crime has been severely criticized by T. Gibbons, particularly because of its lack of "regard for the law or conventional norms and that law enforcement does not contain discretionary responses to negotiation and compromise." He therefore concludes, "It seems unlikely, however, that the economic approach [to crime] can make a significant contribution to an understanding of the actual commission of crime." However, he is clearly an exception. T. Gibbons, "The Utility of Economic Analysis of Crime," *International Review of Law and Economics* 2 (1982): 186.

ing all other influences. An increase in either p_j or f_j would reduce the expected utility associated with a criminal offense, so that

$$\frac{dO_j}{dp_j} < 0, \frac{dO_j}{df_j} < 0 \qquad (8.2)$$

That is, increasing the probability of conviction or the severity of punishment increases the incentive not to commit crimes and so influences the jth individual to commit fewer criminal offenses.

This rational-choice framework is based on the assumption that the person deciding whether or not to commit a crime behaves as if he is responding to the relevant economic incentives. The fact that those who commit certain crimes may differ systematically in certain respects from those who do not commit them does not contradict this basic assumption that both the latter and the former respond to economic incentives. However, this assumption would clearly be inappropriate if a person is insane, since the actions of an insane person are by definition not responsive to normal costs and benefits in a socially acceptable manner. This is indeed the rationale for the use of insanity as a defense to a crime.

The total number of offenses in a community is simply the sum of the offenses committed by all individuals, the sum of all the O_j's. Although the variables p_j, f_j, and u_j are different for each individual j because of differences in such factors as intelligence, education, wealth, and family upbringing, Becker hypothesizes that the total number of offenses, O, can be expressed as the function

$$O = O(p, f, u) \qquad (8.3)$$

where p, f, and u represent the average value of these variables for all individuals in the community. It is assumed that, as for each individual, the number of offenses, O, committed in a community is negatively related to p and f.

Becker's innovative model of rational choice can readily be extended to include other variables that affect the costs and benefits of criminal activities relative to alternative legal activities. One law enforcement variable that should perhaps be included in an extension of his rational-choice framework is the probability that a person will be arrested given that he has committed an offense. That is, irrespective of whether he is later convicted, the embarrassment, anxiety, fear, and temporary restriction of activity associated with arrest in itself provide the individual with an incentive not to commit a crime. Furthermore, a person's perception of the costs associated with a criminal offense may well be influenced by the "visibility" of police patrols. Thus, police activities may act as a direct deterrent on crime over and above the effect they exercise via increasing probabilities of arrest, conviction, and imprisonment.

Equation (8.3) could then be rewritten as

$$O = O\,(a,\, p,\, f,\, u) \tag{8.4}$$

where a represents the average probability of being arrested, once a crime has been committed, for all individuals in the community.

The probability of being arrested, a, is affected by what the police do and how well they do it, and therefore is tied to the police production function, which will be discussed later. But it also is influenced by the prevailing legal system. Specifically, it depends to some extent on the kind of preventive steps that the law tolerates. It makes a great difference, for example, whether police can stop and detain, or at least frisk, suspects on the street in case the officer is convinced that the suspect is preparing to commit a crime or whether the police must be able to prove "probable cause." For example, in *Sibron* v. *New York*, an officer found heroin on the suspect's person, but the court held that the stop-and-frisk that yielded the evidence was unconstitutional. The reason was that the officer had insufficient probable cause for the arrest, since he had merely observed the suspect in the presence of some known heroin addicts in the course of an afternoon and evening.[30] *Sibron* clearly reduces the number of arrests and makes the work of the police more difficult.

The probability of being convicted, p, depends very much on the quality of the arrest made by the police as well as the prevailing legal system and the courts. Not all arrests for serious crimes are of equal quality. For this and other reasons, conviction rates vary greatly among cities. Thus, for example, in the late 1970s in New York, 42% of all felony arrests ended in conviction; in Chicago, 26% in Los Angeles, 46% in Baltimore, 44% and in Washington, D.C., 33%.[31]

What are some of the reasons for low conviction rates? Prosecutors are forced to drop many arrests, most often because of insufficient evidence or poor witness support. Another important factor is the police. For example, in the District of Columbia, more than 50% of all convictions that followed a felony arrest were made by about 10% of the department's officers; 31% of all arresting officers did not make a single arrest that ended in conviction.[32]

---

[30] *Sibron* v. *New York*, 392 U.S. 40 (1968).

[31] Brian E. Forst, "Why Many Arrests Fail to Result in Conviction," *Wall Street Journal* (February 16, 1979): 12.

[32] *Ibid.*

The probability of being convicted is also strongly affected by the prevailing legal system. For example, the exclusionary rule makes it more difficult and therefore more costly for police to obtain convictions. This rule bars from criminal trials evidence obtained from seizure or search made in violation of the Fourth Amendment. The exclusionary rule, it is argued, is necessary in order to combat the incentive of the police to violate the defendant's procedural rights in order to win cases. These rights tend to reduce the probability of successful prosecution at any given expenditure level.

Quite a few state courts have expanded defendants' rights under their state's constitution. In particular, New York's highest court in the 1980s frequently interpreted the exclusionary rule in a manner that made legal arrests increasingly difficult. For example, in *People* v. *Benigno Class,* the court suppressed a loaded handgun that an officer on a traffic stop had found when he reached inside Mr. Class' car to move papers that blocked the vehicle identification number.[33] The court held that the officer had violated Mr. Class' right to privacy — even though the number, required by federal regulations, is specifically intended to remain in public view for police inspection.

Another case, *People* v. *Miguel Torres,* had police, acting on a tip that an armed murder suspect was at a Harlem barber shop, approach the suspect with guns drawn as he entered his car.[34] In the car, officers found a bag containing a loaded gun. The Court of Appeals held that the search of Mr. Torres' car and bag — even when it was reasonable to believe that a weapon was present, and when the officer believed they might be in imminent danger — violated Mr. Torres' rights. Finally, in *People* v. *Melvin Johnson,* the Court of Appeals reversed the conviction of a confessed killer.[35] Mr. Johnson, after his arrest on an informant's tip, had admitted the murder of a store owner during a robbery. The court held that the informant did not meet the legal test of reliability to authorize an arrest warrant. Because the warrant was invalid, the resulting confession was judged inadmissible.

The exclusionary rule is almost unique to the United States. Modifications have often been discussed. Perhaps it should be permissible to introduce all evidence in criminal court trials and, after a verdict has been rendered, the policeman who used illegal evidence could be punished. Or, a panel of judges could determine which evidence, if any, is to be allowed to be introduced. Finally, there could be a good-faith exception. For example, when law enforcement personnel have acted mistakenly but in good faith on reasonable grounds, evidence they have seized would not be excluded.

[33] *People* v. *Benigno Class,* 67 N.Y. 2d 431, 494 N.E. 2d 444, 503 N.Y.S. 2d. 313 (1986).
[34] *People* v. *Miguel Torres,* 77 N.Y. 2d 224, 543 N.Y. 2d 61, 544 N.Y.S. 2d 796 (1989).
[35] *People* v. *Melvin Johnson,* 66 N.Y. 2d 398, 488 N.E. 2d 439, 497 N.Y.S. 2d 618 (1985).

Also, the court's 1985 ruling, which restricts the permissible role of police informants, makes it more difficult to obtain admissible evidence.[36]

Finally, the court itself also influences conviction rates. Thus, for example, 6% of all arrests made in Washington, D.C., in the mid-1970s did not end in a conviction because the defendant fled after the judge set bail conditions that made it feasible to abscond.[37]

Finally, legal income-earning potential, environment, and tastes can also be affected in a variety of ways. In this connection, steps can be taken that aim at increasing the benefits associated with engaging in legal activities rather than merely imposing greater costs on illegal alternatives. For example, the government may be able to lower the level of criminal activity by improving the education of individuals and thereby their income-earning possibilities from legal employment. Alternatively, reducing the level of unemployment will raise a person's chance of gaining legal employment and so increase his expected returns from legal, compared with illegal, alternatives.

In this spirit, Lord Lane, Lord Chief Justice of England and Wales, in his 1983 Darwin Lecture at Cambridge University, suggested that

> Punishment is a sanction that *ex hypothesi* has been unsuccessful. Remedy must be sought much farther back in the history of the delinquent.... The roots of good social behavior, the roots of stability and respect for others are to be found in the home, in a stable family life. A good and stable home provides rules for the child to observe. And family life tends to be more stable when education and employment levels are high.[38]

In line with Becker's rational crime model, two deterrence strategies suggest themselves — reducing the taste for criminal behavior by (1) making criminal acts increasingly costly to law breakers and (2) improving rewards for engaging in legal activities. These two approaches will be explored in sequence.

CRIME DETERRENCE BY RAISING COSTS TO CRIMINALS

In this section, first a model of the criminal justice system is presented, followed by a discussion of police production functions. Next crime deterrence will be examined with emphasis on whether imprisonment pays in the light of econometric studies, in terms of severity versus certainty of

---

[36] *Maine* v. *Moulton*, U.S. 84–797 (1985).

[37] Forst, "Why Many Arrest Fail": 12.

[38] Reprinted in the *Times of London* (November 10, 1983): 12.

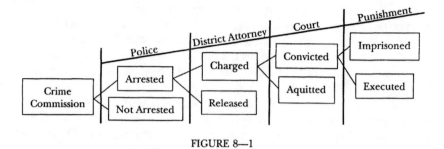

FIGURE 8—1

punishment, as well as capital punishment. Finally, the effect of hand gun control on homicides will be analyzed.

THE CRIMINAL JUSTICE SYSTEM

In order to understand efforts to deter crime, it is necessary to look at the criminal justice system and its main components. The system is best understood by sketching out the sequence of events that can follow the commission of a major crime, shown in Figure 8—1 as a series of branching points. The commission of a major crime can lead to the criminal being either arrested by the police or set free. Once arrested, he can be either charged by the district or city attorney or released. If charged, he can be either convicted in court or acquitted and, if convicted, he can be imprisoned or, in the case of murder, executed.

After a crime has been committed, sequential branching points occur that, if the end of the chain is reached, lead to the imprisonment or execution of the criminal. Thus, the criminal justice system includes such actors as police, district attorney, public defender, court, prison, and even parole agencies.

Phillips has built a simplified econometric model of the criminal justice system.[39] He specified the system as a three-input/two-output technology. Employees in police departments, in corrections, and in such other services as the judiciary and prosecution are the inputs, while imprisonments and average length of time served are the outputs. The system's outputs are perceived as limiting the impairment and losses incurred from crime, as determined by a supply-of-offenses function. As expected, Phillip's study

---

[39] L. Phillips, "The Criminal Justice System: Its Technology and Inefficiencies," *Journal of Legal Studies* 10 (1981): 363–380.

shows that police and correction personnel are complementary inputs in the system. They have highly inelastic factor demands; judges and prosecutors are found to be substitutes, with about unitary elastic demands.

A number of findings with policy implications are indicated — lack of coordination between the different branches of the criminal justice system produces inefficient resource allocation. Also, the larger states in the study ended up having a ratio of imprisonments to time incarcerated that was too high and therefore costly. There were decreasing returns to scale. Twenty-four states were found to produce an efficient output mix, with an average of 2.33 years served in prison for the FBI's seven index felonies. The marginal system cost of incarcerating a prisoner for an additional year was $29,500, which would reduce the number of reported offenses by 92. Finally, the marginal system cost of an additional incarceration was $141,000, a step that would reduce reported offenses by 436, or 187 per year in prison.

Within this model of the criminal justice system, it is possible to analyze federal and state anticrime legislation. For example, since 1980 the United States Congress enacted major anticrime bills about every 2 years, with the 1994 Omnibus Federal Crime Bill addressing both enforcement and prevention. (It, for example, provided $20 billion for additional police and prisons.)

The criminal justice system has produced some unusual results. For example, in 1991, 47% of criminals with one violent felony conviction offense, 31% with two offenses, and 23% with three offenses were not even given prison sentences.[40] According to Petersilia, in 1991, "there were approximately 375,500 offenders convicted of violent crime in prison, and approximately 590,000 outside in the community on probation and parole. Overall, ... nearly three times as many violent offenders (1.02 million) were residing in the community as were incarcerated in prison."[41]

POLICE PRODUCTION FUNCTIONS

The finding that law enforcement variables may exert a deterrent effect on crime would confirm one of the major tenets upon which our criminal law system has always been based. Should empirical research succeed in contributing to our knowledge of the magnitude of this effect, this knowl-

---

[40] John G. Di Iulio, Jr., "Help Wanted: Economists, Crime and Public Policy," *Journal of Economic Perspectives* 10 (Winter 1996): 9.

[41] Joan R. Petersilia, "A Crime Control Rationale for Reinvesting in Community Corrections," unpublished manuscript (University of California — Irvine, April 1995): 19.

edge can assist in the allocation of law enforcement resources so as to maximize society's welfare. Increasing the probability of arresting offenders requires that society incur additional costs. By devoting more resources to police activities aimed at arresting offenders society must forgo the use of those resources in alternative uses, such as education, health services, or personal consumption. Similarly, increasing the average length of prison sentences imposes on society additional costs associated with building and operating penal institutions. In order to compare these costs of increased law enforcement with the benefits resulting from reduced crime rates, we need to know (a) the extent to which increases in specific law enforcement variables will reduce crime rates — that is, the magnitude of the deterrent effect — and (b) the extent to which devoting additional resources to police activities will increase the probability of arrest — that is, the magnitude of the effect that extra police inputs have on the probability that criminals will be apprehended.

Having knowledge of these variables, we can maximize the net benefits to society of allocating resources to various policing activities up to the point where the last dollar of resources devoted to each activity yields a benefit to society (in the form of reduced losses from crime) of $1.

Next I will review some of the empirical research related to measuring this second magnitude, the impact of extra police resources on the probability of arrest. This research involves the estimation of police production functions, where the probability of arrest is regarded as a measure of the output of police activities.

A production function measures the specific service outputs that result from different sets of physical inputs at different scales of operation, under different service conditions, and in the long run, with different states of technology. In more formal terms,

$$O = j(I, S, T) \qquad\qquad (8.5)$$

where O represents output, I represents input factors, S represents service conditions (i.e., the more or less intangible environment within which services are to be rendered), and T represents the state of technology. In the short run, T changes very little, whereas S is largely beyond the control of the relevant police department. Hence, we are primarily interested in measuring the relationship between outputs O and inputs I, holding service conditions S and technology T constant.

But how can police "output" be measured? Several alternative measures of police output have been proposed in the literature. Walzer has used an index composed of the number of police services rendered, such as the number of complaints investigated.[42] Most studies have used arrests as output measures.[43]

However, the probability of arrest suffers from a serious defect as a measure of policy output. It ignores the crime-prevention effect of police activities other than those directed specifically toward the arrest and conviction of criminals. For example, it ignores the crime-deterrent effects of warning potential wrongdoers, guarding people and property, and the general visibility aspect of police patrols. Despite this defect, the probability of arrest or conviction is still the most useful single measure of police output and it best conforms to the rational-choice theoretical framework discussed earlier.

Police production functions have been estimated by a number of economists, including Levitt,[44] Ehrlich,[45] Carr-Hill and Stern,[46] and Chapman et al.[47] Of these the most recent and most sophisticated is the study by Levitt.[48] He uses a panel of large U.S. cities from 1970 to 1992 and finds that a police presence reduces crime for six of seven crime categories examined by him. Adding an officer to a police department is estimated to eliminate 8 to 10 serious crimes. With the help of cost of crime estimates he finds that the social benefit of reduced crime is about $100,000 per officer per year. From these findings he concludes that the number of police in the period 1970–1992 was below the optimal level.

Chapman et al. found police to significantly affect the number of arrests in the city of Los Angeles in 1956–1970.[49] The major contributions were made by nonfield officers and civilian employees in the police department.

EMPIRICAL CRIME DETERRENCE STUDIES

While the police production function can be used to gain insight into the effect of one factor on criminal activities through raising cost to criminals,

[42] N. Walzer, "Economies of Scale and Municipal Police Services: The Illinois Experience," *Review of Economics and Statistics* 54 (1973): 431–438.

[43] An example is Jeffrey I. Chapman et al., "Crime Prevention, the Police Production Function, and Budgeting," *Public Finance* 30 (1975): 197–215.

[44] Steven D. Levitt, *Using Electoral Cycles in Police Hiring to Estimate the Effect of Police on Crime* (Cambridge, MA: National Bureau of Economic Research, Working Paper 4881, 1995): 29.

[45] I. Ehrlich, "Participation in Illegitimate Activities: A Theoretical and Empirical Investigation," *Journal of Political Economy* 81 (1973): 521–565.

[46] R. A. Carr-Hill and N. H. Stern, "An Econometric Model of the Supply and Controls of Recorded Offenses in England and Wales," *Journal of Public Economics* 81 (1973): 289–318.

[47] Chapman et al., "Crime Prevention": 197–215.

[48] Levitt, "Using Electoral Cycles in Police Hiring": 14–23.

[49] Chapman et al., "Crime Prevention": 206.

other factors can play a major role. Many of them have been subjected to empirical analysis. Scholars engaged in such research include Ehrlich,[50] Carr-Hill and Stern[51] of the United Kingdom, Sjoquist,[52] Phillips and Voteys of California,[53] Palmer,[54] Pyle,[55] Freeman,[56] Trumbull,[57] Cloninger,[58] and Tauchen *et al.*[59] These empirical studies find robust evidence of a general deterrent effect flowing from the criminal justice system. However, there are some studies that have been less reassuring. For example, studies by Allison,[60] Walzer,[61] Pressman and Carol,[62] and Pogue[63] found no statistically significant evidence of deterrence, while studies by McPheters and Strong[64] and Swimmer[65] have found limited but relatively weak evidence of deterrence.

Of those who have reviewed both theoretical arguments concerning Becker's theory and its empirical confirmation, Cameron is perhaps the most critical.[66] He offers nine reasons why punishment need not deter crime. They include risk in legal activity, private self-protection, displace-

[50] Ehrlich, "Participation in Illegitimate Activities": 521–565.

[51] Carr-Hill and Stern, "Econometric Model of the Supply and Control of Recorded Offenses": 289–318.

[52] D. L. Sjoquist, "Property, Crime and Economic Behavior," *American Economic Review* 63 (1973): 439–446.

[53] L. Phillips and H. L. Votey, "Crime Control in California," *Journal of Legal Studies* 4 (June 1975): 327–350.

[54] John Palmer, "Economic Analysis of the Deterrent Effect of Punishment: A Review," *Journal of Research in Crime and Delinquency* 14(1) (1977): 4–21.

[55] David Pyle, *The Economics of Crime and Law Enforcement* (London: Macmillan, 1983).

[56] Richard Freeman, "Crime and Unemployment," in J. Q. Wilson, Ed., *Crime and Public Policy* (San Francisco: Institute for Contemporary Studies, 1983): 89–106.

[57] William Trumbull, "Estimation of the Economic Model of Crime Using Aggregate and Individual Level Data," *Southern Economic Journal* 56 (October 1989): 423–439.

[58] Dale O. Cloninger, "Enforcement Risk and Deterrence: A Re-examination," *Journal of Socio-Economics* 23 (1994): 273–285.

[59] Helen Trauchen et al., "Criminal Deterrence: Revisiting the Issue with a Birth Cohort," *Review of Economics and Statistics* 76(3) (1994): 399–412.

[60] J. P. Allison, "Economic Factors and the Rate of Crime," *Land Economics* 48 (1972): 25–30.

[61] Walzer, "Economies of Scale": 431–438.

[62] I. Pressman and A. Carol, "Crime as a Diseconomy of Scale," *Review of Social Economy* 29 (1971): 227–236.

[63] T. F. Pogue, "Effect of Police Expenditures on Crime Rates: Some Evidence," *Public Finance Quarterly* 3 (1975): 14–44.

[64] L. R. McPheters and W. B. Stronge, "Law Enforcement Expenditures and Urban Crime," *National Tax Journal* 17 (1974): 633–644.

[65] G. Swimmer, "Measurement of the Effectiveness of Urban Law Enforcement — A Simultaneous Approach," *Southern Economic Journal* 40 (1974): 618–630.

[66] Samuel Cameron, "The Economics of Crime Deterrence: A Survey of Theory and Evidence," *Kyklos* 41 (1988): 301–319.

ment of incarcerated criminals by new ones, criminals' target income, adaptive behavior, and practical certainty. In addition, he questions the validity of most empirical deterrence studies, since "... much of the literature seems impaired by bias due to measurement error."[67]

Some of the studies that found significant deterrence effects shed light on factors that have policy implications. For example, Tauchen et al. found that crime deterrent measures may be more effective for individuals with limited previous contact with the criminal justice system than for recidivists.[68] Cloninger found that police presence was negatively and significantly correlated with the rate of nonhomicide activities whereas arrest rates were not.[69] Moreover, Levitt found that deterrence is more important in reducing crime than is incapacitation, i.e., placing criminals behind bars so that they are unable to victimize society. Specifically, he found that deterrence explains about 75% of the overall impact of increased arrests on reducing crime.[70]

In the light of the critical examination of Becker's economic model of crime, refinements and modifications have been suggested. They seek to take into account some real life facts facing potential criminals, potential victims, and the criminal justice system. The following are a few examples:

- In relation to teenagers in central cities it appears that many are crime-prone because of their radical present orientation and self-regard.[71] Moreover, members of street gangs often neither fear the stigma of arrest nor incarceration.[72] They are influenced by the drug culture and live by the code of the street.
- According to a model by Witte and Tauchen,[73] individuals choose a level of criminal activity rather than the time to devote to such activities. Moreover, to some extent they have a short time horizon, being used to living a dangerous life.
- The need to involve participation of the community in reporting and fighting crime is important to recognize in modeling crime prevention.[74]

[67] Ibid.
[68] Tauchen et al., "Criminal Deterrence": 411.
[69] Cloninger, "Enforcement Risk and Deterrence": 281.
[70] Steven Levitt, Why Do Increased Arrest Rates Appear to Reduce Crime: Deterrence Incapacitation, or Measurement Error? (Cambridge, MA: National Bureau of Economic Research, Working Paper 5268, 1996).
[71] Mark Fleisher, Beggars and Thieves (Milwaukee: University of Wisconsin Press, 1995).
[72] Di Iulio, Jr., "Why Violent Crime Rates Have Dropped": A 17.
[73] Ann D. Witte and Helen Tauchen, "Work and Crime: An Exploration Using Panel Data," NBER Working Paper 4794 (July 1994).
[74] George Akerlof and Janet Yellen, "Gang Behavior, Law Enforcement and Community Values, Values and Public Policy" (Washington, D.C.: The Brookings Institution, 1994).

Such recognition can lead to emphasis on nontraditional steps toward crime deterrence.

- Eide has suggested to extend Becker's model to account for impulsiveness and alcohol and drug impairment.[75] Toward this end he proposes a rational choice model that merges conventional criminological explanations with rational choice models.
- Dickens points to the fact that crimes have certain temporal characteristics.[76] Potential criminal activity takes place when an individual decides that the probability of detection is low, a period that is followed by one when he fears that it is high. Thus, he has developed a model that shows that increased certainty of punishment deters crime at some parameter values while it raises it at others.

CERTAINTY VERSUS SEVERITY OF PUNISHMENT

Earlier in this chapter, Eq. (8.4) was presented reflecting Becker's argument that the probability of being arrested and convicted on the one hand and the severity of the punishment on the other can affect the number of crimes committed. Now we will turn to the question of whether certainty or severity of punishment can prevent more crimes and do so in a more cost-effective manner. An answer to this question is of more than academic interest, not only for humanitarian but particularly for financial reasons.

Uncertainties about punishment can arise in relation to each and every component of the criminal justice system portrayed in Figure 8—1. For example, the introduction of "determinate" sentencing should increase certainty about the length of incarceration related to specified crimes. On the other hand, there continues to exist great uncertainty about what percentage of the sentence will be served. In 1992 this percentage for the United States was as low as 46% for robbery and as high as 56% for rape.[77] But those aggregates hide the true variations, since overcrowded prisons are forced to release convicts after they have served only a very short time. Potential criminals have little advance information about the prison in which they will serve and its crowding status in the future.

Another uncertainty relates to the apparent ease with which parole violation is treated. Petersilia found that 55% of persons admitted to California

[75] Erling Eide, *Economics of Crime: Deterrence and the Rational Offender* (New York: Elsevier Science, 1994).

[76] Summarized in Cameron, "Economics of Crime Deterrence:" 306–307.

[77] Bureau of Justice Statistics, *Prison Sentences and Time Served for Violence* (Washington, D.C.: Bureau of Justice Statistics, April 1995): 1.

prisons in 1991 were parole violators, a fact that makes fighting crime very difficult.[78]

A number of empirical studies have attempted to estimate the effect of length of sentence on violent crimes. Van Dine et al. analyzed the 342 adult defendants who were charged with violent felonies and whose cases were completed in Franklin County (Columbus), Ohio, in 1973.[79] (Of these defendants, 53% had no prior felony conviction and only 18% had prior violent felony convictions.) Under existing sentencing policies, only about half of the convicted violent offenders were sentenced to serve time. By imposing a mandatory 5-year term on an adult convicted of a felony, adult violent crime was reduced by 18%. If only those who were convicted of violent crimes were given the mandatory 5-year term for the violent conviction and any subsequent conviction, adult violent crime would have fallen by only 6%.

In a second study, Joan Petersilia and Peter Greenwood analyzed 625 adult felons who were convicted in the Denver, Colorado, district court between 1968 and 1970.[80] (Of those defendants charged with violent crimes, only 39% had a prior adult felony conviction and 23% had no juvenile or adult record.) For this cohort, the analysis showed that the imposition of a 5-year mandatory term for every conviction reduced adult violent crime by 31%. If the 5-year mandatory term were restricted to only those convicted of violent felonies, the reduction in adult violent crime would have been 6%.

Petersilia and Greenwood estimated some of the cost implications of sentencing options. The average sentence for those convicted of a violent felony is only 1.3 years (including those who serve no time at all). If every defendant who was convicted of a violent felony was given a 5-year term, the prison population would have to increase by 150% in order to produce a 6% reduction in adult violent crime. Incarcerating criminals for long periods ties up prison resources that might be used more productively, particularly when society is reluctant to build new prisons. Thus, increasing prison terms for some can mean decreasing terms for others, reducing the percentage of convicted criminals sent to prison, or granting earlier parole.

A number of studies have sought to compare the effectiveness of punish-

---

[78] Joan R. Petersilia, "Diverting Non-Violent Prisoners to Intermediate Sanctions," unpublished manuscript (University of California — Irvine, April 1995).

[79] S. Van Dine, *Restraining the Wicked* (Lexington, MA: Lexington Books, 1979).

[80] Joan Petersilia and Peter W. Greenwood, "Mandatory Prison Sentences: Their Projected Effects on Crime and Prison Populations," *Journal of Criminal Law and Criminology* 69 (1978): 604–615.

ment certainty and severity. Witte[81] found from an analysis of prison releases in North Carolina that certainty of punishment had a greater deterrent effect than punishment severity. Similar results were obtained by Grogger[82] in his analysis of a large data set of criminal and employment histories of young male arrestees. He found, "large deterrent effects emanating from increased certainty of punishment, and much smaller, and generally insignificant effects, stemming from increased severity of sanctions."[83]

Should these findings be generally correct, the question of whether three-strike laws are effective means of combatting crimes in particular deserves examination. While in early 1995 more than 30 states had some sort of three-strike laws under serious consideration, California had enacted a law that mandates 25-year-to-life sentences for three-time offenders. The third strike will accrue even for a minor felony, i.e., car theft or, as happened in one case, theft of a pizza.

A RAND study has used a sophisticated computer model to estimate the cost of this law and of some alternatives. One alternative involves increasing the certainty of punishment by guaranteeing convicts full terms.[84] While California's three-strike law is expected to cost about $5.5 billion annually, mainly for building and operating new prisons to house the inmates while reducing crime by about 25%, the guaranteed full-term alternative would accomplish the same reduction, yet for $1 billion less per year.

The RAND report summarizes the efficacy of the two alternatives as follows:

> The full-term alternative would increase sentences for all serious offenders — including first timers who are near the beginning of their criminal careers — and pay for it by not imprisoning many minor felons. Three strikes, in contrast, ignores first-time serious offenders and instead expends a large amount of money keeping older criminals — including many convicted of minor offenses — locked up well past the time when they might have given up crime anyway.[85]

DOES PRISON PAY?

The question of whether the social benefits associated with incarceration exceed its social costs is difficult to answer, particularly in relation to the

---

[81] Ann D. Witte, "Estimating the Economic Model of Crime With Individual Data," *Quarterly Journal of Economics* 94 (February 1980): 57–84.

[82] Jeffrey Grogger, "Certainty vs. Severity of Punishment," *Economic Inquiry* 29 (April 1991): 297–309.

[83] *Ibid.*: 308.

[84] " 'Three Strikes' — Serious Flaws and a Huge Price Tag," *RAND Research Review* 19 (Spring 1995): 1–2.

[85] *Ibid.*: 2.

marginal, rather than the average, cost of crime. Imprisonment results in four classes of social benefits — retribution, deterrence, rehabilitation, and incapacitation. The first three are most difficult to quantify, but the fourth — incapacitation — while difficult, can lend itself to estimates, which a number of studies have attempted to provide. These studies consider the social benefits of incarceration as the values of crimes not committed when a criminal has been placed behind bars. Piehl and Di Iulio,[86] using data developed by Cohen,[87] estimated that the social costs of each incidence of rape in New Jersey was $56,280; robbery, $12,060; assault, $11,518; auto theft, $2,995; and burglary, $1,314. The median social cost of all property and assault crimes, for example, was $70,098, which Piehl and Di Iulio divided by $25,000, the cost of imprisoning one prisoner for 1 year, to obtain a benefit–cost ratio of 2.80.[88] Interesting, moreover, was the finding that the ratio for the prisoner in the 25th percentile was 0.78 and for that in the 10th percentile was 0.07. These results suggest that, while incarceration of the median criminal is socially desirable, it is not so for about 25% of criminals. For this class of criminals alternatives to incarceration, e.g., house confinement, electronic surveillance, or parole, could be considered. In the opinion of Richard Freeman, "even a marginally effective and relatively costly job/crime prevention program for crime-prone groups would also pass a benefit–cost test."[89]

A study by Levitt found that for each 1,000-inmate increase in the prison population, the following annual reduction in crimes will follow: larceny, 9,200; burglary, 2,600; assault, 1,200; robbery, 1,100; auto theft, 700; rape, 53; and murder, 4.[90] Therefore, on average, 15 crimes per year are prevented for each additional prisoner behind bars. Levitt estimated that the average criminal, if on the loose, would impose $53,900 in social costs, which incarceration would prevent. This number is compared to the annual cost of incarceration, which is estimated to be $30,000, thus resulting in a benefit–cost ratio of 1.80. (If the incarceration cost estimate by Piehl and Di Iulio of $25,000 were used, the ratio would increase to 2.16.)

[86] Anne Piehl and John G. Di Iulio, Jr., "Does Prison Pay? Revisited," *Brookings Review* 8 (Winter 1995): 21–25.

[87] Mark A. Cohen, "Pain, Suffering and Jury Awards: A Study of the Cost of Crime to Victims," *Law and Society Review* 22 (1988).

[88] Piehl and Di Iulio, "Does Prison Pay?": 24–25.

[89] Richard B. Freeman, "Why Do So Many Young American Men Commit Crimes and What Might We Do About It?" Journal of Economic Perspectives, 10 (Winter) 1996: 39–40.

[90] "The Effect of Prison Population Size on Crime Rates — Evidence from Overcrowding Litigation," *Quarterly Journal of Economics* 111 (May 1996): 344–347.

CAPITAL PUNISHMENT AS CRIME DETERRENT

An explosive issue that has been at the center of much public controversy concerns the death penalty as a deterrent for the crime of murder. The economist's rational-choice framework and the deterrence hypothesis are especially relevant in the case of murder.[91]

Empirical studies investigating the deterrent effect of the death penalty on homicides have yielded conflicting results. Most prominent among these studies are those by the criminologist Sellin,[92] the economist Ehrlich,[93] and the economist Wolpin.[94] Sellin selected clusters of neighboring states "closely similar" to each other in certain respects. Within each cluster, he then compared homicide rates in those states that had abolished death penalty statutes as opposed to those that had retained such statutes, irrespective of whether the retentionist states actually executed any homicide offenders. He also examined homicide rates before and after abolition of the death penalty in those states where it had been abolished. He found that homicide rates in abolitionist states were not significantly or systematically different from the rates in retentionist states, and so concluded that the death penalty has no measurable deterrent effect beyond that of life imprisonment.

The validity of Sellin's technique of clustering similar states depends heavily on just how "closely" the states within each cluster are "similar" to each other with regard to those variables that are likely to influence homicide rates. To the extent that he failed to identify specific variables that are likely to have the greatest impact on homicide rates, his clustering technique is a weak attempt to hold other influences constant while examining differences in homicide rates.

Ehrlich used more sophisticated regression techniques, within the context of a simultaneous equations model of the supply of homicides and society's defense against homicides. He sought to measure the effect of two law enforcement variables on the number of homicides — the probability of conviction per arrest, and the probability of being executed per conviction. Of particular interest to the capital punishment debate is his finding that

[91] Conversely, it is acknowledged that his rational-choice framework is of much less relevance in the case of lesser homicidal offenses, especially crimes of passion.

[92] T. Sellin, *The Death Penalty* (Philadelphia: American Law Institute, 1959); T. Sellin, Ed., "Capital Punishment," *Federal Probation* 3 (1961): 25; T. Sellin, "Homicides in Retentionist and Abolitionist States," in *Capital Punishment*, T. Sellin, Ed. (New York: Harper, 1967).

[93] I. Ehrlich, "The Deterrent Effect of Capital Punishment: A Question of Life or Death," *American Economic Review* 65 (June 1975): 397–417.

[94] K. L. Wolpin, "Capital Punishment and Homicide in England," *American Economic Review* 68 (May 1978): 422–427.

a 1% increase in the number of executions per homicide conviction on the average reduced the number of homicides by 0.06%. Ehrlich pointed out that this implied that "on the average the trade-off between the execution of an offender and the lives of potential victims it might have saved was of the order of magnitude of 1 for 8 for the period 1933–67 in the United States."[95]

Despite subsequent criticism of Ehrlich's model, structural form, and data, his work represents a comprehensive and sophisticated theoretical and empirical study of the deterrent effect of the death penalty.[96] A note of caution is required regarding the interpretation of Ehrlich's statement about trading off one execution for eight homicides. This statement assumes that the probability of an offender's being executed (given that he is convicted) is independent of the probability that the jury will convict him for murder. In a world where some jurors and judges disagree with the imposition of the death penalty, they may well be reluctant to find an offender guilty of murder if they feel he is likely to be executed. Thus, the deterrent effect of additional executions could be offset by a tendency to convict fewer offenders. The measurement of this offsetting effect, though possibly amenable to empirical research, so far has not been undertaken.

Wolpin undertook an econometric analysis of the deterrent effect of capital punishment, conceptually similar to Ehrlich's work but using 1929–1968 data for England and Wales. He employed ordinary least-squares regression techniques in both linear and logarithmic functional form and found his result quite robust (i.e., unchanged regardless of functional form and time period). Wolpin's conclusions parallel those of Ehrlich in principle, but not in detail. Thus, he finds capital punishment to have had a statistically significant deterrent effect in England and Wales during 1929 to 1968, but the effect is only half as large as that found by Ehrlich in the United States during 1933 to 1967. Specifically, he estimates that four fewer murders are committed, and therefore four lives saved, for each additional execution of a convicted murderer.[97] This effect is relative to the alternative punishment of a prison sentence, generally not exceeding 10 to 15 years.

The Ehrlich and Wolpin studies appear to be consistent with the deterrence hypothesis. A 1978 report by the National Academy of Sciences Panel

---

[95] Ehrlich, "Deterrent Effect": 398.

[96] For criticisms of Ehrlich, and his reply to these criticisms, see the following three articles in *Yale Law Journal* 85 (1975): D. C. Baldus and J. W. L. Cole, "A Comparison of the Work of Thorsten Sellin and Isaac Ehrlich on the Deterrent Effect of Capital Punishment": W. J. Bowers and G. L. Pierce. "The Illusion of Deterrence in Isaac Ehrlich's Research on Capital Punishment": and I. Ehrlich, "Deterrence: Evidence and Inference."

[97] Wolpin, "Capital Punishment and Homicide": 426.

on Research on Deterrent and Incapacitative Effects concludes, "We cannot tell from the studies done so far just how much effect ... capital punishment [has] on the number of ... crimes committed."[98]

HANDGUN CONTROL AND HOMICIDES

For many years, there has been a lively debate about handgun control. This debate can be joined within the general framework of a police production function [Eq. (8.5), presented earlier]. Statutory gun control would change the service conditions S within which the police produce their output.

The arguments in favor of gun control proceed from the premise "that one of the major sources of homicide is assault and that the use of firearms increases both the feasibility of attack and the fatality rate."[99] Phillips et al. have developed a model that gives expression to the implied objective of minimizing both the losses due to crime and the costs of control. Constraints are the budgets of law enforcement agencies and the behavioral relations specifying crime generation and crime control. Two-stage least-squares methods are used to estimate the crime-control and crime-generation equations for homicides.

Phillips et al. found that, based on multiple regression analysis, a 10% reduction in handgun density is associated with a 27.4% reduction in the homicide offense rate.[100] They concluded that, for the sake of social-cost minimization, about 19.5% of California's law enforcement personnel should be assigned to homicide-related activities, although they find the present percentage to be much smaller.

CRIME DETERRENCE BY RAISING LEGAL INCOME

The rational-choice framework that was presented earlier suggests that crime rates can be reduced by increasing legitimate income-earning opportunities and their rewards. These circumstances fall into two major classes — provision of employment opportunities with appropriate rewards, and education and training. Both education and labor market opportunities

---

[98] National Academy of Sciences Panel on Research on Deterrent and Incapacitative Effects, "Deterrence and Incapacitation: Estimating the Effects of Criminal Sanctions on Crime Rates," *Newsletter Assembly of Behavioral and Social Sciences* 6 (March 1978): 3.

[99] L. Phillips et al., "Handguns and Homicide: Minimizing Losses and the Costs of Control," *Journal of Legal Studies* 5 (June 1976): 463–472.

[100] *Ibid.*: 474–475.

and their effects on criminal activities can be analyzed in terms of an individual's behavior or on an aggregate basis.

Evidence exists that when potential criminals face great difficulties in finding legitimate employment, they tend to turn to illegal activities. Over the years, a number of empirical studies have tested hypotheses about the link between crime and economic conditions. Virtually all studies indicate a strong countercyclical pattern for most property crimes.

For example, Yamada examined the relation between 1970 and 1983 quarterly crime data for murder, forcible rape, robbery, aggravated assault, burglary, larceny, theft, and motor vehicle theft on the one hand and labor market conditions on the other. He found that male civilian unemployment rates were strongly and positively associated with most of the crimes studied.[101] This relation was particularly strong for the age group 25 years old and older. The male civilian labor force participation rates also were found to be related to the crime rate, particularly in the case of teenagers. Thus, youth labor force participation rates for both whites and nonwhites, 16 to 19 years old, were more strongly associated with crime rates than the labor force participation rates for males 20 years old and older.

While Yamada used time series data, similar results were obtained by Sjoquist, who examined 53 municipalities with 1960 populations ranging from 26,000 to 200,000.[102] Sjoquist found a significantly positive effect of the unemployment rate on property crime rates (combining robbery, burglary, and larceny) in 1968.

A study by Cook and Zarkin, using 1949–1979 data, related crimes to business cycles.[103] It found that the major movements in crime rates cannot be attributed to the business cycle. Specifically, during recessions there occurred relatively small increases in robberies and burglaries, and negligible increases in murder rates, while auto thefts declined. These findings need not contradict the hypothesis that, as employment opportunities decline, illegal activities tend to increase. Remember that, in recessions, opportunities for property crimes tend to decline, while lower police budgets tend to weaken government's response to crime.

Data from the National Longitudinal Survey of Youth, which samples out-of-school youth not in the military, confirm that youth involved in crime

---

[101] T. Yamada, "The Crime Rate and the Condition of the Labor Market: A Vector Autoregressive Model" (October 1985, mimeographed): 18 pp.

[102] D. L. Sjoquist, "Property Crime and Economic Behavior: Some Empirical Results," *American Economic Review* 63 (June 1973): 439–446.

[103] P. J. Cook and G. A. Zarkin, "Crime and the Business Cycle," *Journal of Legal Studies* 14 (1985): 115–128.

have lower employment than those not participating in crime.[104] Trumbull in his analysis of 1,310 offenders for whom he had complete employment and criminal histories concluded that: "higher rewards for legitimate employment deter future criminal activity."[105] Chiricos also found that joblessness is associated with greater crime.[106] Moreover, Lee found a substantive positive relation between earnings inequality and crime rates across metropolitan areas in 1970 and 1980. He estimated that the increased income inequality in the 1980s induced a 10% increase in crime, as measured by the FBI's Uniform Crime Report Index.[107] Elliot's work suggests that persons engaged in "serious violent behavior" are more likely to refrain from it when they are employed than unemployed.[108]

The current widespread dealing in drugs has raised the importance of providing rewarding legal employment opportunities. Clearly unemployment in the presence of well-paying drug-dealing opportunities further induces criminal activity. For example, Reuter et al. found that drug dealers in Washington, D.C., in 1990 earned $2,000 per month net of expenses, i.e., $30.00 per hour. Consequently, selling drugs was significantly more profitable on an hourly basis than any legitimate jobs available to this class of persons.[109]

Freeman, employing an aggregate analysis, argues that a depressed labor market for low-skilled men in the 1980s and 1990s can explain much of the crime increase of this group during these years.[110] Depending on what data are used, the propensity for criminal acts by noninstitutionalized men increased by 80 to 163% from 1977 to 1992. In 1993, 2.9% of 25- to 34-year-old American men and 12% of black men were incarcerated.[111] At a time when incarceration was on the rise, so were crime and victimization rates. A cogent explanation is that during that period legitimate employment opportunities declined while rewards from crime rose relative to those from legal work. For example, a National Bureau of Economic Research Boston

[104] Freeman, "Why Do So Many Young American Men Commit Crimes?": 35.

[105] Trumbull, "Estimation of the Economic Model of Crime": 435.

[106] Theodore Chiricos, "Rates of Crime and Unemployment: An Analysis of Aggregate Research Evidence," *Social Problems* 34 (April 1987): 187–211.

[107] David Lee, "An Empirical Investigation of the Economic Incentives for Criminal Behavior," B.A. Thesis (Cambridge, MA: Harvard University, 1993).

[108] Delbert Elliot, "Longitudinal Research in Criminology: Promise and Practice," in G. W. Westekamp and H. J. Kernes, Eds., *Cross National Longitudinal Research on Human Development and Criminal Behavior* (Netherlands: Kluwer Academic Publishers, 1994): 189–201.

[109] P. Reuter et al., *Money From Crime. A Study of the Economics of Drug Dealing in Washington, D.C.* (Santa Monica, Calif.: RAND, Drug Policy Center, 1990).

[110] Freeman, "Why Do So Many Young American Men Commit Crimes?": 29–30.

[111] *Ibid.*: 26.

Youth Survey indicates that the proportion of youth that reported to be able to earn more "on the street" than from legitimate employment increased in Boston from 41% in 1980 to 63% in 1989.[112]

For men and women to utilize labor market opportunities effectively, education and training are of the essence. Therefore, investment in education, from Head Start to vocational training and college education, are premier tools for entering the labor market and staying in it. Thus, Trumbull has found that better educated persons are less prone to recidivism than less educated ones, though sex, age, and color admittedly also play a role.[113]

In summary, while not entirely conclusive, empirical evidence confirms that joblessness contributes to crime. Therefore, programs that provide education and training and thereby enhance employability, particularly of crime-prone individuals, together with steps that create for them employment opportunities, are powerful instruments to reduce crime. Freeman suggests that such initiatives offer significant opportunities. He estimates that 2% of the gross domestic product is devoted to crime control and a further 2% is lost to crime. This amounts to $54,000 for each of 5 million persons incarcerated, on probation, or on parole. He concludes that, "the magnitude of the numbers does suggest the potential value of programs to assure that potential criminals have better access to legitimate employment opportunities."[114]

CONCLUSION

In summary, criminal law is predicated on the premise that initial entitlements must and indeed can be protected from criminal encroachment by a specially fashioned class of laws, criminal laws. In order to deter such encroachment and the ensuing negative externalities, society imposes criminal sanctions. Models have been developed by economists to relate deterrence measures to the commission of a crime, and some econometric models have attempted to provide estimates of the deterrent effect.

These models fall into two major classes. One focuses on deterring crime within the criminal justice system by raising the cost of crime commission. The police occupy a key position in the early activities within this system

---

[112] Richard B. Freeman, "Crime and the Employment of Disadvantaged Youth," in George Peterson and Wayne Vroman, Eds., *Urban Labor Markets and Job Opportunity* (Washington, D.C.: Urban Institute, 1992): 201–237.

[113] Trumbull, "Estimation of the Economic Model of Crime": 433.

[114] Freeman, "Why Do So Many Young American Men Commit Crimes?": 40.

and economists have estimated police production functions. They help better understand how police can efficiently carry out their responsibility of arresting criminals and deterring them from engaging in illegal acts. Models exist also for more general crime deterrence studies and quite a few have been empirically implemented. As a result, a better understanding has been gained of what deters crimes. Of particular interest has been whether severity or certainty of punishment is more important and what is the crime deterrent effect of capital punishment. Some efforts have been made to determine whether prison does pay as well as how handgun control affects homicides.

The second class of crime deterrence studies focuses on raising the legal income of potential criminals in the hope of it exceeding their potential illegal income. Education and training are considered as steps toward raising the potential for earning a legal income. Creating labor market opportunities and steps to make them available to potential criminals are further steps that can reduce the taste for criminal activities.

9

ENVIRONMENTAL LAW

INTRODUCTION

Environmental concerns have gained increasing importance. Thus, in 1996 a survey found that 47% of Americans had serious concerns and another 36% had very serious ones about environmental problems.[1] Government has responded in a variety of ways. For example, the Environmental Protection Agency (EPA) in 1996 referred to the Justice Department a record 262 criminal cases against polluters and imposed a record $173 million in fines. Moreover, polluters agreed to spend $1.5 billion to correct violations and prevent future pollution problems.[1a] Between 1973 and 1990 more than 10% of federal crime convictions were for environmental violations.[2]

Sax has raised the question whether, in a modern state, citizens have environmental rights, just as they have rights to decent housing and safe working conditions.[3] If so, he argues the state should assure each individual some level of freedom from environmental hazards. Yet, implementing such rights is not costless and requires balancing conflicting interests. Environmental laws, be they statutory or court-made laws, ideally should be so

[1] E. C. Ladd and K. Bowman, "Public Opinion about the Environment," *Resources* 124 (Summer 1996): 6.

[1a] *Wall Street Journal* (February 26, 1997): C27.

[2] M. A. Cohen, "Theories of Punishment and Empirical Trends in Corporate Criminal Sanctions" *Managerial and Decision Economics* 17 (1996): 399–412.

[3] Joseph L. Sax, "The Search for Environmental Rights," *Journal of Land Use and Environmental Law* 93 (1990): 7.

framed as to balance protection of the environment with other societal objectives.[4] Because of heightened societal interest, environmental law has moved to front stage. The intense attention given to it on the legal scene has resulted from the spread of industrialization and urbanization in many areas of the world. Externalities abound; environmental problems have been emerging at an increasing pace, and society has become concerned, even alarmed, about the degradation of the environment. To cope with these complex problems, property law, tort law, and contract law have been drawn upon in evolving environmental law.

LEGAL ASPECTS OF ENVIRONMENTAL PROTECTION

ENVIRONMENTAL EXTERNALITIES, PROPERTY RIGHTS, AND ENTITLEMENTS

In an affluent, technologically advanced world where the parties engaging in transactions are highly specialized and mobile and live close to one another, everyone's acts affect everyone else. As persons, firms, or governments exercise their property rights or entitlements, they commonly affect the utility or production functions of others. As was stated in Chapter 1, when such exchanges take place outside the market and therefore no appropriate compensation is exchanged, we speak about externalities.

Under conditions of close environmental interdependence, a direct relationship exists between the assignment of property rights or entitlements and the concomitant nature and extent of the externalities. Assignment of private resource rights or entitlements does not necessarily produce the internalization of all externalities. Often internalization of an externality requires government intervention, which must take into consideration assignments of property rights and apply appropriate liability rules. Depending on how these rules affect property rights, the extent to which resources are allocated efficiently will differ. Specifically, more of the externality will be produced if the resource owner responsible for it is declared to have no liability for the damages attributable to this external effect than if he is liable for damages. Moreover, since positive transaction costs inhibit exchange, the disparity between resource allocations at equilibrium and under different assignments of rights in any externality situation increases as transaction costs increase. As the externality situation becomes more complex and the number of resource owners involved in the situation

---

[4] John Ashworth and Ivy Papps, "Should Environmental Legislation Set the Rules Constraining Polluters?," *International Review of Law and Economics* 12 (1992): 79–93.

increases, transaction costs increase and so do deviations from allocative neutrality. In the extreme, transaction costs may be so high that movements away from the initial allocation of resources that is specified by the prevailing system of property rights may be impossible.

In the literature, there is much debate concerning the proper liability rule in the presence of externalities. Mishan favors a liability rule that incorporates a strong bias against the production of externalities when substantial uncertainties exist.[5] Demsetz takes an opposite view: "The greater the uncertainty of effect, the less inclined we should be to require that prior compensation should be paid to those harmed or prior fees be charged of those benefited. The cost of sorting out and measuring legitimate claims in cases of great uncertainty would be so high as to undermine efficient resource use."[6]

These diametrically opposed positions may result from the fact that Mishan regards uncertainty effects as major and irreversible, whereas Demsetz considers them relatively insignificant and reversible. Calabresi acknowledges that either of these conditions might prevail in different externality situations, hence he argues that, in any particular uncertain situation, society should adopt that liability rule for which the market is most likely to correct an error in the initial assignment of property rights.[7] A generalization of this principle is provided by Cheung, who suggests that in uncertain situations the socially most desirable liability rule can be determined by comparing the risk associated with the adoption of each alternative liability rule with all of the other costs and benefits attributable to the adoption of that rule.[8] According to Cheung's principle, since all externality situations do not involve the same degree of uncertainty, different internalization mechanisms will be socially most desirable in different externality situations. Moreover, since communities may exhibit different degrees of risk aversion, they rationally may adopt different internalization mechanisms for essentially identical externality situations.

To the extent that the observed purchasing behavior of a person in a market situation is generally acknowledged to be the most reliable available indication of his economic preferences, it is desirable to adopt those assign-

[5] E. J. Mishan, "The Economics of Disamenity," *Natural Resources Journal* 14 (January 1974): 81–82.

[6] H. Demsetz, "Some Aspects of Property Rights," *Journal of Law and Economics* 9 (October 1966): 64.

[7] G. Calabresi, "Transaction Costs, Resource Allocation and Liability Rules: A Comment," *Journal of Law and Economics* 11 (April 1968): 69–73.

[8] S. N. S. Cheung, "Transaction Costs, Risk Aversion, and the Choice of Contractual Arrangements," *Journal of Law and Economics* 12 (April 1969): 24–29.

ments of property rights that will maximize opportunities to engage in market exchanges promoting the internalization of an externality. In the absence of overriding social considerations, therefore, there is virtue in relying on the negotiated resolution of externality problems wherever voluntary negotiation of the permissible level of the externality is feasible. Feasibility, however, depends on the number of parties involved in the externality situation. The smaller the number, the lower the transaction costs. In turn, when many parties are affected by a particular externality situation and internalization of the externality assumes the nature of a public good for all these parties, the economic and social desirability of governmental intervention is virtually ensured. Thus, all too frequently, externality problems cannot be resolved by negotiated solutions, and other means must be applied, often involving the courts.

COURT-MADE ENVIRONMENTAL LAW

As has been pointed out, the market provides an effective mechanism by which rights or entitlements to the possession and use of goods and services are exchanged. When this exchange of rights or entitlements is complicated by an abundance of externalities that affect many persons and prevent the market mechanism from achieving an economically efficient allocation of resources, government intervention is often called for. Government then takes steps to guide and, if necessary, to adjudicate conflicting property rights and entitlements. High on the list of laws relevant to these circumstances is nuisance law, and this will be explored next.

NUISANCE LAW

The law of nuisance[9] has been applied to determine whether someone's property right or entitlement has been violated.[10] The courts have recognized the need to resolve a deep-seated conflict between two opposing legal principles:

> The law of nuisance plys between two antithetical extremes: The principle that every person is entitled to use his property for any purpose that he sees fit, and the opposing

[9] This section has benefited from F. H. Reuter and P. Kushner, *Economic Incentives for Land Use Control*, EPA-600/S-77-001 (Washington, D.C.: U.S. Environmental Protection Agency, 1977), sect. 2.34–2.53.

[10] A private nuisance has been defined as "an interference with the use and enjoyment of land." W. L. Prosser, *Handbook of the Law of Torts*, 4th ed. (St. Paul, Minn.: West, 1971): 591.

principle that everyone is bound to use his property in such a manner as not to injure the property or rights of his neighbor. For generations, courts, in their tasks of judging, have ruled on these extremes according to the wisdom of the day, and many have recognized that the contemporary view of public policy shifts from generation to generation.[11]

The use of nuisance law as a deterrent to pollution and as a means to internalize the costs of land use has a long history, beginning in English case law.[12] A private nuisance action has been used to abate nearly every common form of pollution: air,[13] water,[14] solid waste,[15] noise,[16] and sight pollution.[17]

The Supreme Court in *Euclid* v. *Ambler*[18] indicated, as early as 1926, that "a nuisance may be merely the right thing in the wrong place, like a pig in the parlor instead of the barnyard."[19] In general, "a nuisance may undoubtedly arise from a land use incompatible with the surrounding neighborhood."[20] Thus, the first element of a nuisance is the unreasonable use of one's land as determined by the character of the neighborhood. Certain activities that may be perfectly reasonable in industrial areas or in the country are not suitable in residential communities. Courts have found that a powder mill,[21] a factory,[22] or a stable,[23] if located in residential areas, are nuisances, but these same activities are purely permissible in the proper setting.

Once it has been determined that the *activity is unreasonable for the area,* it must also be proven that the *interference is substantial.* For instance, a slight amount of noise or smoke is permissible,[24] but the activity will be considered a nuisance if it is sufficient to "interfere with the ordinary comfort of human existence."[25] The Supreme Court of New Hampshire considered

---

[11] *Antonik* v. *Chamberlain,* 81 Ohio App. 465, 475, 78 N.E.2d 752, 759 (Ct. App. Summit County 1947).

[12] William Aldred's Case, 77 Eng. Rep. 816 (K.B. 1611).

[13] *Campbell* v. *Seaman,* 63 N.Y. 568 (1876).

[14] *Johnson* v. *City of Fairmont,* 188 Minn. 451, 247 N.W. 577 (1933).

[15] *Lind* v. *City of San Luis Obispo,* 109 Cal. 340, 42 P. 437 (1895).

[16] Hennessey v. *Carmony,* 50 N.J. Eq. 616, 25 A. 374 (1892).

[17] See "Torts — Aesthetic Nuisance: An Emerging Cause of Action," *New York University Law Review* 45 (November 1970): 1075–1097.

[18] *Euclid* v. *Ambler Realty Co.,* 272 U.S. 365 (1926).

[19] *Ibid.:* 388.

[20] *Township of Bedminster* v. *Vargo Dragway, Inc.,* 434 Pa. 100, 253 A.2d 659 (1969).

[21] *Cumberland Torpedo Co.* v. *Gaines,* 201 Ky. 88, 255 S.W. 1046 (1923).

[22] *Riblet* v. *Spokane Portland Cement Co.,* 41 Wash. 2d 249, 248 P.2d 380 (1952).

[23] *Johnson* v. *Drysdale,* 66 S.D. 436, 285, M.W. 301 (1939).

[24] Prosser, *Handbook:* 79.

[25] *Holman* v. *Athens Empire Laundry Co.,* 149 Ga. 345, 351, 100 S.E. 207, 210 (1919).

substantial harm to be that "in excess of the customary interferences a land user suffers in an organized society. It denotes an appreciable and tangible interference with a property interest."[26] Both of these required elements introduce the possibility that a landowner will be able to externalize the costs of his land use.

Nuisance law permits two general forms of remedy: damages and injunctive relief. Normally, only if the damages cannot be determined or if the nuisance would require continued litigation will the court permit injunctive relief. In two cases, *Boomer* v. *Atlantic Cement Co.*[27] and *Baldwin* v. *McClendon*,[28] the courts permitted the payment of damages that would compensate the injured party, not only for the past and present, but for future injury as well.

In *Boomer*, the defendant operated a large cement plant near Albany, New York, and neighboring landowners sought an injunction and damages to compensate for costs imposed on their properties from dirt, smoke, and vibration emanating from the plant. The court found the defendant guilty of a nuisance in that the company was making an "unreasonable" use of its land. This use created such externalities upon neighboring landowners that in order to maintain the relative economic position of all the parties before the court, the defendant had to pay for damages inflicted.

But the plaintiffs in *Boomer* also asked the court to enjoin the defendant from continuing the nuisance; on the facts of the case and the state of technology in cement production, this would have required the factory to shut down. The court denied the plaintiffs' motion for an injunction, noting that the defendant's investment in the plant was in excess of $45 million and that it employed 300 people.

There are two doctrines that a court may apply to deny an injunction and possible damages even after a nuisance is found: the *balancing-the-equities doctrine* and the *coming-to-the-nuisance doctrine*.

The doctrine of balancing the equities sometimes requires a court to deny a remedy to the plaintiff even if a nuisance is otherwise proven. The courts have examined the harm alleged by the plaintiff and compared it to the harm that the defendant and society would suffer if the defendant had to cease operations. Thus, in *Clifton Iron Company* v. *Dye*,[29] the development of mining interests was judged to be more important than the pollution the defendant caused by his operations. Some earlier cases have similar holdings. For example, in *Pennsylvania Coal Co.* v. *Sanderson,* the court found,

---

[26] *Roble* v. *Lillis,* 112 N.H. 492, 299 A.2d 155, 158 (1972).

[27] *Boomer* v. *Atlantic Cement Co.,* 26 N.Y. 2d 219, 257 N.E.2d 870, 309 N.Y.S. 2d 312 (1970).

[28] *Baldwin* v. *McClendon,* 292 Al. 43, 288 S.2d 761 (1974).

[29] *Clifton Iron Co.* v. *Dye,* 87 Ala. 468, 6 So. 192 (1888).

The plaintiff's grievance is for a mere personal inconvenience; and we are of the opinion that mere private personal inconveniences ... must yield to the necessities of a great public industry, which, although in the hands of a private corporation, subserves a great public interest. To encourage the development of the great natural resources of a country trifling inconveniences to particular persons must sometimes give way to the necessity of a great community.[30]

Similarly, the defendant's own financial interests must be examined:

If the resulting damage ... because of the nuisance cannot be avoided, or only at such expense as would be practically prohibitive to a person in the enjoyment of his own land, he (the defendant) may not be required to abate the nuisance.[31]

In this Pennsylvania case, the commonwealth was attempting to stop the pollution of a stream, but lost because of its inability to formulate a practical plan of abatement.

The coming-to-the-nuisance doctrine prevents the plaintiff from recovering because "one who voluntarily places himself in a situation whereby he suffers an injury will not be heard to say that his damage is due to the nuisance maintained by another."[32] Thus, a person who moves next to a golf course cannot complain that golf balls are falling on his property.[33]

Taking (with Just Compensation) versus Applying the Police Power

In framing laws that are designed to deal with a nuisance, it is necessary to make a decision as to whether or not the police power should be applied. The police power has been described by the Supreme Court as,

one of the most essential powers of government, one that is least limitable. It may, indeed, seem harsh in its exercise, usually is on some individual, but the imperative necessity for its existence precludes any limitation upon it when not exerted arbitrarily.[34]

Yet this power can be in conflict with another fundamental tenet of American law, the Fifth Amendment of the Constitution of the United States, which prohibits the taking of property without just compensation. This provision is a "seemingly absolute protection" against the possibility

[30] *Pennsylvania Coal Co.* v. *Sanderson,* 113 Pa. 126, 6 A. 459 (1886).

[31] *Commonwealth* v. *Wyeth Laboratories,* 12 Pa. Commw. Ct. 327, 315 A.2d 648, 653 (1974).

[32] *Oetjen* v. *Goff Kirby Co.,* 38 Ohio L. Abs. 117, 124, 49 N.E.2d 95, 99 (Ct. App. Cuyahoga County, 1942).

[33] *Patton* v. *Westwood Country Club,* 18 Ohio App. 2d 137, 247 N.E.2d 761 (1969).

[34] *Hadachek* v. *Sebastian,* 234 U.S. 394, 410 (1915).

of confiscation by the government of a private party's property without compensation.

In *Pennsylvania Coal Co.* v. *Mahon,* the Supreme Court held that the police power qualifies the protection granted under the Fifth Amendment. Justice Holmes, speaking for the Court, concluded,

> The natural tendency of human nature is to extend the qualification more and more until at last private property disappears.... We are in danger of forgetting that a strong public desire to improve the public condition is not enough to warrant achieving the desire by a shorter cut than the constitutional way of paying for the change.[35]

Since the decision in *Pennsylvania Coal Co.* v. *Mahon,* the state courts have struggled to strike the proper balance between the police power qualification and the seemingly absolute prohibition against taking property without paying just compensation.

But under what circumstances does diminution of property value warrant compensation?[36] The Supreme Court, in *Pennsylvania Coal Co.* v. *Mahon,* stated the diminution-of-value test as follows:

> Government hardly could go on if, to some extent, values incident to property could not be diminished without paying for every such change in the general law.... One fact for consideration ... is the extent of the diminution. When it reaches a certain magnitude, in most cases if not all cases there must be an exercise of eminent domain and compensation to sustain the act.[37]

Since the *Pennsylvania Coal* decision, courts have sought to determine what magnitude of diminution is the "certain magnitude" mentioned by Justice Holmes. Courts have concluded that neither financial hardship nor substantial diminution is sufficient for a taking. They have instead required that "a property owner be unable, permanently, to use his property ... and is therefore deprived of all beneficial use thereof."[38] Despite what appears to be an insurmountable burden for a plaintiff, many property owners in environmental cases have succeeded in satisfying the test.

In *Morris County Land Improvement Co.* v. *Township of Parsippany–Troy Hills,* zoning regulations had created meadowlands to promote flood control.[39]

---

[35] *Pennsylvania Coal Co.* v. *Mahon,* 260 U.S. 393, 413 (1922).

[36] See, Bruce A. Ackerman, *Private Property and the Constitution* (New Haven: Yale University Press, 1977).

[37] *Pennsylvania Coal Co.* v. *Mahon,* 260 U.S. 413.

[38] *Bureau of Mines of Maryland* v. *George's Creek Coal and Land Co.,* Md., 321 A.2d 748, 762 (1974).

[39] *Morris County Land Improvement Co.* v. *Township of Parsippany–Troy Hills,* 40 N.J. 539, 193 A.2d 232 (1963).

The uses permitted the plaintiff were very limited and severely reduced the property's value. The New Jersey Supreme Court concluded that the regulations "are clearly far too restrictive and as such are constitutionally unreasonable and confiscatory."[40] The court, in determining the property's value, examined not only its existing value as a swamp, but its potential value if filled. For that reason there was a great diminution of value, which resulted in a taking without compensation.

In *State* v. *Johnson*, the Maine State Wetlands Control Board attempted to prohibit the filling of coastal wetlands.[41] The landowner argued that such a regulation made his property "commercially valueless land."[42] The Supreme Court of Maine agreed, holding that the prohibition amounted to a taking of property without just compensation and an unreasonable exercise of the police power. As in the *Morris* case, the value of the property included its potential after landfill.

In *Dooley* v. *Town Plan and Zoning Commission of Town of Fairfield*,[43] the plaintiff's property was zoned as a floodplain with a limited number of uses, and, in fact, the court found that "use of the plaintiff's land has been, for all practical purposes, rendered impossible."[44] The diminution in value was estimated to be approximately 75%, which the Supreme Court of Connecticut found to be a taking without just compensation.

On the other hand, an early case permitting extreme diminution of value within the police power is *Hadachek* v. *Sebastian*.[45] Despite the plaintiff's loss of nearly 90% of the value of his property, the Supreme Court in 1915 found no taking, commenting that the exercise of the police power is sometimes "harsh."

Courts have again begun to permit substantial diminution, verging on total deprivation, without compensation. In *Turnpike Realty Co.* v. *Town of Dedham*,[46] the zoning board had established a floodplain district. The case was very similar to the cases just mentioned, but the result was vastly different. The diminution of the plaintiff's land was approximately 90%, but the Massachusetts Supreme Court concluded,

> We realize that it is often extremely difficult to determine the precise line where regulation ends and confiscation begins. The result depends on the "peculiar circum-

---

[40] *Ibid.*: 242.

[41] *State* v. *Johnson*, 265 A.2d 711 (Me. 1970).

[42] *Ibid.*: 716.

[43] *Dooley* v. *Town Plan and Zoning Commission of Town of Fairfield*, 151 Conn. 304, 197 A.2d 770 (1964).

[44] *Ibid.*: 772.

[45] *Hadachek* v. *Sebastian*, 239 U.S. 394, 410 (1915).

[46] *Turnpike Realty Co.* v. *Town of Dedham*, 284 N.E.2d 891 (Mass. 1972).

stances of the particular instance.". . . In the case at bar we are unable to conclude, even though the judge found a substantial diminution in the value of petitioner's land, that the decrease was such to render it an unconstitutional deprivation of property.[47]

STATUTORY ENVIRONMENTAL LAW

Nuisance litigation is cumbersome and costly for dealing with modern environmental problems, because the problems tend to be the result of multiple causes, involving scientifically complex issues and having widespread effects with many victims. Seldom are the cause-and-effect relations simple and remedies unique and obvious. Matters are further complicated by the fact that potential plaintiffs tend to bear relatively small parts of the social costs of a large problem and, therefore, have weak incentives to bring costly lawsuits that promise limited rewards.

All too often, the courts are poorly equipped to deal with difficult environmental issues, often requiring considerable scientific expertise to either rule on complicated environmental issues or oversee an ongoing program of technological controls, or both.

In the opinion of Dukemenier and Krier, "nuisance litigation is ill-suited to other than small-scale, incidental, localized scientifically uncomplicated pollution problems."[48] Admittedly, some efforts have been made to overcome the shortcomings of nuisance litigation by using class action suits.

The main alternative is environmental legislation, which on first consideration might appear difficult to enact. Since an individual's efforts on behalf of statutory pollution control can have only an infinitesimal effect on himself, "free riding" on efforts by others would produce virtually costless environmental benefits. This "free rider" problem should stand in the way of organizing large groups of environmentalists, while rent-seeking industrial interest groups should dominate the environmental scene. But, in fact many environmental statutes have been enacted, a fact explained by Farber.[49] His argument rests on an identifiable symbiotic relationship between legislators and such environmental groups as the National Wild Life Federation and the Sierra Club, with about 850,000 and 370,000 members, respectively. Environmental legislation is enacted because of strong public demand, which is effectively exploited by ideological and credit-seeking politicians. Farber points to a quid pro quo — environmental groups benefit officials by brokering information during the enactment

---

[47] *Ibid.*: 894.

[48] Jesse Dukemenier and John Krier, *Property* (Boston: Little, Brown, 1981): 956.

[49] Daniel H. Farber, "Politics and Procedure in Environmental Law," *Journals of Law, Economics and Organization* 8(1) (1992): 59–81.

process and assisting in the implementation of laws, while the legislation promotes the groups' growth.

Among the environmental statutes, the most important ones seek to mitigate air and water pollution, and address waste management and toxic substance problems. There are other environmental statutes, e.g., related to noise pollution, which are mainly local, and will not be taken up. The various environmental statutes are responsible for a 46% (or 1.3 billion pound) decline in release of toxic chemicals into the nation's environment between 1988 and 1997.[50]

AIR POLLUTION STATUTES

The first federal foray into the air pollution arena was the Air Pollution Control Act of 1955. It was followed by the Clean Air Act of 1963,[51] which was amended in 1967, 1970, 1977 and most importantly again in 1990. The 1990 amendments enacted massive programs for new and existing point sources that greatly expanded the number of facilities subject to point source regulation. The current law can be divided into six parts: (1) National Ambient Air Quality Standards (NAAQS) designed to insure that air quality throughout the United States is adequate to protect public health and the public welfare; (2) a program for preventing significant deterioration of air quality in those areas of the country that are currently clean; (3) complex requirements for stationary sources of air pollution; (4) strict inspection and enforcement programs for stationary sources; (5) tailpipe emission standards for mobile sources of air pollution and the regulation of fuels that are burned by such sources; and (6) programs for limiting production of air pollutants that are depleting the stratospheric ozone layer.

Air pollution statutes, though often controversial, have significantly improved air quality. For example, between 1986 and 1995 concentrations of carbon monoxide, sulfur dioxide, ground-level ozone, nitrogen dioxide, particulate matter, and lead have all decreased, some dramatically.[52]

WATER POLLUTION STATUTES

As far back as the 1940s, Congress took action designed to control water pollution, enacting the Federal Water Pollution Control Act of 1948; it looked upon the states as having primary responsibility in this area. Recognizing states' ineffectiveness, the Act was amended a number of times and

---

[50] "EPA Says Release of Toxic Chemicals Fell 46% Since 1988," *Wall Street Journal* (May 21, 1997): A16.
[51] 42 U.S.C. §§1857–1857 like in (1964).
[52] The *Economist* (March 15, 1997): 29.

in 1977, it was renamed the Clean Water Act.[53] A further amendment occurred in 1987 to prohibit all unpermitted discharges into the waters of the United States (including the territorial sea) of pollutants from point sources, to impose effluent limitations on dischargers, and to require state-wide planning for control of pollution from nonpoint sources. Other statutes address ocean dumping, oil pollution, coastal zone management, and safe drinking water.

Over the years, water control strategy has shifted from reliance on tech-nology-based standards to an emphasis on water quality standards. The latter, often expressed in specific numerical criteria, e.g., attainment levels, have been turned into the driving regulatory force implemented by the EPA. Technology-based standards are set by the EPA and apply uniformly to all dischargers within each covered industrial category regardless of the nature of the receiving waters. Water quality standards, in contrast, are set by individual states, subject to EPA approval, and thus can vary from state to state.

Water pollution statutes have had positive effects in that water quality in the United States has improved markedly in recent years.[54]1 Still, about 20% of the point sources of water pollution are neither in compliance with their permits nor have attained the goal of "fishable and swimmable waters." On the positive side, between 1972 and 1985, the number of Americans served by secondary waste-water treatment facilities rose from 85 to 127 million.[55]

WASTE MANAGEMENT STATUS

The principal statutory authorities that regulate waste management prac-tices are contained in the Resource Conservation and Recovery Act (RCRA) and the Comprehensive Environmental Response, Compensation and Lia-bility Act (CERCLA) codified at 42 U.S.C. §§9601–9675. It was substantially revised in 1984 by the Hazardous and Solid Waste Amendments (HSWA). Because CERCLA creates the federal Superfund, it is often referred to as the Superfund legislation. It was substantially amended in 1986 by the Superfund Amendments and Reauthorization Act (SARA), and reautho-rized in 1990. RCRA and CERCLA supplement each other. RCRA provides for cradle-to-grave regulation of hazardous waste substances and is to pre-

[53] Pub. L. 92-500, 33 U.S.C. §1251 et. seq.

[54] Jackson B. Battle and Maxine I. Lipeles, *Environmental Law: Water Pollution*, 2d ed. (Cincin-nati, OH: Anderson Publishing Co., 1993): 20.

[55] Council for Environmental Quality, *Twentieth Annual Report* (Washington, D.C.: Govern-ment Printing Office, 1990): 7–11.

vent releases of hazardous wastes. CERCLA is to clean up releases of a broader class of hazardous substances. They each employ very different means to pursue their goal. RCRA employs a regulatory approach, while CERCLA is founded on a strict liability scheme.[56]

TOXIC SUBSTANCE REGULATION

Toxic substance regulation involves protection of human life in the face of great uncertainties. "Toxic" is a term applied on the basis of a substance's ability to cause serious adverse health and environmental effects at low levels of exposure. Almost 60 substances commonly found in our environment are known to have toxic effects at some level of exposure.[57] Concern about them rose as society learned more about the seriousness of their effects on living organisms.

The Federal Insecticide, Fungicide, and Rodenticide Act was originally passed in 1948 and was significantly strengthened by two amendments.[58] With passage of the Toxic Substances Control Act and the Resource Conservation and Recovery Act in 1976,[59] standards and procedures could be established for control of toxic substances from their creation to disposal. The need for such standards became more pressing as knowledge of earlier use and disposal practices unfolded. Frightful examples were the Hudson River with its massive contamination by PCBs, and Love Canal, where discarded chemical wastes endangered the health of hundreds of families.[60]

---

[56] CERCLA empowers the EPA to respond to the actual or threatened release of a hazardous substance either by conducting the cleanup itself and suing a wide range of responsible parties for reimbursement, CERCLA §§104 and 107, 42 U.S.C. §§9604 and 9607, or by issuing an administrative order or seeking a court order requiring the responsible parties to conduct the cleanup themselves, CERCLA §106, 42 U.S.C. §9606. A party that receives an administrative order requiring it to cleanup a CERCLA site cannot challenge the order until an enforcement action is brought against it, §113(h), and if it fails at that time to prove that it had "sufficient cause" for not complying with the order, it is liable for up to $25,000 per day in civil penalties for such noncompliance, §106(b)(1), as well as treble damages if the EPA proceeds to conduct the cleanup and sues for reimbursement, §107(c)(3).

[57] Robert V. Percival, *Environmental Regulation: Law, Science and Policy*, 2d ed. (Boston: Little, Brown, 1992): 427.

[58] U.S. Code 1998 Title 7, §§135 et seq.

[59] U.S. Code 1988 Title 15, §§2601 et seq., and U.S. Code 1988 Title 42, §§6901 et seq.

[60] There exist many other statutes that regulate toxic substances. For example, under the Federal Insecticide, Fungicide, and Rodenticide Act (SDWA), the EPA regulates contaminants in public drinking water systems; section 112 of the Clean Air Act requires the EPA to regulate emissions of hazardous air pollutants; and under the Clean Water Act, the EPA regulates toxic water pollutants. Other agencies also have regulatory authority, e.g., the Food and Drug Administration, the Occupational Safety and Health Administration, the Consumer Product Safety Commission, and the Nuclear Regulatory Commission.

Principal provisions of the Toxic Substances Control Act authorize the EPA
to require the testing of any chemical substance on finding, for example,
that it is toxic and either may present an unreasonable risk of injury to
health or the environment or may result in substantial human exposure.
It requires data, 90 days in advance, indicating that a new chemical substance will not present an unreasonable risk, and it can prohibit manufacturing a dangerous substance or sue to seize it.

ECONOMIC ANALYSIS

Already in the 1970s Baumol and Oates expressed concern about elements
in our economic system that act as systematic inducements to abuse of the
environment. They pointed to "detrimental" externalities as a key cause
of our most serious environmental problems. When firms' activities result
in detrimental externalities and do not pay the costs they impose on others,
the market mechanism does an imperfect job of protecting the environment.[61]

In order to determine an optimal intervention, we must carefully define
the economic and legal relationships between property rights and entitlements on the one hand and externalities on the other hand. In line with
the *Restatement of Property*, which defines *right* as "a legally enforceable claim
of one person against another," a person who has a property right or
entitlement is legally able to compel another to commit or not to commit
a given act.[62] In the abstract, when one person's activity causes damage to
another person's property rights (i.e., imposes negative externalities), the
owner of the rights can force the person causing the damage to cease the
activity or pay for any damage incurred. Such externalities, which can
impose costs on (or avoid benefits to) persons who hold property rights
or entitlements, can take many forms relative to such environmental conditions as air, water, solid waste, noise, or view. What, then are the conditions
of optimal intervention?

If the assumptions that underlie the economist's model of perfectly
competitive markets were satisfied in real life, all impacts on the natural
environment, no matter who was responsible for them, would be appropri-
ately incorporated into the decisions of each party in those markets. However, these assumptions are not met, in part because of the very existence

---

[61] William Baumol and Wallace Oates, *Theory of Environmental Policy: Externalities, Public
Outlags and the Quality of Life* (Englewood, Cliffs, N.J.: Prentice-Hall, 1975).
[62] Restatement of Property, §1.

of externalities. The externalities of concern here do not result from the performance of malicious acts by decision makers but are, for the most part, produced incidentally in the pursuit of a legitimate activity. The presence of externalities prevents the market mechanism from reaching an economically efficient allocation of resources. Thus, when parties to a transaction generate externalities but fail to consider their implications in making the decision, the resource allocation is unlikely to be Pareto optimal. Hence, it will be theoretically possible to reallocate resources and increase the welfare of at least one member of society without decreasing that of any other member. For example, if a manufacturer pollutes the air, adversely affecting the health and welfare of people living in the neighborhood, and fails to incorporate these external costs into his production decisions, including those dealing with smoke-generation decisions, then the manufacturer's equilibrium level of pollution will tend to exceed the economically efficient level. Under such conditions, efficiency increases if the manufacturer reduces his pollution to a level at which the cost of additional pollution abatement exceeds the gain accruing to neighbors therefrom and if the abatement is financed exclusively from the gains obtained by the manufacturer's neighbors as a result of this smoke reduction.

In theory, such a solution can be negotiated under contract law if a very small number of parties are involved. The principle of this solution is stated by Coase:

> The traditional approach has tended to obscure the nature of the choice that has to be made. The question is commonly thought of as one in which A inflicts harm on B and what has to be decided is: how should we restrain A? But this is wrong. We are dealing with a problem of a reciprocal nature. To avoid the harm to B would inflict harm on A. The real question that has to be decided is: should A be allowed to harm B or should B be allowed to harm A? The problem is to avoid the more serious harm.[63]

This principle can be applied to our example: Unrestricted generation of smoke by a manufacturer gains him additional profits while imposing external costs on his neighbors; pollution-control activities provide gains to the firm's neighbors while imposing smoke-abatement costs on the manufacturer. Thus, the external effect is caused by both the resource owner who generates the effect and the resource owner who receives it. Optimal resource allocation demands that both of these resource owners take into account all external effects related to their resource decisions. This situation

---

[63] Ronald Coase, "The Problem of Social Cost," *Journal of Law and Economics* 3 (October 1960): 1–2.

obtains if those who seek to modify the behavior of a second party engage in a trade with that party, moving both to preferred positions where all additional mutually agreeable trades are available and thus a Pareto optimum prevails.

However, trade requires a careful assignment of resource rights in externality situations. Such determination will indicate either that the manufacturer possesses the right to generate any quantity of smoke that he deems desirable or that his neighbors possess the right to an environment that contains at most a specified level of smoke, possibly zero. Once these rights are assigned, and if these rights are transferable and rigidly enforced and no costs are associated with the negotiations and enforcement, then any particular assignment of resource rights will produce an economically efficient resource allocation.[64] Under such conditions, the stipulated property-right assignment provides incentives to one of the parties in the externalities situation to seek changes in the externality-producing activity by offering inducements to modify its behavior.

Since the marginal cost associated with any particular increase in the production of an external effect is unaffected by resource-right assignment, the very same economically efficient resource allocation can be obtained as long as the differences in wealth distribution that are associated with the various systems do not affect demand patterns. In short, if the income elasticity of demand is zero in all markets, including the market for the external effect, and if the cost of negotiating and enforcing transactions is zero, the market resolution of any externality problem will be both economically efficient and allocatively neutral with respect to the assignment of liability. However, several studies have demonstrated that the asserted allocative neutrality of alternative assignments of resource rights will not prevail when some of the resource owners who are involved in the externalities situation are merely consumers, when the income elasticity of demand for at least some goods in the economy is not zero, or when the costs of negotiating and enforcing transactions are positive.[65] Since one or more of these conditions tend to prevail in real life, negotiated resolutions

---

[64] Property rights with respect to liability damages are transferable if the government enforces liability rules only upon appeal by one of the parties involved in the externalities situation. Such an enforcement policy introduces the possibility of exchange between these parties.

[65] F. T. Dolbear, "On the Theory of Optimum Externality," *American Economic Review* 56 (March 1967): 95–97; W. J. Samuels, "The Coase Theorem and the Study of Law and Economics," *Natural Resources Journal* 14 (January 1974): 6–12; and A. Randall, "Coasian Externality Theory in a Policy Context," *Natural Resources Journal* 14 (January 1974): 43–44.

of externality situations are unlikely to be allocatively neutral with respect to alternative assignments of property rights.

COST-BENEFIT ANALYSIS

When environmental amenities are not traded in markets, their value is not registered and since therefore the amenities do not move to the most highly valued uses, government often intervenes. Its decisions can be aided by a cost–benefit analysis. It allows comparisons of social benefits with their opportunity costs and ultimately can lead to socially desirable resource allocation. Not only are cost–benefit analyses undertaken explicitly, but an empirical study of EPA decisions finds that the EPA has acted as if both costs and benefits influence its selection of regulatory standards.[66]

What are the benefits that are expected from pollution control and other environmental initiatives? The major classes relate to population longevity and health, crop and lifestock production, and recreation values. Measuring benefits poses major difficulties. Nevertheless, air pollution-control benefits — health and longevity — have been measured. For example, Lave and Seskin showed in a study of 117 Standard Metropoliton Statistical Areas (SMSAs) that air pollution was a significant factor in explaining the variation in total death rate.[67] In efforts to place monetary values on life, mainly two approaches have been used. One method observes market transactions in which people actually purchase or sell changes in their risk levels. A second method relies on interviews in which people are asked about hypothetical situations. When such a contingent valuation method is employed, the questionnaire elicits the willingness of respondents to pay for (generally) hypothetical projects or programs.[68]

Rather than measuring directly the effect of air pollution control on health, longevity, crop yields, etc., real estate values can provide an indirect measure. For example, hedonic housing price functions discussed in Chapter 3, which include levels of pollutants, could prove a useful tool. Also, the benefits from water pollution control that accrue in terms of improved recreational opportunities have been measured by Clawson and Knetsch, who used a travel-cost approach that calculates the value of recreation in

[66] George L. Van Houtwen and Maureen L. Cropper, "When Is Life Too Costly to Save? The Evidence from Environmental Regulations," *Resources 114* (Winter 1994): 6.

[67] L. B. Lave and E. P. Seskin, *Air Pollution and Human Health* (Baltimore: Johns Hopkins University Press, 1977): 238–239.

[68] Portney Paul, "The Contingent Valuation Debate: Why Economists Should Care" *Journal of Economic Perspectives* 8(4) (Fall 1994): 3–117.

terms of the distance that people are willing to travel to recreational facilities and expenses they were willing to incur in doing so.[69]

Costs associated with initiatives to improve the environment relate to present and future undertakings. The latter pose special difficulties since future control technologies are shrouded in uncertainty and so are their capital costs of control equipment, as well as its repair and maintenance. Since the opportunity cost concept guides costing environmental programs, some costs are particularly difficult to estimate. For example, in damming a river, recreation opportunities to fish, raft, bike, etc., are lost.

Decisions about environmental initiatives, as well as their legal review, can make use of cost–benefit analysis, which works in the following manner: the more relevant environmental alternatives are identified and for each alternative all benefits and costs are listed, evaluated to obtain dollar figures, and adjusted by a discount rate to determine their present value. The present values of the social costs and benefits of each alternative are compared, and the one with the highest overall excess of social benefits over social costs in terms of present values is chosen. It is the socially optimal alternative. In most instances, difficulties exist because of serious evaluation problems, absence of clear-cut guidelines for the selection of discount rates, and a host of theoretical issues.[70] When there are many intangible benefits and costs related to an environmental initiative, it might be helpful, after presenting estimates of quantifiable benefits and costs, to list intangible ones and offer some qualitative evaluation. Since cost–benefit analyses are so very sensitive to the chosen interest rate, calculations for two or three different rates might be presented. Note that the higher the discount rate, the smaller the significance of benefits and costs that accrue in the future. Moreover, Weitzman has argued that since environmental concerns tend to increase, it would be a mistake to hold the discount rate constant over time.[71]

INSTRUMENTS FOR PROTECTING THE ENVIRONMENT

The main instruments presently in use, particularly in mitigating air and water pollution, fall into two main classes: price and quantity instruments. The latter include command-and-control regulation and the trading in

---

[69] Marion Clawson and Jack Knetsch, *Economics of Outdoor Recreation* (Baltimore: Johns Hopkins University Press, 1996).

[70] For a summary of some of the problems common to most of welfare economics, see John V. Krutilla and Anthony C. Fisher, *The Economics of Natural Environments* (Baltimore: Johns Hopkins University Press, 1975): 28–35.

[71] Martin L. Weitzman, "On the Environmental Discount Rate," *Journal of Environmental Economics and Management* 26 (1994): 200–209.

emission permits assigned by a central agency. The price instruments include Pigouvian effluent taxes or fees and subsidies.

The efficacy of these instruments must ultimately be judged in terms of the attainment of the overall efficiency in the economy. An optimum level must not take into account merely the costs and benefits of pollution abatement, but also those associated with the activities from which pollution emanates. Thus, it would seek to achieve the overall optimum pollution level for the economy. Usually, a higher level of government mandates achievement of a specified pollution target. In the United States, the Federal government's EPA sets the standards. But it is a local agency that ultimately is responsible for implementing the mandated standards. Toward this end, local agencies must select the instrument that is most likely to meet the pollution abatement objectives efficiently.

The tax-fee alternative is the most important price instrument, which has two alternatives. One involves periodic taxes that are paid after or at the time firms or people impact on the environment. These *ex post* taxes can be distinguished from *ex ante*, lump-sum taxes. In both instances, a tax should be levied equal to the marginal net damage, that is, the difference between marginal social and private costs.[72]

For example, where a factory's pollution damages a laundry, the *ex post* tax levied on the factory should equal the damage its smoke caused the laundry during the preceding period. The tax restrains factory smoke emission, and the costs of operating the factory, including pollution control, are internalized to the factory owner, a step consistent with optimal resource allocation. Imposing *ex post* pollution taxes becomes increasingly difficult and costly the more polluters there are and where polluters are mobile, e.g., cars.

An *ex ante*, lump-sum tax is set at a level equal to the discounted present value of the damage expected to be caused by a given activity in the future. In the presence of great uncertainties about future circumstances surrounding a pollution source during its lifetime, determining the proper *ex ante* tax-fee is particularly difficult. Examples are construction permit, rezoning, and sewer connection fees.

A second price instrument, though rarely used, is subsidies, basically the obverse of the polluter's fee approach. Selective cash grants can be made to polluters in return for their restricting emissions to an optimal degree. These cash grants could in principle be equivalent to the off-site costs imposed by increments of waste discharge and could vary with conditions as well as pollutants. Since the subsidy instrument resembles the polluter's

---

[72] A. C. Pigou, *The Economics of Welfare* (New York: Macmillan, 1932).

fee scheme, though its approach is the opposite, the criticism of tax-fees would also apply here. The strongest criticism has been advance by Mills, who declares,

> They are simply payments for the wrong thing. The investment credit proposal will illustrate the deficiency that is common to others. An investment credit on air pollution abatement equipment reduces the cost of such equipment. But most such equipment is inherently unprofitable in that it adds nothing to revenues and does not reduce costs. To reduce the cost of such an item cannot possibly induce a firm to install it.[73]

Theorists have also shown that subsidization will be less effective than taxation in inducing the internalization of external diseconomies, but it will be more effective than taxation in inducing the internalization of external economies.[74] Moreover, subsidization is likely to be inefficient, in that it will frequently stimulate the purchase of special equipment when other methods might be superior. Furthermore, taxpayers' feelings of equity might be violated, since the industrial firm, in not having to consider pollution abatement a cost of production in the same sense that labor and capital are, would rely on payments raised at least partially by higher taxes on other taxpayers.

The second approach relies on such quantity instruments as command-and-control regulation, sometimes in conjunction with emission permit trading. These instruments modify the behavior of potential polluters directly. Examples are outlawing use of high-sulfur coal, prescribing the installation of scrubbers on factory stacks, and limiting motor vehicle exhaust emissions to a specified number of grams per mile. Once a regulatory program is in place, it is backed by civil and/or criminal penalties. In short, regulations tell polluters how and/or how much to control their production activities. Legal sanctions are designed to achieve compliance.

A key question is the determination of the pollution limit, i.e., the cap deemed desirable by society. Cost–benefit analysis can again help determine the optimal use of society's scarce resources by trading off environmental amenities against other goods and services. Specifically, it involves weighing the social costs of environmental amenities against their social benefits.

---

[73] E. S. Mills, "Federal Incentives in Air Pollution Control," *Proceedings, National Conference on Air Pollution* (December 12–14, 1966): 576.

[74] F. T. Dolbear, "On the Theory of Optimum Externality," *American Economic Review* 56 (March 1967): 90–103, G. A. Mumey, "The 'Coase Theorem': A Re-examination," *Quarterly Review of Economics and Statistics* 85 (November 1971): 718–723; and R. A. Tybout, "Pricing Pollution and Other Externalities," *Bell Journal of Economics and Management Science* 13 (Spring 1972): 252–266.

Theoretically, once society has chosen an overall maximum permissible level of a particular pollutant (e.g., carbon monoxide), then the most efficient method to achieve the desired level is to have each polluter reduce his level of pollution output until the marginal costs of an incremental decrease in pollution are the same for all polluters.

I will next turn to command-and-control regulation in conjunction with trading in emission permits, particularly in the case of air pollution.[75] Beginning in the early 1980s, governments have been experimenting with emission permit (or pollution right) markets as a means to reduce the costs of achieving a given emission reduction goal.[76] A permit to emit a given pollutant is issued to polluting firms, which are then free to reduce emissions and sell their unneeded permits or to buy permits rather than reduce emissions, depending on which is more cost-effective. Like with all instruments using market-based incentives, marginal costs of compliance are equalized among polluting firms. This occurs when emission control burdens are transferred to firms with low control costs. As a result, a specified level of aggregate emission control is attained by the use of relatively fewer total resources.

While such a trading system can be less costly than most other pollution control instruments, transactions costs can be quite high. Such costs stem from information search, bargaining between emission permit buyers and sellers, and monitoring enforcement, although the latter occurs mainly to government. Transaction costs can significantly affect the quantity and pattern of trading and hence the total cost of pollution control. The choice between emission permit trading and other instruments must be made on a case-by-case basis.[77]

Recent evidence suggests that emission permit trading authorized under Title IV of the 1990 Amendments to the Clean Air Act is reducing (SO_2)

[75] S. Atkinson and T. Tietenberg, "Market Failure in Incentive-Based Regulation: The Case of Emissions Trading," *Journal of Environmental Economics and Management* 21 (1991): 17–31.

[76] For example, the South Coast Air Quality Management District, responsible for controlling air pollution in much of Southern California, i.e., an area with a population of about 14 million, adopted an emissions trading program. Specifically, its Board adopted in 1993 an emissions trading program for oxides of nitrogen (NO_x) and oxides of sulfur (S_x) known as RECLAIM — Regional Clean Air Incentives Market — for 393 firms. Under RECLAIM, the District determines the overall amount of permissible pollution for the basin and then distributes to each of the firms a given number of pollution permits. Firms polluting less than the number of permits they were endowed with can sell the excess permits to firms in the opposite situation.

[77] Robert N. Stavins, "Pollution Charges for Environmental Protection Policy Link between Energy and Environment," *Annual Review of Energy and Environment* 7 (1992): 187–210.

emission by nearly one-half.[78] This emission reduction is achieved at about one-half to one-third of the cost compared to that of instruments used during the first 20 years of federal air pollution control. Flexibility is the main reason for this salubrious outcome.

COMPARISON OF TAX-FEES WITH REGULATION IN CONJUNCTION WITH TRADING IN EMISSION PERMITS

The relative merits of quantity instruments, such as trading in emission permits, on the one hand, and price instruments such as effluent tax-fees, on the other, are affected by a variety of factors. They include transaction costs, incorrectly set emission permits and fee levels, strategic behavior — including collusion and entry denial to competitors, interest group distortions, and distorting revenue effects. Both price and quantity instruments involve high transaction costs. Those of price instruments are particularly high, since it is extremely difficult and costly to correctly estimate the tax-fees' effect on polluters and therefore on pollution levels. If decision makers are risk averse, they will tend to set fees too high and thereby unduly damage the local economy. As flawed estimates are made, frequent and costly fee adjustments will be necessary. These transaction costs are likely to be significantly higher than those of a quantity instrument that requires issuance of emission permits and establishment of a market in which they are traded.

Closely related to the transaction cost issue is the damage done by setting incorrect tax-fees and permit levels. In addition, there is also the issue of strategic behavior, which comes into play in the absence of accurate information to all market participants. This issue is likely to be most pressing with trading permits, particularly if they are of relatively long duration or are bankable. Then new entrants must purchase them from existing, perhaps well-heeled, permit holders with an excess of permits, and permit purchasers can withhold permits from the market for the purpose of preventing the entry of potential competitors. No counterpart to this problem exists in relation to fees.

Furthermore, powerful interests can significantly affect the setting of pollution caps, permits, and tax-fees. Interest groups, for example, will tend to exert pressure to have relatively high caps. Fewer opportunities appear to exist for interest group distortions in relation to price rather than quantity instruments. Finally, the revenue effect of pollution fees over time poses

[78] Dallas Burtraw, "Trading Emissions to Clean the Air: Exchanges Few but Savings Many," *Resources* 122 (Winter 1996): 3.

efficiency concerns. What are we to do once these tax-fees have produced the called-for abatement goals? If they are abandoned, pollution increases will be ignited, and if they are kept, uncalled-for fund transfers from the private to the public sector occur.[79]

ENVIRONMENTAL REGULATIONS, PRODUCTIVITY, AND COMPETITIVENESS

Grave concerns are common about the effects of environmental laws on how well firms and industries perform in such an environment. Some claim that such regulations impose significant costs, impair productivity gains, and interfere with American competitiveness abroad. In fact, when the effect of regulations was tested empirically by Gray and Shadbegian in relation to paper, oil, and steel plants, they found that from 1975 to 1985 the more regulated the plant, the smaller its productivity and productivity growth.[80] Specifically, a $1 increase in compliance cost was associated with a 3 to 4% reduction in (total factor) productivity.

While the long-run social costs of environmental regulation may be major and affect adversely productivity, Jaffe et al. in their review article concluded that "studies ... to measure the effect of environmental regulation on net exports ... have produced estimates that are either small, statistically insignificant, or not robust to tests of model specification."[81] The finding that such regulations have minor, if any, effects on competitiveness and economic growth can be attributed to two factors. Even in heavily regulated industries environmental costs are small and such regulations tend to be about the same in most industrialized countries. Moreover, a study by Hall et al. of the effects of air pollution control on Southern California found positive effects. From 1964 to 1990 air quality significantly improved, while the economy grew more than that of the nation, i.e., 85 versus 53%, and manufacturing jobs grew 17%, while they declined 4% percent nationally.[82]

[79] Horst Zimmermann, "The Revenue Effect of Environmental Charges," *Zeitschrift für Angewante Umweltforschung* 7 (1993): 26–36.

[80] Wayne Gray and Ronald Shadbegian, *Environmental Regulation and Manufacturing Productivity on the Plant Level* (Cambridge, MA: National Bureau of Economic Research, 1993).

[81] Abram B. Jaffe et al., "Environmental Regulation and the Competitiveness of U.S. Manufacturing: What Does the Evidence Tell Us?" *Journal of Economic Literature* 33(1) (March 1995): 157–158.

[82] Jane Hall et. al., *The Automobile, Air Pollution Regulation and the Economy of Southern California* (Fullerton, CA: Institute for Economic and Environmental Studies, 1995): 53–116.

CONCLUSION

Environmental law has grown out of society's concern with defining, enforcing, and allocating environmental property rights and entitlements, a complex task because of the interrelated and, therefore, nonexclusive nature of environmental resources. By their inherent nature, the use of environmental resources generates a host of externalities, thereby making specific enforceable rights to their usage difficult to define. They are therefore difficult to exchange and reallocate to their highest valued alternative use.

Courts and legislatures have been called on to intervene. They have applied nuisance laws for a long time. But since nuisance laws and its litigation are cumbersome, statutory environmental law has supplemented court-made law. Thus, beginning in the early 1970s, statutes in relation to air, water, and noise pollution as well as waste management and toxic substance disposal have been enacted. In these undertakings, and their agency-issued regulations, increasing use is being made of cost–benefit analysis toward reaching efficient resource decisions in environmentally sensitive areas. To protect the environment, two major classes of instruments have been developed — quantity instruments, which include command-and-control regulation alone and in conjunction with emission permit trading, and price instruments, which include the levying of Pigouvian effluent fee-taxes and subsidies. The efficacy of each of those instruments much depends on a host of factors, including transaction cost, difficulty of setting correct tax-fee and permit levels, strategic behavior, interest group distortion, and distorting revenue effects.

10

ANTIMONOPOLY LAW

Contract law, as was discussed earlier, is based on the premise that all parties to a transaction are reasonably equal in bargaining power. This equality of bargaining power is a prerequisite — a necessary though not sufficient condition — for a competitive market, where important characteristics of a competitive market are:

1. A large number of firms
2. Homogeneous products
3. Free entry into and exit from the market
4. Independence of decisions among firms
5. Perfect knowledge

Economists differentiate between perfect and pure competition. *Perfect competition* requires all five characteristics; for *pure competition*, some economists consider the first four characteristics essential; others, merely the first two. In the absence of pure or perfect competition, markets are monopolistic or oligopolistic to varying degrees, depending on whether the industry has one or a small number of members.

However, as E. S. Mason has effectively argued, lawyers and economists use the word *monopoly* (and therefore the word *competition*) in distinctly different ways.[1] For lawyers, the term *monopoly* is used as "a standard of

---

[1] E. S. Mason, "Monopoly in Law and Economics," *Yale Law Journal* 47 (November 1937): 34–49.

evaluation," designating a situation not in the public interest *Competition*, in comparison, designates situations in the public interest. For the lawyer, monopoly means a restriction of the freedom of business to engage in legitimate economic activities.

To an economist, the distinction between monopoly and pure competition is the differing ways in which market transactions occur and resources are allocated under the two. A monopolist (or oligopolist) is able to influence the market price. Consequently, firm output decisions are made keeping in mind their potential effect on price. A (pure) competitor, conversely, cannot affect the market price; as a result, in the abstract, he seeks to maximize profits by producing until marginal cost equals price.

A firm with monopoly power will produce at a lower output level and charge a higher price than an identical firm in a competitive market. Clearly, total surplus could be increased by forcing a monopolist to act like a competitive firm, yet whether such coercion could or should be adopted is a difficult question. It is imperative to ask not only whether a firm has market power but also why it has such power.

Besides questions of efficiency, issues of social justice and equity may also be relevant in evaluating the effects of monopolies. The domination of an industry by a single firm may be undesirable, apart from effects on efficiency. For instance, to allow a single firm to dominate an industry vital to national security may grant the firm's owners more political power than is in society's interest.

Why should government interfere with the sanctity of a contract? The reason is simple. When there exists great inequality in bargaining power, a contract, even if freely arrived at, can have major ill effects on others who are not parties to it. Government intervention, it can be argued, is then needed to champion resource-allocation efficiency.

Some authors have expressed strong opinions on these issues. For example, R. H. Bork argues,

> The present misshapen look of antitrust doctrine is due in large measure to the Supreme Court's habit of regarding business efficiency as either irrelevant or harmful. Insufficient regard for efficient methods of production and distribution meant that hardly any business practice challenged could survive.[2]

Clearly, as will be seen, this is not the only view of antimonopoly laws. Walter Adams reaches the conclusion that the enforcement of antitrust laws by the Justice Department and the Federal Trade Commission "have

[2] R. H. Bork, "Vertical Constraints: Schwinn Overruled," 1977 *Supreme Court Review*, P. Kurland and G. Caper, Eds. (Chicago: University of Chicago Press, 1977): 172.

had a salutary deterrent effect on many forms of anticompetitive behavior."[3] Phillip Areeda and Donald Turner, in their five-volume treatise on antitrust law, conclude that it is socially desirable to reduce otherwise persistent monopoly power not based on economies of scale, and they voice serious concern about the detrimental effects of barriers to entry resulting from monopoly power.[4]

In exploring the law and economics of antimonopoly law, I will examine the role played by incentives to monopolize markets and review key antimonopoly laws. This will be followed by a review of instruments commonly used to gain monopoly power. They include horizontal mergers and conglomerates, cooperation among competitors, price discrimination, and government-induced price fixing and entry foreclosing. Finally, the rather new issue of antitrust policy toward high-tech firms in a global economy will be examined.

THE ECONOMIC INCENTIVE TO MONOPOLIZE MARKETS

In theory, the existence of a perfectly competitive equilibrium relies upon the fulfillment of a number of restrictive assumptions, some of which were discussed earlier. Individual firms are assumed to be identical in every respect, each producing at minimum long-run average total cost. Consequently, the market supply curve is equal to the summation of the individual firms' marginal cost curves. The solution is depicted as point A in Figure 10—1, at the intersection of the market demand and supply curves. Output equals Q_c and price equals P_c.

A monopolist also equates MC and MR to maximize profits. In Figure 10—1, if we now assume that a single monopolist has the same marginal cost curve as the summation of MC curves of the competitive industry, we can compare the monopoly and competitive solutions. Since the monopolistic firm is not a price-taker, the firm knows its output decision will determine the market price and, consequently, the profitability of the firm. As a result, the monopolist, also equating MR to MC, maximizes profits by choosing a lower output level Q_m and a higher price P_m than that found in a competitive market. In a monopolistic market as compared to a perfectly competitive market, total surplus is reduced by the value of the triangle ABD.

[3] Walter Adams, "Antitrust and a Free Economy," in *Industrial Concentration and the Market System,* Eleanor M. Fox and James T. Halverson, Eds. (American Bar Association, 1979): 43.

[4] Phillip Areeda and Donald F. Turner, *Antitrust Law,* Little Brown, Boston (1978 and 1980).

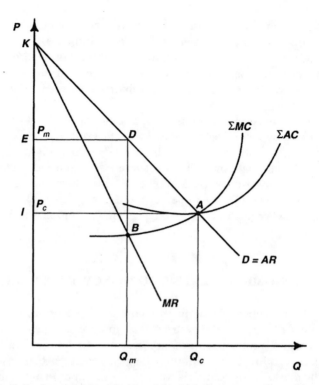

FIGURE 10—1 Profit-maximizing solutions of the single-firm monopolist and the competitive firm. (Key: *MC*, marginal cost function; *AC*, average cost; *MR*, marginal revenue function; *D = AR*, demand or average revenue function; P_m, price, and Q_m, output of the monopolist; P_c, price, and Q_c, output, of the competitive firm.)

A fundamental question is why other firms do not enter monopolistic industries and compete away much or all of the monopoly profits until the competitive outcome is achieved. There are several reasons why other firms will not enter. First, average costs of production may be falling over a long range of production levels, meaning that very large firms have cost advantages. If there are increasing returns to scale, then the industry may be composed of a single firm. This is considered a natural monopoly, since it is the nature of the technology that engenders this outcome.

Second, there may exist significant economies of scale, meaning that it is cheaper for firms to produce at higher output levels. The distinction between economies of scale and increasing returns is that the former does not refer to the production process but rather to factors including the prices of inputs, large fixed-cost expenditures such as advertising and research and development, and other similar factors.

Third, firms may have patents on certain products forbidding other manufacturers to produce the same product.

These and other barriers to entry enable firms to enjoy monopoly power. How much a firm is willing to spend to create and maintain monopoly power (expenditures include political lobbying against antitrust laws, technological research to maintain a comparative advantage, etc.) depends to a large extent on the additional profits to be gained by having the market power. This rests mainly on the industry elasticity of demand. Specifically, an industry where demand is highly inelastic offers much higher potential profits for monopoly firms.

Beside the difficulty of isolating the causes of monopoly power, it is difficult to determine how much market power individual firms have. There is much disagreement about the relationship between concentration and profit rates. Stigler has shown that monopoly and concentration are positively correlated.[5] Demsetz, however, argues that profit rates may be less the result of concentration than of superior performance by firms.[6]

A BRIEF OUTLINE OF ANTIMONOPOLY ACTS

Antimonopoly law, more commonly referred to as *antitrust law*, is derived from broad statutory guidelines provided mainly in the Sherman, Clayton, and Federal Trade Commission (FTC) acts.

Section 1 of the Sherman Act provides that every contract, combination, or conspiracy in restraint of trade among the several states is illegal. Section 2 outlaws single-firm monopolization. Thus, Sherman Act standards parallel Mason's legal definition of monopoly, cited earlier in the chapter. There is wide agreement that a per se approach toward conspiratorial conduct to fix prices is justified. To the extent that conspiracies are effective, the chance of vigorous price competition is reduced.

The Clayton Act limits undertakings that tend to lessen competition substantially or create a monopoly. Horizontal mergers have been judged on almost a purely structural basis and have been found illegal whenever an increase in the centralization of market power is a probable result. The test for vertical mergers has been the degree to which customers or suppliers

---

[5] G. J. Stigler, *Capital and Rates of Return in Manufacturing Industries* (Princeton, N. J.: Princeton University Press, 1963): 78.

[6] H. Demsetz, "Economics as a Guide to Antitrust Regulation," *Journal of Law and Economics* 19 (August 1976): 374.

would be foreclosed from the part of the market represented by one of the merging firms. (On the basis of *FTC* v. *Proctor and Gamble Co.*[7] courts find anticompetitive implications in overall firm size as well as in relative size in a given market.)

Section 2, amended by the Robinson–Patman Act, prohibits price discrimination.[8] This currently contested provision, which can prohibit the lowering of prices, has led to the businessman's lament that he cannot lower prices, "administer" prices by keeping them constant, or raise prices without violating some antitrust law.[9] Section 3 makes many tie-in arrangements illegal. These are sales or leases of products on condition not to buy from competitors. Section 7, amended by the Celler-Kefauver Act of 1950, renders corporate mergers and acquisitions illegal if they substantially lessen competition.[10] Finally, Section 8 prohibits individuals from being board members of competitors.[11]

The FTC Act gives the Federal Trade Commission jurisdiction over Sections 1 and 2 of the Sherman Act and over some provisions of the Clayton Act.[12] In addition, Section 5 of the FTC Act forbids "unfair methods of competition" and, in some cases, this includes violation under any other antitrust provision.

For a variety of reasons, the antitrust acts are not all-encompassing. Two major economic groups have been exempted.[13] First, agricultural cooperatives do not come under these acts. Most likely, Congress was persuaded that a host of small farmers exposed to the vagaries of nature and the often not insignificant monopsony power of those who purchase from farmers deserve protection.[14]

Labor unions also are exempted from prosecution under the antitrust acts. This was not always the case. Initially, the Sherman Act was applied to unions. However, matters changed in the early 1930s, when the Norris–La Guardia Act virtually eliminated the labor injunction and the Wagner Act of 1935, in fact, encouraged the formation of labor unions.

Over its more than 100-year history, antitrust policy has not followed a steady, consistent course. During the first half of the century, the courts

---

[7] *FTC* v. *Proctor and Gamble Co.*, 386 U.S. 568 (1967).

[8] 15 U.S.C. §13.

[9] 15 U.S.C. §13, 15 U.S.C. §1, 15 U.S.C. §130.

[10] 15 U.S.C. §18.

[11] 15 U.S.C. §19.

[12] 15 U.S.C. §41–58.

[13] Additionally, the McCarran–Ferguson Act exempts the insurance industry.

[14] *Antitrust Treatment of Agricultural Cooperatives* (North Central Regional Research Project NC-117, 1983).

adopted an aggressive antitrust policy, based on what some refer to as a populist view. Its thrust was to advance competition so as to protect viable, small, locally owned businesses. More recently, the emphasis has shifted toward promoting economic efficiency. The efficiency view is that such a policy is in the best interest of consumers, even if it leads to considerable concentration of economic power. The great challenge remains, i.e., to balance the populist and efficiency views of antitrust policy.

Although U.S. antitrust policy in recent years has emphasized efficiency, the antitrust agencies have been quite active. For example, the Antitrust Division of the United States Department of Justice in 1995 filed 60 criminal cases; corporations and individuals were forced to pay $42 million in fines.[15]

WAYS TO MONOPOLIZE MARKETS: MANY ROADS LEAD TO ROME

Firms have traveled different roads toward enhanced monopoly power. Perhaps the single most direct one is consolidation, be it through merger or creation of conglomerates. A second method involves various forms, often secret, of cooperation among competitors, cartels being the outstanding example. A third method relies on price discrimination, including predatory pricing, while a fourth employs a variety of instruments to foreclose entry into the industry, e.g., vertical integration, advertising, and such vertical restraints as exclusive dealing, tie-in arrangements, and reciprocal buying. Last, government has taken a number of steps that induce firms to fix prices and/or foreclose entry.[16]

HORIZONTAL MERGERS AND CONGLOMERATES

Mergers result when one firm takes over one or more other firms, often in the same industry. When the takeover comprises firms on a single level of the production–distribution system, we talk about *horizontal mergers*. From 1972 to 1996, U.S. mergers varied from a high of about 6,000 in 1996 to

---

[15] Carl Shapiro, "Antitrust Policy: Toward a Post Chicago Synthesis," *Jobs and Capital* 6 (Winter 1997): 13.

[16] Phillip Areeda and Louis Karplow, *Antitrust Analysis* (Boston: Little, Brown, 1988); and John E. Kwoka and Lawrence J. White, Eds., *The Antitrust Revolution: The Role of Economics*, 2nd ed. (New York: Harper Collins, 1994).

a low of 1,700 in 1991, involving asset values of $500 billion and $70 billion, respectively.[17]

Figure 10–1 can also be applied to represent the horizontal merging of a number of competitive firms into a single-firm monopolist under the most simplified assumptions. Accordingly, creation of a single-firm monopoly leads to price and profit increases, and quantity and consumer surplus declines. A welfare loss to the public has occurred, since the output formerly produced and desired by consumers under competitive conditions is no longer being produced under monopoly conditions. Under these simplified assumptions, horizontal mergers are inefficient and therefore undesirable.

However, the merged firm might incur scale economies and obtain some input factors below the price paid before the merger. Lower cost functions then will result. Although under these conditions there will be monopoly profits, consumers may benefit from lower prices.

Combining competitive firms and consequently capturing a larger market share would normally be associated with a decline in consumer welfare, as prices would increase and output decline. Yet, if by combining smaller firms, a corporation was able to reap the benefits of economies of scale, consumer welfare could even increase as profits rose (though it would remain below the level that would prevail if the newly more efficient producer were forced to act like a competitor).

Conglomerate mergers bring together two or more enterprises engaged in unrelated lines of business, in terms of either activities or products. In this connection, it is particularly helpful to recognize that markets and firms are alternative instruments to complete related transactions. On a priori grounds, it is not clear which alternative is more efficient. Much depends on the costs of writing and executing complex contracts across a market compared to costs incurred when the transactions are carried out within a single firm. Williamson suggests that antimonopoly policy with respect to conglomerate acquisitions focus on those mergers that impair potential competition and those involving giant firms that do not dispose of comparable assets at the time of their acquisition.[18]

However, it must be realized that mergers into a single-firm monopoly are extremely rare. Most mergers lead to oligopoly positions, and the behavior of oligopolistic markets is substantially less clear than that of single-firm monopolists. Thus, whatever, limited analytical conclusions were drawn concerning the behavior of mergers into single-firm monopolies become

[17] Bob Becker and Paige Korenich, *Industry Mergers and Acquisitions* (Los Angeles: Arthur Andersen, 1997): 2.

[18] O. E. Williamson, "The Economics of Antitrust: Transaction Cost Considerations," *University of Pennsylvania Law Review* 122 (June 1974): 1491.

even less clear in relation to oligopoly. Nevertheless, the 1950 amendment of Section 7 of the Clayton Act, which seems to place exceedingly stringent limitations on mergers between competitors, tends to be defended as necessary to prevent further increases in oligopoly.[19]

In this connection, *FTC* v. *Procter and Gamble Co.*,[20] a product-extension merger that was ruled illegal, is of interest. Procter and Gamble sought to expand into the household liquid bleach market by acquiring the assets of Clorox, the leading producer of liquid bleach. One argument by the Court was that Procter and Gamble was a potential entrant in the market and knowledge of this fact kept the price competitive in the industry. (The Court also felt that Procter and Gamble's huge assets gave it unwarranted leverage in the market and the power of predatory pricing.) Posner describes potential competition as two concepts: perceived potential competition and actual potential competition. "Together they are a principal, perhaps the principal, basis on which mergers are challenged today on antitrust grounds."[21]

Actual potential competition refers only to those firms that will enter the market even if price does not rise, so it is perceived potential competition that discourages firms from raising their prices, since these are the firms that would enter the market. The more perceived potential competition there is, the more elastic is the industry supply curve, the more elastic is the firm demand curve, and the less monopoly profits are available to the present firms. Consequently, any merger that would lower the number of potential competitors concurrently raises the opportunities to earn monopoly profits. Yet if there are many firms that are potential competitors, the elimination of one should have little effect on the ability to earn monopoly profits. The possible gains in efficiency of the merger must be compared with any decrease in competition.

In *United States* v. *Penn–Olin Chemical Co.*,[22] Penn and Olin decided to form a joint venture in order to compete in the production of sodium chlorate. Section 7 of the Clayton Act, prohibiting anticompetitive mergers, was applied instead of Section 1 of the Sherman Act. The Supreme Court stated that it was probable that one but not both of the companies would have entered the market separately, hence there would appear to be no competitive loss. However, the other firm would have remained at the edge of the market as a potential competitor, exerting downward pressure on price.

[19] Richard A. Posner, *Economic Analysis of Law,* 4th ed. (Boston: Little, Brown, 1992): 298.

[20] *FTC* v. *Procter and Gamble Co.*, 386 U.S. 568 (1967).

[21] Posner, *Economic Analysis of Law,* 4th ed.: 303.

[22] *United States* v. *Penn–Olin Chemical Co.*, 378 U.S. 158 (1964).

In *Citizen Publishing Co.* v. *United States*,[23] the two major Tucson newspapers formed a joint operating agreement. By most economic tests, the agreement created productive efficiencies and was ancillary to the creation of these efficiencies, since it went no further than a merger. At the same time, it also would eliminate some competition, since the effect would have been a reduction in the number of independent newspapers from two to one in Tucson. However, one of the papers was in bad financial shape. Under the failing-company doctrine, an exception could be made if failure was imminent. Without the merger, there would be only one paper. However, the Supreme Court did not accept this argument.

In 1992, the Department of Justice and the Federal Trade Commission issued a set of Horizontal Merger Guidelines superseding earlier ones. These guidelines incorporate the two agencies' merger enforcement policies subject to Section 5 or 7 of the FTC Act, or Section 1 of the Sherman Act. Their unifying theme is that mergers should not be permitted to create or enhance market power, so as to confer on a seller the ability profitably to maintain prices above competitive levels for a significant period of time. The guidelines describe the analytical process used to determine whether to challenge a horizontal merger: assessment of whether (1) the merger would significantly increase concentration and result in a concentrated market; (2) the merger, in light of market concentration, would raise concern about potential adverse competitive effects; (3) entry would likely deter competitive effects of concern; (4) efficiency gains would result that otherwise cannot be achieved; and (5) but for the merger, either party to the transaction would be likely to fail and exit the market.

Assessment of market concentration, which is considered an indicator of potential competition effects of a merger, is carried out by focusing on the number of firms in a market and their respective market shares. For this purpose, the FTC uses the Herfindahl–Hirschman Index (HHI) of market concentration. The HHI is calculated by summing the squares of the individual market shares of all the participants.

In evaluating horizontal mergers, the FTC will consider both the postmerger concentration and the increase in concentration resulting from the merger. If the HHI is expected to be below 1,000 after the merger, the market is considered unconcentrated; if 1,000–1,800, moderately concentrated; and if above 1,800, highly concentrated. If the postmerger HHI is above 1,800 and merger is expected to increase it by more than 50 points, the merger raises significant competitive concerns.

---

[23] *Citizen Publishing Co.* v. *United States*, 394 U.S. 131 (1969).

Thus, while the tendency in recent years has been to provide helpful guidelines for companies who contemplate mergers, quite a few hard-to-quantify issues also play a role. For example, are there synergies and, if so, how important are they; and how credible are efficiency gains claimed to result from the merger, and how likely are they to be passed on to consumers?

CARTELS

When competitors seek to enter secret agreements to either fix prices or divide markets, they often form cartels. These, unlike mergers, do not beneficially affect production costs. Cartels tend to engage in two major activities of concern to antimonopoly policymakers — horizontal price fixing and horizontal market division, Agreement exists that it is socially desirable for government to prevent cartels from engaging in conspiracies to fix prices, rig bids, or allocate markets; such practices can injure consumers, enhance economic power, and reduce efficiency.[24] However, actually determining the existence of a conspiracy remains a major challenge. For example, it is not enough to observe two or more firms charging identical prices, submitting identical bids, or repeatedly allocating markets among bidders.[25] Instead some tangible evidence of collusive action is required.

HORIZONTAL PRICE FIXING

Entering an agreement to fix the price is unlikely to lower the cost functions of the colluding firms. Most likely, substantial transaction costs of monitoring and policing the behavior of cartel members will result. Costs may therefore be higher than before.

In the first important antitrust case, *United States* v. *Addyston Pipe and Steel Co.,*[26] involving cartelization and price fixing, a group of producers of cast iron cartelized, with all business being referred to a central authority that decided the price for the work. Members of the cartel then bid internally for the job and the central authority divided up the profits. Judge Taft noticed that no economies of scale or other productive efficiencies were

[24] Shapiro, "Antitrust Policy": 13.
[25] Note that when firms participate in what economists call a "Supergame," i.e., repeated competition, a mutually beneficial outcome, i.e., a Pareto frontier, may result without any explicit agreement.
[26] *United States* v. *Addyston Pipe and Steel Co.,* 85 Fed. 271 (6th Cir. 1898).

involved in the cartel and therefore ruled it illegal. More important, for purposes of the Sherman Act, horizontal price fixing and horizontal market division are identical and illegal per se.[27] Additionally, Judge Taft formulated the doctrine of *ancillary restraints*. He stated that agreements that are ancillary to the purpose of the contract and no wider than necessary to create efficiency should be held valid. These valid common-law agreements include agreements by retiring partners not to compete with the firm, agreements by a partner not to compete with a pending partnership, contracts by a seller of a business not to compete with the buyer in derogation of the purchase price, and others.

Another doctrine formulated shortly thereafter is the *rule of reason*. After determining that a contract creates efficiencies and that the restriction is ancillary to the contract, the court looks into the purpose and effect of the agreement. In *United States* v. *Chicago Board of Trade*,[28] Justice Brandeis determined that a call rule, limiting the hours that differing bids could be made, was permissible. The rule created efficiencies and was ancillary to the purpose to enhance noneconomic values. Therefore, Justice Brandeis concluded that the purpose and effect of the rule was not significantly anticompetitive. This rule has economic rationale since presumably the anticompetitive effect of a contract between two firms, with a small market share, will be minimal. Those firms would be trying to expand their output, not restrict it. The purpose part of the test may not be so valuable. Presumably, any businessman would seek to restrain output and gain monopoly profits if he could; therefore, almost all activities of firms will have, as one important purpose, the enhancing of profits.

United States v. *Socony Vacuum Oil Co.* represented the next major legal development.[29] The major oil companies tried to restrict the output of "hot" oil from Texas by contracting with small producers in an effort to keep the price up. There was no integration of productive facilities and no efficiencies were created; hence, the agreement should have been ruled invalid, as it was. However, the Supreme Court went further, declaring that all price-fixing agreements are per se illegal, regardless of whatever efficiencies might have been created. Here the investigation of agreements centered around the question of whether the particular

---

[27] An activity is considered per se illegal under the antitrust acts if it is said to be so, "by and of itself." An alternative is the rule of reason, which requires a weighing of the relevant circumstances of a case to decide whether a restrictive practice constitutes an unreasonable restraint competition [*Monsanto Co.* v. *Spray-Rite Service Corp.*, 465 U.S. 752 (1984)].

[28] *United States* v. *Chicago Board of Trade*, 246 U.S. 231 (1918).

[29] *United States* v. *Socony Vacuum Oil Co.*, 310 U.S. 150 (1940).

contract fit within the per se rule, not whether it was economically efficient. This by and large is the state of the law today with respect to horizontal price-fixing agreements.

HORIZONTAL MARKET DIVISION

Horizontal market divisions, which cut up the market among competitors, were also ruled illegal per se in *United States* v. *Sealy, Inc.*[30] Sealy was a tradename combine that advertised nationally for a group of regional mattress producers. In order to increase local sales efforts, a market division arrangement, which prevented the producers from selling in neighboring territories, was part of the agreement. A price fix was also imposed to enforce the market division and reduce the incentive to shift the mattresses to neighboring areas. Since the price restriction was only on Sealy mattresses — a very small part of the market — there was no attempt to fix the price of mattresses in general. The real purpose of the market division was to eliminate free rides by nonadvertising sellers. Local advertising would suffer, it was argued, if some retailers could obtain the benefits of advertising paid for by the participating retailers. The Supreme Court held both the price fixing and market division per se illegal despite the creation of advertising efficiencies. The creation of a property right in information about Sealy and its enforcement through trademark advertising was destroyed.

The Supreme Court, in *United States* v. *Topco Associates, Inc.*, probably contributed to inefficiency.[31] Several small grocery chains formed a voluntary contract association in order to get volume discounts from wholesalers. Although no restriction of output by these small retailers was possible, the Court called the arrangement a naked restraint of trade. The Court most likely confused intrabrand and interbrand competition. Clearly, intrabrand restrictions such as Topco imposed here on its own retailers (or as Safeway does on its stores to prevent their competing with each other) have minimal impact on competition and are common practice. Horizontal interbrand restrictions are clearly suspect, but none were present here since only one association was involved. The efficiencies of Topco were created to increase output, not restrict output, as the Court itself noted. Still, the territorial restrictions on the use of the Topco trademark were found to be horizontal in nature and illegal per se.

[30] *United States* v. *Sealy, Inc.*, 388 U.S. 350 (1967).
[31] *United States* v. *Topco Associates, Inc.*, 405 U.S. 596 (1972).

PRICE DISCRIMINATION

Firms with monopoly power can also charge different prices to different purchasers. To do so, the firm must have some knowledge of consumers' willingness to pay and be able to prevent resales. While under some circumstances price discrimination can be socially desirable, with output approximating that of a competitive market, some firms practice predatory pricing as well. It occurs when a firm with substantial market power sells below cost in some markets and, after competitors are forced out, sets a high monopoly price. Predation is relatively rare since it tends to be costly to the predator and seldom succeeds.[32] According to *Brooke Group Ltd.* v. *Brown and Williamson Tobacco Corp.*, for the court to hold that predation occurred, two prerequisites under the Robinson–Patman and Sherman Acts must be met: (1) the price must be below an appropriate measure of cost and (2) it must be capable of leading to supracompetitive prices and profits that would offset or recoup the alleged predator's investment in below-cost prices.[33]

Williamson has shown that welfare assessment is quite complicated.[34] I will attempt to reproduce the Williamson argument here. Figure 10—2 assumes large-scale economies in relation to the size of the market; the average cost curve falls precipitously over a considerable output range. The unregulated, profit-maximizing monopolist who charges the uniform price to all customers will restrict output to Q_m, well below the social optimum of Q^*. The monopolist who segregates his market so that each customer pays his full valuation (given by the demand function) for each unit of output is inclined to add successive units of output until the price paid for the last unit equals marginal cost. The fully discriminating monopolist will thus favor the social optimum Q^*. At the same time, undesirable income redistribution is likely to take place.

So far zero transaction costs to achieve discrimination are assumed. However, in most cases, price discrimination will require substantial expenditures to reveal customers' true preferences and to prevent resale by those who paid little to those who are forced to pay dearly. Thus, the firm that seeks to engage in price discrimination, although possibly benefiting from scale economies, may incur major costs in connection with its price-discriminating schemes. Clearly, there can be both types of cases, those where the transaction costs are smaller than the savings due to scale economies, and vice versa.

---

[32] *Matsushita Electric Industrial Company* v. *Zenith Radio Corp.*, 475 U.S. 574 (1986).

[33] *Brooke Group Ltd.* v. *Brown and Williamson Tobacco Corp.*, 113 S. Ct. 2578 (1993).

[34] Williamson, "Economics of Antitrust": 1447–1449.

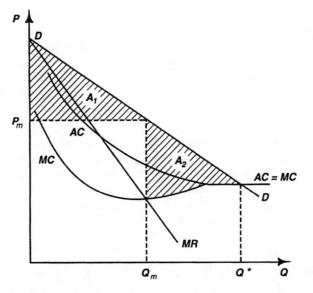

FIGURE 10—2 Effects of price discrimination on output; Q^* is the socially optimal output. (See key to Figure 10-1 for definitions of variables.)

So much for a static analysis. However, predatory price discrimination, as has been mentioned, is a strategy designed to reduce competition by easing out competitors. Once this is accomplished, the monopolist thus strengthened may raise prices and reduce output in a socially undesirable manner. This part of the analysis is similar to that presented earlier regarding monopolization through merger.

The attitude of the courts has been influenced mainly by the Robinson–Patman Act, which prohibits discrimination only when the effect may be to lessen competition substantially. In some earlier cases, price differentials hurting one or more competitors were assumed to hurt competition by presumably contributing to the easing out of competitors.[35] Examples are *Corn Products Refining Co.* v. *A. E. Stealey Mfg. Co.*[36] and *Federal Trade Commission* v. *Morton Salt Co.*[37]

In *Texaco* v. *Hasbrouck*, the Court held that granting substantial discounts to two distributors, not justified by lower costs, violated the Robinson–

[35] Peter Asch, *Economic Theory and the Antitrust Dilemma* (New York: Wiley, 1970): 344.

[36] *Corn Products Refining Co.* v. *A. E. Stealey Mfg. Co.*, 324 U.S. 746 (1945).

[37] *Federal Trade Commission* v. *Morton Salt Co.*, 334 U.S. 37 (1948).

Patman Act.[38] However, in other cases the Court held that price discrimination was not predatory. For example, in *Matsushita Electric Industrial Co.* v. *Zenith Radio Corp.,* U.S. manufacturers of consumer electronic products had charged that Japanese firms conspired to charge high prices in Japan and low prices in the United States in order to drive plaintiffs from the market.[39] The Court rejected a predatory pricing conspiracy as "by nature speculative." The Court reviewed the necessary conditions for successful predation, noting that defendants must have a prospect of achieving monopoly, monopoly pricing must not result in quick entry by new competitors, and firms must be able to maintain monopoly power long enough to recoup their losses and harvest some additional gain. Thus, the alleged predation must be credible. Likewise, in *Brooke Group Ltd.* v. *Brown and Williamson Tobacco Corp.* the Court held that cutting prices of generic cigarettes did not injure competition.[40]

FORECLOSING ENTRY

A number of techniques have been used that may, to varying degrees, bar firms from entering an industry. Such techniques can also ease out competition among existing firms in an industry. They include vertical integration, advertising, and such other vertical restraints as exclusive dealings, tie-ins, reciprocal buying, and boycotts.

VERTICAL INTEGRATION

A vertically integrated firm controls a number of successive stages of the production–delivery process. The emergence of vertical arrangements of firms, in addition to being explainable by profit-maximizing models (as represented in Figure 10—1), can also be explained by transaction cost economics. Transaction cost economics considers cost minimization and efficiency as the driving force in the choice among vertical contractual and organizational arrangements, acknowledging the potential for foreclosure and market monopolization. Relying on a contractual approach, in particular a paradigm of incomplete contracts, facilitates the evaluation of alternative contractual arrangements. Recent scholarship has shown that different

---

[38] *Texaco* v. *Hasbrouck,* 110 Ct. 2535 (1990).

[39] *Matsushita Electric Industrial Co.* v. *Zenith Radio Corp.,* 475 U.S. 574 (1986).

[40] *Brooke Group Ltd.* v. *Brown and Williamson Tobacco Corp.,* 113 S.Ct. 2578 (1993).

vertical contractual arrangements can have different effects on costs as well as on the quantity and quality of goods and services offered customers.[41] While vertical contractual arrangements can prove anticompetitive, this outcome is likely to occur mainly when in one or more horizontal levels of transactions the arrangements significantly reduce competition.

Transaction cost economics can complement the microeconomics employed by the Chicago school of law and economics. The latter's concern about unwarranted attacks on vertical arrangements is based on the argument that such arrangements neither created nor enhanced market power. While the Chicago School seeks to explain why vertical arrangements have little effect on firms' monopoly power, transaction cost economics offers reasons for such arrangements to arise as cost-reducing responses to specific transactional characteristics.

A vertically integrated firm can make it increasingly difficult for other firms to enter the industry. Williamson has pointed to two situations in which a substantial disadvantage to potential entrants may arise.[42] One is the presence of a dominant firm or of otherwise strong concentration in the industry. The second involves moderately concentrated industries in which collusion has been successfully effected.

But even in concentrated industries, vertical integration is not to be condemned per se. For example, when there are two stages in the production process of a particular final good, vertical integration would be objectionable if stage H were competitively organized except for the vertical integration by the dominant firm in stage I of the industry. As a result, the residual, nonintegrated sector of the stage II market may be so small that only a few firms of efficient size can serve the stage II market. Firms that would otherwise be prepared to enter stage I would therefore be discouraged for fear "of having to engage in small numbers bargaining, with all the hazards that this entails, with these few nonintegrated stage II firms."[43] Additionally, entering into a vertically integrated industry may be unattractive if potential entrants lack stage II-related experience and therefore would incur high capital costs. For this reason, Williamson concludes that permitting leading firms to integrate stages I and II is anticompetitive, in entry aspects at least.

The situation is different where scale economies at both stages are known to be large in relation to the size of the total market. Severing vertical connections then will not deter those contemplating entry into one of the

[41] Paul L. Joskow, "The Role of Transaction Cost Economics in Antitrust and Public Utility Regulatory Policies," *Journal of Law, Economics, and Organization* 7 (Spring 1991): 53–83.

[42] Williamson, "Economics of Antitrust": 1461–1462.

[43] *Ibid.*: 1462.

stages, since entrants will not have to incur the adverse capital costs attached to entry at an unfamiliar stage.

Vertical integration in industries with low to moderate degrees of concentration often has few disadvantages. Under such conditions, firms entering either stage can expect to strike competitive bargains with firms in the other stage, since no single integrated firm enjoys a strategic advantage with respect to such transactions.

In *Brown Shoe Co., Inc.* v. *United States*,[44] the Supreme Court held that a lessening of competition in a vertical merger arises "primarily from foreclosure."[45] Rather than holding that the size of the market share that was foreclosed in itself determined whether a merger was illegal, the court found it necessary to look further into the historical and economic background of affected markets.

The Court noted that though the shoe industry was atomistic, Brown's share of the national manufacturing market was 5% to 6% and Kinney's retail sales were 2%. Thus, vertical integration would not have produced an overwhelmingly large firm. Although the Court found the industry highly competitive, it held that retaining vigor in competition cannot immunize a merger if the trend in the industry is toward oligopoly. Since Congress had revised Section 7 to preserve competition and prevent the formation of oligopolies, the Court found the merger suspect. It concluded that "the trend towards vertical integration in the shoe industry, when combined with Brown's avowed policy of forcing its own shoes upon its retail subsidiaries, may foreclose competition from a substantial share of the markets ... without producing any countervailing competitive, economic or social advantages."[46] The Court's reading of congressional intent led Chief Justice Warren to conclude,

> The retail outlets of integrated companies, by eliminating wholesalers and by increasing the volume of purchases from the manufacturing division of the enterprise, can market their own brands at prices below those of competing independent retailers. Of course, some of the results of large integrated or chain operations are beneficial to consumers.... But we cannot fail to recognize Congress' desire to promote competition through the protection of viable, small, locally owned businesses. Congress appreciated that occasional higher costs and prices might result from the maintenance of fragmented industries and markets. It resolved these competing considerations in favor of decentralization. We must give effect to that decision.[47]

---

[44] *Brown Shoe Co., Inc.* v. *United States*, 370 U.S. 294 (1962).
[45] *Ibid.*: 328.
[46] *Ibid.*: 334.
[47] *Ibid.*: 344.

In the *Brown Shoe* decision, the Court was searching for standards under which a lessening of competition because of vertical integration could be inferred. It apparently judged the competitive effect of the vertical integration purely in terms of its effect on the structure of relevant markets. Therefore, Asch concluded that "if it were found to be anticompetitive on this basis not even an expectation of improved market performance could save it from Section 7 prohibition. This strict view was undoubtedly influenced strongly by the Court's reading of Congressional intent."[48]

ADVERTISING

Advertising also has been pointed to as a method to increase monopoly power, mainly by establishing barriers to entry into the industry. It is argued that advertising makes possible effective product differentiation and prevents potential competitors from entering the industry. Before developing the latter argument in detail, it should be pointed out, however, that advertising can have distinctly positive effects. For example, by providing information, advertising can serve an important requirement of competition.

A theoretical argument tying advertising to entry barriers has been advanced by Comanor and Wilson.[49] They argue that new firms have higher costs than established firms at every level of output. Firms new to the industry, in addition to the production costs and advertising costs incurred by all firms, must also spend money on advertising to gain market penetration.

Comanor and Wilson tested their hypothesis indirectly. Assuming that large-scale advertising, by foreclosing entry, would increase profits, they engaged in empirical analyses of the relationship between rates of return and advertising intensity as measured by firms' advertising-to-sales ratios. Comanor and Wilson and a number of other studies treating advertising as a current expense found a strong positive relationship between advertising and profits.[50] However, there are two studies that treat advertising as an investment. One, by Weiss, confirms the earlier results of a strong positive

[48] Asch, *Economic Theory*, 300.

[49] W. S. Comanor and T. S. Wilson, "Advertising, Market Structure and Performance," *Review of Economics and Statistics* 49 (November 1967): 423–440.

[50] L. S. Esposito and F. F. W. Esposito, "Foreign Competition and Domestic Industry Profitability," *Review of Economics and Statistics* 53 (November 1971): 343–353; W. G. Shepherd, "The Elements of Market Structure," *Review of Economics and Statistics* 54 (February 1972): 25–37.

relationship between advertising intensity and profits.[51] A study by Ayanian employs a set of advertising depreciation rates to recalculate rates of return for a group of heavy advertisers by capitalizing their past advertising expenditures. Anayian does not find a statistically significant relation between these corrected rates of return and firms' advertising intensities.[52] Telser, studying the relationship between advertising intensity and concentration, could not find it to be statistically significant.[53] Nevertheless Turner, the former assistant attorney general in charge of the Department of Justice's Antitrust Division, was convinced intuitively that heavy advertising promotes industry concentration and may thus harm competition.[54]

OTHER VERTICAL RESTRAINTS

A number of vertical restraints are available to firms who do not undertake full vertical integration. Although exclusive dealing arrangements, tie-in arrangements, reciprocal buying, and boycotts differ, under certain circumstances all can ease out competitors. In some instances, these instruments may also act as barriers to entry into the industry.

While exclusive vertical dealing and tie-in arrangements will be taken up in some detail below, I will offer only a few words about reciprocal buying and boycotts. Reciprocal buying relies on an explicit quid pro quo arrangement between the buyer and the seller. A boycott involves a concerted, collective refusal to have dealings with a party. The objective of the collaborators who ban together often is to gain market power over competitors with the purpose of coercing or destroying them. If that is the case, the boycott would be condemned by a simple per se approach under Section 1 of the Sherman Antitrust Act. An example is *Eastern States Retail Lumber Dealers Association* v. *United States*,[55] in which a group of retailers agreed not to buy from a supplier who entered into the retail business in competition with members of the retail group. Since this involved a simple arrangement for the sole purpose of excluding competing wholesalers from the retail market, the Court had little trouble in invalidating the boycott. On

---

[51] L. W. Weiss, "Advertising, Profit, and Corporate Taxes," *Review of Economics and Statistics* 51 (November 1969):421–430.

[52] R. Ayanian, "Advertising and Rate of Return," *Journal of Law and Economics* 19 (October 1975): 479–506.

[53] L. G. Telser, "Advertising and Competition," *Journal of Political Economy* 72 (December 1964): 537–562.

[54] D. F. Turner, *Advertising and Competition* (address delivered before the Briefing Conference of Federal Controls of Advertising and Promotion, June 1966, mimeographed).

[55] *Eastern States Retail Lumber Dealers Association* v. *United States,* 234 U.S. 600 (1914).

the other hand, organized distribution of information about a firm or its orders, as a means of curbing abusive business conduct, was upheld by the Court.[56]

Exclusive Vertical Dealing Arrangements

Under an exclusive vertical dealing arrangement, a manufacturer will sell to a retailer only if the latter agrees not to carry products produced by a competitor. With this arrangement, the manufactuer is attempting to reduce interbrand competition in order to increase his profits. Let us review two early court decisions involving exclusive dealing arrangements. The Standard Oil Company of California had entered into exclusive supply contracts with 5937 independent service stations binding them to fill their entire requirement from the company. It was the largest seller of petroleum products in the area, and the service stations involved in the exclusive contract comprised 16% of total area outlets. Standard's competitors practiced similar dealings, and only 1.6% of the area service stations were supplied by more than one company. In *Standard Oil of California and Standard Stations, Inc.* v. *United States*,[57] the Supreme court ruled that the exclusive requirement contracts created a "potential clog on competition"[58] and were in violation of Section 3 of the Clayton Act. The Court stated that inclusive requirement contracts — unlike tying arrangements — might prove to be desirable. Yet because of serious difficulties encountered in applying the necessary tests, a presumption was made against contracts involving a substantial share of business. Though the Court seemed to argue for a rule-of-reason approach, it actually applied a per se test modified by the significance of commerce affected.[59]

In *Tampa Electric Co.* v. *Nashville Coal Co.*,[60] the Tampa Electric Company and the Nashville Coal Company had entered into a contract in which the former agreed to fill its entire coal requirements from the latter for a period of 20 years. The Supreme Court in 1961 did not find the requirement contract in violation of Section 3. Although the Court held the contract to amount to exclusive dealing, it decided such contracts were not illegal per se. The sum of the contract amounted to less than 1% of the relevant market and this was not considered sufficient to imply a Section 3 violation. Thus, the Court did not rule out that exclusive dealing arrangements could

---

[56] *Cement Manufacturing Protective Association* v. *United States*, 268 U.S. 588 (1925).

[57] *Standard Oil of California and Standard Stations, Inc.* v. *United States*, 337 U.S. 293 (1949).

[58] *Ibid.*: 314.

[59] Asch, *Economic Theory:* 351–352.

[60] *Tampa Electric Co.* v. *Nashville Coal Co.*, 356 U.S. 320 (1961).

have positive benefits and, for this reason, such arrangements should be judged under a rule-of-reason approach.

If the Court's view of exclusive dealing arrangements was unclear in 1961, matters did not get much better after that date. In *White Motor Co.* v. *United States*,[61] the company was accused of employing written dealer agreements that limited dealer resales to specified geographical areas and reserved all sales to government to White alone. The Supreme Court reversed the summary judgment for the government and remanded for trial. The majority felt it had insufficient information to know whether the elimination of rivalry restricted output, as a cartel would, or created efficiency and therefore might be permissible. Unfortunately, an out-of-court settlement prevented a final judicial determination that might have recognized that, depending on the forms taken by vertical restraint or market division, efficiencies might result and make the per se rule inappropriate.

In *United States* v. *Arnold, Schwinn and Co.*,[62] the following were the facts: Arnold, Schwinn and Co. sold bicycles it manufactured in a variety of ways but always insisted that its wholesalers sell only within assigned territories and only to retailers franchised by Schwinn and that its retailers sell only to ultimate consumers. The decision to adopt this exclusive vertical dealing arrangement was taken when Schwinn was the industry leader with a 22.5% market share.

The Supreme Court held that "the antitrust outcome does not turn merely on the presence of sound business reason or motive," but upon the question whether "the effect upon competition in the marketplace is substantially adverse."[63]

The Court expressed concern that Schwinn had used both customer and territorial exclusionary clauses, and held the latter per se illegal. Economists are not of one mind about the effects of mandating exclusive territories, Permitting a single dealer to market a specific product can have efficiency effects. In the eyes of Posner these effects are positive on the distribution system and such restrictions, therefore, should be legal per se.[64] However, Cartensen and Dahlson find this practice to stifle competition and reduce consumer welfare.[65] An empirical study of the beer industry finds that

---

[61] *White Motor Co.* v. *United States*, 372 U.S. 253 (1963).

[62] *United States* v. *Arnold, Schwinn and Co.*, 388 U.S. 365 (1967).

[63] *Ibid.*: 378.

[64] Richard A. Posner, "The Next Step in Antitrust Treatment of Restricted Distribution: Per Se Legality," *University of Chicago Law Review* 48 (1981): 6.

[65] Peter C. Cartersen and Richard F. Dahlson, "Vertical Restraints in Beer Distribution," *Wisconsin Law Review* 40 (1986): 1.

such vertical restraints, while encouraging promotional activities, raise beer prices though without a significant change in consumption.[66]

In *Continental TV* v. *GTE Sylvania, Inc.*,[67] the Court broke new ground. In 1962, Sylvania decided to sell directly to retailers, few in number, and adopt a dealer "elbow room" policy; in order to limit competition between resellers of Sylvania products, it spaced its franchisees. To prevent encroachment by another dealer, Sylvania representatives made it clear orally that a franchise was for a specified location only. Continental TV of San Francisco, one of its most successful dealers, opened a shop in Sacramento, where it had no franchise, and moved Sylvania sets from franchised locations to Sacramento. There it infringed on Handy Andy, a very successful Sacramento franchise. When Continental did not withdraw its Sylvania sets from Sacramento, its franchises everywhere were canceled. Continental then filed suit against Sylvania claiming violation of Section I of the Sherman Act.

The Supreme Court upheld an appeals court opinion that the location clause used by Sylvania was not per se unreasonable. Justice Powell, writing for the five members of the majority, declared, "*Per se* rules of illegality are appropriate only when they relate to conduct that is manifestly anticompetitive,"[68] or when a practice or agreement displays a "pernicious effect on competition and lack of any redeeming virtue."[69] Justice Powell cited examples of distributive efficiencies that must be considered "redeeming virtues." Manufacturers may then use them, for example, to induce retailers to engage in promotional activities or to provide service and repair facilities necessary to the efficient marketing of their products. Here he referred to the "free-rider" phenomenon.

Turning to the question of whether to extend the *Schwinn* per se rule to nonsale transactions, Justice Powell noted that vertical restrictions of a nonprice variety did not meet the standard for per se illegality.

Tie-in Arrangements

A tie-in arrangement provides that the buyer can purchase one product — the tying good — from the seller only if he agrees to purchase another good — the tied good — as well. Section 3 of the Clayton Act is

[66] Tim R. Sass and David S. Saurman, "Mandated Exclusive Territories and Economic Efficiency: An Empirical Analysis of the Malt-Beverage Industry," *Journal of Law and Economics* 36 (April 1993): 153–177.

[67] *Continental TV* v. *GTE Sylvania, Inc.*, 97 S. Ct. 2549.

[68] *Ibid.*: 2558.

[69] *Northern Pacific Ry. Co.* v. *United States*, 356 U.S. 1, 5 (1958).

directly applicable to tie-in arrangements. It declares it to be illegal for a person to lease or sell commodities "on the condition, agreement or understanding that the lessee or purchaser thereof shall not use or deal in the goods ... of a competitor or competitors of the lessor or seller where the effect ... may be to substantially lessen competition or tend to create a monopoly in any line of commerce."[70] However, the legal position toward tie-in arrangements is somewhat clouded by the fact that under Section 5 of the FTC Act, the arrangement, to be illegal, must merely be unfair to competitors. Hence, under the FTC Act standard almost any agreement can be unfair.

Some argue that, in many circumstances, the existence of tie-in arrangements actually increases allocative efficiency and should therefore be permitted under the Clayton Act. For example, Markovitz states:

> Any assessment of the allocative efficiency or competitive effect of tying agreements must be based on realistic assumptions about the way in which the defendants would respond to the tie-in prohibitions. (Would they abandon the strategy or adopt a more costly way of doing it?)[71]

One particular use of tie-ins that may enhance efficiency is their use as devices to control quality. If tie-ins lower the monitoring costs of protecting the reputation of a frachise or the quality of complements used along with the tying good, they may be considered efficient.[72]

Several important court cases have involved tie-in arrangements. In *Federal Trade Commission* v. *Brown Shoe Co.*, the defendant agreed to provide certain services if the dealer would agree to buy its shoes.[73] Clearly, Brown did not want the dealer buying another company's shoes to take a free ride on the services Brown provided. The Supreme Court voided the arrangement, giving the FTC under the FTC Act wide latitude to attack these *de minimis* arrangements in their incipiency.

Another case is *Fortner Enterprises* v. *United States Steel Co.*[74] United States Steel provided Fortner with cheap 100% financing in its construction of prefabricated homes. Fortner was then obligated to buy the products of United States Steel for the production of the homes. Presumably, Fortner would not have obtained the financing without the latter agreement. The

---

[70] 15 U.S.C. §14.

[71] R. S. Markovitz, "The Functions, Allocative Efficiency and Legality of Tie-ins: A Comment, *Journal of Law and Economics* 28 (May 1985): 387–404.

[72] B. Klein and L. F. Saft, "The Law and Economics of Franchise Tying Contracts." *Journal of Law and Economics* 28 (May 1985): 345–362.

[73] *Federal Trade Commission* v. *Brown Shoe Co.*, 384 U.S. 316 (1966).

[74] *Fortner Enterprises* v. *United States Steel Co.*, 394 U.S. 495 (1969), and 51 L. Ed. 2d 80 (1977).

Supreme Court concluded that United States Steel had no monopoly over money and that Fortner would not have agreed to accept a higher price for houses if they were not getting a lower price for credit.[75] Clearly, a firm with a cost advantage can either lower the price for the product and impose a tie-in or keep the price the same with no tie-in.

In *Eastman Kodak Co.* v. *Image Technical Services,* the manufacturer of photocopying equipment, who also sold replacement parts and services, was accused of unlawfully tying the sale of service for Kodak machines to the sale of parts in violation of Section 1 of the Sherman Act.[76] Kodak did so by limiting availability of parts to independent service organizations (ISOs), thereby making it difficult for them to compete in servicing Kodak equipment. The ISOs contended that "Kodak has more than sufficient power in the parts market to force unwanted purchases [in] the tied market service."[77] Some parts are available solely through Kodak, enabling it by this action to increase its share of the service market. The Court found sufficient evidence of a tying arrangement and concentrated on whether it was an illegal arrangement with appreciable economic power in the tying market. It acknowledged that a lack of market power in the primary equipment market does not preclude, as a matter of law, the possibility of such power in derivative after markets. Since Kodak had not proved that its parts, service, and equipment activities are components of one market, the equipment market disciplines the other markets to price competitively, or any anticompetitive effects of Kodak's are outweighed by competitive effects, the Court remanded for Kodak to prove its economic theory.

Criticism has been voiced of the Court's ruling, particularly by economists. For example, Shapiro argues that the tie-in practice of Eastman Kodak, which had only a 15–20% market share (much smaller than that of Xerox and IBM, its main competitors), would have allowed it to compete more effectively with the latter.[78] The result would have been lower prices for consumers. Moreover, forcing Eastman Kodak to sell its parts, some of which were patented, to rivals, and thereby making available their patented innovations to rival firms, could have a chilling effect on its willingness to innovate. Thus, forcing a manufacturer of durable equipment requiring much research and development to alter its aftermarket strategy, to reduce likely antitrust action, can be inefficient.

---

[75] 394 U.S. 495, 499 (1969), quoting *Northern Pacific Ry. Co.* v. *United States,* 356 U.S. 1, 5–6 (1958).

[76] *Eastman Kodak Co.* v. *Image Technical Services,* 112 S. Ct. 2072 (1992).

[77] *Ibid.:* 2078.

[78] Shapiro, "Antitrust Policy": 16–17.

Tie-in arrangements can also be viewed as a price discrimination or cartel reinforcement device. In *IBM* v. *United States,* IBM charged a single price for a given computer but required the purchase of its cards used by the machine.[79] For cards, it charged a varying price based on the quantity purchased. In this case, it appears IBM used the cards as a counting device. If intensive users tend to have more inelastic demand for the computer, then tying the purchase of the cards to the purchase of the computer can achieve the goal of discriminatory pricing for the computer.[80]

However, IBM did not have a monopoly. Remington was a major competitor. Thus, IBM and Remington entered into an arrangement whereby neither sold to the other's lessees. Therefore, the tie-in exclusive dealing arrangement was a horizontal cartel reinforcement device.

By and large, the Court has applied a harsher standard to tie-in than to exclusive vertical dealing arrangements. Nonetheless, although the Court has declared on several occasions that tying is per se illegal, a loose definition of per se has often been applied. Actual tie-ins have been found illegal only when monopolistic power in the market for the tying good or substantial market foreclosure in the tied good existed.[81]

GOVERNMENT-INDUCED PRICE FIXING AND FORECLOSURE

Various statutes have injected government into a situation where its activities clearly interfere with the competitive behavior of markets. Retail sales maintenance laws will be discussed as an example of government-induced price fixing and occupational licensing as an example of steps to bar entry into certain professions.

It should be noted that government engages in many other activities of a similar nature. For example, there are the minimum wage laws. Public utility regulation is another area of intervention where government establishes prices and stipulates performance.

A further interesting part of government's role in antimonopoly laws relates to exceptions. Thus, Section 6 of the Clayton Act declares that

> nothing contained in the antitrust laws shall be construed to forbid the existence and operation of labor, agricultural or horticultural organizations, instituted for the purpose

---

[79] *IBM* v. *United States,* 298 U.S. 131 (1936).

[80] W. S. Bowman, Jr., "Tying Arrangements and the Leverage Problem," in *Economic Analysis and Antitrust Law,* eds. T. Calvani and J. Siegfried (Boston: Little, Brown, 1979): 243–244.

[81] Asch, *Economic Theory:* 357–358.

of mutual help ...; nor such organizations, or members thereof, be held or construed to be illegal combinations or conspiracies in restraint of trade under the antitrust laws.[82]

This provision has been declared by Asch as "the clearest departures from the procompetitive orientation of the antitrust laws.[83] Yet the provision covers a significant part of the American economy. In 1977, for example, about 27% of all farm products were sold by agricultural cooperatives operating under antitrust exception.[84]

RESALE PRICE MAINTENANCE

Resale price maintenance exists when manufacturers set a price floor below which retailers cannot resell their products. These agreements may serve to enhance the monopoly power of the participants. For example, retailers may push for a resale price floor to enforce a horizontal price fixing arrangement, or manufacturers of a given product may fix prices among themselves and use retail price restrictions to assure adherence to the price-fixing conspiracy.[85]

Yet, resale price maintenance may serve to increase allocative efficiency by providing manufacturers with a low-cost means to control the quality of their products. Eliminating intrabrand price competition among retailers may induce them to engage in nonprice forms of competition. Examples include better service facilities, more knowledgeable sales people, etc. The fact that all retailers are subject to the minimum price restrictions eliminates any free-rider problem that could exist if some retailers offer information that consumers can use to purchase the good at a lower price somewhere else. Lessening of intrabrand price competition will harm the consumer who desires the good at the lower price, especially if substitutes are unavailable.

Since the early 1900s, the legal attitude toward artificial resale price fixing has changed a number of times. When, soon after the turn of the century, a drug manufacturer sought to establish a resale price below which no retailer was permitted to resell the product, the Supreme Court declared resale price maintenance illegal. Thus, in 1911, the Court held in *Dr. Miles Medical Co.* v. *John D. Park and Sons Co.*[86] that since the result of this practice

---

[82] 15 U.S.C. §617.

[83] Asch, *Economic Theory:* 373.

[84] R. Smith, "Are Ag. Co-ops Overly Healthy," *Los Angeles Times*, December 18, 1977.

[85] E. Gellhorn, *Antitrust Law and Economics* (St. Paul, Minn.: West Publishing Co., 1951): 255–261.

[86] *Dr. Miles Medical Co.* v. *John D. Park and Sons Co.*, 220 U.S. 373 (1911).

was the same as if the retailers had gotten together and agreed what price to charge, which would be illegal price fixing, resale price maintenance, too, was illegal per se. But in 1931, California passed the first statute exempting resale-price-maintenance agreements from prosecution under state antitrust laws. The statute allowed manufacturers to set a retail price below which no resale of their product could be made. When some retailers who declined to sign price-maintenance agreements ignored the price specification of the manufacturer, California added a nonsigner provision in 1933. As a result, all resellers had to adhere to the resale price established by the manufacturer as long as one reseller within the state had signed a price-maintenance contract. Other states rapidly passed similar legislation, which was upheld in 1939 by the Supreme Court.[87] According to the Court, a manufacturer's right to protect his "goodwill" justified this so-called "fair-trade" legislation. The Miller–Tydings Acts, an amendment to the Sherman act, exempted from prosecution resale-price-maintenance contracts in interstate commerce, whenever such contracts were permitted in the reseller's state.

When, in 1951, the Supreme Court in *Schwegmann Bros.* v. *Calvert Distillers Corporation*[88] weakened resale price maintenance, Congress in 1952 passed the McGuire–Keough Act as an amendment to Section 5 of the FTC Act. Under this act, resale-price-maintenance contracts in interstate commerce are permissible when legal under state law; such contracts may be enforced against nonsigning retailers whenever one retailer in the state signs and the rest are notified.

In 1975, the Federal Trade Commission's order directing Corning Glass Works to stop using a secondary boycott clause was affirmed by the Court of Appeals for the Seventh Circuit.[89] It prohibited Corning to require that its wholesalers (selling in signer-only states) sell only to dealers with a valid fair-trade agreement. As a consequence, fair-trading manufacturers lost their legal right to prevent firms in fair-trade states from supplying discounters in signer-only fair-trade states.[90] In the same year, Congress passed Public

---

[87] *Old Dearborn Distilling Co.* v. *Seagram Distillers Corp.*, 299 U.S. 183 (1936).

[88] *Schwegmann Bros.* v. *Calvert Distillers Corp.*, 340 U.S. 928 (1951).

[89] *FTC* v. *Corning Glass Works*, 509 F.2d 293 (7th 1975).

[90] An economic study has raised serious questions concerning the correctness of the Court's decision. It found that Corning stockholders did not benefit from the decision, sales fell in spite of increased advertising expenditures, and competitors did not incur consistent stock market reaction. Its principal agent analysis concluded that Corning was less motivated by antimonopoly concerns than a desire to expand distribution of its products and services, all with salubrius welfare effects [Pauline M. Ippolito and Thomas R. Overstreet, "Resale Price maintenance: An Economic Assessment of the Federal Trade Commission's Case Against the Corning Glass Works," *Journal of Law and Economics* 34 (April 1996): 285–328].

Law 94-145 ending fair-trade-law provisions and eliminated the authority of the states to enforce their own fair-trade laws.[91]

The argument against fair-trade laws is that they legalize price fixing, restrict competition, and result in higher retail prices. According to Asch, "In effect, fair-trade laws exempt vertical price fixing from antitrust prosecution. The only rationale for such laws is that active price competition is regarded as dangerous by those who would be forced to compete."[92]

Resale price maintenance can also take the form of prohibiting manufacturers from capping prices retailers charge for their products. This prohibition was in force until the United States Supreme Court, in a unanimous 1997 decision, reversed a 30-year-old decision.[93] *State Oil Company* v. *Barkat U. Khan and Khan & Associates, Inc.* allows manufacturers to place limits on prices retailers and franchises can charge, as long as the manufacturers can show that they are not stifling competition. The result could be advantageous to consumers, because of possibly lower and more uniform prices.

OCCUPATIONAL LICENSING

The states have long exercised their police power to provide for occupational licensing of law and medicine. During the latter part of the 1890s, states began to extend licensing control over more and more occupations, including physicians, psychologists, attorneys, dentists, architects, veterinarians, optometrists, pharmacists, real estate brokers, and plumbers.

Licensing legislation is usually initiated by the occupational groups themselves rather than by the public. They argue that professional licensing is needed to protect an unwary public from unscrupulous and unethical practices. Only competent individuals should be permitted to engage in a particular practice. Opposition has usually come from other occupational groups, which feel that such licensing may jeopardize their own interests.

Following Rottenburg, many economists have looked upon occupational licensing as limiting the supply of trained labor to the market.[94] In order to restrict supply, entry costs into the market are increased, be it by additional required schooling, lower pass rates on licensing examinations, citizenship

---

[91] In 1988, the Court appeared to relax the ban when it ruled in a case where a retailer that had cut prices had its supply terminated. The Court held that because there was not agreement on price among the other competing retailers and the manufacturer, antitrust laws had not been violated. [*Business Electronics Corporation* v. *Sharp Electronics Corporation*, 485 U.S. 717 (1988)].

[92] Asch, *Economic Theory:* 384.

[93] *State Oil Company* v. *Barkat U. Khan and Khan & Associates, Inc.*, S.Ct. 96–871 (1997).

[94] S. Rottenburg, "The Economics of Occupational Licensing," in *Aspects of Labor Economics* (New York: National Bureau of Economic Research, 1962).

requirements, training quotas, prior experience requirements, residency requirements, age limits, character qualifications, or other restrictions. Each restrictive device reduces the supply of trained practitioners and tends to raise the costs to consumers of employing licensed professionals. An income redistribution takes place from consumers to those possessing a license. The result is an excess of persons seeking entry into the occupation, encouraging illegal markets and often unequal returns between practitioners depending upon their pre- or postrestrictiveness entry to the occupation.

But the other side of the coin is that occupational licensing increases the quality of services and its uniformity. Yet, in a broader setting, the quality of services can decline because the higher prices engender substitution incentives. Consumers may react and substitute self-service or no service for professional services. Thus, whether occupational licensing raises quality, and, if so, whether this positive result more than offsets the increased cost of the service, is an empirical question.[95]

Holen studied dentistry and found that licensing appears to increase quality.[96] His conclusion was, "even allowing for restriction of entry, licensing appears to be beneficial. Further evidence that licensing benefits consumers is provided by their willingness to pay higher prices when standards are high."[97]

A second study, by Carroll and Gaston, reached somewhat different conclusions.[98] Their empirical studies covered real estate brokers, attorneys, sanitarians, electricians, optometrists, veterinarians, plumbers, and pharmacists. The results for the last four groups were entirely inconclusive. Somewhat better results were obtained for the first four occupations. The results are summarized as follows:

> there existed a strong negative association between per capita numbers of an occupation and per capita service received. Further, almost as consistently, restrictive licensing appeared to significantly lower the stocks of licensees. There is, then, evidence from several professions and trades that indicates that restrictive licensing may lower service quality.[99]

---

[95] Jeffrey M. Perloff and Klass T. van't Veld, *Modern Industrial Organization*, 2d ed. (New York, Harper, 1994) 693–696.

[96] Arlen Holen, *The Economics of Dental Licensing* (Washington, D.C.: Public Research Institute of the Center for Naval Analyses, October 1977).

[97] *Ibid.*: 67.

[98] S. L. Carroll and Robert J. Gaston, *Occupational Licensing* (Knoxville: University of Tennessee, 1977, mimeographed).

[99] *Ibid.*: 41.

A study by Kleiner and Kudrle, using powerful econometric techniques of analysis, examines the effects of licensing dentists.[100] To measure the restrictiveness of state licensing requirements, the study used the pass rate on the state's licensing examination and whether the state licensing board gives reciprocity or endorsement to dentists from other states. The study found that in states with more restrictive licensing laws for dentists, dental health is no higher than in states with less restrictive laws, but dental service prices are higher. Specifically, if a state were to raise restrictiveness from the low to the high pass level (which is below 80%), dental prices would rise 14–16 %, while dentists' incomes would rise 10%.

The federal courts have been largely unsympathetic to constitutional challenges to licensing legislation. For the most part, they have been unwilling to pass judgment on the reasonableness of state economic regulations. For example, in *Ferguson* v. *Skrupa*, the Supreme Court stated, "It is now settled that states have the power to legislate against what are found to be injurious practices in their internal and business affairs, so long as their laws do not run afoul of some specific federal constitutional prohibition, or of some valid federal law."[101] Neither have state courts halted the expansion of occupational licensing. Nevertheless federal antitrust agencies have been moving more boldly in attacking occupational licensing boards. Suits have been filed against the American Bar Association, the National Society of Professional Engineers, the American Institute of Certified Public Accountants, the American Institute of Architects, and the American Society of Anesthesiologists. California, in 1976 passed the Public Members Act, which requires all professional and occupational boards other than those of the healing arts and accountancy to have a majority of public members.[102]

REMEDIES

Once an illegal act has been found to have taken place, the court often issues an injunction to discontinue the practice in question. Such a restriction, even if combined with positive conduct requirements, is frequently insufficient. Moreover, there is no mechanism for policing the firm to see whether the court ruling is indeed consistently and fully implemented. Therefore, rather than insisting on divestiture, courts have in some cases

[100] Morris Kleiner and Robert Kudrle, *Does Regulation Improve Outputs and Increase Prices: The Case of Dentistry* (Cambridge, MA: National Bureau of Economic Research, NBER Working Paper No. 5869, 1997).

[101] *Ferguson* v. *Skrupa*, 372 U.S. 726 (1963).

[102] California S.B. 21-13 and California A.B. 41-32.

threatened divestiture within a given time period unless satisfactory struc-tural changes are carried out. For example, in *United States* v. *Eastman Kodak Co.*,[103] consent decrees were entered requiring that the company split the tie-in between its color film and color-film-processing activities. Eastman Kodak was to divest itself in 7 years of any processing facilities in excess of 50% of national capacity, but divestiture would *not* be required if in 6 years it was shown that purchasers of Eastman color film had easy access to processors other than Eastman. When, in 1961, the government and the company agreed that independent processors had captured more than 50% of the market, divestiture was set aside.

In criminal cases, frequently involving conspiracy, those who are found guilty can be fined or even incarcerated. Fines are usually small in compari-son to the wealth of the firm, and prison sentences are infrequent.

Class action has been permitted in those cases where the effects of violation are so widely diffused among consumers that none has an incentive to bear the costs of a suit. Class action permits persons who would be affected by a decree, but are so numerous that it would be impossible or at least impracticable to bring them all in as parties, to seek judgment as a "class" though only some members of the class may be parties to the suit, the judicial opinion may bind all members of that class. Class action provides economies of scale as well as enhanced power to plaintiffs. But class action can also lead to frivolous harassment of defendants. The impor-tance of class actions has been rapidly increasing.

SOME FURTHER ECONOMIC CONSIDERATIONS

Economists have been concerned with providing tools to evaluate the per-formance of firms with monopoly power. With their help they seek to indicate why, when, and, if so, in what form to intervene and when not. They also have shown interest in understanding better the monopoly problem in highly dynamic and innovative industries with relative ease of entry, e.g., the high-tech information industry.

Efforts to develop performance criteria have focused on how increased monopoly power affects allocative and productive efficiency, and to com-pare their relative changes. Productive efficiency is the physical efficiency of the input–output production transformation and allocative efficiency is the price efficiency of optimal resource allocation. Under competitive mar-ket conditions the sum of consumer and producer surpluses cannot increase

[103] Trade Cas. Par. 67, 920 (W.D. N.Y., 1954).

by antitrust action. When firms have monopoly power, antimonopoly action can only increase the total surplus if it raises allocative efficiency more than it reduces productive efficiency. Since monopoly power reduces allocative efficiency, before taking antitrust action, we must take into account the firm's monopoly power (and its allocative efficiency reducing effect) as well as its effect on productive efficiency. Specifically, in evaluating the overall effect of an antitrust action it is necessary to estimate its probable net effect on the total surplus as well as such transaction costs as are associated with prosecuting, defending, and deciding the antitrust case.

Thus, the focus is on estimating and comparing allocative and productive efficiency. If this is done on a case by case basis, the rule of reason is applied, and if it is done across the board, the per se rule is applied. If in this type of analysis, a firm is held to have violated an antitrust act, a number of remedies are available. They include divestiture, injunction to discontinue the practice, fines (which can include triple damages), and incarceration.

The desirability of antitrust action has been reconsidered by some economists, who have pointed to evidence that a firm's economic performance is not necessarily closely associated with market structure and monopoly power.[104] They point to some very large firms, e.g., IBM and AT & T and some highly concentrated markets, e.g., the information industry, which have been extremely innovative and productive, and have benefited consumers. They also note the vigorous price competition between Coca-Cola and Pepsi Co., which control three-quarters of the soft-drink sales.

The attitude toward antimonopoly laws and their enforcement appears to have undergone a major change in the 1990s. There is no change in the objective, which is to prevent any firm from exercising undue market power, i.e., having the ability to set prices higher than competition would allow. The concern remains predation against competitors. Until recently, market control was at the heart of the matter. The view was that if one firm charges unrealistically low prices to drive out another, consumers benefit. Yet the predator cannot sustain monopoly profits for long, since new competitors will be attracted into the market.

Recent thinking has raised questions about defining the correct market. For example, in the competition between British Airways and American Airlines, is the relevant market travel between the United States and Europe

---

[104] Paul A. Samuelson and William D. Nordhaus, *Economics* (New York: McGraw-Hill, 13th ed., 1989): 623–624.

or the United States and Britain? The focus has also shifted from simple market share to building models of strategic competition among oligopolists.[105] These models take into account whether an alleged predator raises rivals' costs, reduces rivals' revenues, and whether two or more markets are linked so that a monopolist in one market can boost profits in another. Clearly the view before the 1990s was critical of government activism and often held antitrust suits to be unwarranted, if not altogether counterproductive. The new view supports tougher antitrust enforcement. Nowhere is this difference in outlook more compelling than in relation to high-tech industries, issues that will be taken up next.

ANTITRUST POLICY TOWARD HIGH-TECH INDUSTRIES

The emergence in the 1990s of a multitude of high-tech firms, especially in the computer software and cyberspace industries, calls for a reexamination of existing antitrust policies. Some laws are more than 100 years old and were developed to address mainly monopoly, problems in manufacturing, public utilities, and retailing.

The monopoly problems posed by high-tech industries do not relate so much to prices charged customers, especially not in the short run, than enabling start-up firms, who may only work in garages and labs, to break into the market. Moreover, monopolists should not be allowed to start the race for a new and improved product with an artificial, monopoly-related advantage over their competition. If the competitors in high-tech industries would be characterized as participants in a series of 100-yard sprints, no single firm should be permitted, because of its market power, to create a situation where it would start the next race significantly ahead of its competitors. Such a condition could come about when a high-tech firm misuses its market position in the industry, e.g., locks in users, or threatens its customers to retaliate if they use competitors' new products.

Software and cyberspace industries are good examples of the challenges facing existing antitrust policy. They appear perhaps more invention- than price-driven. Their pace of innovation is often mind-boggling. These industries benefit from a number of natural advantages that can be detrimental to competition in the longer term. The following are important:

---

[105] J. A. Hausman, "Competition in Long-Distance and Telecommunications Equipment Markets: Effects of the M.F.J.," *Managerial and Decision Economics* 16 (July–August 1995): 365–383.

1. Computer networks, even more than networks of railroads, electricity, and natural gas transmission, use an interconnected web of fixed infrastructure where consumers benefit from network growth and externalities. For example, the larger the telephone network, the more users that can phone others as well as be phoned. Similarly, network externalities can result from the use of a common or compatible computer language and word-processing program. Standards for compatibility in computer software yield network externalities and yet such standards are continually undergoing change and improvement.
2. When one firm's technology is widely used, it will incur significant network externalities. The wider the use, the more difficult it is for competitors, possibly with better products, to enter the market. Any customer who considers change to another product will be required to incur huge costs in replacing software and retraining staff.
3. In a dynamic software or cyberspace industry, set-up costs, i.e., initial costs to make the program work, are disproportionately high, and can prevent moves to a new technology.
4. Firms in such industries, while subject to ever-increasing returns and the emergence of technical standards, gain two major benefits — the successful monopolist will directly profit, and start the next technological contest with an advantage over competitors.

Under these circumstances, there is the potential for anticompetitive practices to occur, particularly when the innovator, benefiting from scale economies, succeeds in locking in users to a particular technology. (An example is Microsoft and its Windows Operating System.) As a consequence, potentially superior operating systems can be locked out and a degree of market predestination or "path dependence" can occur. The resulting anticompetitiveness may deserve antitrust intervention that is speedy, effective, and in the public's interest. But perhaps not, when the ease of entry into the industry by such "up-starts" as Netscape and Sun Microsystems can create a competitive environment. While it is important for antitrust policymakers and enforcers to recognize the unique character of high-tech industries, unwarranted or heavy-handed government intervention is to be avoided by those considering reform.

The advance of technology may in time be unkind to firms who today may appear to have a monopoly. Not unlike International Business Machine Corporation, they might find themselves left behind with their monopoly that is by-passed by new technology. Quite possibly antitrust action would not have been needed.

In the late 1990s, some government agencies became alarmed about potentially anticompetitive practices of two giants — Microsoft Corporation, in the software industry, and Intel Corporation, in the semiconductor industry.[106] Both have been highly innovative and productive. Nevertheless in May 1998, the United States Department of Justice filed an antitrust suit against Microsoft. They accused Microsoft for using its monopoly power in Windows operating systems to gain control of the Internet browser market. Specifically, the suit alleged that there is a broad pattern of predatory conduct and a scheme by Microsoft to extend its software monopoly into cyberspace. Twenty states have taken similar legal action.

In June 1998, the Federal Trade Commission filed an antitrust suit against Intel Corporation, alleging that Intel used its monopoly power to cement its dominance over the microprocessor market. Specifically, Intel is accused of illegally withholding, in a discriminatory and exclusionary way, key intellectual property, while taking in about 80% of industry, wide revenues for microprocessors in 1997. The FTC alleged that when such computer manufacturers as Compaq, Digital Equipment Corporation, and Intergraph sought to enforce their microprocessor patents, Intel retaliated by withholding information and threatening to cut of the supply of chips. It is argued that if Intel can prevent other firms from enforcing their patents, these companies will have little incentive to invent new features in microprocessors to challenge Intel's dominance.

CONCLUSION

More than 100 years ago, Congress became concerned about the tendency of firms in certain industries to acquire strong monopoly power, and it enacted laws to cope with excesses, most prominently the Sherman, Clayton, and FTC acts. Various antitrust laws have been designed to address moves to gain undue monopoly power through horizontal mergers and formation of conglomerates, secret cooperation in the form of cartels, price discrimination, and foreclosure of entry into industries. However, government itself also has taken some steps that create artificial monopolies, e.g., resale-price maintenance and occupational licensing. Legal and economic aspects of these undertakings are examined.

Economists have worked with lawyers in antimonopoly matters for longer than in any other legal field. Dissatisfaction with the status of antimonopoly law is widespread. In part, this stems from major disagreements between

---

[106] "Microsoft Accused,", *The Economist* (May 23, 1988): 21–23; and "Intel: Paranoia Time," *The Economist* (June 13, 1998): 62–63.

those who hold a populist view and those with an efficiency view, with the latter prevailing in the recent past. Many practitioners and scholars in the antitrust arena favor a blending or synthesis of the two dominant views.

During much of the existence of antitrust laws, a large number of cases reached the courts, but in recent years the volume has fallen off. A major reason is that today firms contemplating steps that could possibly be held in violation of one or another of the antitrust laws tend to bring their plans to the attention of the Antitrust Division of the Department of Justice or the FTC. Thus, these agencies can advise firms contemplating steps that could violate antitrust laws whether these plans are likely to withstand scrutiny. Firms then can either drop their plans or negotiate mutually acceptable compromises.

Yet, an antitrust policy that basically was formulated to address monopoly practices of very large manufacturers, be it in the steel or oil industry, might require review when applied to high-tech firms in a dynamic microchip age. For example, firms in the information and knowledge industries, with their breathtaking innovation pace and relative ease of entry, may require new policies. The dynamism and inventiveness of such firms may offer society the greatest gains if government regulation is kept to a minimum.

11

DISCRIMINATION LAW

INTRODUCTION

While discrimination is the essence of economics — people display their preferences by discriminating among goods, services, investments, etc. — some types of discrimination evidenced in the labor or the housing markets pose special problems that have been recognized by legislatures and courts. Some of these problems are primarily moral in nature, while others have a major economic content.

Our concern is with the possibility that individuals are accorded different treatment on the basis of their race, religion, sex, national origin, and age. Discrimination can relate to such issues as employment (i.e., hiring, discharging, compensation, terms, conditions, or privileges), education, housing, credit, or child custody.

In this chapter, I will focus on employment discrimination, reverse discrimination, and housing discrimination. In each instance, legal issues will be taken up first; they will be followed by an economic analysis.

EMPLOYMENT DISCRIMINATION[1]

Employment discrimination is said to exist when members of one or more groups, commonly defined by race, sex, age, religion, or national origin,

---

[1] This section draws heavily on Barbara Schlei and Paul Grossman, *Employment Discrimination Law,* 2d ed. (Washington, D.C.: Bureau of National Affairs, 1983).

are denied the employment opportunities and/or wages accorded other groups, regardless of qualifications.

My examination of employment discrimination will focus on discrimination by race and, to a lesser extent, sex. It should not be difficult for the reader to apply the legal discussion as well as the economic theory and analysis to other bases of discrimination. Likewise, parts of the economic theory of discrimination developed in relation to employment are also applicable to other issues such as housing and education.

EMPLOYMENT DISCRIMINATION LAW

Laws dealing with discrimination go back to the days after the Civil War, when Congress enacted a series of civil rights statutes designed to lend force to the newly ratified Thirteenth, Fourteenth, and Fifteenth Amendments. In recent years, three of these statutes — now codified as 42 U.S.C. §1981, §1983, and §1985 — have been used to attack employment discrimination. They are commonly referred to as the Civil Rights Acts of 1866 and 1871.

A second wave of antidiscrimination activity took place in the mid-1960s, culminating in the passage of the Civil Rights Act of 1964, and especially its Title VII. To some extent, the Acts of 1866 and 1871 and the Act of 1964 complement one another. The 1964 Act addresses situations not covered by the earlier acts. At the same time, the Acts of 1866 and 1871 provide plaintiffs with compensatory and punitive damages, while also making available jury trials under certain circumstances.

In addition to some housing discrimination laws that were enacted in the 1970s and 1980s (see later, the discussion of housing discrimination), subsequently the Civil Rights Act of 1991 was enacted.[2] It's purpose was to deal with job discrimination.

The major antidiscrimination statutes are the Act of 1866 (or 1870) and that of 1964. Let me start by summarizing the scope and coverage of the Civil Rights Act of 1866 (42 U.S.C. §1981). It provides

All persons within the jurisdiction of the United States shall have the same right ... to make and enforce contracts, to sue, be parties, give evidence, and to the full and equal benefit of all laws and proceedings for the security of persons and property as is enjoyed by white citizens, and shall be subject to like punishments, pains, penalties, taxes, licenses, and exactions of every kind, and to no other.

[2] Pub. L. No. 102–166, 105 Stat. 1071 (Supp. 1991) (codified as amended in scattered sections of 2 U.S.C. and 42 U.S.C.).

This statute (and some companions) were originally enacted as §1 of the Civil Rights Act of 1866,[3] pursuant to the Congressional power to eradicate slavery provided by the Thirteenth Amendment, which had been ratified in 1865. After ratification of the Fourteenth Amendment in 1868, the statute was reenacted in 1870[4] in order to remove any doubt of the constitutional authority of Congress to pass such legislation. Thus, the statute has been referred to as the Civil Rights Act of 1866 or 1870, or, in its modern form, as §1981.

Initially, §1981 was narrowly interpreted to apply only to public acts of discrimination. Only in 1968 (more than 100 years after passage of the statute) did the Supreme Court, in *Jones* v. *Alfred H. Mayer Co.*, hold that purely private acts of discrimination were covered by the 1866 act.[5]

The Court confirmed this view in the landmark case of *Johnson* v. *Railway Express Agency, Inc.*,[6] stating: "[I]t is now well settled among the federal courts of appeals — and we now join them — that §1981 affords a federal remedy against discrimination in private employment on the basis of race."[7]

There are other sections to the early Civil Rights Act. For example, §1983, §1985, and §1986 were originally §1 of the Civil Rights Act of 1871, also known as the Ku Klux Klan Act.[8] It provided that "no *State* shall make or enforce any law which shall abridge the privileges or immunities of citizens of the United States; nor shall any *State* deprive any person of life, liberty or property without due process of law; nor deny to any person within its jurisdiction the equal protection of the laws."[9] Section 1983 reaches only persons acting "under color of" state law and does not reach purely private conduct, nor does it reach conduct of federal agencies and officials in most instances.

Next I will turn to Title VII of the Civil Rights Act of 1964, referred to hereafter as Title VII. Under Title VII, it is an unlawful practice for any employer, employment agency, or labor organization to discriminate against a person on the basis of race, color, religion, sex, or national origin. This prohibition covers such issues as hiring, discharging, compensation, terms or conditions, or privileges of employment; failure to refer; causing

---

[3] Act of April 9, 1866, Ch. 31, §1, 14 Stat. 27.
[4] Act of May 31, 1870, Ch. 114, 16, 18, 16 Stat. 144.
[5] 392 U.S. 409 (1968).
[6] U.S. 454, 10 FEP 817 (1975).
[7] *Id*, at 459–60, 10 FEP at 819.
[8] Act. of April 20, 1871, Ch. 22, §1, 17 Stat. 13.
[9] U.S. Const., Amendment 14, §1. The purpose of the legislation is clear from its title: "An Act to Enforce the Provisions of the Fourteenth Amendment to the Constitution of the United States, and for Other Purposes," 17 Stat. 13.

an employer to discriminate; and printing or publishing a discriminatory employment notice or advertisement. However, it is up to the plaintiff to show that there was a causal connection between a basis and the issue.

There exist four general categories or theories of discrimination by which the causal connection between basis and issue may be proven. They are (in order of their historical development): (1) disparate treatment;[10] (2) policies or practices that perpetuate in the present the effects of past discrimination;[11] (3) policies or practices having an adverse impact not justified by business necessity;[12] and (4) failure to make reasonable accommodation to an employee's religious observance or practices.[13]

The first theory of discrimination is disparate treatment on the basis of race, color, religion, sex, or national origin and is viewed by Congress as prohibited. This concept of disparate treatment is well stated by the Supreme Court in *Teamsters* v. *United States.*

"[d]isparate treatment"... is the most easily understood type of discrimination. The employer simply treats some people less favorably than others because of their race, color, religion, sex or national origin. Proof of discriminatory motive is critical, although it can in some situations be inferred from the mere fact of differences in treatment. [Citation omitted.] Undoubtedly disparate treatment was the most obvious evil Congress had in mind when it enacted Title VII ... [14]

The determining factor is that treatment differ between blacks and whites, women and men, or Catholics and Protestants. The treatment may involve

---

[10] Examples include an absolute refusal to consider browns for employment, paying a woman a lower wage than that paid a man for the same work, and discharging a black employee for an offense for which whites are given lesser or no discipline.

[11] A classic example is a departmental seniority structure where the employer has departments of varying desirability. If, prior to the relevant time frame, the employer hired minorities only into the least desirable departments and, thereafter, either flatly barred transfers between the departments or required a forfeiture of seniority as a condition of transfer, a minority employee would be effectively locked into an undesirable department, in which he had originally been placed as a consequence of discrimination. The legality of the seniority structure would then depend on whether it was bona fide.

[12] Examples include: (1) a general intelligence test as a prerequisite for hire that disqualifies substantially more blacks than whites and that cannot be shown to be job-related in the sense that it accurately predicts successful job performance; (2) a requirement of a high school diploma as a prerequisite for hire where fewer blacks than whites have such a diploma and the diploma cannot be shown to be job-related; and (3) selection for promotion by white foremen based on subjective criteria that result in blacks not being promoted.

[13] An example would include discharging a religious Jew for refusing to work on the Sabbath where an accommodation to the employee's religious practices would not work an undue hardship on the conduct of the employer's business.

[14] 431 U.S. 324, 335–336 n. 15, 14 FEP 1514, 1519 (1977).

promotion or provision of facilities. According to Barbara Schlei and Paul Grossman, no importance is attached to whether

> the employee is a good or bad employee, or whether the employer is fair or unfair. For example, a violation of Title VII would be proved under the disparate treatment theory by evidence that a female plaintiff was discharged for four unexcused absences in accordance with a company rule that all persons with four unexcused absences are discharged, but similarly situated male employees were not discharged after four unexcused absences. However, if similarly situated male employees were also discharged in such circumstances, there would be no violation of Title VII. In both situations, it is irrelevant whether the plaintiff was a bad employee or a good employee. General conceptions of whether or not it is fair to discharge someone for four unexcused absences are similarly not determinative.[15]

In a disparate treatment case, the plaintiff must prove that he was treated differently because of his protected basis, for example, his race. Specifically, according to the Supreme Court in *McDonnell Douglas Corp.* v. *Green*,[16] the plaintiff must establish a prima facie case; the defendant must offer a legitimate, nondiscriminatory reason for its actions; and the plaintiff must establish that this supposedly legitimate, nondiscriminatory reason was a pretext to mask an illegal move.

Consequently, in hiring proceedings, the prima facie case would have to be established in the following manner:

> The complainant in a Title VII trial must carry the initial burden under the statute of establishing a prima facie case of racial discrimination. This may be done by showing (i) that he belongs to a racial minority; (ii) that he applied and was qualified for a job for which the employer was seeking applicants; (iii) that, despite his qualifications, he was rejected; and (iv) that, after his rejection, the position remained open and the employer continued to seek applicants from persons of complainant's qualifications....[17]

The second and third stages would then proceed as follows:

> After a plaintiff establishes such a prima facie case, the "burden then must shift to the employer to articulate some legitimate, nondiscriminatory reason for the employer's rejection." [Citation omitted.] If some such reason is advanced by the employer, the focus returns to the plaintiff so that he can "be afforded a fair opportunity to show

---

[15] Schlei and Grossman, *Employment Discrimination*: 13.
[16] *McDonnel Douglas Corp.* v. *Green*, 411 U.S. 792, 5 FEP 965 (1973).
[17] *Id.* at 802, 5 FEP at 969.

that (the employer's) stated reason for (the employee's) rejection was in fact pretext."
[Citation omitted.][18]

Since *McDonnell Douglas Corp.* v. *Green,* the Court has made it clear that the burden of proof remains with the plaintiff. The employer's sole obligation at the second stage is simply to articulate a legitimate, nondiscriminatory reason. He does not need to establish by a preponderance of the evidence that its proffered reason was the real reason or that the person selected was more qualified than the plaintiff.[19]

Most litigation relates to the third stage, where the plaintiff must establish that the justification given by the defendant for his actions is in fact pretext. The plaintiff can provide direct evidence of motive, which, however, is seldom possible, or statistical evidence or, most commonly, comparative evidence. In relation to the latter, the plaintiff offers a comparison of treatment between protected group members and majority group members, while seeking to show that the treatment of protected group members was inferior compared to that accorded majority group members.[20]

The second of the theories of discrimination related to the perpetuation in the present of the effects of past discrimination. This category, together with the third (to be discussed below), have been perhaps the most important developments associated with Title VII.

Perpetuation of the effects of past discrimination through devices that are neutral on their face has been clarified in *Quarles* v. *Philip Morris, Inc.*[21] Two black employees of Philip Morris, Inc., brought action against the company, Local 203 of the Tobacco Workers International Union, and the president of the union, to enjoin them from intentionally engaging in unlawful employment practices by discriminating on the ground of race. According to the court,

> The company had numerous departments, of which the lower paying were primarily black and the higher paying primarily white. Historically interdepartmental transfers

[18] *Davis* v. *Weidner,* 596 F.2d 726, 729, 19 FEP 668, 670 (7th Cir. 1979) (sex discrimination termination case; general order and allocation of proof in disparate treatment cases described). See also *Smith* v. *University of North Carolina,* 632 F.2d 316, 23 FEP 1739 (4th Cir. 1980) (no requirement that employer prove by a preponderance of evidence that legitimate, nondiscriminatory factor was the motivating force).

[19] *Texas Dept. of Community Affairs* v. *Burdine,* 450 U.S. 248, 25 FEP 113 (1981).

[20] A good example is *Slack* v. *Havens,* where the court accepted comparative evidence of the treatment of four black women who alleged to have been discriminatorily discharged due to their race, in violation of the Civil Rights Act of 1964. [7 FEP 885 (S.D. Cal. 1973) affirmed, in part, remanded on other grounds, 552 F.2d 1981, 11 FEP 27 (9th Cir. 1975).]

[21] *Quarles* v. *Philip Morris, Inc.,* 279 F. Sup. 505, 1 FEP 260 (E.D. Va. 1968).

were totally prohibited.... The plaintiff, Douglas H. Quarles, has been employed by Philip Morris for nine years. He is a laborer in the prefabrication department earning $2.22 per hour. He sought a job as a truck driver, which pays $2.58 an hour, in the warehouse shipping and receiving department, where eight or ten truck drivers are assigned. A Negro has never been employed as a permanent truck driver.... An employee does not need to ascend the ladder of progression in the department to get a truck driver's job. He must have merit, ability and seniority within the department to bid successfully.... Quarles was not denied the job for lack of ability. There was no provision in the collective bargaining agreement that would allow him to transfer from the prefabrication department, where approximately 92 per cent of the employees were Negro, to the warehouse shipping and receiving department, where approximately 86.1 per cent were white....

The plaintiffs contend that Quarles and other Negroes hired before January 1, 1966, are deprived of opportunities to advance because of their race. They do not seek to oust white employees with less employment seniority from their jobs, but they do seek to be trained and promoted to fill vacancies on the same basis as white employees with equal ability and employment seniority.

The Court held

that the defendants have intentionally engaged in unlawful employment practices by discriminating on the ground of race against Quarles, and other Negroes similarly situated. This discrimination, embedded in seniority and transfer provisions of collective bargaining agreements, adversely affects the conditions of employment and opportunities for advancement of the class.

Adverse impact not justified by business necessity is the third legal theory of discrimination. In this connection, Section 703(a) of the Civil Rights Act of 1964 provides

It shall be an unlawful employment practice for an employer — ... (2) to limit, segregate, or classify his employees in any way which would deprive or tend to deprive any individual of employment opportunities or otherwise adversely affect his status as an employee, because of such individual's race, color, religion, sex, or national origin....

(h) Notwithstanding any other provision of this title, it shall not be an unlawful employment practice for an employer ... to give and to act upon the results of any professionally developed ability test provided that such test, its administration or action upon the results is not designed, intended, or used to discriminate because of race, color, religion, sex, or national origin....

Based on this section, the Court offered one of its most important employment discrimination rulings in *Griggs* v. *Duke Power Co.*[22] In it, the Court

---

[22] *Griggs* v. *Duke Power Co.*, U.S. 424, 3 FEP 175 (1971). Actually, the *Griggs* decision was preceded by a lower court decision finding violations of Title VII on the *Griggs* theory. See Judge Irving Hill's decisions in *Gregory* v. *Litton Sys., Inc.*, 316 F. Supp. 401, 2 FEP 842 (C.D. Cal. 1970), *aff'd as modified*, 472 F.2d 631, 5 FEP 267 (9th Cir. 1971) (uniform and evenhanded application of company policy not to hire individuals who have been arrested with greater frequency than whites, and business necessity, defined to be a practice or policy essential to the safe and efficient operation of the business, not shown).

addressed the question of whether an employer is prohibited by the Civil Rights Act of 1964, Title VII, from requiring a high school education or passing of a standardized general intelligence test as a condition of employment in or transfer to jobs when: (*a*) neither standard is shown to be significantly related to successful job performance; (*b*) both requirements operate to disqualify Negroes at a substantially higher rate than white applicants; and (*c*) the jobs in question formerly had been filled only by white employees as part of a long-standing practice of giving preference to whites.

Suit had been brought by a group of incumbent Negro employees against Duke Power Company. The company's Dan River plant was organized into five operating departments; (1) Labor, (2) Coal Handling, (3) Operations, (4) Maintenance, and (5) Laboratory and Test. Negroes were employed only in the Labor Department, where the highest paying jobs paid less than the lowest paying jobs in the other four "operating" departments in which only whites were employed. Promotions were normally made within each department on the basis of job seniority. Transferees into a department usually began in the lowest position.

The Court established that

> In 1955 the Company instituted a policy requiring a high school education for initial assignment to any department except Labor, and for transfer from the Coal Handling to any "inside" department (Operations, Maintenance, or Laboratory). When the Company abandoned its policy of restricting Negroes to the Labor Department in 1965, completion of high school also was made a prerequisite to transfer from Labor to any other department....
>
> The Company added a further requirement for new employees on July 2, 1965, the date on which Title VII became effective. To qualify for placement in any but the Labor Department it became necessary to register satisfactory scores on two professionally prepared aptitude tests, as well as to have a high school education. Completion of high school alone continued to render employees eligible for transfer to the four desirable departments from which Negroes had been excluded if the incumbent had been employed prior to the time of the new requirement. In September 1965 the Company began to permit incumbent employees who lacked a high school education to qualify for transfer from Labor or Coal Handling to an "inside" job by passing two tests — the Wonderlic Personnel Test, which purports to measure general intelligence, and the Bennett Mechanical Aptitude Test. Neither was directed or intended to measure the ability to learn to perform a particular job or category of jobs. The requisite scores used for both initial hiring and transfer approximated the national median for high school graduates.

The Court ruled that Duke Power Company had engaged in employment discrimination. It held that "good intent or absence of discriminatory intent" is not a defense, that "the Act proscribes not only overt discrimination but also practices that are fair in form, but discriminatory in operation," that "the touchstone is business necessity," and that "an employment practice which operates to exclude Negroes" and which "cannot be shown to be related to job performance" is unlawful.

However, in 1989 the Court in *Wards Cove Packing Co.* v. *Alioto*[23] greatly modified and, in the eyes of some, eviscerated the 1971 *Griggs* decision. *Wards Cove* made proof of discrimination by plaintiff more difficult. It no longer allowed proof for intentional discrimination to be unnecessary in order to show that hiring practices had a discriminatory effect or "disparate impact." Though preserving the "disparate impact" rule, *Wards Cove* shifted the burden of proof. Plaintiff must show that certain employment practices were not required for conduct of business, rather than, as before, employer having to demonstrate that the practices were necessary. Moreover, plaintiff must identify specific employment practices that produced the discrimination.

In the same year the Court struck down Virginia's set-aside plan, which reserved 30% of government contracts for minorities.[24]

ECONOMICS OF EMPLOYMENT DISCRIMINATION

Discrimination laws that were discussed earlier aim at making America a color, gender, and age-blind society. Yet to date in most labor markets wage as well as employment rate differences among certain groups are common. Many circumstances may be responsible for these differences. Discrimination can be one factor.

As was earlier indicated, employment discrimination exists when one class of people is denied access to higher paying jobs on the basis of characteristics unrelated to their actual performance. Wage discrimination exists when the individuals of one particular class are paid less than are the individuals of another class for doing identical jobs; or when the job structure of a firm segregates workers by race, ethnicity, religion, or sex, paying the workers of one class less than others, although the two have about the same job. Women appear to be particularly affected by the latter type of wage discrimination.

The following numbers can describe existing differences, which in many cases have shrunk during much of the past three decades: In 1996 the black/white unemployment rate ratio was 2.4, down from 2.6 in 1960.[25] In 1995 the median weekly earnings of black males were 73% of those of

[23] 448 U.S. 448.
[24] *City of Richmond* v. *Croson,* 488 U.S. 469 (1989).
[25] U.S. Bureau of Labor Statistics, *Employment and Earnings* 8 (January 1991): 5, 178, 212–213.

white males, while similar figures for females were 86%.[26] In the same year, the median weekly earnings of white females were 73% of those of white males and for blacks the figure was 86%. For all employed women, weekly earnings as a persent of men's had risen from 62% in 1979 to 76% in 1995.[27] Some of the earnings differences may be due to discrimination, as is suggested by a 1991 study by the Urban Institute. It sent "testers" on hundreds of job searches in Chicago and Washington, D.C., in response to "help wanted" ads. Both black and white applicants used similar "scripts" to describe to employers their work experience, education, and skills.[28] While 66% of the interviews failed to generate a job offer for either black or white applicants, 15% of interviews led to a job only for the white applicant, and 5% only for the black applicant. Generalizing to the entire work force, black workers incur higher search costs, look longer for a job, and will tend to settle for less desirable, lower paying jobs than do white workers.

A review of participation in key professions also shows great race and gender differences. In 1990, 2.3% of all male physicians in the United States were black (up from 1.8% in 1970).[29] For females, the percentages were 1.2% and 0.04%. For black lawyers, the percentages were very similar. For college faculty, the black male and female percentage was 2.4% in 1990, up from 1.9% for males and 2.6% for females.

Having established that differences with regard to race and gender, wage, and employment exist, I will turn to a search for reasons. Economists attempt to explain wage difference from the supply and demand side and thereby place the problem into a general labor market framework. On the supply side, wage differences can be explained in terms of the age and sex mix, labor force participation, and level of education and experience, among other variables. Black and Hispanic workers usually are younger than white workers; black and Hispanic women usually participate in the labor force at higher rates than do white women; and whites usually are better educated than blacks and Hispanics. Because age and education are positively correlated with earnings, we would expect earnings of whites to be higher than those of blacks and Hispanics. Further reason is that blacks,

[26] U.S. Department of Commerce, *Statistical Abstract of the United States, 1996* (Washington D.C., 1996); 426.

[27] U.S. Department of Labor, "Earnings Differences Between Women and Men," *Facts on Working Women*, No. 93–5 (Washington, D.C., December 1993): 2; and No. 96-2 (September 1996): 12.

[28] M. A. Turner et al., *Opportunities Denied, Opportunities Diminished: Racial Discrimination in Hiring,* Report No. 91-9 (Urban Institute: Washington, D.C., 1991).

[29] Andrew Hacker, "Good-bye to Affirmative Action," *New York Review of Books* (July 11, 1996): 26.

perhaps mainly because of their socioeconomic situation, have inferior opportunities of investing in themselves.

And in terms of gender, it is a fact that women only recently have entered the labor force in increasing numbers. As a result they tend to be younger, less experienced, and have lower seniority and therefore earn lower wages than male workers. Such differences in income can be explained by human capital theory, which seeks to explain differences in earnings among different classes of workers, e.g., between white and black men, and men and women, on the basis of differences in their personal characteristics. According to the human capital approach, the price of labor in the form of wages and salaries in each market, like all other prices, should in equilibrium (and in the absence of discrimination) equal the value of labor's marginal product. In line with this theory, discrimination would exist whenever there was inequality in earnings between two classes of employees that could not be explained in terms of differences in their personal characteristics (other than race and sex) and therefore their ensuing economic contribution or productivity. In other words, from the supply side, wage differences not accounted for by differences in productivity would point to discrimination.

Turning to the demand side, minority members may have occupations for which there is little demand compared to available supply. They also may suffer from the venerable policy "last hired, first fired." Thus when wage or employment differences of black and white or female and male workers cannot be explained from either the supply or demand side, the residual can be attributed to discrimination. There exists little empirical research that estimates this discrimination-related difference, although it has been surmised to be between 5 and 15% of the whites' wage permium.[30]

Economists have developed two main theories of discrimination[31] — a demand related theory based on "taste for discrimination" and advanced by Becker[32] and a second called statistical discrimination. The latter is associated with Arrow[33] and with Phelps.[34] According to Becker's taste for

---

[30] E. D. Williams and R. H. Sander, "The Prospects for 'Putting America to Work' in the Inner City," *Georgetown Law Review* 81 (5) (June 1993): 2029.

[31] Other theories include that by Spence based on "signaling," where the relationship between education and ability is different for different groups (Michael A. Spence, *Market Signaling: Information Transfer in Hiring and Related Screening Processes* (Cambridge, MA: Harvard University Press, 1974). Another group of theories uses search models (Robert T. Masson, "Cost of Search and Racial Price Discrimination," *Western Economic Journal* 11 (1973): 167–186.

[32] Gary Becker, *The Economics of Discrimination* (Chicago: University of Chicago Press, 1957).

[33] Kenneth J. Arrow, "The Theory of Discrimination, "in *Discrimination in Labor Markets*, O. Ashenfelter and A. Rees, Eds. (Princeton, N.J.: Princeton University Press, 1973): 3–33.

[34] Edmund S. Phelps, "The Statistical Theory of Racism and Sexism," *American Economic Review* 62, (September 1972): 659–661.

discrimination concept a person acts "as if he were willing to pay something, either directly or in the form of a reduced income, to be associated with some persons instead of others."[35] This can take a number of forms in the labor market. Employers may dislike hiring certain groups of individuals; employees may dislike working with certain groups of individuals; customers may dislike buying from firms owned by or employing members of certain groups.

In the Becker model, a discriminating employer is assumed to place a cost on employing members of minority groups. Let Ww be the wage paid to whites and Wb the wage paid to blacks; assume all workers have the same VMP, where VMP is the value of an employee's marginal product. In a world without discriminating employers, all workers would earn equal wages, where $Ww = Wb = VMP$. Yet, if employers did discriminate, they would attach an extra nonpecuniary cost d (called the discrimination coefficient) to the cost of employing minority workers. As a result, they would hire minority workers until $Wb(1 + d) = VMP$ and $Wb = VMP/(1 + d) < Ww$. Minority workers with the same productivity as white workers would be paid less than whites, owing to the positive value of the discrimination coefficient. In an empirical study, Barry Chiswick found that the hypothesis that white male workers act as if they have a taste for discrimination against minorities is supported for the United States.[36] The labor market could be affected by discrimination among labor substitutes (workers who perform the same tasks) or labor complements (a foreman and a group of unskilled workers). If white workers attach a cost to working with minority individuals — especially working for a minority foreman — they will demand higher wages $[Ww = W(1 + d)]$. In essence, the cost of hiring minority employees, even for a nondiscriminating employer, would exceed Wb, since the white employees would have to receive additional compensation. This would have adverse effects on the demand for minority workers.

There is arguably less tendency toward the elimination of wage discrimination in markets characterized by monopoly conditions, where employers have significant freedom to lower their profits in order to earn nonpecuniary returns. Posner argues that one way for regulated monopolies to avoid a profit ceiling (regulated monopolies are often restricted as how much profit they can earn) is to gain nonmonetary income[37] The tighter the

[35] Becker, *Economics of Discrimination*: 14.

[36] Barry Chiswick, "Racial Discrimination in the Labor Market: A Test of Alternative Hypotheses," in *Patterns of Racial Discrimination*, George M. von Furstenberg, Ann R. Horowitz, and Bennett Harrison, Eds. (Lexington, Mass.: D.C. Heath and Company, 1974), vol. 2: 101–120.

[37] Richard A. Posner, *Economic Analysis of Law*, 4th ed. (Boston: Little, Brown, 1992): 651–653.

labor market and the greater the competitive pressures on individual firms, the more quickly wage differentials should be eliminated.

Taste-based analyses are quite good at explaining discrimination in situations where individuals interact, and, thus, tastes matter. However, can they explain discrimination in impersonal transactions, e.g., obtaining home loans? For such cases a second theory is offered.

Statistical discrimination approaches recognize that observability of an employee's productivity is imperfect. As a consequence people use an individual's race or gender as a proxy for individual characteristics. If such categories are based on data rather than prejudice, these proxies can provide low-cost signals. For example, a mortgage company might be reluctant to lend to a black person in the belief that blacks generally have relatively high default rates. And using the race proxy is less costly than researching the individual's credit history.

Measuring discrimination has proved to be very difficult, whether regression analysis or audits are used. Regression analysis suffers from the fact that certain variables, e.g., quality of employee, are extremely hard to quantify. Other variables may have been overlooked.[38] But audits pose problems too. In an audit, two individuals equal in all respects save one, such as race or gender, sequentially visit an employer, rental agent, or loan officer to detect whether there is disparate treatment. They, too, pose problems of reliability, e.g., that the two individuals are indeed similar in all respects save one.[39]

Economic explanations and theories of discrimination, thus, have serious shortcomings. Arrow concludes "that market-based explanations will tend to predict that racial discrimination will be eliminated. Since they are not, we must seek elsewhere for non-market factors influencing economic behavior."[40] He suggests that a more fruitful approach might be based on the general principle "that beliefs and preferences may themselves be the product of social interactions unmediated by prices and markets."[41]

If available theories to explain discrimination are inadaquate, if not flawed, and if so are efforts at measurement, whether by regression analysis or audit, present antidiscrimination policies might stand review. Specifically, should Heckman be correct in claiming that "the evidence from the

---

[38] J. Yinger, "Evidence on Discrimination in Consumer Markets," *Journal of Economic Perspectives* 12 (Spring 1998): 23–40.

[39] J. J. Heckman, "Detecting Discrimination," *Journal of Economic Perspectives* 12 (Spring 1998): 101–116.

[40] K. J. Arrow, "What Has Economics to Say About Racial Discrimination?," *Journal of Economic Perspectives* 12 (Spring 1998): 93.

[41] *Ibid.*: 97.

current U.S. labor market is that discrimination by employers alone does *not* generate large economic disparities between blacks and whites,"employment antidiscrimination laws will not do.[42] Instead, greater emphasis should perhaps be placed on the quality of education, particularly in the early years of schooling, and on the home environment of minorities.

Should discrimination, however, exist in labor markets, it would be desirable to outlaw it. Efficiency would be enhanced when employees are hired, paid, and promoted strictly according to their productivity. And the potential gains from the elimination of discrimination are not confined to the present minority employees. Higher parental incomes and expectations of greater job opportunities should induce minority children to acquire more education. Effective antidiscrimination legislation could very well have a cumulative effect toward raising the well-being of minority groups, thus making it worth even a considerable expenditure.

Some scholars fear that antidiscrimination laws can turn out to perpetuate some types of discrimination, if not be altogether counterproductive. The most extreme position is that of Epstein, who claims that such laws harm the interest of blacks.[43] He argues that the government should allow firms and private individuals to make employment decisions in whatever way they see fit. Antidiscrimination laws merely infringe on individuals' right to freedom of contract. If freedom to contract is maximized, social welfare will also be maximized. Hence, restrictions on freedom decrease overall social welfare. Competitive markets, rather than antidiscrimination laws, will protect the victims of discrimination because firms can maximize their profits if they do not arbitrarily discriminate. Competition, thus, should eliminate all invidious forms of discrimination.

Epstein's views have been attacked widely. For example, Siegelman points out that Epstein was very selective in his choice of philosophers on which to base his theory.[44] Moreover, while other studies have shown either that antidiscrimination laws can be efficient or that statistical discrimination is inefficient, the real issue is not efficiency, but achieving a just or fair world. Siegelman also points out that if Epstein was right that competition will eliminate discrimination, why has it not done so historically?

Ayres, in response to Epstein's arguments, demonstrates that invidious forms of discrimination can persist in competitive markets even when gov-

[42] Heckman, "Detecting Discrimination": 112.

[43] Richard A. Epstein, *Forbidden Grounds: The Case Against Employment Discrimination Laws* (Cambrigde, Mass.: Harvard University Press, 1992).

[44] Peter Siegelman, "Shaky Grounds: The Case Against the Case Against Antidiscrimination Laws," *Law & Social Equity*, 19 (1994): 725–741.

ernment has not mandated disparate treatment.[45] In the housing and automobile markets, for example, he finds strong evidence that race discrimination is not cost-justified and competition has failed to eliminate invidious discrimination in employment. Finally, Issacharoff argues that Epstein's *Forbidden Grounds* fails for lack of a normative basis for his contractarian notions of liberty and commitment to aggregate social utility as the standards by which to measure civil rights laws.[46] Unless one subscribes to libertarian ideals about regulation, Epstein's thesis will thus not be satisfying. Also, Epstein addresses neither how blacks in the pre-1964 South were supposed to acquire a "normal distribution" of talents, which the model in his book relies upon, nor the effect of discrimination on the acquisition of human capital for individual minority group members.

More limited institutional concerns have been expressed by Williams and Sander.[47] They fear that discrimination laws can perpetuate stereotyping of minorities by not allowing employers to rely on screening devices with disparate impact on minorities while not being justified by "business necessity" (see *Griggs* v. *Duke Power Co.*).[48] With a steady narrowing of the credential gap that was so important in *Griggs*, lack of reliable tests to predict future job performance, and threat of lawsuit should racial difference emerge, employers are likely to turn to interviews, in which prejudice and statistical discrimination can be pervasive. Williams and Sander have a second concern that relates to their observation that most discrimination suits are not filed by job applicants but by fired, not promoted, or mistreated job holders. Thus, the Civil Rights Act of 1991, which makes suits by job applicants more promising, covers a very small portion of employment discrimination. Finally, it has been suggested that employers, who fear discrimination suits, have an incentive to rely on higher screening standards for minorities, thus hiring fewer of them.[49]

LEGAL CONSIDERATIONS OF REVERSE DISCRIMINATION

Reverse discrimination can be, and often is, the direct byproduct of affirmative action designed to remedy past discrimination. It results when there

[45] Ian Ayres, "Alternative Grounds: Epstein's Discrimination Analysis in Other Market Settings," *San Diego Law Review* 31 (1994): 67–133.

[46] Samuel Issacharoff, "Contractual Liberties in Discriminatory Markets [Review of *Forbidden Grounds: The Case Against Employment Discrimination Laws*, By Richard Epstein]," Texas Law Review 70 (1992): 1219–1259.

[47] Williams and Sander, "Prospects for 'Putting America to Work'": 2056–2057.

[48] *Griggs* v. *Duke Power Co.*, 401 U.S. 424 (1971).

[49] J. Donohue and P. Siegelman, "The Changing Nature of Employment Discrimination Litigation," *Stanford Law Review* 43 (1991): 1017, 1024–1028.

is a zero-sum game, as, for example, when under an affirmative action program some black students are given preference to whites in their admission to medical or law schools. Since, if qualifications alone determined admission, fewer blacks would have been admitted, an affirmative action program, by increasing the number of blacks, reduces the number of whites who are admitted to the program. The issue of reverse discrimination is complex, perplexing, and wrought with tensions.

In relation to affirmative action measures and their ensuring reverse discrimination effects, two different schools of thoughts exist. One school, which was predominant in much of the 1970s and early 1980s, allowed remedies that were race and gender conscious. Their purpose and justification were to remedy identified past discrimination. Difficult questions are whether such discrimination had to have been committed by the employer in question or can the discrimination have been societal? There are further questions: Can racial preferences be used by employers who themselves have not discriminated in order to remedy societal discrimination by according preferential treatment to persons who were never judicially determined victims of discrimination? And, if race may be a factor in employment decisions, how much of a factor, for how long, and in what situations?

Support for a color- and gender-conscious policy was eloquently stated by Chief Justice Warren Burger, when he said for the majority[50]:

> The objective of Congress in the enactment of Title VII [of the Civil Rights Act] is plain.... Practices, procedures, or tests neutral on their face, and even neutral in ... intent cannot be maintained if they operate to "freeze" the status quo of prior discriminatory practices.

Further support for this school comes not only from those who consider it a political decision about unfair treatment of groups in the past, who therefore deserve encouragement and opportunities, but also from those who call for a moral reading of the constitution. They interpret the "Equal Protection" clause of the Fourteenth Amendment to require taking account of past legal and political practices.

The second school, which has found strong support in the mid-1990s, advocates a society that is totally color and gender blind. Accordingly, affirmative action programs deserve to be dismantled. This position underlies for example, California's Proposition 209 (which deliberately mimics the language of the 1964 Civil Rights Act) and was approved by the voters in 1996. This constitutional amendment goes with the grain of recent Court decisions that have reduced the scope for racial preferences. Supporters

[50] *Griggs* v. *Duke Power Co.*, U.S. 424, 430–431 3 FEP 175 (1971).

claim that their aim is to give everybody a fair chance of getting ahead and advocate "nonexclusionary" affirmative action, based on individual needs rather than on group claims of stereotypes.

While most reverse discrimination takes place in the context of affirmative action, some can be outside this context. For example, there are a number of cases involving disparate treatment against majority group persons unrelated to employer efforts to engage in affirmative action. An example is *McDonald* v. *Santa Fe Trail Transportation Co.,*[51] which is based on the *Griggs* v. *Duke Power Co.,* case discussed earlier. In the latter, a unanimous court held

> [T]he Act does not command that any person be hired simply because he was formerly the subject of discrimination, or because he is a member of a minority group. Discriminatory preference for any group, minority or majority, is precisely and only what Congress has proscribed. What is required by Congress is the removal of artificial, arbitrary, and unnecessary barriers to employment when the barriers operate invidiously to discriminate on the basis of racial or other impermissible classification.

In *McDonald* v. *Santa Fe Trail Transportation Co.,* the Supreme Court was asked to determine whether a complaint alleging that white employees charged with appropriating property from their employer were dismissed from employment, while a black employee similarly charged was not dismissed, involved reverse discrimination. Thus, the Court faced the question of whether §1981, which provides that "[a]ll persons shall have the same right ... to make and enforce contracts ... as is enjoyed by white citizens ..."[52] affords protection from racial discrimination in private employment to white persons as well as nonwhites. The Court concluded that discrimination against whites was prohibited by Title VII and §1981 of the Civil Rights Act of 1866.

However, of particular interest is reverse discrimination in the affirmative action context. Two Supreme Court cases overshadow all others — *Regents of the University of California* v. *Bakke* of 1978 and *United Steel Workers of America* v. *Weber* of 1979.

A narrow reading of Title VII appears to prohibit discrimination against any and all groups, including majority groups. This becomes clear from an examination of the legislative history of Title VII and its §703(J). This position is well articulated by Justice Powell when he stated in *Bakke,* "Preferring members of any one group for no reason other than race or ethnic origin is discrimination for its own sake, this the Constitution forbids."[53]

---

[51] *McDonald* v. *Santa Fe Trail Transportation Co.,* 427 U.S. 273, 12 FEP 1577 (1976).
[52] 427 U.S. 273.
[53] *Regents of the University of California* v. *Bakke,* 438 U.S. 265, 307, 17 FEP 1000, 1017 (1978).

In spite of this, various courts have approved preferential treatment for minorities. Thus, in both the *Bakke* and *Weber* cases, a majority of justices of the Supreme Court agreed to sustain preferences in appropriate cases. However, the question remains under what factual circumstances are preferences appropriate.

In *Bakke,* the Court ruled on the legality under Title VII of the 1964 Civil Rights Act and the Equal Protection Clause of a medical school admissions program at the University of California at Davis that set aside a fixed number of places for minorities. The Court held,

> In summary, it is evident that the Davis special admissions program involves the use of an explicit racial classification never before countenanced by this Court. It tells applicants who are not Negro, Asian, or "Chicano" that they are totally excluded from a specific percentage of the seats in an entering class. No matter how strong their qualifications, quantitative and extracurricular, including their own potential for contribution to educational diversity, they are never afforded the chance to compete with applicants from the preferred groups for the special admission seats. At the same time, the preferred applicants have the opportunity to compete for every seat in the class.
>
> The fatal flaw in petitioner's preferential program is its disregard of individual rights as guaranteed by the Fourteenth Amendment. *Shelley* v. *Kraemer,* 334 U.S. 1, 22 (1948). Such rights are not absolute. But when a State's distribution of benefits or imposition of burdens hinges on the color of a person's skin or ancestry, that individual is entitled to a demonstration that the challenged classification is necessary to promote a substantial state interest. Petitioner has failed to carry this burden. For this reason, that portion of the California court's judgment holding petitioner's special admissions program invalid under the Fourteenth Amendment must be affirmed.[54]

However, at the same time, the Court also held that while the specific admissions program was unlawful, not all admissions programs according consideration to race need to be unlawful. In this respect, five justices agreed that some uses of race in university admissions are permissible. They did not deny the possibility for the University of California to establish race-conscious programs in the future. As a matter of fact, the *Bakke* opinion written by Justice Powell explicitly points to university admissions programs that take race into account in achieving the educational diversity valued by the First Amendment. To accomplish this objective, the Court argued that the assignment of a fixed number of places to minority group is not necessary. Specifically, the Court pointed to the fact that Harvard College has expanded the concept of diversity to include students from disadvantaged economic racial and ethnic groups. It thus recruits not only Californians or Louisianans, but also blacks, Chicanos, and other minority stu-

[54] *Ibid.*

dents. Emphasis on achieving educational diversity, rather than the use of quotas of minorities, appears to the Court acceptable.

In 1996 the Fifth Circuit court struck down a University of Texas Law School admissions policy that gave preference to black and Mexican–American applicants.[55] Four white applicants claimed they had been denied admission under a system that used an index based on grades and LSAT scores, which required an index of at least 199 for whites and only 189 for minorities. The panel held that the law school "may not use race as a factor in deciding which applicants to admit in order to achieve a diverse student body, to combat the perceived effects of a hostile environment at the law school, to alleviate the law school's poor reputation in the minority community, or to eliminate any present effects of past discrimination."

In *United Steel Workers of America* v. *Weber,* the Supreme Court ruled on whether it was permissible to have under Title VII a voluntary, collectively bargained selection ratio for craft trainees. Specifically, the case involved a master collective-bargaining agreement covering terms and conditions of employment at fifteen Kaiser Aluminum and Chemical Corporation plants. Part of the agreement was an affirmative action plan to eliminate conspicuous racial imbalances in Kaiser's then almost exclusively white craft work force. The collective-bargaining agreement reserved for black employees 50% of the openings in an in-plant craft training program until the percentage of black craft workers was commensurate with the percentage of blacks in the local labor force. The Court ruled that Title VII does not permit such race-conscious affirmative action plans in the private sector even though it is designed to eliminate manifest racial imbalances in traditionally segregated job categories.[56]

There remains the question of what type of preference plans will the Court permit. In this connection, in 1986, the Court in *Wygant* v. *Jackson Board of Education*[57] held unconstitutional a layoff preference plan that permitted black public school teachers to keep their jobs while white teachers with more seniority were laid off. However, in two other cases, *Sheet Metal Workers Local 28* v. *EEOC*[58] and *Fire Fighters Local 93* v. *City of Cleveland,*[59] the Court indicated that minority hiring and promotion goals may sometimes be imposed by federal judges on employers or unions that are guilty of discrimination.

[55] *Hopwood* v. *State of Texas,* 78 F.3d. 932 (5th Cir. 1996).
[56] *United Steel Workers of America* v. *Weber,* 443 U.S. 193, 20 FEP 1 (1979).
[57] *Wygant* v. *Jackson Board of Education,* U.S. 40 FEP 132 (1986).
[58] *Sheet Metal Workers Local 28* v. *EEOC,* U.S. 41 FEP 107 (1986).
[59] *Fire Fighters Local 93* v. *City of Cleveland,* U.S. 41 FEP 139 (1986).

It is important to evaluate affirmative action programs on the grounds of economic efficiency as well as equity. The effects of affirmative action on economic efficiency are difficult to measure. In the short run, the act of hiring less qualified employees and paying them wages that exceed their marginal productivity is likely to engender some welfare losses. And, concurrently, denying employment or promotion to a skilled white male, in effect stopping him from utilizing all of his skills, also generates welfare losses. (The same holds true in the case of school admissions policies. Affirmative action may preclude more qualified whites from attending a particular school, their "optimal choice," while permitting less qualified minorities to attend. And, in the case of education, the admission of unqualified minorities to programs that they will be unable to complete can cause losses to the minority students, who forego other opportunities to be educated and trained.) In short, the Court will not tolerate layoffs as a remedy for existing discrimination, while possibly acquiescing to preferential hiring, promotion, and transfers. The reason appears to be that, in the eyes of the justices, the last three actions, which are less harmful and costly to the white majority than are layoffs, are acceptable if balanced against the benefits that accrue to minority members.

ECONOMICS OF REVERSE DISCRIMINATION

On first view, affirmative action appears to cause significant welfare losses, in some cases to the same minorities it was designed to help. Yet there are likely to be situations where long-run efficiency gains from applying affirmative action outweigh the costs to the individuals immediately affected. In particular, the existence of affirmative action programs will encourage minorities to invest more in themselves, since these programs are tangible proof of the elimination of labor market discrimination. In this sense, the skill level of the labor force is not predetermined but in fact depends on available employment opportunities. A second potential benefit of affirmative action is that by expanding minority participation in jobs that have greater decision-making power, the interests of minorities might be better represented. This can have efficiency ramifications if biases, especially in the political process, had caused inefficient allocations of resources.

On equity grounds, the case for or against affirmative action and the issue of reverse discrimination rest upon which of the two schools of thought, discussed earlier, one embraces: equal treatment, which mandates color and sex blindness, or color and sex consciousness in order to remedy past injustices and avail minorities of more equal opportunities.

Supporters of the first school of thought believe that affirmative action programs are discriminatory and unfair to whites and, as such, are prohibited by U.S. law. Proponents of the second view, conversely, reject the equal treatment view, since "it fails to accommodate for the present and continuing effect of past discrimination."[60] These people believe that the antidiscrimination laws justify the use of affirmative action as a means of remedying a long history of discrimination against certain groups, even though it is acknowledged that some white individuals, particularly white males, will be harmed in the process. In this spirit, Robert Belton, in describing the dissenting opinion in *Bakke*, writes,

> The theory of Brennan, White, Marshall and Blackmun is that a racial classification that operates to the disadvantage of whites is not the same as one that operates against blacks and other minorities. The purpose of the equal protection clause, by this line of reasoning, is to protect a discrete and insular minority. It is intended to help the kind of group that is least able to protect its own interest through the political process and so must be protected from the tyranny of the majority."[61]

Some empirical work exists on whether affirmative action actually engenders significant welfare losses. Jonathan Leonard used aggregate production functions to examine whether affirmative action or Title VII had a significant effect on productivity in the U.S. economy in the years 1966 and 1977.[62] Utilizing pooled cross-section data, Leonard concluded that neither affirmative action nor Title VII litigation has had a significant impact on productivity. The low significance levels of most of the tests, combined with the aggregate nature of the study, make the results less than conclusive.

A second study by Richard Freeman used time series data in arguing that a significant part of this increase was due to affirmative action.[63] In this equation, the explanatory variable that measured the per nonwhite worker cumulative expenditure of the equal opportunity employment commission had a large and significant coefficient. The result suggests that antidiscriminatory activity, from 1965 to 1971, on average, was associated with increases in the black–white income ratio of 15% for males and 27% for females. Freeman's work was subjected to a great deal of criticism.[64]

---

[60] Robert Belton, "Discrimination and Affirmative Action: An Analysis of Competing Theories of Equality and Weber," *North Carolina Law Review* 59 (March 1981): 541.

[61] *Ibid.*: 579.

[62] Jonathan S. Leonard, "Antidiscrimination or Reverse Discrimination: The Impact of Changing Demographics, Title VII, and Affirmative Action on Productivity," *Journal of Human Resources* 19 (Spring 1984): 145–174.

[63] Richard Freeman, "Changes in the Labor Market of Black Americans, 1948–1972," in *Brookings Papers on Economic Activity* (Washington, D.C.: The Brookings Institution, 1973): 67–120.

[64] *Ibid.*: 129–131.

James P. Smith and Finis Welch found little reason to accept the findings that affirmative action had played an important part in the relative increase in blacks' earnings.[65] Instead, they argued that the evidence revealed an irregular but clearly positive trend of the growth in black incomes relative to white incomes from 1944 to 1984. Smith and Welch attribute most of the rise in relative black earnings to black northward migration and improvement in the quality of the education of blacks. They found that while affirmative action had increased the proportion of blacks in covered firms (covered firms are those firms that have more than 100 employees or federal contracts above $50,000 and at least 50 employees), it had a negligible effect on the relative incomes of blacks. Smith and Welch reached three basic conclusions regarding the effects of affirmative action on the earnings of blacks:

> First, affirmative action apparently had no significant long-run effect, either positive or negative, on the male racial wage gap. The relative rate of improvement in black incomes, after affirmative action was instituted, is consistent with the speed of improvement that occurred before it was instituted.
>
> Second, affirmative action had a significant but short-lived positive effect on wages of young black workers. Their wages increased dramatically from 1967 to 1972, but the gains eroded by 1977.
>
> The final wage impact of affirmative action was a pro-skill bias. The positive wage effects of affirmative action on black males appear to be limited to young black college graduates.[66]

A further study of the effects of the antidiscrimination programs on the welfare of minority workers was conducted by Andrea Beller.[67] She hypothesized that the goal of eliminating wage discrimination encouraged firms to reduce minority employment, but the employment provisions in the antidiscrimination legislation required firms to increase minority employment. This conflict could encourage firms to take other measures (e.g., become more capital intensive or relocate plants in predominantly white areas) that would not increase the welfare of minorities but would enable firms to comply with the letter of the law. Beller found that enforcing the employment provision increased relative black employment and wages, while enforcing the wage provision lowered them. She concluded that,

---

[65] James P. Smith and Finis Welch, *Closing the Gap: Forty Years of Economic Progress for Blacks* (Santa Monica: RAND Corporation, 1986): 1–26.

[66] *Ibid.*: 95.

[67] Andrea H. Beller, "The Economics of Enforcement of an Antidiscrimination Law: Title VII of the Civil Rights Act of 1964," *Journal of Law and Economics* 21 (October, 1978): 359–380.

between 1960 and 1970, the effects of the wage provision were stronger and, consequently, that affirmative action had been unsuccessful in raising the welfare of blacks.

Coate and Loury empirically explored the question of whether affirmative action policies can bring continuous labor-market gains to minorities without becoming a permanent fixture.[68] They argue that much depends on whether affirmative action can eliminate negative stereotyping of minority workers by causing employers to believe that minorities' productivity has risen because of such action. Their empirical results suggest that even if groups are identically endowed *ex ante,* affirmative action can lead employers to perceive correctly the groups to be unequally productive, *ex post.* A major reason is that job preferences can entice employers to patronize minorities, thereby reducing their incentives to acquire the necessary skills.

HOUSING DISCRIMINATION

Housing discrimination is said to exist when members of a minority group, most frequently a racial group, are denied housing that is available to other groups, regardless of formal qualifications. One of the results can be segregation and an artificial settlement pattern in America's communities. Moreover, racial housing discrimination and its accompanying segregation can affect a neighborhood's physical appearance, add costs to a host of transactions, and narrow social contacts. Thus, not only does discrimination violate norms of fairness, but it has serious social and economic side effects. My examination of housing discrimination will first focus on race and thereafter on age and family status.

RACIAL HOUSING DISCRIMINATION

Housing discrimination, especially against blacks, is practiced in a number of ways: brokers withhold information from black customers; they show houses only in black, fringe, or changing neighborhoods; they steer blacks only into certain neighborhoods and not into others; they misrepresent the price or terms of the transaction; they delay showing a house until a white buyer or tenant is found; or they inform potential black buyers that a house was sold or rented when it was not.

---

[68] Stephen Coate and Glenn C. Loury, "Will Affirmative Action Eliminate Negative Stereotypes?," *American Economic Review* 83 (5) (December 1993): 1220–1240.

Pettigrew confirmed the existence of racial prejudice regarding housing. His racial attitude surveys of the late 1960s found 35% of whites indicating that they would or might move, and 51% that they would object, if a black family moved in next door.[69] If many blacks moved into their neighborhood, 71% of whites said that they would or might move. Moreover, 43% of whites asserted that whites have the right to exclude blacks from white neighborhoods and 63% opposed laws forbidding discrimination in housing. Surveys of blacks taken at the same time indicated that 74% of blacks preferred neighborhoods with both black and white residents, whereas 16% preferred black neighborhoods.

Although discrimination appears to have decreased, using 1989 housing audit data, Page found still significant racial discrimination in rental and ownership housing resulting from biases of real estate agents.[70] Thus, such agents were found to have provided blacks access to about 80% of the units made available to whites. A comparable figure for Hispanics was 90%.[71] In such cities as Cincinnati and Denver the access for blacks was as low as 60%. Since blacks and Hispanics are excluded from many housing locations, they tend to be forced to pay more under an artificially reduced housing supply and spend more money and time traveling to work and school.

Furthermore, a housing discrimination survey of 25 large metropolitan areas with central city populations in excess of 100,000 and where at least 12 and 7% of the population were black and Hispanic, respectively, produced the following findings[72]: In 1989 black and Hispanic renters faced a 39 and 36% probability, respectivity, of being denied information about housing availability, and a 17 and 16% probability, respectively, of being told that the advertised unit is no longer available, even though it was available to comparable whites. For blacks and Hispanics the index of unfavorable treatments in completing the renting transaction was 44 and 42%, respectively.

A direct result of housing discrimination is segregation, specifically that within metropolitan areas, where blacks are highly concentrated in the central cities. Segregation has only slightly changed since 1960. The index of dissimilarity, which measures the percentage of blacks who would have

[69] Thomas F. Pettigrew, "Attitudes on Race and Housing: A Social-Psychological View," in *Segregation in Residential Areas*, Amos H. Hawley and Vincent P. Rock, Eds. (Washington, D.C.: National Academy of Sciences, 1973).

[70] Marianne Page, "Racial and Ethnic Discrimination in Urban Housing Markets: Evidence from a Recent Audit Study," *Journal of Urban Economics* 38 (1995): 183–206.

[71] *Ibid.*: 202–203.

[72] Marjorie Turner, *Housing Discrimination Study — Synthesis* (Washington, D.C.: U.S. Department of Housing and Urban Development, 1991).

to move into white areas to achieve full integration, has fallen steadily but modestly in major urban areas over the past 30 years: 88% in 1960, 87% in 1970, 81% 1980, and 77% in 1990[73] Indeed, Williams and Sander argue that the continuing high level of segregation is a major culprit in the plight of urban blacks, i.e., joblessness, crime, and drugs. They conclude "If we could substantially erode housing segregation, we could, plausibly, erode these other problems in the process."[74]

RACIAL HOUSING DISCRIMINATION LAW

A number of federal statutes and their ensuing court rulings are aimed at the elimination of discriminatory housing activities.[75] In terms of historical sequence, they are Section 1982 of the Civil Rights Act of 1866, Title VI of the Civil Rights Act of 1964, Title VIII of the Civil Rights Act of 1968, and the Equal Credit Opportunity Act of 1974 amended in 1976.[76]

The United States Supreme Court, in the landmark case of *Jones* v. *Alfred H. Mayer Co.*,[77] interpreted Section 1982 of the Civil Rights Act of 1866[78] to be a valid exercise of congressional power to eliminate "badges and incidents of slavery [including] all racial discrimination in private as well as public housing."[79] Section 1982 declares: "All citizens of the United States shall have the same right, in every State and Territory, as is enjoyed by white citizens thereof to inherit, purchase, lease, sell, hold, and convey real and personal property."[80]

Jones was decided 2 months after the passage of Title VIII of the Civil Rights Act of 1968, and the decision considered some of the differences in the coverage of Section 1982 and Title VIII. In the Supreme Court's opinion, the enactment of Title VIII was not intended to and did not "effect any change, either substantive or procedural, in the prior statute," and the Court concluded that the two statutes are independent of one another.[81]

---

[73] Williams and Sander, "Prospects for 'Putting America to Work'": 2022.

[74] *Ibid.*: 2059.

[75] For more details, see David Falk and Herberg M. Franklin, *Equal Housing Opportunity* (Washington, D.C.: Potomac Institute, 1976).

[76] The material in this section draws heavily on United States Commission on Civil Rights, *The Federal Fair Housing Enforcement Effort* (Washington, D.C.: U.S. Government Printing Office, 1979).

[77] *Jones* v. *Alfred H. Mayer Co.*, 42 U.S.C. §1982 (1970).

[78] 392 U.S. 409 (1968).

[79] 392 U.S. 409, 410 (1968).

[80] 42 U.S.C. §1982 (1970).

[81] 392 U.S. 409, 416–417 (1968).

Unlike Title VIII, Section 1092 was created as private right of action and does not apply to housing discrimination based on religion, sex, or national origin.

Title VI of the Civil Rights Act of 1964 prohibits discrimination in any program or activity receiving federal financial assistance.[82] It states, "No person in the United Staes shall, on the ground of race, color, or national origin, be excluded from participation in, be denied the benefit of, or be subjected to discrimination under any program or activity receiving Federal financial assistance."[83] In some instances, Title VI prohibits housing discrimination. For example, when local governments use federal financial assistance to operate low-income housing, they are prohibited by Title VI from practicing discrimination on the basis of race, color, or national origin in renting housing.

Title VIII of the Civil Rights Act of 1968,[84] also referred to as the "Fair Housing Act," is by far the most important legislation prohibiting discrimination based on race, color, religion, sex, and national origin in the sale or rental of most housing.[85] It covers activities of all segments of the real estate industry, including real estate brokers, builders, apartment owners, sellers, and mortgage lenders, and extends to federally owned and operated dwellings and dwellings provided by federally insured loans and grants. Title VII prohibits such discriminatory activities as:

- Refusal to sell or rent a dwelling[86]
- Discrimination in the terms, conditions, or privileges of the sale or rental of a dwelling[87]
- Indicating a preference, limitation, or discrimination in advertising[88]

---

[82] 42 U.S.C. §§2000d–2000d-6 (1970).

[83] *Ibid.*

[84] U.S.C. §3601-19, 3631 (1970 and Supp. V 1975).

[85] Exempted from Title VIII are single-family homes sold or rented without the use of a broker and without discriminatory advertising; rooms or units in dwellings with living quarters for no more than four families, provided that the owner lives in one of them and does not advertise or use a broker [42 U.S.C. §3603(b) (1970)]. In addition, religious organizations and affiliated associations are free to give preference in selling or leasing housing to persons of the same religion, provided that the property is not owned or operated for a commerical purpose and provided that the religion itself does not restrict membership on account of race, color, sex, or national origin. Private clubs and religious organizations that are not open to the public and that incidentally operate noncommercial housing may limit occupancy of the housing to their members [42 U.S.C. §3607 (1970)].

[86] 42 U.S.C. §3604(a) (Supp. V 1975).

[87] 42 U.S.C. §3604(b) (Supp. V 1975).

[88] 42 U.S.C. §3604(c) (Supp. V 1975).

- Representation to a person or persons that a dwelling is unavailable[89]
- Denial of a loan for purchasing, constructing, improving, or repairing a dwelling[90]
- Discrimination in setting the amount or other conditions of a real estate loan[91]
- Denial of access to or membership in any multiple-listing service or real estate brokers' organization[92]

The act also prohibits such forms of discrimination as blockbusting — convincing owners to sell property on the grounds that minorities are about to move into a neighborhood — and steering — the process of directing a racial, ethnic, or religious group into a neighborhood in which members of the same group already live.[93] It also provides that it is unlawful for any bank, building and loan association, or other institution engaged in making real estate loans to deny a loan or other financial assistance for purchasing, constructing, repairing, or maintaining a dwelling or to discriminate against borrowers in fixing the amount, interest rate, duration, or other terms or conditions of such a loan because of an applicant's race, color, religion, national origin, or sex.[94]

Another major piece of legislation mandating fair housing is the Equal Credit Opportunity Act (ECOA).[95] This 1974 act, as amended in 1976, makes it unlawful for creditors to discriminate against any applicant with respect to any aspect of a credit transaction, including any mortgage transaction, on the basis of race, color, religion, national origin, sex, marital status, age (provided the applicant has the capacity to contract), or because all or part of the applicant's income derives from any public assistance program.[96] With regard to discrimination in mortgage finance on the basis of race, religion, sex, or national origin, ECOA covers many of the same violations that are covered by Title VIII.

---

[89] 42 U.S.C. §3604(d) (Supp. V 1975).

[90] 42 U.S.C. §3605 (Supp. V 1975).

[91] *Ibid.*

[92] 42 U.S.C. §3606 (Supp. V 1975).

[93] 42 U.S.C. §3604(e) (Supp. V 1975).

[94] 42 U.S.C. §3605 (Supp. V 1975).

[95] 15 U.S.C. §1691–1691f (1976).

[96] 15 U.S.C. §1691a(a) and (2) (1976). As it was originally passed in 1974, ECOA prohibited credit discrimination based on sex or marital status. The 1976 amendment added race, color, religion, national origin, age, and receipt of public assistance as prohibited based of discrimination.

ECONOMICS OF HOUSING DISCRIMINATION

Housing discrimination by race has at least three economic effects, all of which often interact. One effect takes the form of housing segregation, the second, housing price differentials, and the third, inefficient resource use. They will be taken up in turn.

There are different theories to explain why the residences of ethnic minorities, particularly blacks, are physically separated from those of other groups. The first involves border models of racial prejudice and urban structure that can be traced to Becker and Bailey's work. Becker's work on discrimination concluded that whites would be willing to pay a premium to live among whites, a premium that is greater than the premium that blacks would be willing to pay to live among whites.[97] The reason is white residents' fear of social and personal implications and economic losses likely to result from the influx of minorities into their neighborhoods. Whites fear not only that the entry of nonwhites would seriously damage the social status of their neighborhood but also that it would persuade many white families to move out of the neighborhood and thus disrupt established association patterns.[98] In addition, whites fear that property values in their neighborhood would fall if minority groups were permitted to enter.

This fear would lead to whites consistently outbidding blacks for housing in white areas and the consequent preservation or extension of segregated living patterns. Unfortunately for the theory, segregation can also be explained by the opposite phenomenon, namely, that blacks are consistently willing to outbid whites for the privilege of living among blacks. It is therefore unclear whether the higher-bid hypothesis is evidence of discrimination of whites against blacks or of blacks against whites, unless one assumes that the blacks' effective demand for integration is less strong than that of whites for segregation. It seems reasonable to assume from all of the information we have that whites discriminate against blacks.

Martin Bailey looked at the logical result of including race in utility functions and developed a model in which residential segregation had already been achieved, with one section in a city allocated to whites and another allocated to blacks.[99] His aim was to discover what the difference

---

[97] Becker, *Economics of Discrimination*: 59; Martin J. Bailey, "Note on the Economics of Residential Zoning and Renewal," *Land Economics* 35 (1959): 288–290.

[98] Luigi Laurenti, *Property Values and Race* (Berkeley and Los Angeles: University of California Press, 1961): 37.

[99] Bailey, "Economics of Residential Zoning": 288–290.

in the price of housing would be, if any, and what caused prices to change relative to each other in the two areas. Bailey assumed that whites were willing to pay extra to live away from blacks and that blacks were indifferent. Four housing prices can be generated in such a model: prices to blacks and to whites in the interior of each area and at the boundary between the areas. Because blacks are indifferent, the boundary and interior prices to blacks are equal. But, since whites are willing to pay a premium for living among whites, the price to whites at the boundary between the areas will be lower than the interior price to whites. If, as some people have asserted, blacks pay more for housing, then, at the boundary, the blacks' bid price will exceed the whites' asking price. If real estate brokers are rational, the boundary will expand into the whites' area. This process will continue until the boundary price to whites rises and the boundary and interior prices to blacks fall so that all three are equal. At that point, however, the interior prices to whites will be greater than the other three. This seems inconsistent with the assertion that blacks pay more for housing than do whites. Another way of saying this is that, even if the prices to blacks were higher than the prices to whites, the situation would be unstable. The only stable equilibrium under Bailey's assumptions occurs when the prices to whites are higher than those to blacks, consistent with the prediction of Becker's model.[100]

Bailey's border model was extended and incorporated by Courant and Rose-Ackerman into a more general model of an urban area.[101] Both incorporate the same prejudice assumptions that Bailey used into an equilibrium model of an urban area. But they do not make Bailey's assumptions about complete segregation and about blacks preferring to live near whites, which is contradictory. Courant's simulations suggest that high-income blacks have an incentive to hop over whites, unless white prejudice is extremely strong, and that they are willing to pay at least 40% more for their housing in order to live as far from blacks as possible.

I will next turn to the amenity models, which look at prejudice as a disutility from living with members of another race. Yinger argued that this view of prejudice is analogous to the more general formulation of

---

[100] The evidence of higher prices for blacks and Bailey's conclusions of higher prices for whites are not necessarily inconsistent. The apparent inconsistency could come from a chronically greater rate of expansion of the housing demand of blacks relative to that of whites. The differential growth in demand could come either from greater rates of immigration of blacks than of whites or from the greater increases of income of blacks than of whites in the presence of an income-elastic demand for housing.

[101] Paul M. Courant, "Urban Residential Structure and Racial Prejudice," Discussion Paper #62 (Ann Arbor: Institute of Public Policy Studies, University of Michigan, 1974); Susan Rose-Ackerman, "Racism and Urban Structure," *Journal of Urban Economics* 2 (1975): 85–103.

a neighborhood amenity, the reason for the name of such models.[102] The amenity models by Yinger and Schnare assume that households are directly concerned about the racial composition of their own location but not about that of other locations.[103] These models borrow from Schelling's tipping model.[104] Tipping occurs when a recognizable new minority invades a neighborhood in sufficient numbers to cause the current residents to begin evacuating. There is a major difference between the amenity models and the Schelling tipping model, in that the amenity models are concerned about housing prices and racial segregation in an entire urban area rather than in a single neighborhood. From this amenity model, two major conclusions can be derived, which, however, can also be derived from a border model. One conclusion is that, with realistic assumptions about black preferences, no pattern of complete segregation is in equilibrium. The second conclusion is that whites value neighborhood stability and do so because, without a stable equilibrium in a competitive market, whites find it rewarding to purchase stability by discriminating against blacks.[105]

Finally, there are exclusion models, associated with Downs, Kain, and Stengel.[106] These models assume housing markets to be split into black and white submarkets, physically separated, since sellers in the white market refuse to sell to blacks. Exclusion is so all-pervasive that the sellers in border neighborhoods will sell only to blacks when the price differential between the submarkets is extremely high. As a result, a large black–white price differential exists in equilibrium. These models are unable, however, to explain why exclusion is so pervasive and specifically why blockbusters do not open border neighborhoods to blacks except when the price differential has disappeared.

---

[102] John Yinger, "Prejudice and Discrimination in the Urban Housing Market," in *Current Issues in Urban Economics*, Peter Mieszkowski and Mahlon Strasheim, Eds. (Baltimore, Md.: Johns Hopkins University Press, 1979): 432.

[103] John Yinger, "Racial Prejudice and Racial Residential Segregation in an Urban Model," *Journal of Urban Economics* 3 (1976): 383–406; Ann B. Schnare, "Racial and Ethnic Price Differentials in an Urban Housing Market," *Urban Studies* 13 (1976): 107–120.

[104] Thomas Schelling, "A Process of Residential Segregation: Neighborhood Tipping," in *Racial Discrimination in Economic Life*, Anthony Pascal, Ed. (Lexington, Mass.: Lexington Books, 1972): 157–184.

[105] Yinger, "Prejudice and Discrimination in the Urban Housing Market": 436–437.

[106] John F. Kain. "Effect of Housing Market Segregation on Urban Development," in *Savings in Residential Financing: 1969 Conference Proceedings*, Donald P. Jacobs and Richard T. Pratt, Eds. (Chicago: U.S. Savings and Loan, 1969): 89–108; Michelle Stengel, *Racial Differentials: Market Separation and the Ghetto Housing Market* (East Lansing: Michigan State University Press, 1976).

Some of the theories that can explain housing segregation can also shed light on why racial minorities, particularly blacks, pay more for their homes than whites. Empirical studies have produced strong evidence regarding black and white housing price differentials. King and Mieszkowski found that whites pay 7.5% less in the boundary zone than in the white interior.[107] According to findings by Yinger, housing prices dropped as the percentage of blacks increased in both largely white and boundary areas.[108] A housing price drop of 6% was associated with every 10 percentage points of increase in the black population in largely white areas, whereas the comparable price decline was 9% for every 10 percentage points of increase in the black population in boundary areas. A study by Robert Schafer found that whites paid less in ghetto, transition, and central city white areas than in white suburbs.[109]

Although there have been inquiries into the relationship between racial composition and prices in the black submarket, these inquiries have been inconclusive.[110] Yet there is reliable evidence of a substantial black–white housing price differential within submarkets. Studies by Galster detected differentials varying from a low of 8% to a high of 51%.[110] Convincing evidence has also been offered that blacks consume smaller amounts of housing attributes than do whites with similar incomes and life-cycle characteristics, that is, they live in lower quality housing. Among the largest differentials are those relating to the conditions of a house and its neighborhood, but there is very little difference between blacks and whites in their use of square footage or floor area.[111]

There can be little doubt that housing discrimination can be associated with inefficiencies. As housing choices of minority families are restricted, minorities are denied efficient access to the kind of housing they prefer and particularly its location. Serious impediments result to finding efficient access to employment opportunities. Not only do time and money costs of travel to work increase unnecessarily for minority workers, but they can turn out to be prohibitive. For example, blacks living in the Watts area of

---

[107] Thomas A. King and Peter Mieszkowski, "Racial Discrimination, Segregation, and the Price of Housing," *Journal of Political Economy* 81 (1973) 590–606.

[108] John Yinger, "The Black–White Price Differential in Housing: Some Further Evidence," *Land Economics* 54 (1978): 187–206.

[109] Robert Schafer, "Racial Discrimination in the Boston Housing Market," *Journal of Urban Economics* 6 (1978): 176–196.

[110] George C. Galster, "A Bid-Rent Analysis of Housing Market Discrimination," *American Economic Review* 67 (1977): 144–155.

[111] John F. Kain and John M. Quigley, *Housing Market and Racial Discrimination* (New York: National Bureau of Economic Research, 1975); Mahlon R. Straszheim, *An Economic Model of the Urban Housing Market* (New York: National Bureau of Economic Research, 1975).

Los Angeles until recently had virtually no public transportation available to allow them to find gainful employment outside their area. The unusually high unemployment in Watts was argued to have been a major factor responsible for the 1965 Watts riots.[112] Housing segregation also affects educational opportunities. Elementary and secondary education in ghettoes and barrios tends to be of poor quality, and higher education opportunities are often geographically far away. Thus, all three effects of racial housing discrimination impede human capital growth among members of minority groups.

AGE DISCRIMINATION

Age discrimination is mainly of concern to tenants with children and to senior citizens in relation to gainful employment. I will address the tenant issue, since it has been more important than that of employment.

The right of a landlord to choose a tenant has been increasingly circumscribed by law. The U.S. Supreme Court has deemed the categories of race, national origin, and alienage as "suspect."[113] These classifications effectively prevent most housing discrimination in which the state can be deemed to be involved.[114] Moreover, state legislatures have enacted antidiscrimination legislation, which has expanded the number of these classes and lessened the requirement of state involvement.[115]

In recent history, serious attention has been given to age discrimination in housing. Until the 1970s, landlords were usually free to both select and evict tenants on the basis of whether or not they had children. Then, due

[112] For an in-depth study of the Watts riots of 1965, see *Los Angeles Riots*, Nathan Cohen, Ed. (New York: Praeger, 1970): 1–142.

[113] See *Graham* v. *Richardson*, 403 U.S. 365 (1971). After deeming a class "suspect," the Court then employs strict scrutiny in making its determination as to whether the discrimination is violative of the Constitution (*Id.* at 372). A state, in order to overcome this hurdle, would then need to show that a compelling state interest is actually furthered by the discriminatory classification, and that no less restrictive alternative exists to achieve the state's interest. See L. Tribe, *American Constitutional Law* (1977): 983.

[114] Currently, there is a question as to the requisite state action needed in order to invoke the Fourteenth Amendment. It has been suggested that simply utilizing the court system to enforce an unlawful detainer action where there are age discrimination motives present on the part of the landlord might be sufficient to meet this prerequisite. For a more thorough analysis, see B. Dunaway and T. Blied, "Discrimination Against Children in Rental Housing: A California Perspective," *Santa Clara Law Review* 21 (1979): 38–40.

[115] 1963 Cal. Stat. 3823 [repealed 1977, current version at Cal. Gov't. Code §§12900–12996 West 1980 and Supp. 1983]. A statute such as this does not confront the issue of requisite state action since it is aimed at private individuals.

to the growing sentiment against age discrimination in housing, several states enacted antiage discrimination statutes.[116]

Moreover, many local jurisdictions within states that do not have antiage discrimination statutes have enacted their own ordinances.[117] The courts have also taken an interest in local control of the ability of families with children to obtain housing. The United States Supreme Court, in *Moore* v. *City of East Cleveland,* went so far as to provide definitions of what constitutes a family and what classes of individuals are permitted to live together in one dwelling.[118]

The federal government does not have a clear policy with regard to housing discrimination against children. The Fair Housing Act[119] and the Age Discrimination Act[120] avoid direct reference to housing discrimination against children. The National Housing Act of 1950,[121] however, does have a provision that requires landlords to certify that they do not discriminate against families with children in housing that was built with federally insured mortgage loans.[122]

In 1982, the California Supreme Court, in the case of *Marina Point, Ltd.* v. *Wolfson,*[123] interpreted the California Civil Rights Act as preventing housing discrimination against children. Although the tenants in *Wolfson* argued on several statutory and constitutional grounds that age discrimination in housing is prohibited,[124] the court found that the strongest basis for this position rested upon California's Unruh Civil Rights Act.[125] The Unruh Act provides that "[a]ll persons ... are entitled to ... full and equal accommodations in all business establishments."[126] California courts have

---

[116] Ariz. Rev. Stat. Ann. §§33-1317 (West Supp. 1982–1983); Conn. Gen. Stat. §46a-64a (1982); Del. code Ann. tit. 25, §6503 (1974); D.C. Code Ann. §1-2515 (1981); Illinois Human Rights Act, §3-104 Ill. Rev. Stat. ch. 68, §3-104 (1981); Mass. Gen. Laws Ann. ch. 141B, §4(6)(a) (West 1982); Mich. Comp. Laws §37.2102–.2130 (Supp. 1982–1983); Minn. Stat. §363.03, subd. 2(1)(a)-(1)(b) (1982); N.Y. Real Prop. Law 236 (McKinney Supp. 1982–1983); 1981 N.J. Laws ch. 3233, §2.

[117] For a nationwide listing of many of these municipalities, see Comment, "Why Johnny Can't Rent — An Examination of Laws Prohibiting Discrimination Against Families in Rental Housing," *Harvard Law Review* 84 (1981): 1829, 1929 n4.

[118] 431 U.S. 494, 496 n.2 (1977).

[119]Fair Housing Act, 42 U.S.C. §§3601–3631 (1976 and Supp. II 1978).

[120] Age Discrimination Act of 1975, 42 U.S.C. §§6101–6107 (1976 and Supp. II 1978).

[121] 12 U.S.C. §§1701–1750g (1976 and Supp. V 1981).

[122] 12 U.S.C. §1713(b).

[123] *Marina Point, Ltd.* v. *Wolfson,* 30 Cal. 3d 721, 640 P.2d 114, 180 Cal. Rptr. 446, cert. denied, 103 S. Ct. 129 (1982).

[124] *Id.* at 727–30, 640 P.2d at 118–20, 180 Cal. Rptr. at 500-02.

[125] Unruh Civil Rights Act, Cal. Civ. §Code 51 (West 1982).

[126] *Ibid.*

interpreted the phrase "business establishments"to include housing,[127] though it is doubtful whether the legislature specifically intended such an application.[128] Even more problematic is the question of whether the legislature intended the Unruh Act to cover age discrimination. Certainly, age discrimination is not explicitly mentioned in the enumerated prohibitions against discrimination on the basis of "sex, color, race, religion, ancestry or national origin."[129]

A number of arguments have been advanced in opposition to antiage discrimination laws. For example, in 1971, in the case of *Flowers* v. *John Burham & Co.*,[130] a California appellate court determined that, because of childrens' "independence, mischievousness, boisterousness and rowdyism," age discrimination within housing was not arbitrary discrimination.[131] Also, the dissent in *Wolfson* argued that regulations regarding children are reasonable and rationally related to the services performed by the landlord when it has been determined that the apartment complex has been constructed for all-adult housing and its facilities are ill-adapted for use by children.[132] Thus, landlords are faced with two costs associated with the *Wolfson* decision: Not only will landlords be prohibited from choosing tenants on the basis of whether or not they have children, but they will also be forced to incur expenses to alter their premises to accommodate children.

Although states have shown concern about housing discrimination for many years, comprehensive federal legislation arrived only with enactment

---

[127] See *Flowers* v. *John Burham & Co.*, 21 Cal. App. 3d 700, 98 Cal. Rptr. 644 (1971); see also *Burks* v. *Poppy Constr. Co.*, 57 Cal. 2d 463, 370 P.2d 313, 20 Cal. Rptr. 609 (1962); *Swain* v. *Burkett*, 209 Cal. App. 2d 684, 26 Cal. Rptr. 286 (1962).

[128] See Horowitz, "The 1959 California Equal Rights in 'Business Establishments' Statute — A Problem in Statutory Application," *Southern California Law Review* 33 (1959–1960): 260, 286–294: but see *Burks* v. *Poppy Constr. Co.*, 57 Cal. 2d 463, 468–70, 370 P.2d 313, 315–317, 20 Cal. Rptr. 609, 611–613 (1962). In 1983, the California Supreme Court found that a condominium owners' association was a "business establishment" within the meaning of the Unruh Act [*O'Connor* v. *Village Green Owners Ass'n.*, 33 Cal.3d 790, 662 P.2d 427, 191 Cal. Rptr. 320 (1983)]. The Court held that the fact that the association, through a board of directors, employed a professional property management firm, obtained insurance for the condominium owners, provided maintenance and repair services, and collected fees for its services, was enough to make the association a "business establishment" within the meaning of the act (*Id.* at 796, 662 P.2d at 430–431, 191 Cal. Rptr. at 323–324). Indeed, the court found the functions performed by the association to be analogous to those performed by landlords (*Id.*).

[129] Cal. Civ. Code §51 (West 1982).

[130] *Flowers* v. *John Burham & Co.*, 21 Cal. App. 3d 700, 98 Cal. Rptr. 644 (1971).

[131] *Id.* at 703, 98 Cal. Rptr. at 645 (1971).

[132] 30 Cal. 3d at 746–747, 640 P.2d at 130–131, 180 Cal. Rptr. at 512.

of the Fair Housing Amendments Act of 1988.[133] It prohibits landlords to refuse to rent or show a house or apartment to a family with children younger then 18 years old, or to require such a family to pay higher rent, impose restrictions, or create unfair barriers not required of someone without children. However, under some circumstances families with children can be excluded, e.g., in "housing for older persons." There are two classes of such housing: (1) "62 or over housing," if all tenants in the housing complex are 62 years or older, and (2) "55 or over housing," if at least 80% of all units in the complex have at least one occupant 55 years or older and there exist significant facilities and services to meet the needs of older people.[134]

Thus, age discrimination laws relating to housing have been mainly directed at tenants with children and at senior citizens. The interests of these two classes of tenants can be in serious conflict. Senior citizens favor a tranquil life, which often becomes an impossibility with young children as close neighbors, while young families, like all families, want to be free to live wherever they choose. Arguments in favor of such laws include the serious impact on family stability as well as a deep psychological effect on children. Moreover, since most minority families have many children, child discrimination might be disguised racial discrimination and no doubt contributes to such discrimination.

ECONOMICS OF AGE DISCRIMINATION

Traditional economic theory tends to indicate that landlords in highly competitive housing markets will seldom, if ever, refuse to rent to families with children. In such a setting, a landlord could satisfy his distaste for families with children only at the expense of a higher vacancy rate. Therefore, housing markets with age discrimination probably contain some elements of monopoly. The landlord has some locational monopoly as well as some market power due to any unique characteristics his building may have. More important, exclusionary maximum-density zoning laws and slow-growth policies of local governments, combined with a growing demand for housing rentals, have tended to widen the gap between the quantity of dwellings supplied and those demanded. While rents should have adjusted to this situation and helped to close these gaps, in reality, price adjustments

---

[133] Pub. L. No. 100-430, 102 Stat. 1625.

[134] Since concerns had been voiced concerning the vagueness of the facilities and services requirement of "55 or over housing," Public Law 104-76 was enacted in 1995 eliminating this requirement.

in the housing market have been slow. This result is due to some of the same institutional features discussed earlier, as well as the existence of long-term leases.

Microeconomic analysis of welfare effects can utilize a demand-and-supply housing stock model. Since children impose costs on landlords, e.g., for heightened repair and maintenance, the supply curve shifts upward as the number of children increases. With children affecting negatively the utility of some aged tenants, their demand function will shift downward. The welfare effect of such laws depends on the relative importance of tenants who enjoy children in their building compared to those who are ill-affected and, if so, by how much.

CONCLUSION

The scope of discrimination and segregation is vast and so is the area that potentially can be covered by antidiscrimination and antisegregation laws. Efforts in this chapter, therefore, had to be selective. Both when examining employment and housing discrimination, my discussion focused on race and, to a lesser extent, on gender, age, and family situation and no attention was paid to religion and national origin. Furthermore, discrimination in education, although an important topic, was given short shrift. I hope that the tools provided can be applied to the neglected areas.

There were two periods when the nation was deeply concerned about the treatment of minorities, i.e., in the 1860s and 1960s, and major federal discrimination laws were enacted. Economic analysis of the extent of discrimination in employment and wages has provided new insights, as has research on the effects of discrimination. While most would agree that discrimination has negative efficiency effects, there is no unanimity about the extent to which antidiscrimination laws had lasting positive effects. In recent years, concern about reverse discrimination, especially flowing from affirmative action programs, has been on the increase.

Housing discrimination, and segregation associated with it, also have been the subject of much economic research. In addition to discrimination models built by economists, efforts to better understand race and gender discrimination have been undertaken. How to accommodate young families with children in the same housing complex with senior citizens has been a vexing problem. Legislatures have sought to mitigate the conflict between these two groups by enacting the Fair Housing Amendments Act of 1988 allowing "62 or over housing" and "55 or over housing." The costs and benefits of these provisions are not easily assessed.

In summary, in recent years legislatures and courts have been active in addressing discriminatory practices. And so have economists. Their analytic and empirical work has focused on better understanding the nature of particular types of discrimination, the forces that tend to be responsible for it, and its major economic effects, as well as the effects associated with laws designed to prevent discrimination.

INDEX

Printed in the United States
84923LV00003BA/22/A